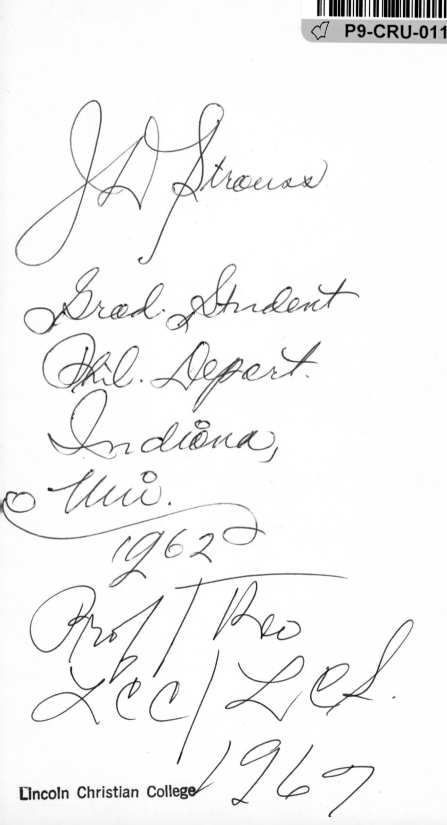

Religions
in a
Changing World

Religions

in a

Changing World

A Presentation of World Religions
in the Mid-Twentieth Century—
Facing the onslaughts of rising nationalism,
Communism, and increasing mass
communication

HOWARD F. VOS, Th.D., M.A., *Editor*

MOODY PRESS • CHICAGO

Preface

SOME WILL ASK, "Why another book on world religions? Don't we have enough of them now?"

There are indeed many good books on world religions. But most of them take the comparative religions approach. That is, Christianity is viewed as just another of the religions of the world. It, like the rest, has its weak points and strong ones. It constitutes only one of the many ways to find peace of mind and eternal bliss. To a true believer in Christ, this view of Christianity is inadequate. Secondly, many of the works now in print do not treat all the great living religions of the world. They may deal with any number from one to ten. Thirdly, a large percentage of works now available has been written by one man or woman. Presumably one person could not in a lifetime become an authority on several religions of the world. Fourthly, except in one or two instances, current works on religion have not attempted to present their subject in the light of current affairs.

Therefore, the editorial staff of Moody Press decided to publish a study of world religions that would meet some of these objections. To begin with, all the major living religions of the world were allotted space. Communism, which has its faith, its saints, its bible, and its method of salvation merited inclusion.

Then a group of writers was chosen. Their qualifications included personal experience in dealing with followers of the religions about which they were to write and an academic knowledge of those re-

5

ligions. Obviously, writers who could measure up to such a standard would come largely from the ranks of foreign missionaries. And
it was advisable that they should, because for the average Christian,
non-Christian religions constitute a missionary problem, rather than
a mere cultural or intellectual pursuit.

Writers were instructed to include some historical facts concerning the founding of the religion with which they were dealing, a statement of the way in which the teachings of that religion fall short of
Christianity, and some advice on winning adherents of that religion
to Christ. Also, to give the work current significance, observations
were to be made concerning the effect of such forces as nationalism
and communism on the religion under discussion. It is this placing
of world religions in their political context that prompted the title
Religions in a Changing World. Advice was given concerning the
length of the chapters, but no absolute limits were set. More space
was assigned to the chapters on Japan and China because they were
to describe the total religious picture of those lands. Such a procedure was thought to be much more realistic than devoting separate chapters to Buddhism, Taoism, Confusianism, and the like.
Often an individual is an adherent of more than one of those religions at the same time. Perhaps the reader will feel that an undue
amount of space has been given to the lesser religions of India, but a
greater abbreviation of those studies would have resulted in a sacrifice of clarity.

Although the book is designed as a text for students in Bible
institutes, Christian colleges, and seminaries, it is written in such a
way that laymen without background in this field will find it
valuable.

Contents

Fig. 1.—One of the most significant developments of the modern religious scene is the political resurgence of Islam. Even in many countries where Islam is not in power politically there are many Mohammedan worshipers. In India, for instance, 35 million Mohammedans remain. Here 200,000 of them gather for prayer in Calcutta. (Courtesy of World Wide Photo.)

For humanity sweeps onward: where today the martyr stands,
On the Morrow crouches Judas with the silver in his hands;
Far in front the cross stands ready and the crackling fagots burn,
While the hooting mob of yesterday in silent awe returns
To glean up the scattered ashes into History's golden urn.

From "The Present Crisis"
JAMES RUSSELL LOWELL

I.

Worlds in Transition

by HOWARD F. VOS

IN PRODUCING A WORK ON WORLD RELIGIONS, one faces much the same problem as the editor of a weekly news magazine. The world and its institutions are in transition; patterns of events are changing rapidly. Past developments may be recorded and interpreted, but trends of the present are not so easily discernible. Predictions for the future are risky indeed. Great changes are occurring within some religions; a few even seem to be in danger of passing off the scene. And nationalism and Communism are drastically altering the societies among which religions find their adherents.

To say that civilizations are in ferment would hardly seem to be necessary. Yet amidst the peace and cushioned prosperity of America, one sometimes needs to be startled into the reality of such a fact. For the Western powers summer is over. The trees of empire no longer stand unmolested among the nations and spread their leaves in the

HOWARD F. VOS, A.B. (Wheaton College), M.A. (Northwestern University), Th.M., Th.D. (Dallas Theological Seminary) is Associate Professor of History at Trinity College, Chicago. He is author of six books on Biblical and historical themes.

warm sunshine. Autumn has come. The chilling winds of emergent nationalism and Communism have blown away the leaves one by one. And some of the trees are dead or decaying. The saplings of social, economic, political, intellectual, and religious institutions are also being denuded of their former glory. Unrest is everywhere apparent. As the leaves drop from the trees, they tumble helter skelter across the countryside. Occasionally they pile up against a hedge or alongside a fence; a pattern of world events seems to be developing. Then comes a gust of wind and scatters the pile in a dozen directions. About all that the observer can say is that winter is on the way. Dark and cold days are ahead for those nations which have enjoyed world political supremacy. Dark and cold days are ahead too for Christian missions, which have benefited greatly from this favorable political context. The time seems to have just about ended when Christian missions could virtually pick an area for conquest and join battle with the Kingdom of Darkness almost unchallenged by the political power of other religious forces and protected by an imperial government.

But it is not enough to say that the world political and religious scene is very much in transition. In order to be of help to the student and informed layman, it is necessary to trace briefly the picture as it now seems to be developing. As already noted, the two factors which have most complicated the religious situation are nationalism and Communism. Where Communism has taken over, Christianity generally has suffered persecution. At least it has been subjected to strenuous efforts to strangle its effectiveness. Christians usually have been cut off from sources of money, workers, and supplies from the West. It has been the practice to convert Christian private schools into state schools, and in many cases to close theological schools. This does not mean, however, that Christianity has lost out behind the Iron Curtain. In some cases, as Christianity has been divorced from association with Western culture, it has tended to become a more national religion and therefore to have greater appeal. Moreover, as foreign missionaries have been removed, local leaders have been forced to shoulder the responsibility of leadership, and laymen have found greater expression in evangelistic efforts. Too, foreign workers do enter such Communist countries as Yugoslavia for brief itinerant ministry. Some theological schools, as for instance the seminary of the Reformed Church in Hungary, remain open.

Where nationalistic movements have resulted in the creation of new states, the religious body with the largest number of adherents tends to assume leadership and establish a state religion. Moslems predominate in Pakistan and Indonesia, Hindus in India, and Buddhists in Burma. Therefore Christian work does not enjoy the freedom which existed under friendly British or Dutch governments. In many of the new nations the religious situation is further complicated by the instability of the government. Shaky economies give rise to increased Communistic effort. Political and economic difficulties, along with Islamic pressures, have created a particularly uncertain situation in Indonesia during the last couple of years.[1]

An especially momentous aspect of the rise of nationalism has been the political resurgence of Islam. Territory lost to Christian powers during later medieval and modern times has rapidly come under the control of Mohammedan governments again during the last few years. Egypt has won freedom from Britain, Syria from France. Their United Arab Republic seeks to woo Jordan and Iraq, also freed from Britain, and Tunisia, now independent of France. Tunisia, for the moment, prefers friendship with the West. Iraq professes a desire for independence. Jordan totters and may have fallen into the Damascus-Cairo orbit by the time this book comes off the press. Lebanon, half Moslem and half Christian, shivers in the valley of indecision. Indonesia, not long out of the nest of Dutch Empire, tries her wings among the world community of nations. So far, her internal economic and political troubles have prevented her from being very vocal in world affairs.

In saying that Moslem political power is resurgent, we do not necessarily mean that the religious devotion of individual Mohammedans is increasing. Such is not generally the case. All over the

[1]The growth of literacy in Indonesia points up another problem for the religions of the world. According to a national whom the editor recently met, the rate of illiteracy has dropped from 97 per cent to 75 per cent since Indonesian independence. In other areas of the world progress in literacy has been equally significant. This advance makes it increasingly difficult for some religions to hold a hitherto uninformed constituency in line. In such places Communism has deluged the newly literate with propaganda, yet Christianity has found it difficult to meet the challenge. In addition, radio has been used widely for exploitation of both literate and illiterate. This is true especially in the Middle East. Whole nations are swayed in the balances by Communism, Islam, Christianity and other forces that seek to win them. To which ideas that they read or voices that they hear will the masses respond?

Middle East, and in North Africa as well, there is a growing laxness in performing some of the religious duties of Islam. This does not signify, however, that Islam as a religion is losing ground. Particularly in the interior of Africa adherents are increasing as missionaries from such institutions as the University of Cairo penetrate the interior with their gospel. In fact, in many areas of Africa conversions to Islam outstrip those to Christianity.

This missionary advance without conquest is a new phase of Islam. Islam has always sought to win converts with the sword. Holy War (al Jihad) is one of the pillars of the Faith. With Israeli defeats of Arab forces in the Middle East, much of the enthusiasm for a Mohammedan Crusade has been lost, however. And Moslems have taken a lesson from the successful, peaceful methods of Christian missionaries.

Whether the Mohammedan nations will be able to resist the incursions of Communism is an open question. Many informed observers feel that there is not sufficient dynamic within this monotheistic religion to hold the faithful in line when the economic shoe pinches. Such a view seems to be supported by the fact that in Indonesia Communists are particularly strong among labor groups, which are largely Moslem. Much will depend on the ability of Moslem[2] governments to raise the standards of their subjects. The fate of the large number of Moslems behind the Iron Curtain is even more uncertain, especially since our sources of information are scant. Large numbers of Moslems live in Southeastern Europe (1,500,000 in Yugoslavia, for instance), China, and the Soviet Union. Russia's approximately 20,000,000 have been subjected to especially severe pressures. For the most part their schools have been closed or converted into State schools; many of their mosques, with support cut off, have been forced to close. It may be supposed that in a generation or so most of the separate Moslem community of Southern Russia will have been assimilated.[3]

Islam broadly denotes whatever is fundamentally Mohammedan, whether religion, culture, form of government, people, or territory. Strictly, *Islam* means "surrender of soul" to God according to the teachings of Mohammed. A *Moslem* is one who has made this surrender of soul to God, one who has adopted the religion of Islam. *Mohammedan* is the common term given to those who embrace the faith of Islam or Mohammed the Prophet.

In recent years there has been concern over Moslem missionary efforts in North America, especially in connection with the erection of a new Islamic Information

Of particular importance to the Arab nations, especially those of the Middle East, is the rise of the new state of Israel. In fact, animosity to Israel has been one of the chief factors contributing to the united action of Arab nations. Within Israel, motivation may not be any more clearly religious than among her Arab neighbors. Interest in Zionism is generally political, cultural or humanitarian. The majority of the leaders are secular-minded and are not interested in establishing a theocracy. Government schools do teach religion, but mainly because the history of the Jews cannot be taught without it. Among the common people interest in religion varies. Certainly orthodox Jewry can claim only a very small percentage of the citizenry. As to the influence of Communism in Israel, the great majority of the population are anti-communist. Communal villages scattered across the land are not to be taken as evidence of a widespread feeling for Communistic views. They are merely an indication of a unity of purpose. They are socialistic experiments in which one is free to leave the community as he wishes.

Release of the great sub-continent of India from British suzerainty spawned a whole new series of problems for that area. It can be fairly well demonstrated that Indian nationalism was created during British rule by the effectiveness of British unification efforts and by antipathy to British rule. It has often been said that the various elements in Indian life could agree on nothing except that the British must go. When the English left, therefore, one of the chief cohesive factors disappeared from India. In fact, even before the British left they agreed to a partition of India into Pakistan and India. Soon war broke out between Moslem, Hindu, and Sikh. Following this came probably the greatest population exchange in all of history. Millions were forced from their homes to live under a more favorable government—Moslems to Pakistan and Hindus and Sikhs to India. Great was the loss of life during the war and migration.

In this movement the Sikhs suffered very severely. They lost all of their wealth in the Western Punjab (which became part of Pakistan), including their temples. The economic strain of re-location

Center in Washington, D.C. Reports made by Moslems in this country estimate the number of Moslems in North America to be between 30,000 and 70,000, including many converts.

did not permit construction of worship centers in the East Punjab and in other areas where the Sikhs settled. Thus was hastened the trend toward irreligion which began among them before the war. Deprived of their old religious centers, the Sikhs have been increasingly attracted by the Hindu temples around their new homes. Unless Sikhism is revitalized it faces the danger of being assimilated by Hinduism. Sikhs have also been attracted to Communism in substantial numbers. Since they have been in the vanguard of the nationalistic movement they have been exploited by Communists, who endeavor to turn all foment into a victory for themselves.

Jainism and Zoroastrianism, other India religions have not been influenced by Communism, however. The former is repelled by Communistic use of force; a true Jain would not want to kill anything. Zoroastrians have an exalted monotheistic theology. In addition, adherents of both of these faiths are among the more well-to-do of India and operate many of her business concerns; so for economic reasons they have no sympathy with Communism. Jainism today is steadily declining in numbers and, like Sikhism, faces assimilation by Hinduism. Zoroastrianism or the Parsi religion is known as the museum piece among the religions of the world. Only about 100,000 remain; therefore its influence is not great. But it does not give promise of passing off the scene in the near future.

Hinduism is predominant in India—both religiously and politically. Under Gandhi, Hinduism stood at the forefront of the Indian nationalistic movement. During those years Hinduism not only became more self-conscious politically, but great changes occurred within the religion itself. Numerous reform movements arose within Hinduism for the purpose of eliminating some of the grosser and more objectionable features of the religion. The success of these movements has tended to make Hinduism more respectable and to rob Christian missionaries of some of their ammunition formerly available in dealing with Hindus. Another important development was the breakdown of the caste system, at least officially. It must be admitted, however, that in actual practice much of the old system remains. Curiously enough, while this social adjustment would seem to have removed one of the great talking points of the Communists, such has not been the case. Under the caste system upper classes assumed more of a responsibility for those on lower rungs of the social ladder. With the increasing atomization of society and individualism of outlook, the poor are often less well taken care of and therefore a target for Marxist propaganda. Although Hinduism is something of a deterrent to Communism, it is too amorphous to be effective, especially with an economically dynamic China to the north. The economic battle is severe in India, and the land could turn Communistic in spite of religious deterrents.

To the east of India is another land that has won her independence since World War II—Burma. The religious picture in Burma is vastly different from that of India; in Burma about ninety per cent of the population is Buddhist. And though religious toleration is practiced, Buddhism has a special status by constitutional provision. In fact, Buddhism in Burma is enjoying a revival of considerable proportions; this revival has the full blessing of the government. While economic and political problems have been very serious and Communist infiltration sizable, the government has been gradually righting the ship of state—especially in the defeat of armed bands of Reds. One cannot predict, however, whether Buddhist power and improving economic conditions will be able to prevent the country from going Communistic.

To the east of Burma, in Thailand, Buddhism is also experiencing something of a revival, but not to the extent that it is in Burma. In Indo-China, on the other hand, Buddhism has little vitality. In the southern part of the country it has little strength, whereas in the northern part it was fairly active until the Communists took over. No doubt Buddhism in northern Indo-China will suffer much the same fate it has in China. Perhaps it should be mentioned in passing that Southeast Asian Buddhism is known as the Hinayana form and represents much more the original form of Buddhism. In this branch of the religion salvation is won by stern effort, and it is believed that only a limited number will attain the final end. To offer greater hope to the masses, there is greater emphasis on reincarnation in Hinayana Buddhism; if one does not attain to the righteous state in this life he has another chance. The northern branch of Buddhism, practiced in China and Japan, is known as the Mahayana form. It is much more lax in its demands upon the individual than the Hinayana form, holds that many more will reach the state of bliss, and puts less stress on reincarnation.

Buddhism has not enjoyed a post-war prosperity in China as it has in Burma and Thailand. Communist opposition to Buddhism is quite systematic. Most temples and monasteries have been suppressed; a few remain open under the guise of freedom of religion. Taoism, the more mystical strain in Chinese religion, has suffered an even worse fate. Decadent before the war and revolution, it has been virtually destroyed under the Red regime. Operating temples are almost non-existent, as is the case with monasteries. Occasionally a Taoist priest performs some service, such as conducting a funeral. Confucian teaching was decadent and largely gone before the revolution in China; now it is virtually non-existent. The temples are almost all closed; its moral teachings are fast being eradicated from the educational fabric, and the ancestral cult is also on the way out. Islam has fared a little better because of large numbers of closely knit communities and the pressure of pan-Islamic opinion. The Communist bloc has been sensitive to the aims and views of rising Moslem political power in the world. As in Russia, the Communists have tolerated Christianity but have subjected it to strict control. Hundreds of thousands of Chinese Protestants have refused to join the state church and have suffered accordingly. But Roman Catholics have suffered most in China because of their tight organization, the issue of Papal headship, and their refusal to join the reform movement. A few Roman Catholic churches remain open in the cities as show places of religious toleration. In general Chinese life is being rapidly secularized under the impetus of a materialistic Communistic philosophy. The Chinese economic revolution is dynamic; an informed observer recently returned to this country from China says that their industrial revolution dwarfs the Russian Revolution.

Travelling farther east, one comes to Japan. There the main religion is Shinto. Under American occupation, Shinto was disestablished and the union of religion and state dissolved. Education was freed from the control of Emperor and Shrine. Subsidies to the temples ceased and some of the temple lands were distributed among the people. These acts of the Occupation Government were less devastating to Shinto than once was supposed. Before the war most State subsidies were discontinued, and few temples or shrines lost more than ten per cent of their income as a result of occupation decrees. Most of the religious centers have not had to curtail their activities drastically. It is obvious, then, that the Occupation Government did not destroy Shinto. Even though Shinto's official grip on the people was greatly reduced, the household altars (the real strength of Shinto) were not destroyed. And the veneration of ancestors and Shinto family solidarity continued.

One of the most significant recent developments in Japan has been the rise of new sects—many of them offshoots of Shinto or Buddhism. Some of these number hundreds of thousands of adherents. Another important development is that since the control of the Occupation Government has been lifted there are signs of restoration of the power of State Shinto. It is even possible that the former regimentation of the educational system may return. Communism has also invaded Japan and is vying with Shinto for control of the Japanese. It is a real question whether the family solidarity of Shinto, the deep devotion of the Japanese to the Emperor, and other deterrents in Japanese religion and society will be able to stem the tide.

Something more should be said in this introductory statement concerning the position of Christianity in the world. Christendom is divided into three main branches: Roman Catholicism, Eastern Orthodoxy, and Protestantism. It is hard to present accurate generalizations concerning any of these groups, but certain observations may be made. Romanism apparently is losing out in some areas and gaining in others. Recently the Roman Church has evidenced concern over the loss of her grip on many of the laymen: a large number are merely nominally Catholic. This has been especially true in such countries as Spain and France. In several other countries that have long been known as Catholic strongholds, the rise of atheism and scientific materialism have pulled large numbers from the ranks of active supporters of the Church. Witness for instance the great power of the Communist party in Italy. In Brazil the growth of Protestant churches is particularly rapid. In fact, the increase of Protestants all over Latin America has caused grave concern to Pope John XXIII.

While Romanism may lose popular support in some areas, this is not generally matched by a decline in political power; that has been on the increase in many areas of the world. Moreover, numerical support in some countries has multiplied greatly. In many of our large cities the percentage of Catholics has increased greatly during recent decades; in some cases it approximates fifty per cent. In Holland, a traditionally Calvinistic country, the balance has been slowly swinging to the Catholics. Of the approximately ten million in the country, about four million are Protestant, about four million are Catholic, and about two million unchurched. Others report the total population to be rather evenly divided between Protestants and Catholics. In Germany, with a large percentage of the Protestant area swept behind the Iron Curtain, the balance of power has swung to the Catholics. In Northern Ireland the number of Catholics has been increasing rapidly; within the foreseeable future they may be able to win an election in favor of union with the rest of the Island. Behind the Iron Curtain Romanism has lost ground, but the result everywhere has not been disastrous. In Poland, for instance, the Catholic Church has been one of the greatest bulwarks against the success of Communism.

Eastern Orthodoxy has lost heavily with the advance of Communism in Europe. In Russia, as elsewhere behind the Iron Curtain, many churches have been closed. The flow of young people into the Church has been greatly curtailed, and a large number of theological schools has been closed. Outside of the Iron Curtain countries a spiritual revitalization of the Church has been initiated with the "New Life" movement. And especially in the United States a considerable numerical growth is taking place.

Protestantism is a vast mosaic. That being the case, it is hard to speak in general terms concerning all denominations. Certain trends can be observed, however. The old purely naturalistic liberalism has been found inadequate for a dying world. In its place has arisen a neo-supernaturalistic Neo-Orthodoxy. This theological viewpoint has even invaded some conservative strongholds. Second, World War II has rather effectively killed the remnants of an optimistic, postmillennial theology, with its idea of man bringing in a utopia. Third, the problems of the world have brought Protestants together increasingly; the ecumenical movement has become widespread. Many groups have united. Lastly, the foreign missionary endeavor has been changed radically. Nationalism has forced the severance of ties between many churches planted on foreign fields and the parent organizations; Communism has forced many fledgling groups of Christians to go on their own, perhaps long before they were ready for it. In such countries as China and Russia, Christians are living under conditions typical of the early church period. Persecution is rampant. They cannot look to any security in this world. The role of the missionary is more and more becoming that of an assistant to nationals, a specialist to help a national church prepare for complete independence. Especially in Africa mission boards are seeking to establish indigenous works; in the last few years much mission property has been deeded to nationals and many positions of leadership turned over to them. Today the greatest remaining opportunity for pioneer evangelism lies among the animistic tribes[3] people of the world, many of whom do not even have a language reduced to writing. But even among animistic groups the time is short; nationalism and Communism are rapidly making inroads.

The time has come for Christians to make an agonizing re-appraisal. Communism has engulfed almost half the world's population. Nationalistic fervor has reduced the welcome formerly accorded to the missionary. Arab nationalism and Moslem solidarity have closed many a door to the Christian message. Shinto seems on the way back to power in Japan. Resurgent Buddhism rears its head in Southeast Asia. In some of the lands of the Reformation the handwriting is on the wall; a definite drift back into the Roman fold is noticeable. Scientific materialism and atheism are everywhere opposing the Christian message. Where do we go from here? Will the Gospel be able to turn the world upside down as it did in the first centuries of our era?

[3]Animism may be generally defined as spirit worship; it also involves magic, fetishism, and taboo.

Fig. 2.—A witch doctor at work in Indonesia. Lying behind him is a sick woman. He is calling on Satan for deliverance, and is being assisted in his ritual by men beating gongs and drums. His assistants are out of the range of the camera. (Courtesy of the Christian and Missionary Alliance.)

The Animist knows of no greater misfortune than to die without
descendants, for such an one has nobody who feels bound to serve
and honour him after his death. The dead demands, with the
instinct of self-preservation, that the living honour him; and he
compels them to do so by afflicting them. Ancestors are honoured
because one's own well-being is dependent on them.

—WARNECK

II.

Animism

by H. VIRGINIA BLAKESLEE

R UN, RUN TO OUR HOUSE, do not look up to the clouds," cried the
old man as a loud clap of thunder rumbled through the surrounding hills. He had been told to look after the children while
their mothers were away doing a day's cultivating in their far-away
gardens. "God is stretching himself and cracking his joints. He is
making ready to chase away and destroy his enemies. If you look
up to see him, he will strike you dead," said the old man to the children who were by this time quaking with fear as they huddled together around the fireplace in their dark hut.

This man is an Animist. He believes in a god who is the creator
and giver of all things. This god takes notice of the behavior of
people. While he lives in the sky, he has temporary homes in the
mountains where he rests during his visits to inspect the earth to
bring blessing or punishment to people. He takes little interest in
individuals, yet at the four crises of life—birth, initiation, marriage,

H. VIRGINIA BLAKESLEE is a graduate of the Hudson River Institute (Claverack, N. Y.) and the Atlantic School of Osteopathy.
After practicing her profession for two years in Altoona, Pa.,
she went to Africa in 1911. There she served until retirement in
1954 with the Africa Inland Mission, chiefly among the Kikuyu
people. Her book, *Beyond the Kikuyu Curtain,* is based on this
work.

and death—communications are established with god on behalf of the individual. The high god is more concerned with a race or village of people than with individuals. If all goes well, prayer is not made to god, for it is believed he is well pleased with the people and their dwellings. However, when the elders meet to plan a public affair or to decide on a course of action in emergencies, as when the people are in great distress because of a prolonged drought or a widespread epidemic affecting the people or the flocks, an appeal is made through prayer to him for guidance, help, and deliverance.

Believing the temporary, official abiding place of god on earth to be on certain mountains, the Animists choose certain trees to symbolize the mountains. The trees are held to be sacred and under them the people worship and offer their sacrifices when occasion demands.

In the study of Animism, one begins to touch the depths of heathendom. Who can describe Animism—that oldest, vaguest, most widespread of all pagan religions? It is older than history, deeper than reason. It has no written laws or creeds. It varies from place to place. It is said that Buddhism has been superimposed on a foundation of Animism and that Animism has altered the local characteristics of Buddhism in Burma. It is probable that Buddhism in China and Tibet, Hinduism in India, Islam, and even the survival of pagan superstitions in Christianity, may be traced to the same source.

Animism may be simply defined as "spirit worship." And it is applied to the most primitive forms of religion. Tribes involved in Animism have not learned to assign human or animal forms to their gods, but rather view them as spirits inhabiting stones, trees, water, the hills, and the air around themselves and the sky above. Conscious life is ascribed to all natural objects. Animists also believe in the continued existence of the human soul after death and in the activity of the soul in the disembodied state around the area where the person spent his earthly life. Therefore Animism comes to involve ancestor worship, as well as fetishism and magic.

Animistic people in some countries, as in Africa, do not have a priesthood. It is the duty of certain wise elders, believed to be endowed with miraculous powers to perform and lead the people in sacrificial ceremonies to their most high god. These seers are thought to be in direct spiritual communication with god who gives them new revelations and instructions, usually during sleep. The wise men, it is said, will bring disaster to a community if they use their supernatural powers for personal advantage. Animistic worshipers in Burma, China, Tibet, India, and islands of the Far East have priests who commit to memory and offer traditional prayers to a supreme being on behalf of the people.

It is considered to be the duty of parents to instruct their children in all the religious ethics and social customs on which the worship of their god depends. Thus religious beliefs and traditions are acquired and firmly entrenched in the minds and lives of the people from early childhood on.

For an illustration of how an Animistic ceremony is carried on, come with me to a certain African district inhabited by Animists. Last year's food supply is exhausted, grain bins are empty. Gardens have turned to dust. The cattle and sheep are dying of starvation. Children are crying for food. The garden lands have been prepared for seed sowing. The people have waited long but the relentless sun shines on. A group of second-rate elders have met to determine the cause of the prolonged drought. They call for the older elders and seers.

"Have you received any message from god as to the cause of this drought; does he tell you what we have done to displease him that he withholds the rain?" they ask.

"We have had no word from god," reply the seers solemnly.

"Return to your villages, meet us here in the morning, it may be god will this night reveal to you what we have done to anger him."

In the morning one seer reports a communication from god. "Bring a brown sheep without spot or blemish, no matter how young," he commands. A brown lamb is brought. The owner is carefully questioned as to how he became the owner of the lamb. Was the mother bought by grain cultivated on land lawfully owned; or with honey from a beehive made from the wood of a sacred tree? This point settled, the character of the owner of the lamb is investigated. Is he known to be honest and trustworthy? Has he ever committed theft, murder, rape, or had any connections with witchcraft? That settled, the question is raised as to who will be chosen to take part in the offering of a sacrifice to god for rain. Old elders who are believed to have only the good of the people at heart are chosen. Several old women considered to be past the age of mischief common to womanhood are named. Two small children, a boy, and a girl of about six years, are also selected. Children of this age are thought to be free from worldly sins of mind, heart, and body. A sacred tree under which the sacrifice for rain is to be made must be carefully selected. Five days and five nights hence the sacrifice will take place. The public is notified. On the sixth day they will communicate with the great god. Meantime, no one is permitted to ford a river or stream. No stranger may arrive or depart on the day of communion. All quarrels or disputes are banned. Peace must prevail in the district lest the sacrificial ceremony be defiled and refused by the great god.

The eve of the sacrifice has arrived. The elders and seers gather in the village of the leading elder. Here come the lamb and the two children. Honey-beer is being prepared to be placed near the fire to ferment during the night. The day of the ceremonial sacrifice has dawned. The milk of a ceremonial cow is milked into a small calabash. The honey-beer is strained into a similar calabash. Now an old elder, followed by the boy carrying the milk and the girl the honey-beer, moves down the path to lead the procession. The lamb with eyes covered follows the children. Next come the elders and old women. The procession moves slowly toward the tree of god. At the tree the leading elder takes the two calabashes from the children. Holding them aloft and facing a sacred mountain, he utters this prayer: "Reverend Elder [god] who lives on the mountain; you who cause the mountains to tremble and rivers to flood; we offer this sacrifice to you that you may bring rain and posterity." After each clause of this prayer the elders chant in chorus—"Peace, we beseech you, god, peace be with us."

Now the leader sips the contents of the two calabashes and spits it over his right and left shoulders for the ancestral spirits to feed upon. It is believed they are the keepers of the tree of god in the midst. The procession now moves around the tree seven times, sprinkling the milk and beer on the trunk. On the eighth time round, all sit down in a circle. The lamb is brought and placed on its back. The children put their thumbs on the lamb's throat to signify the lamb was killed with undefiled hands. Elders strangle it, the blood is drawn into a calabash, the fat is rendered on a nearby fire and poured into a calabash. The intestines of the lamb are tied around the tree trunk with the blood and the fat. Small bits of meat are placed in a heap for the great god, the remainder is roasted and consumed by the elders and children. Leaves of sweet smelling bushes are placed on the fire. As the smoke ascends, the elders chant a prayer. Taking with them a small quantity of the contents of the lamb's stomach to be used in a planting ceremony, the procession moves homeward.

Controlling Principles of Animism

The universal basis of Animistic religion is fear. The Animist lives in constant terror, night and day, of spirits he believes to surround him. They are responsible for everything that happens to him. There are no natural causes. All life in its minutest detail is saturated with fear of spirits. At birth, marriage, house-building, seedtime and harvest the spirits must be honored. The living are tormented by the fear of their disembodied dead, the spirits of whom may hover about the village to haunt it. Offerings through sacrifice are made to induce the spirits of the departed one to go away to its abiding place. They are believed to live in unusual places such as strange rocks, a sacred tree, a waterfall or springs of medicinal waters.

The people feared a waterfall that tumbled over the rocks near a mission station in Africa. The spirits were thought to live in nearby rocks. Tribal elders were greatly agitated when schoolboys burned off surrounding grass in preparing a plot on which to plant wattle trees. The elders declared this act had offended the spirits, and in retaliation they had caused an epidemic of dysentery occurring about the same time.

Fear of spirits is manifested in countless ways. Charms are bought from the medicine men and worn on the wrist, arm, or ankle, to counteract the curse of the "evil eye." Sickness is feared because of its all too frequent consequences. Death is the greatest fear of the Animist. He does not believe death ends existence, but he has no idea of life after death.

The medicine man is called to determine the cause when misfortune or sickness befalls a village or community. He casts lots to discover the spirits responsible, and then proceeds to find the reason for causing the trouble and the spirit requires to appease its anger. The family may have had a feast and failed to give a portion to their departed. If this is found to be the case, the feast must be repeated and a portion set out in a secluded place. The offended spirit is asked to partake that the family may know friendly relations have been resumed. An elder is delegated to hide near the secluded spot to watch for the spirit. When a mongoose or hawk appears to devour the offering, the elder returns to report that the grieved spirit has been appeased. If an epidemic does not end and the people or sheep and cattle do not regain health and strength after all the instructions of the medicine man have been carried out, the cause of the trouble is believed to be the work of evil spirits hiding in the bushes of the district to harass the people by mass attack. The winds they say, carry these spirits from ridge to ridge and from village to village. Whirlwinds of dust are said to be the evil spirits, or the spirits of women, making ready for an attack.

Come to a certain district of Africa and see what takes place in this event. The elders and seers have held their consultation. They announce the only way to end the epidemic is to prepare an all out battle against the evil spirits to drive them away. The people are told to prepare to attack in the evening of a certain day as the moon is rising. This is supposed to be the most favorable time. At the sounding of the war horns in the various districts, men, women and children rush from their villages in wild excitement, armed with clubs, sticks and weapons. Forming in ceremonial fighting units, they all begin to beat the bushes in ceremonial rhythm, shouting and screaming as they slowly march toward the river. Blasts from the war horn halt the crowds at the river bank. "Have you collected all the evil spirits with their diseases on your side?" calls out one of the leaders.

"Yes, and those which tried to hide we have beaten and brought with us," replies the leader from the opposite bank. As the war horns are blown for the last time, the crowd on both sides of the river with piercing screams throw their clubs into the river, shouting as they do so—"Evil spirits, we have crushed you. We sink you in the river. Let the waters carry you far from us. You will go forever and never return." Shaking the dust from their garments and feet that no malicious spirit escape by clinging to them, they march homeward singing lustily in the vain hope their efforts may have freed their villages from dangerous spirits. The Animist, it has been said, "resembles a captivated slave pledged to a satanic system, from which he struggles hopelessly to be delivered."

FRUITS OF ANIMISM

Animism is a satanic system. Animists are dominated and controlled by the powers of Darkness. Said Warneck, one of the greatest authorities on the subject, "The place of God is taken by demons, who are feared and worshiped." It has been said there are three great *I*'s in spiritism: infidelity, insanity, and immorality.

Many missionaries bearing the Light of the world to Animistic people for the first time have had experinces similar to that recorded of Jesus in Mark 5. An African in French Equatorial Africa, listening to a Gospel record being played by a missionary, suddenly pointed in the direction of the gramophone, "Look, look," he cried in terror, "Cetani is there." His panic-stricken countenance gave evidence that he saw a manifestation of opposing demons.

On hearing the name of Jesus mentioned by pioneer missionaries, Africans of the Akamba tribe of Kenya Colony fell down crying, "The disease of Jesus." "A blackness of darkness," described by Peter (II Peter 2:14 A.S.V.) beclouds the minds of Animists. "Satan hath blinded their minds."

They are totally blind to the beauties and charm of the handiwork of God in nature all about them. Bishop Tucker, Uganda, sought diligently to discover in the African some sense of an appreciation for the beautiful in nature. Walking along the path on a safari, he saw one day to his delight one of his porters stoop down to pluck a brilliant gloriosa lily. But alas, the next moment he beheld the porter wiping his nose. The lovely lily was left in a crumpled mass by the wayside.

Animism seems to rob its adherents of any conception of humanity, mercy, kindness, or love. A mother must take her dying child to the bushes, leave it there and return to her village. In New Guinea small girls, unsalable because their bodies are wrecked by yaws, are taken to the jungle to shriek in vain for help until they perish. In Africa the old and infirm are taken to the depths of a forest. Given a bit of food and a fire, they are told to wait beneath a tree until their escort returns from an engagement. He never returns. In a certain tribe of Kenya the sick and dying were not allowed to die in the village. They were taken to the bush. The hyenas found them. In a Congo Logo village, if a mother dies, the infant is buried alive with her.

One of the outstanding characteristics of spirit worship or communion with spirits is uncleanness. In the ranks of Animists chastity is unknown. Adultery is not considered on moral grounds but is forbidden because the woman is the purchased property of her husband or the family into which she has married. Promiscuous intercourse among the unmarried youth is encouraged by tribal elders. There is no sin in the moral sense. A Congo Zande youth, when the guilt of his sin was explained to him, replied simply, "My heart has no eyes." Sin to the Animist is failure to conform to tribal custom or taboo. Moral evil is regarded as good if it does not infringe upon tribal customs. Some African tribes in their primitive state are remarkably free from lying and thieving not because of a differentiation between good and evil, but because it is taboo and offends tribal custom. The victims of Animism perish in physical, moral, and spiritual ruin.

EFFECTS OF CIVILIZATION

A mighty upheaval began when the first agents of civilization invaded Animistic lands. In some cases the people were roughly treated. Slave trading and the rubber atrocities caused them much suffering. Today with hurricane violence and speed the Animistic pattern of life is being shaken to the core. It can never be the same again. The entrance of trade, the influx of settlers, and the rule of Western governments have all contributed to a modification of the Animistic way of life.

The heralds of the Gospel, the most revolutionary force of all, followed economic and political penetration of Animistic areas. Mission schools and dispensaries sprang up here and there, thus opening wide the door to knowledge. The entrance of light revealed superstition, ignorance, disease and immorality. A remedy was offered. As the missionary sought to pull down these strongholds of evil and suffering, he preached a power that gave a more abundant way of life.

But conflict could not be avoided. The youth who heard and believed the truths of the Gospel refused to participate in village and communal ceremonies and sacrifices. Animistic religious ceremonies are invalid unless all male members of the family are present. Tribal elders and fathers strongly objected to their young people joining missions or going to school. Many boys and girls were disowned and disinherited for refusal to break with the new way of life.

When the forces of civilization had been unleashed, sections of the Animistic world were turned upside down and inside out. A thirst for knowledge developed among the youth. Many professed to believe the truths taught, but at heart used the mission school as a bridge to knowledge for material gain. Thus there arose a vast number who had lost faith in and were unrestrained by tribal beliefs and customs, but had no desire to accept the Christian standards of morality, honesty, and behavior. Here was a fertile field for agents of unrest and discontent to sow the seed of subversive movements of many varieties, religious and political.

Before the advent of civilization, the drinking of intoxicating liquor was confined to tribal elders and old women only. Custom and ancient law forbade a young man to get drunk. He was severely punished and ridiculed by his age group if he broke custom. Extensive advertising of the products of Western brewing companies produced in their midst is responsible today for the widespread drunkenness among young men and women of Animistic descent. Venereal diseases were unknown in Animistic tribes of East Africa until the invasion of civilization.

But there is a brighter side. It is not to be concluded that the civilizing forces did not bring with them many good results. The rapid rise in population gives evidence of the improvement in health and hygiene due to the teaching of the youth in schools, hospitals, dispensaries, and maternity centers. Famines, which before the advent of civilization slew Animists by the thousands, have been banished. The fear of sudden night raids by neighboring tribal enemies is a thing of the past. The warrior class is now engaged in learning improved methods of agriculture. They are interested in growing new money crops, investigating good business methods and outlets for the disposal of new produce. But the speed of progress in some parts has undoubtedly been too rapid and has in some cases produced an unbalanced outlook.

The most dynamic of the good results is the calling out from among Animistic peoples of a Church, the Body of Christ, united in a fellowship which transcends all tribal and denominational barriers. They know Whom they have believed and are persuaded God is not only Creator but Sovereign of all He has made. They are convinced that the powers of darkness are limited and temporary because Christ on Calvary's cross won a victory over them. They believe every detail of their lives concerns Him: that He allows Satan and men to go their way, within limits, for the present; but a day is surely coming when the Christ Who was crucified, resurrected and ascended will come to reign in righteousness and truth on this earth.

It is a witnessing Church. Many of its members have sealed their testimony with their blood. The gates of Hell have not been able to prevail against them nor have the forces of evil been able to move them from their faith in their Redeemer.

ANIMISM *versus* COMMUNISM

With the disintegration of Animistic tribal life and the impact of modern civilization, a strong spirit of nationalism has developed. Almost overnight some Animistic people have leaped the chasm of progressive development and are feeling their way to take their place among the nations. Nationalism influencd by Communism is pressing in at all points. Trained communistic agents are taking advantage of the rising tides of nationalism, tensions, and unrest to spread their propaganda and channel the current to flow their way.

The Viet Namese for the most part are Animistic. During the recent war, many of them went over to Communism. They have been led to believe they have been sold out by Western Powers. In other parts of the East many young people are breaking with their traditional beliefs. They are in an ideological vacuum, ready for the Gospel, Communism, or some other philosophy of life. Red agents are working feverishly to buy up all opportunities. The Animistic world trembles on the brink of a tremendous crisis.

In many Animistic tribes of Africa, Communistic agents not only revive but organize forces to compel people who have emerged from the bondage of Animism to return to their traditional practices and beliefs. The world has heard of the tragic results in one African tribe of one million and a quarter souls, the the Kikuyu. With the exception of a small group of staunch Christians, they were forced back into a barbarianism more horrifying than that of Animism. Today their wisest disillusioned leaders know that the development and progress of their ambitious, progressive people has been retarded for many years to come.

Rev. Ronald K. Orchard, a secretary of the International Missionary Council, at a meeting of the Institute of Missionary Research held in Uppsala, Sweden, reported a revival of Asia's old religions, spreading even to Europe. Could the same forces be operating in Africa to bring about a revival of Animism?

THE MISSIONARY PROBLEM

Every known tribe of Animists recognizes the existence of a creator and teaches various mythological ideas of his character and the story of creation. In practice they remind one of Paul's assertion that their paganism represents not the first step in assent to a true worship, but the tragic results of being deceived into an acceptance and practice of a substitute for a worship of a God once known (Rom. 1:18 ff.).

The missionary to Animists is engaged in a grim conflict with the rulers of the darkness of this world. He must bear in mind that he is being sent to captives in chains. His problem is not the helpless Animist, but the powers that hold the sinner captive. The missionary has been provided with weapons and the authority of One capable of setting the captive free by breaking his chains. It is essential for the bearer of the Good Tidings to know the omnipotence of his Commander, and to be skillful in the use of weapons and authority provided him. With a sympathetic approach and understanding of the plight of the people to whom he is sent, the ambassador for Christ will find in the breast of the Animist a faint knowledge of the true God and the worship from which he and his people have fallen. He will discover feelings that lie buried and crushed by the enemy of their souls, feelings which the truth of the living God has power to revive and restore if the messenger is guided and controlled by the Holy Spirit.

For an idea of how to approach adherents of Animism, untouched by civilization or the Gospel, come with the writer to one of their villages. A group of old elders and several old women are sitting on low, three-legged wooden stools as we enter their village. They are dignified, conservative, well satisfied with their affairs and those of their forefathers. After the usual greeting, we sit down on the stools offered us and listen to their conversation. They are talking about the weather, the crops, their sheep and goats.

"Are there sheep in the country you come from?" asks one old elder with an amused smile.

"Yes, but our sheep are not like yours. They have long, curly wool."

"Here the sun is too hot for our sheep to grow that kind."

"I see you have killed one of your sheep," I said, pointing to a nearby skin stretched out and pegged down to the earth with wooden pegs to dry in the sun.

"Yes, we have killed a sheep," replied the owner of the village.

"Why have you killed this sheep?" I asked.

Lifting his eyebrows and shrugging his shoulders he looked at me for a long minute with a sagelike expression. I knew he was saying to himself, "It's no good trying to tell white people why we kill sheep; they cannot understand our affairs."

"We have killed a sheep because we wanted some meat to eat. Do you not eat the meat of a sheep?" he asked naïvely.

"I do eat sheep meat; it is very good," I replied. Now I remember the old elder's daughter was very ill the last time I visited this village. "Is your daughter now well, has she gone to the gardens with the women?" I asked.

"*Kai.* Have you not heard? My daughter died."

"Ah, now I know why you have killed this sheep. If I should tell you about a village in a land where there is no pain or sickness or death, would you like to go to live in that village?"

"*Titheru* [truly]," cried the man with a low chuckle and sparkling eyes. "If you could tell where to find a village like that, we would pack all our things on our backs and move into that village to-morrow."

"*Titheru,* I know of such a village, and I know the path leading to it. I heard in my village far over the seas that your people had never

heard of this village and no one had pointed out to you the way leading thereto.

"I am on my way to that village myself, but I have stopped off to
live among you for a few years to tell you about the village and the
path. I would be sorry to have you miss it because no one had told
you the way to reach it. God made this very beautiful village I am
telling you of. He wishes all the people of the world to come to live
with Him there. He sent His Son to this world one time to say, 'In
my Father's house are many mansions, I go to prepare a place for
you.' But there is one thing that prevents God from allowing any
of us from this world to enter His village. You elders understand
all about that thing. It is *thauhu;* you know *thauhu* is uncleanness,
defilement. We call it sin and we are all defiled by sin. But God
loved all the people of the world and love always finds a way. When
you saw your daughter's sickness was unto death, you took her to the
bushes to die there lest her death defile your village. You sent your
oldest son to build a fire and sit near her to ward off the prowling
hyenas."

"Yes, that is our custom," assented the old elder.

"You did not allow your son to return to your village until after
you had called the witch doctor to do a cleansing ceremony on him.
From time to time you have your village and people cleansed by the
witch doctor. You kill a sheep. He dips a bunch of leaves into its
blood, touches all vessels and people of your village with it. Backing
to the outer boundary of the village with the leaves held behind him,
he shakes them violently. You believe he has taken away all uncleanness with the blood of the sheep. He pronounces your people and
your village clean. After that, you are careful to allow nothing defiling or unclean to enter. Is it not strange that you people think
the same thoughts of your village that God thinks about His? I know
why you killed the sheep of this skin drying here in the sun. The
witch doctor took of its blood to sprinkle upon your son there in the
bushes separated from the fellowship of his father's village because
of defilement. Do you elders say the blood of a sheep is stronger than
the blood of a man?"

"No," they answer in chorus, "the blood of a man is the stronger."

"There again you think the thoughts of God. He said the blood
of bulls and goats could never take away the sin and defilement of

man. He said it must be the blood of a man who was clean, pure,
and undefiled. Among all tribes and nations of the world not one
man could be found to meet these requirements, for all had sinned.
He knew of only One, His best beloved only begotten Son. Because
of His love for you and me and all the people of the world alienated
from the fellowship of His village by sin and wicked works, He was
willing to give His Son. He sent Him down to this sin-cursed world
to live among men and women. He taught them the words of God.
One day a group of people led Him away to a cross where they
crucified Him. A soldier pierced His side and the blood trickled
down. From that day to this God has said to the people of the world:
'Behold the Lamb of God, which taketh away the sin of the world.'
If you will believe in the blood of the Lamb of God in the very same
way you have believed in the blood of this sheep the witch doctor
has killed, God will take away all of your defilement and in His
sight you will be clean. He can then receive you into His village.
When the witch doctor sprinkled your son with the blood of this
sheep, did he see his defilement roll away into the bushes, or feel it
leave him?"

"No, he did not see or feel it."

"Why then did you think it was gone?"

"We believed the words of the witch doctor when he said: 'It is
finished, he is clean.' "

"That is the way I know my sin and defilement have gone. God
said: 'When I see the blood of the Lamb upon your heart; that is,
when you believe it has power to cleanse you, I will pass over your
sin; I will remove it as far as the East is from the West; I will remember it against you no more forever; I will blot it out.' I have
believed the words of God. Could you not, too, believe the words of
the true and living God?

"You old men know what it means for one to become the way of
another one. Sometimes when I want to go places in these bushes
I get lost. There are many narrow paths running in different directions. I do not know which one to take. One day I met Kamau and
asked him to direct me to Kinyanjui's village."

" 'Follow me,' he said, 'I will lead you to his village.'

"I followed him. He led me over a rough way. My feet were
bruised by the rocks. Great overhanging vines with long, clawed

thorns scratched my arms and face and tore my clothing. We crossed unbridged rivers, waded muddy bogs, climbed steep hillsides. I did not murmur or complain. I followed Kamau, because I had been lost and he knew the way. By and by he led me into Kinyanjui's village. Kamau that day was my way. In the same way the Lord Jesus, the Son of God, said to the people of this world: 'I am the way, the truth, the light.'

"Having trusted His blood to take away your sin and defilement, if you will follow Him day after day, year after year, it may be He will lead you over a rough path. The elders of your district may rise up against you; they may take your sheep and garden land from you. But if you will follow Jesus and trust Him to help you, He will strengthen you day by day. Some day when you are sick, they may roll you up in your old red blanket and carry you to the bushes. Your village people from time to time will peer out to the spot where they placed you. When they see the blanket no more moves up and down they will say to your people, 'Njuguna is dead.' But you will not be dead. He who is your Way, your Truth, your Life will have come for you to bear your spirit away to His village where there is no pain, no sickness, no death; and you will live with Him there forever."

And hearing, the Animists understand.

It is estimated that there are about 175,000,000 Animists in the world today. Who will carry to them the Good News of Jesus, who was anointed to deliver captives?

BIBLIOGRAPHY

ANDERSON, J. N. D. (ed.) *The World's Religions.* London: Inter-Varsity Fellowship, 1950.

BEWES, T. F. C. *Kikuyu Conflict.* London: The Highway Press, 1953.

BLAKESLEE, H. VIRGINIA. *Beyond the Kikuyu Curtain.* Chicago: Moody Press, 1956.

HOUGHTON, A. T. "Animism," in *The World's Religions.* London: Inter-Varsity Fellowship, 1950.

HOWELLS, WILLIAM. *The Heathen: Primitive Man and His Religions.* Garden City: Doubleday & Co., 1948.

KENYATTA, JOMO. *Facing Mount Kenya.* London: Martin Secker & Warburg, 1953.

SOPER, EDMUND DAVIDSON. *The Religions of Mankind.* New York: Abingdon Press, 1938.

WARNECK, J. *The Living Christ and Dying Heathenism.* Trans. from German by Neil Buchanan. Grand Rapids: Baker Book House, 1954.

Fig. 3.—A Rabbi at Tel Aviv presides at the Feast of Hanukkah (about December 25), which commemorates the rededication of the Temple at Jerusalem following the victory of Judas Maccabeus over the Syrians. (Courtesy of the Consulate General of Israel.)

III.

Judaism

by Jakob Jocz

JUDAISM BELONGS to the great historic religions of the world. For its influence, spirituality, ethical idealism and monotheistic vision of God, it may easily claim a place of its own among the great religious systems.

ORIGIN

Unlike many other religions, Judaism cannot properly be traced to a founder. Its roots lie deeply buried in the Old Testament, more particularly in the Pentateuch. It is a mistake to regard Moses as the founder of Judaism. Though he holds a unique position in the synagogue, its authority is not vested in his person, but in God. Moses is only the instrument of God's will, otherwise there is no religious significance attached to him. Judaism knows of no other founder but God. Israel's religion is based upon election: this means that the religious Jew regards his knowledge of God as a special act of revelation. That act of revelation he primarily associates with the Giving of the Law at Mount Sinai. But it is equally a mistake to confuse Judaism with the religion of the Old Testament, for Judaism is a departure from it in some important points.

Born in Lithuania of Hebrew Christian parentage, Dr. Jakob Jocz obtained undergraduate training in Frankfurt/M, Germany. He was ordained in the Anglican Church and served as a missionary in Warsaw. He came to England before the Second World War and held a pastorate in London. He earned his Ph.D. and D. Litt. degrees at the University of Edinburgh. In 1954 he was chosen President of the International Hebrew Christian Alliance. Dr. Jocz has since moved to Toronto where he directs the Nathanael Institute. He is the author of the books: *The Jewish People and Jesus Christ* and *A Theology of Election—Israel and the Church.*

A. The Sacrificial System

With the destruction of the Temple by the Romans in A.D. 70, the sacrifices ceased. Gradually prayer and study of the Law came to be looked upon as a substitute for sacrifices. This is already implied in ancient Rabbinic literature. Rabbi Sheshet (fourth century) used to pray in the evening after a fast day: "O Lord of the world . . . I have fasted today, and through this fasting my blood and my fat have been decreased. Deign to look upon the part of my blood and my fat which I have lost through my fasting as if I had offered it to Thee, and forgive my sins in return." But even Johanan b. Zakkai, one of the leading teachers of the first century who is reputed to have saved Judaism after the fall of Jerusalem by establishing a Rabbinic academy at Jabneh, was already at a loss to understand the meaning of the sacrifices except in terms of obedince to an ordinance of God.[1]

Once this central aspect of the Old Testament religion had fallen away, Judaism changed from a priestly cult to a "legal" system. The process set in long before the first century, but reached its culmination with the disappearance of the Temple. This is indicated by the waning power of the priests and the gradual rise to authority of the scribes and Pharisees in Maccabean and post-Maccabean times. When the Temple finally disappeared, Judaism became emancipated from the hegemony of the priesthood, and the task of leadership fell to the Rabbinic scholar. This meant a democratization of religious life, but it also meant a significant break from the Old Testament tradition. The priesthood was hereditary—the priests were descendents from the house of Aaron of the tribe of Levi—the rabbis were mainly men of the people who attained to their position by scholastic achievement and personal piety, irrespective of pedigree. The son of the humblest family could become an important Rabbinic authority, as is the case with Rabbi Akiba (*ca.* 50-137) who, according to tradition, was a humble herdsman and later became the most famous rabbi.

The position of Judaism in respect to the sacrifices is not clearly defined. Reform Judaism omits from the prayer book every reference to the sacrifices and regards all sanguinary ceremonies as an expression of a more primitive religious consciousness. But orthodox Juda-

---

[1] Cf. Jewish Encyclopedia, Vol. X, p. 628b.

ism makes constant references to the sacrifices in its liturgy and prays
for the day of the restoration of the Temple.

In orthodox Jewish communities, the descendants of the house
of Aaron still enjoy certain prerogatives: they take precedence in the
public reading of the Law; they pronounce the priestly benediction;
they act in the ceremony of the redemption of the first-born, and
avoid contact with a corpse. But in every other respect there is
no distinction between priests and laymen in the synagogue. All
Israelites are equals. The rabbi is not a priest in the Roman Catholic
sense: he is a "layman" who has the authority of teaching by virtue
of his learning and by the general consent of the congregation. The
synagogue is "congregational" and democratic.

B. The Law

The connection between Mosaic Law and Judaism is not always
obvious to an outsider. Rabbinic law is related to Mosaic Law in a
curious way. Between the two are centuries of gradual development
in a certain direction. To the Jew, *Torah* implies much more than
the literal commandment of the Mosaic Code. It is derived from a
verb which means "to point," "to direct," "to shoot at": *Torah* therefore implies both receiving direction from a higher authority and
also aiming at fulfillment. Compliance with the will of God is the
underlying principle of Judaism. The synagogue believes that
God's will for the Jew is deposited in the Old Testament, but chiefly
in the precepts of the Mosaic Code. It is the rabbis' task to elucidate
these precepts and to apply them to the changing conditions of daily
life. The result is an elaboration of Mosaic Law which in some
instances is almost a denial of its original purpose. We will return
to the subject at a later stage.

C. Mediation

The omission of sacrifices and the specifically Rabbinic concept of
Torah resulted in another significant change. Mediation is an underlying principle in the Old Testament approach to God. The
whole Temple cult expressed the concept of *indirect* approach. The
worshiper could only come to God by the mediation of the sacrifices, the priest, and the Temple. In the synagogue the position
is different. Here mediation has almost completely fallen out;

Judaism is built upon immediacy of approach. Every Jew by virtue
of his descent is a son of God and has direct approach to Him.
Judaism takes this direct relationship between Israel and God for
granted. It is founded upon the covenant-relationship between
Israel and God. For this reason, Judaism knows nothing about conversion in terms of spiritual regeneration. A Jew is born a Jew and
needs no conversion. If he turns his back upon God, all he needs to
do is *return* (the Hebrew meaning of *repentance*) and mend his
ways. Even the "conversion" of proselytes is not conversion in the
Christian sense. The proselyte *accepts* the Law and by virtue of
submitting to it he is received into the synagogue.

We see thus something of the internal difference between the Old
Testament religion and Rabbinic Judaism.

Literary Sources

Every normal synagogue consists of two parts: the *bet ha-keneset*
(house of assembly) and the *bet ha-midrash* (house of study). In
the house of assembly the most prominent place is given to the Scroll
of the Law. This signifies the importance the synagogue attaches to
the Pentateuch. But in the house of study, there are shelves filled
with Rabbinic books, all concerned with the elucidation of Mosaic
Law. The literary sources of Judaism are therefore vast. This is
understandable considering the age of the Jews and the nature of
their religion, for Judaism is not a static faith; it grows and devel-
ops, ever adapting itself to changing conditions. For this reason it
shows the need of redefining itself and restating its position from
time to time.

Next to the Old Testament, and particularly the Pentateuch, must
be placed the Mishnah (lit., "repetition"). It was compiled by
Rabbi Judah the Patriarch at the close of the second century A.D., and
represents a collection of legal traditions derived from the Mosaic
Code. It has binding force, and forms the foundation of Rabbinic
law. Next to the Mishnah come the Babylonian and Jerusalem
Talmuds (lit., "teaching"), which are mainly a commentary on the
Mishnah but which contain a wealth of Jewish tradition and folklore. They represent, in addition to ancient traditions, the opinions
of scholars from the third to the fifth centuries. The code which
comprises a complete digest of Jewish law and practice is called

Shulhan Aruk (lit., "Prepared Table"), compiled by Rabbi Joseph Karo and first published in 1565. The *Siddur* (lit., "order") which is the daily Prayer Book, and the *Mahzor* (lit., "cycle") which contains the order of services for the great festivals, reflect the mass of Jewish religious sentiment as expressed in liturgy and worship.

Torah

It is usual to translate *Torah* with "Law" but this lends itself to misunderstanding. For the Jew, Torah has a much wider connotation. It first means the Scroll of the Pentateuch, but it also means the whole bulk of Rabbinic teaching based upon Mosaic Law, and it also means the whole mode of Jewish life and practice as established by tradition. "Torah," says Rabbi Epstein in his book on Judaism, "connotes the whole body of Jewish teaching, legislation, practices, and traditions that have proceeded from the interpretation and reinterpretation from the laws of the Bible according to the light of reason, and the principles of righteousness, justice, and equality, as well as any adaptations or modifications made by the spiritual leaders of the people applicable to changed conditions of life—economic, domestic, social."[2] This wide description of what the Jew means by Torah reveals the inadequacy of describing it simply as "Law"—it is a way of life, a direction, and a goal.

The rabbis divide the *Torah* into two main parts: the written Torah (i.e., the Pentateuch), and the Torah which was handed down by word of mouth from generation to generation. According to Rabbinic tradition, the "unwritten law" also goes back to Moses and Mount Sinai and enjoys the same authority as the written Law. The unwritten Torah carries the traditional interpretation of the written Torah and is inseparable from it. This means in practice that "the authority for the interpretation and reinterpretation of the Torah is vested in the people of Israel."[3] The rabbis act on Israel's behalf, and God Himself respects their decisions. They are the direct heirs of the prophets, and the decrees of the Great *Bet Din* (Supreme Court) have authority to modify and in some cases to set aside the written Torah. The principle which guides the rabbis in their decisions is that God gave the Law for man to live by, not to die by. When a law therefore becomes burdensome it must be cir-

[2] I. Epstein, *Judaism*, p. 40.
[3] *Ibid.*, p. 41.

cumvented; for this purpose the rabbis invented a number of legal
fictions. Thus Hillel (first century B.C.) instituted the *prosbul*—a
legal instrument executed in court whereby a creditor secured his
debts during the sabbatical year, though the Law decreed universal
release. This was done in order to prevent hardship, as creditors
were reluctant to lend money for fear of forfeiting their claim.
Another device is called *erub* (lit., "combination") whereby the
prohibition to carry objects beyond four yards, or to walk more than
2,000 yards on the Sabbath day is overcome. It consists of a legal
fiction whereby a whole area is declared to be one single domain.

PRACTICING THE LAW

The rabbis have reduced the commandments of the written Law
to 613 precepts: of these 365 are negative—things a Jew must not do—
the number corresponding to the number of days in the solar year;
the remaining 248 are positive—things a Jew must do—the number
corresponding, according to the Rabbinic view, to the 248 bones in
the human body. It means that every day of the year and with every
member of his body a Jew is obliged to keep the Law. In addition,
the rabbis have decreed seven precepts which are not directly derived from the Mosaic Code: thanksgiving for every enjoyment, washing of hands, lighting of Sabbath candles, preparing the *erub* for
Sabbath transfer, the special hallel on holy days, burning of Hanukkah lights (in memory of the rededication of the Temple at the time
of the Maccabees), and the reading of the Book of Esther on Purim
(the festival of the defeat of Haman). Of this multitude of precepts, Rabbinic tradition has it 611 were given through the meditation of Moses (611 is the numerical value of Torah in Hebrew),
whereas the first two commandments of the Decalogue were given by
the mouth of God Himself.[4]

From this it is obvious that Judaism is a religion of practice rather
than creed. Rabbinic law has closely defined Jewish life from the
cradle to the grave. A Jewish boy enters the Covenant through
circumcision when eight days old and becomes a "son of the Law"
when thirteen years of age. From that moment he is pledged to the
Torah till he breathes his last. All his life he remains a marked man;

---

[4]For a detailed list of the whole body of commandments see Jewish Encyclopedia,
Vol. IV, 181*b* ff.

loyalty to the Law drives a wedge between him and the Gentile world. The food restrictions separate him from table-fellowship not only with Gentiles, but even with nonpracticing fellow Jews. He is kept aware of his religious obligations by every possible device— by the *arba kanfot* (lit., "four corners"), a small garment with fringes worn underneath the usual clothing (cf. Deut. 22:12), by the uncut "corners" of his beard (Lev. 19:27), by the prohibition to shave (Lev. 21:5), by the wearing of a head covering all the waking hours and even at night—out of reverence for God, by the putting on the phylacteries (cf. Deut. 6:8, 9) for prayer, by wearing a tallith (prayer shawl), by observing the Law regarding the mezuzzah (a small roll of parchment containing the text from Deut. 6:4 ff. and some other texts, affixed to every doorpost of a Jewish home), by eating kosher food, etc.

These precepts are not conceived as voluntary aids, but as carefully defined duties. The rabbis took nothing for granted. Once the Law prescribed a precept, they defined it in every detail. To give an example: the Law prescribes the wearing of *zitzit* (fringes) ; the rabbis lay down the number of threads, the number of knots, the length of the fringes, under what conditions does a fringe cease to be a valid fringe, etc.[5]

Another example is the question of the Sabbath rest. The Law forbids work on the Sabbath. The rabbis have worked out a table of thirty-nine main divisions of labor which are forbidden on the Sabbath day, such as knotting or unknotting, sewing two stitches, writing two letters of the alphabet, etc. Under the heading "separating" we are told: "It is forbidden to put food which is mixed with worthless matter into water in order that the worthless matter sink to the bottom or float on the top, as that is 'separating.' "[6] Even the placing of an egg in hot sand so that it gets cooked is breaking the Sabbath.[7] The Mishnah goes as far as to define what kind of burdens animals are allowed to bear on the Sabbath day.

We have already hinted that some laws have become so over-elaborated by Rabbinic casuistry as to lose their original purpose. A case in point is the law regarding kindness to animals: "Thou shalt

[5]G. Friedlander (trans. and ed.) *Laws and Customs of Israel*, p. 6.
[6]*Ibid.*, p. 260.
[7]Danby, *Mishnah*, Shabbat, 3.3.

not seethe a kid in its mother's milk" (Exod. 23:19). This law has been interpreted to mean a prohibition of eating milk and meat at the same time. The rabbis have gone so far as to insist upon complete separation of dishes so that dishes and utensils used for meat must never be used for milk foods, and vice versa—even to the saltcellar. If one has eaten of meat or even of a dish prepared with meat, that person must not partake of milk food before an interval of six hours.[8] This gives some indication of how seriously the Jew treats the "Law" and how keenly he is concerned with its fulfillment in every detail.

Here, perhaps, is the place for pointing out the religious difference between the Jewish male and female. Whereas the pious Jew is occupied with keeping the Law every waking hour of the day, the Jewish woman, by comparison, has few duties to perform. Orthodox Judaism is essentially a religion for the male. Jewish custom requires a quorum of ten male Jews for public worship; if one single Jew is missing all the women of Jewry cannot substitute for the missing Jew. The congregation in the synagogue consists mainly of men; women are only allowed in the galleries. They have no vote (although this is now gradually changing) and can hold no office. A Jewess cannot even be a witness in court, whether in civil or criminal cases.[9] Her sphere of activity is strictly confined to the home. Here her main religious obligation is to prepare food according to Rabbinical law, to bring up the family in the Jewish way of life, and to be a good mother and wife.

THE HOME

Although the synagogue is the center of the community's worship, the home has a special place in the religious life of the Jew. There is a specific atmosphere about an orthodox Jewish home, because it is in the home where Judaism is really practiced. The mezuzzah on every doorpost is already a sign that here the Law is taken seriously. An important place in a Jewish home is the kitchen, because food plays a special part in the practice of Judaism. We have noted the strict separation of milk and meat. This in itself entails most meticulous housekeeping, as all utensils and dishes must be kept separate.

[8]*Laws and Customs*, p. 96.
[9]Cf. J. Jocz, *Judaism and the State of Israel*, p. 14f.

But there are other complications in respect to food. During the eight days of Passover (Nisan 15–22) all kitchen utensils, all plates, dishes, etc., are replaced by crockery specially kept for the occasion, so that no particle of leaven can contaminate the food. In addition, because of the prohibition of blood, laws concerning the salting and soaking of kosher meat require most meticulous attention.[10] But above all, it is the Sabbath which gives to the Jewish home special significance.

For the Jew, the Sabbath begins on Friday night when the first star becomes visible. But preparations for the Sabbath start early in the morning. This weekly occurrence is an important landmark in the spiritual life of the Jew. The atmosphere of a truly pious home on Friday night is one of the most beautiful features of Judaism. Even the poorest home becomes transformed and, in the glow of the Sabbath lights, Jews have found comfort and hope even in the most distressing times. With the burning candles, the glass of wine, the two white loaves on the festive table, something of the peace of eternity enters the home, no matter how stormy the world outside may be. Even more impressive is the Paschal Meal celebrated on the night of Nisan 14, when the whole family sits down to re-joice in the redemption from slavery. Passover is called in the synagogue *hag ha-herut*—the Festival of Freedom—and is essentially the festival of the home. In the *Seder* (lit., "order," "rite") the Jewish family re-lives the fate of the Hebrew people on their way from slavery to freedom, and keeps alive the great hope of redemption. But above all, it is the home where the pious Jew, wrapped in his prayer shawl and dressed with the phylacteries, prays to the God of the fathers and thus "sanctifies" His holy name. The center of the Jewish home is the table: "The festive table on Friday night merely demonstrates the function which this family table fulfills during the whole week. The table unites the family and has the power which formerly the altar of the Temple possessed—to bestow sanctity."[11] It is at the family table that the pious Jew blesses the God of Israel for every gift and every enjoyment.

[10]Cf. *Laws and Customs*, 67ff.
[11]Ignaz Maybaum, *The Jewish Home*, p. 35.

The Synagogue

For the Jew there is no special sanctity attached to the building as such. The synagogue is only a convenient place of assembly; it is only the presence of the worshiping community which gives significance to the building. The most important article in the synagogue is the Scroll of the Law. This roll of parchment, handwritten by an expert and carefully examined so that there is not the slightest error, decorated with ornaments, wrapped in mantles, and placed behind a curtain against the east wall (toward Jerusalem) is the symbol of all Jewish piety. It forms the center of attention, and the taking out of and the reading from the Scroll is the most solemn act of the Jewish service.

The Ark is opened.

Reader takes the Scrolls of the Law and says:
   Blessed be He who in His holiness gave the Law to His people Israel.

Reader and Congregation say:
   Hear, O Israel: the Lord our God, the Lord is One. One is our God; great is our Lord; holy is His name.

Reader:
   Magnify the Lord with me, and let us exalt His name together.

Reader and Congregation:
   Thine, O Lord, is the greatness, and the power and the glory, and the victory, and the majesty: for all that is in the Heaven and in the earth is Thine; Thine, O Lord, is the kingdom, and the supremacy as head over all. Exalt ye the Lord our God, and worship at His footstool: holy is He. Exalt ye the Lord our God, and worship at His holy mount; for the Lord our God is holy.

After the reading of the Law, the Scroll is "elevated" (*hagbahah*) for the Congregation to see, and all say:

   This is the Torah which Moses set before the children of Israel, according to the commandment of the Lord by the hand of Moses. It is a tree of life to them that grasp it, and of them that uphold it everyone is rendered happy. Its ways are ways of pleasantness, and all its paths are peace. Length of days is in its right hand: in its left hand are riches and honor. It pleased the Lord, for His righteousness' sake, to magnify the Law and to make it honorable.

The synagogue's liturgy is built round the Eighteen Blessings (since the beginning of the second century there are nineteen blessings) .[12] These benedictions can be divided into three parts: praise, petitions and thanksgiving. The Psalms play an important part in the synagogue's service. Another important feature is the Shema (lit., "hear") —beginning with the words: "Hear, O Israel . . ." (Deut. 6: 4-9) ; to this passage is added the text from Deuteronomy 11:13-21 and Numbers 15:37-41. The declaration of God's unity which the Jew believes to be expressed in the Shema is the most solemn act in Jewish worship: "Hear, O Israel, the Lord our God, the Lord is One."[13] After this verse the formula is interjected: "Blessed be His name, whose glorious kingdom is forever and ever." This sentence of praise pervades the synagogue's prayers and finds full expression in the Kaddish (lit., "hallowing") Prayer in which God's name is sanctified:

Reader:

Magnified and sanctified be His great name in the world which He hath created according to His will. May He establish His kingdom during your life and during your days, and during the life of all the house of Israel, even speedily and at a near time, and say ye, Amen.

The Kaddish Prayer occupies a central part in Jewish worship and like no other prayer expresses the peculiar genius of Judaism.

THE JEWISH YEAR

The Jewish sacred year is the most important link with the past. From festival to festival the individual Jew and the whole community experience personally the whole drama of Israel's Old Testament history. This, perhaps, is the strongest link between the synagogue and the Old Testament tradition. But the sacred year includes more than the Old Testament feasts and commemorates some outstanding events in the long history of the Jewish people. These events are seen in the light of God's providence and have, therefore,

[12]Cf. J. Jocz, *The Jewish People and Jesus Christ*, 51ff.
[13]It is doubtful whether this is a correct translation of the word *ehad* in Deut. 6:4; the English R.V. suggests several translations.

religious significance. It is not possible in this short chapter to give
a detailed description of all the feasts and fasts; all we can do is just
mention them briefly.

A. Rosh Hashanah—New Year[14]

This festival is the beginning of the civil year, though it falls in
the seventh month Tishri (September-October). According to the
Pentateuch, the beginning of the sacred year is really Nisan (March-
April) the first month in the Jewish calendar which roughly corresponds to April. New Year is an important festival and lasts two
days. It is regarded as a time of judgment and a day of remem-
brance and inaugurates the ten Solemn Days which end with the
Day of Atonement. It is a time of heart-searching and penitence,
and the solemnity of the festival is marked by the blowing of the
ram's horn (*shofar*).

B. Yom Kippur—Day of Atonement (tenth day of Tishri)

This is the most important day of the year in the life of a pious
Jew. It is the climax of the Ten Days of Penitence and is spent in
fasting for twenty-five hours so that not even a drop of water may be
taken to moisten one's lips. Jews believe that on this most solemn
day God "seals" man's fate about life and death, about prosperity
and adversity. The day is spent in the synagogue in prayer and in
penitence. The Hebrew word for "repentance" is *teshubah* and
means "returning" or "turning." Yom Kippur is a time of turning
to God in humble acknowledgment of sin and in prayer for forgiveness. One prayer is specially interesting to a Christian:

> Most merciful God is Thy name! Most gracious God is Thy
> name! We are called by this name! O Lord, grant our re-
> quest for Thy name's sake. Grant it for the sake of Thy
> truth . . . grant it for the sake of the young children at school.
> . . . Grant it for the sake of sucklings at the breast, who have
> not sinned. Grant it for the sake of weaned infants who
> have not transgressed; for the sake of orphans and widows.
> Grant it for Thy own sake, if not for ours; O grant it for
> Thy sake, and save us.

[14]Since the Jewish calendar is a lunar calendar, its equation with the Gregorian
calendar (the one in common use) varies. Approximations appear in parentheses after
Jewish festivals.

The fast concludes with the blast of the ram's horn announcing the conclusion of the day.

C. The Three Pilgrim Feasts

In old times, in accordance with the injunction: "Three times in the year shall all males appear before the Lord," the following festivals were used for pilgrimage to Jerusalem: Tabernacles, Passover, Feast of Weeks.

1. Tabernacles (Succoth)

This festival lasts nine days, from Tishri 15-23 (October).[15] The middle days of the festival are only half-holidays. The last day is of special significance, for it is the Rejoicing of the Law. On this day the synagogue completes the reading of the Torah, divided into weekly sections throughout the year, and immediately recommences to read it again. It is a day of great rejoicing in which children take a special part. The Scrolls are carried about in procession through the synagogue, and young and old dance and rejoice.

Tabernacles seems to be a fusion of two festivals: Jews build booths in memory of the wandering through the wilderness, but also express the agricultural nature of the feast by the "four species" consisting of a citron, a palm-tree branch, myrtle branches and branches of the willow; these are brought into the synagogue and waved in every direction "proclaiming thereby that the world is God's and that His dominion is everywhere."[16]

2. Passover (March-April)

This is really the first of the pilgrim feasts. We have put it second only because we began the year with the month Tishri and not with Nisan. Jews frequently speak of Passover as *Ḥag ha-matzot*—the Feast of Unleavened Bread. This festival too has an agricultural aspect which is connected with the "counting of the omers" beginning at the second night of Passover for forty-nine days. The "omer" was the offering of the first fruit of the winter barley before the new corn could be eaten. But this is only secondary; the main meaning of the feast is to commemorate deliverance from slavery in Egypt. Its special feature is the Paschal Meal celebrated in every Jewish

---

[15]In the land of Israel the festival lasts only seven days. It became the custom to add extra days in the Diaspora to all the festivals except Yom Kippur. Cf. Oesterley and Box, *The Religion and Worship of the Synagogue*, 348.
[16]Yaacov Vainstein, *The Cycle of the Jewish Year*, 95.

home. The order of this delightful family service is called *Seder*
(lit., "order") and the book which gives the details of the *Seder*
is called *Haggadah* (lit., "narration"). On this occasion the whole
story of the flight from Egypt is told by word of mouth and symbolic
actions. Most Christians hold that it was at a *Seder* that Jesus Christ
broke the bread and passed round the cup in anticipation of His
death which was to bring greater freedom than the one from national
bondage. In the Diaspora this festival lasts eight days, when no
leaven may be eaten.

3. Feast of Weeks (*Shabuoth*)

This festival marks the completion of the week of weeks—forty-
nine days from the second day of Passover—*i.e.*, the fiftieth day after
the first day of Passover, hence the Greek name "Pentecost." It lasts
two days in the Diaspora and only one day in the land of Israel, and
in Biblical times it was the main agricultural feast marking the wheat
harvest (about June). In the synagogue, *Shabuoth* is celebrated as
the season of the Giving of the Law. The Book of Ruth is read after
the morning service to remind the Jew that the Gentile world has
also a claim upon the God of Israel and that the Torah has universal
application. With these associations in mind the giving of the Holy
Spirit to the Church in Jerusalem on Pentecost gains special significance. The Holy Spirit of God through faith in Jesus Christ was
to renew Israel's heart to understand the Torah in a new way and
to preach it to the nations.

D. Historical feasts

Two more feasts play an important part in the Jewish calendar,
though neither was instituted by Moses: Ḥanukkah ("Dedication")
(December; frequently coincides with Christmas) and Purim
(? Lots) (February-March; one month before Passover). Ḥanukkah
is in memory of the rededication of the Temple after the Maccabean
victory over the Syrian armies in 165 B.C. According to tradition
there was found in the Temple only one cruse of oil fit for use because it was undefiled and intact with the seal of the high priest.
Such a cruse would usually suffice for one single day, but by a miracle
it lasted for eight days. Ḥanukkah has therefore become the Festival
of Light. A special Ḥanukkah lamp is lit in every Jewish home,
adding one candle each successive night until eight candles are lit.

On the Sabbath of Hanukkah the lesson from Zechariah is read in the synagogue: "Not by might nor by power, but by my Spirit, saith the Lord of Hosts" (Zech. 5:6) .

Purim is celebrated in memory of the deliverance from the hands of Haman as recorded in the Book of Esther. The day before is observed as a minor fast, but the day itself is kept in a spirit of rejoicing; in fact, it is Jewry's carnival. The Book of Esther is read in the synagogue, and God is praised for His miraculous dealing with His people.

E. The synagogue observes four major fast days in addition to Yom Kippur (October) and a number of minor fasts.

The major fasts commemorate the beginning of the siege of Jerusalem, the breach made in the wall, the destruction of the first and second Temples (according to tradition on the same day, Ab 9) , and the martyrdom of Gedaliah (cf. Jer. 41) . Pious Jews are also wont to fast on Monday and Thursday after the festive seasons of Passover and Tabernacles.

THE TEACHING OF JUDAISM

We can here only indicate very briefly the main tenets of the synagogue.

Life. The basic principle dominating the Jewish faith is that God is One and that He is the sole and only Creator of Heaven and earth. He is the Source of life and everything exists by His will. The sovereignty of God runs through the whole liturgy. The Morning Prayer for every day commences with the Yigdal—"Magnified and praised be the living God"; and is followed by the *Adon olam*—"He is Lord of the universe."

Life is the most precious gift to the religious Jew. To preserve one human life is equal to preserving the whole world; and conversely, to destroy one human life is equal to destroying the whole world. Life to the Jew has a wider connotation than physical existence; it includes the spiritual and moral aspects as well. Judaism is essentially a moral religion infused with optimism. Matter is not a vehicle of evil but was created for man's blessing. To live the pious life is to enjoy the gifts of God and to bless the Creator for them. "The Holy Spirit rests on him who has a joyous heart," is a Rabbinic saying. A special point is made on Jewish festivals of eating fruits and dainties and of encouraging others to do likewise.

Death. A people attached to life naturally shies from death. Death is the most terrible calamity to the Jew. There is something characteristically Jewish about the horror of death. It may be that this relates to the fact that the Jew faces judgment on the strength of his own merits, whereas the Christian pleads the merits of Jesus Christ. There is also the fact that the Old Testament has only veiled and indirect references to the life after death. Bereavement is thus a major tragedy in the Jewish family. The Jewish customs of mourning are designed to express the maximum of grief. After death it falls upon the son of the deceased, or another member of the family, to recite the Kaddish Prayer at a public place of worship. Great importance is attached to this rite. It is not uncommon to hire a stranger to recite the prayer where there are no relatives left. It is of some interest that the Kaddish Prayer makes no reference to death, except at the burial service. The Kaddish is a glorious ascription of praise. "Blessed, praised and glorified, extolled and honored, magnified and lauded be the name of the Holy One, blessed be He." With this doxology the Jew surrenders to the omnipotent will of God. Although he professes that God will quicken the dead, the resurrection is not a personal experience but a pious hope. Judaism is usually described as ethical monotheism. The same could be said of Christianity, but Jewish monotheism has its own peculiar feature. Judaism understands the unity of God in almost a numerical sense— every emphasis is given to the affirmation that God is One. The Maimonidean Creed (twelfth century) defines the unity of God in the second article: "I believe with perfect faith that the Creator, blessed be His name, is a unity and that there is no unity in any manner like unto His."

God. Together with the unity goes the invisibility and incorporeality (spirituality) of God. The second commandment has taken deep roots in the Jewish consciousness. The Jew shies from any visual portrayal or even symbol of God. This is the reason for the lack of art in the synagogue. Pious Jews have even gone so far as to refuse to be painted or photographed in case it should lead to idolatry. There can be no pictures in the synagogue. The eternal, omnipo-

tent, just, good, holy and perfect God is beyond all human appre-
hension. The God of Israel is naturally the God of all creation,
but He is in a special way Israel's God. The recurring phrase in the
liturgy is "Our Father, our King." The synagogue blesses the God
of the universe who has chosen Israel from all nations and has given
him His Law.

Sin. For Judaism, sin is not an inherent flaw in human nature
but only a deficiency which can be remedied. Man need not sin
if he observes the Law and walks humbly with God. The synagogue
therefore repudiates Original Sin as a non-Jewish conception; it
looks upon sin not as a state but as an *act.* Judaism thus speaks of
sin in the plural: *aberot,* trespasses. Man may go wrong and fall
short of the mark, but he is also able to make amends and restore
the balance. He makes his own atonement, and God graciously for-
gives. This does not mean that the pious Jew knows nothing about
grace, but it is grace to cope with the requirements of the Law and
to live up to the high ideal. The Jew knows that God's forgiveness
is conditioned by man's repentance, hence the tremendous importance of the Day of Atonement. Repentance is thus the clue to
the divine—human relationship. It is, as it were, the mechanism
whereby man adjusts himself to the Creator. Behind this ethical
rationalism is the conviction that man is sufficient to cope with his
situation. Salvation from sin in the Christian sense is entirely foreign to the synagogue.

Messiah. The Jewish concept of sin makes a Saviour as the Christian understands it utterly unnecessary. The Jewish Messiah does
not save from sin but is a wise leader anointed by God to gather
Israel and to restore him to his former glory. The Messiah will be
under the strict authority of the Law and practice it in all detail.
The Law is above the Messiah and can never be rescinded. Nevertheless the Messianic hope is deeply ingrained into the faith of the synagogue and recurs constantly in the liturgy, but in spite of this, Judaism is not committed to a personal Messiah; the Messianic ideal is
more important than the Messiah's Person. Liberal Judaism has
completely abandoned the idea of a personal Messiah and only believes in the Messianic Age—the golden time of the future which
will come about by man's heroic effort. Messiah to the synagogue

is therefore not a superhuman Being, though pious Jews still pray for His coming every day.[17]

THE CHRISTIAN ASPECT OF JUDAISM

In spite of the fact that the synagogue has much in common with the Church there is a deep gulf dividing them. The primary issue concerns the Person of Jesus Christ. The Church makes stupendous claims for Jesus of Nazareth, the synagogue emphatically denies these claims. But apart from this the "salvation" offered in the New Testament is not the kind the Jew expects or needs. The pious Jew already knows himself as a son of God and claims direct approach. At best, for the Jew, Jesus can occupy a position equal to the sages and teachers of Israel. Every other claim is to him blasphemy. The Christian doctrine of the Trinity clashes with the Jewish doctrine of the Unity which admits of no variation in the Godhead. Even had the synagogue accepted the Messiahship of Jesus, it would still have to deny the doctrine of the Trinity; otherwise it would cease to be the synagogue and become the Church. To Judaism, Jesus can only be a man; no decisive religious significance can be attached to His Person.

To the Church, God's *ultimate* dealing with man is in His Son, Jesus Christ. It is for this reason that Christ is the end of the Law (cf. Rom. 10:4). Christians believe that God is no respecter of persons; He does not deal with Jews in one way and with Gentiles in another. The Christian missionary enterprise is borne by the conviction that God deals with *all* men on an equal footing. The truth is one and indivisible. If the synagogue is right, then Jesus is a false Messiah. The Church knows Him to be true, and she sees God, sin and life in the perspective of His cross and passion. Seen in this light, she discovers in the Jewish atttiude man's self-sufficiency before God. Only in the shadow of the cross and in the light of the resurrection is it possible to assess Judaism correctly. From this perspective, Judaism appears to be the highest expression of man's autonomy before God. This is the constant danger of religion: "They have a zeal of God, but not according to knowledge" (Rom. 10:2).

[17]J. Jocz, *The Jewish People and Jesus Christ*, 281ff.

THE POSITION OF JUDAISM IN THE MODERN WORLD

The Judaism we have described above is the one which has held sway over the majority of the Jewish people for centuries. But the emancipation movement of the Jewries in Europe in the last century has initiated a revolution which is in process of changing the whole aspect of Jewish life. Closer contact with Western culture has served to emphasize the discrepancy between Rabbinical Judaism and the modern world. As a result many Jews have left the synagogue altogether, but others have tried to introduce reforms which would bring Judaism in harmony with the modern age. The reform movement began in Eastern Europe but took shape in Germany. It gradually spread to England, and in America it took several forms. The father of American Reform Judaism is undoubtedly Isaac Mayer Wise (1819-1900) who organized the first Conference of Reform Rabbis at Cleveland in 1855. This conference was followed by the one at Philadelphia in 1889 when a uniform program of reform was accepted. Reform Judaism repudiates the national ideal and favors a purely religious concept of Israel. It accepts only the ethical teaching of the Mosaic Code and gives a spiritual interpretation to many of the tenets of Judaism such as belief in a bodily resurrection. It rejects the dietary laws and with it most of traditional law. Reform Judaism, in its extreme form, is not any more a religion of Torah but rather an ethical system with a monotheistic philosophy behind it.[18] Between the two extreme movements, orthodoxy and reform, there is also a moderate body of opinion which strives to combine progressiveness with tradition. This conservative group had once a large following in Germany and is an important factor in American Jewry. Its origin goes back to the founder of the historic study of Judaism, Leopold Zunz (1794-1886). But Zunz belongs to the more extreme wing of reform; it was Zacharias Frankel (1801-1875), the chief rabbi of Dresden, who managed to combine a progressive attitude to learning with personal loyalty to Jewish tradition. *Die Monatsschrift für Geschichte und Wissenschaft des Judentums,* which he founded, exerted an enlightening and deepening influence upon educated Jewry. This "positive historical Judaism," sometimes referred to as the "historical school," found its great pro-

[18]Cf. M. Simon, *Jewish Religious Conflicts,* p. 137f.

tagonist in the Jewish historian Heinrich Graetz (1817-1888). It
was Graetz's conviction that it is possible to make historic Judaism
compatible with the modern outlook. But even Graetz was too much
committed to negative criticism to be able to form a more positive
synthesis. It was left to Solomon Schechter (1847-1915), a Roumanian
Jew with a chassidic background, who came to England as the tutor
in Rabbinics to Claude Montefiore, and later became Reader of
Rabbinics in Cambridge, to carry on the struggle. In 1901 Schechter was appointed president of the Jewish Theological Seminary in
New York, and he set himself the task of counteracting the extremes
of Reform Judaism. In fact, Prof. Bentwich describes him as the
leader of the Jewish Counter Reformation.[19] He was not only a man
of learning but of piety and became a great influence in American
Jewry, chiefly among the youth. But even he failed to achieve a
synthesis.[20] It is therefore true to say that religious Jewry is at
present in a state of transition. Orthodox Judaism is steadily losing
ground, but both reform and conservative Judaism is only attracting
a fraction of the increasingly secularized Jewish population. Large
numbers of Jews are outside all religious groups. In England, "fund-
raising" or some other kind of social service has become a substitute
for faith in God.[21] In Israel, where the reform movement is recent
and orthodox Judaism is in bitter opposition to modern trends, the
bulk of the population is indifferent if not hostile to traditional religion. This does not mean that the Jews are irreligious; only that
in the crucible of modern life Judaism is unable to withstand the
heat and is crumbling.[22] The modern Jew is in search of new values
and of new spiritual insight. There are indications that the Bible is
once again coming to his rescue and providing an answer to his
deepest need. What form the Judaism of the future will take is as
yet undecided, but it is for the Christian Church to see to it that the
treasures of the New Testament and, above all, the Person of Jesus
Christ remain not hidden to the Jew in his quest for truth.

[19]Cf. Norman Bentwich, *Solomon Schechter*, p. 207f.
[20]Prof. Bentwich remarks: "He was more successful in exposing the cant of reform
than in revealing the content of conservative Judaism," *ibid.*, 343.
[21]Cf. M. Friedman (ed.), *A Minority in Britain*, p. 186.
[22]Cf. J. Jocz, *Judaism and the State of Israel.*

BIBLIOGRAPHY

Authorised Daily Prayer Book of the United Hebrew Congregations of the British Empire, transl. S. Singer. London: Eyre & Spottiswoode, Ltd., 1914.

BENTWICH, NORMAN. *Solomon Schechter.* Cambridge: The University Press, 1938.

DANBY, H. *The Mishnah.* Oxford: Clarendon Press, 1933.

EPSTEIN, I. *Judaism.* London: The Epworth Press, 1939.

FRIEDLANDER, GERALD. *Laws and Customs of Israel.* (Trans. and ed.) London: Shapiro, Vallentine & Co., 1921.

FRIEDMAN, ed. *A Minority in Britain.* London: Vallentine, Mitchell & Co., Ltd., 1955.

Jewish Encyclopedia. 12 vols. New York 10 and London: Funk. & Wagnalls Co., 1906.

JOCZ, J. *The Jewish People and Jesus Christ.* London: S.P.C.K., 1954.

———. *Judaism and the State of Israel.* London: International Hebrew Christian Alliance, 1952.

MAYBAUM, IGNAZ. *The Jewish Home.* London: James Clarke & Co., Ltd., 1945.

OESTERLEY, W. O. E., and BOX, G. H. *The Religion and Worship of the Synagogue.* London: Sir Isaac Pitman & Sons, Ltd., 1911.

SIMON, MAURICE. *Jewish Religious Conflicts.* London: Hutchinson's University Library, 1950.

VAINSTEIN, YAACOV. *The Cycle of the Jewish Year.* Jerusalem: World Zionist Organization, 1953.

FIG. 4.—The new Islamic Center in Washington, D.C. (Courtesy of Islamic Center.)

Praise be to Allah, Lord of the Worlds,
The Beneficent, the Merciful.
Owner of the Day of Judgment,
Thee (alone) we worship; Thee (alone) we ask for help.
Show us the straight path,
The path of those whom Thou hast favoured;
Not (the path) of those who earn Thine anger nor of those who
go astray.

SURA 1, the *Koran*

IV.

Islam

by WILLIAM McELWEE MILLER

WHEN JESUS CHRIST COMMANDED His followers to go into all the world and make disciples of all nations, there were no Mohammedans in existence. The religion of Mohammed did not make its appearance till six centuries after the time of Christ. Today there are more than 300,000,000 in the world, about one-seventh of the human race, who believe in Mohammed as their Prophet and who call themselves Moslems.[1] Every Christian who takes seriously the Great Commission must be concerned about these millions of his fellow men who do not recognize Jesus Christ as their Saviour and Lord. In order to love them as he should, and to help them to know God's love as revealed in Christ, it is necessary for him to know something about them and their beliefs and practices. The purpose

WILLIAM McELWEE MILLER, A.B., M.A. (Washington and Lee University), B.D. (Princeton Theological Seminary), D.D. (Wand L. University), is a missionary to Iran with the United Presbyterian Church U.S.A. Going to Iran in 1919, he served at Meshed, Teheran, Tabriz, and Resht, and is now once more in Teheran. He is Chairman of the Board of Evangelism of the Synod of the Evangelical Church of Iran, and of the Church Council of Iran. He has written an English book on Bahaism, has translated an Arabic Shi'ite Creed into English, has prepared commentaries in Persian on Luke, John, Acts, Romans and I Corinthians, has written a Persian History of the Early Church in the Roman and Iranian Empires, and a Persian textbook on evangelism.

[1] *Islam* is an Arabic word which means "to submit," "to yield" (to the will of God). A *Moslem* (or Muslim) is one who submits, that is, one who believes on Mohammed and follows the religion of Islam.

61

of this chapter is to give to Christians in America the information they need to enable them to share intelligently in the task of sending the Good News of Christ's salvation to the followers of Mohammed.

However, it is evident that it is impossible in one brief chapter to give an adequate account of a religion which has spread over a large part of Africa, the Near East, and Asia and which has a history of more than thirteen centuries. It includes in its fold civilizations as different as the primitive Moros of the Philippines and the cultured university graduates of Cairo and Beirut, and theological beliefs which are as far apart as are those of the Roman Catholics of Colombia and the Unitarians of New England, or of the Mormons of Utah and the Presbyterians of Scotland. Hence it should be understood that the religion described in this article is chiefly that variety of Islam which the author has known in Iran, and it is inevitable that some of the statements about Islam which are true for Iran and some other lands will not be entirely correct for the whole Moslem World. However, every effort has been made to draw a picture which though incomplete is accurate in outline.

HISTORICAL DEVELOPMENT

A. Mohammed, the Founder of Islam

Some religions had no founder and have developed without being greatly influenced by any one individual. But that is not the case with the religion of Islam. While the followers of this religion do not usually call themselves "Mohammedans," it is as appropriate to give them this name as it is to call the followers of Jesus Christ "Christians." Mohammed has profoundly influenced the private lives and shaped the destinies of the countless millions of people who, during the past 1,300 years, have looked to him as their divinely appointed leader. Therefore, it is impossible to understand Islam and its adherents without knowing something of Mohammed.

About the year A.D. 570 there was born in the city of Mecca near the west coast of Arabia a boy who was named Mohammed, which means "praised." His father Abdullah ("Slave of Allah") died before his son was born, and the mother Amina died when Mohammed was only six years old. The child was brought up first by his grandfather and then by his uncle, Abu Talib, who were members of the influential tribe of Quraish in Mecca. The boy sometimes took care of the flocks in the desert, as Moses and David had done long before, and sometimes went with the camel caravans carrying merchandise from Arabia to Syria, thus coming in contact with people of a higher civilization and a better religion than that of the heathen Arabs. Later Mohammed entered the employ of a wealthy widow named Khadija, and was so faithful in attending to her business affairs that when he was about twenty-five years of age and she about forty, Khadija decided to marry him. The marriage seems to have been a happy one, and Mohammed was greatly helped and encouraged by his faithful wife. During the twenty-five years that she lived with him he took no other wife. Several children were born of this marriage, but only one daughter named Fatima survived. Mohammed gradually became a man of influence in his native town.

At that time the people of Arabia were idolaters. They believed in a supreme god whom they called Allah, but along with Allah they worshiped a number of other gods and goddesses. The religious center of Arabia was Mecca, and in Mecca was a small temple called the Kaaba in which were numerous idols which were worshiped by the Arabs. Built into the wall of the Kaaba was a Black Stone, a meteorite, which was considered very sacred. The heathen Arabs used to make pilgrimages to the Kaaba and go around it seven times and kiss this Black Stone. There were Jews and Christians in various parts of Arabia at that time, but those who knew the one true God failed to make Him known to the heathen. If the followers of Christ had made disciples of the people of Arabia as He commanded them to do, Mohammed would probably have been a Christian and might have rendered a great service to the cause of Christ. But although he learned much from the Jews and something from the Christians whom he met, he never heard the true Gospel of salvation and so not only missed the way himself but also led astray a great multitude of people.

Mohammed was a religious man. He was acquainted with a group of men in Mecca who were dissatisfied with idolatry and wanted to follow what they called "The Religion of Abraham" and, like them, he used sometimes to retire to a cave three miles distant from Mecca for meditation. He had no doubt been influenced against the evils of idolatry by what he heard from Jews and Christians. And as he thought about these things a great passion arose in his heart to save his people from the false religion which they practiced and to teach them the true religion. One day when Mohammed was asleep in the cave he thought he saw the angel Gabriel in the form of a young man and heard a voice saying, "Recite thou in the name of thy Lord." Mohammed replied that he was not a reciter, but the angel repeated the command three times and pressed his body so hard that he thought he would die. He was so frightened by this experience that he told his wife and his friends, but they assured him that as God's Word had formerly come to Moses and other prophets so it had now come to him. Mohammed was forty years old when he had this first revelation.

After a time other revelations followed. Sometimes he saw Gabriel, sometimes he heard the noise of a bell and through it the words of Gabriel were brought to him. His whole frame would then become agitated, and perspiration would roll down his face. Sometimes he would fall on the ground and foam at the mouth, as one having a fit. It seems that for a time Mohammed was in doubt as to whether his revelations were from God or from Satan, but Gabriel assured him that he was indeed the prophet of God and must recite the words which were spoken to him.

The words recited by Mohammed were later written down by his friends and followers, and after his death were collected in a book which was called *The Qur'an* (Koran), that is, The Recitation. It is generally believed that Mohammed was unable to read or write. The Koran as we now have it is divided into 114 Suras (chapters), some short and some very long. The earlier Suras were short, but when the Koran was arranged by Mohammed's successors the shorter Suras were placed last, so they are not now in chronological order. One of the best of the earlier Suras is Number 93, "The Brightness." Rodwell translates it as follows:

> In the name of God, the Compassionate, the Merciful
>> By the noonday brightness,
>> And by the night when it darkeneth!
>> Thy Lord hath not forsaken thee, neither hath He been displeased.

And surely the Future shall be better for thee than the Past,
And in the end shall thy Lord be bounteous to thee and
   thou shalt be satisfied.
Did he not find thee an orphan and gave thee a home?
And found thee erring and guided thee,
And found thee needy and enriched thee.
As to the orphan therefore wrong him not,
And as to him that asketh of thee, chide him not away;
And as for the favors of thy Lord tell them abroad.

Until recently Moslems have not translated the Arabic Koran into other languages on the ground that it must be read only in Arabic and cannot be translated. During the last few years, however, several translations have appeared.

The early Suras proclaim the unity and greatness of Allah the one true God, foretell the Resurrection and the Day of Judgment and picture the delights of a sensual Paradise and the tortures of the damned in Hell.

The first person to believe on Mohammed as the Prophet of Allah was his wife Khadija, who often comforted and encouraged him when men opposed him. Then Ali, the fourteen-year-old cousin of Mohammed who lived in his home, became a Moslem. Ali later married Mohammed's daughter Fatima and was one of the great leaders of Islam. Zaid, a slave who had been freed by Mohammed and had then become his adopted son, was the next to believe. The first person outside the family to become a Moslem was Abu Bakr, a respected merchant, whose adherence to the cause was a great encouragement to the Prophet of Islam. Abu Bakr later gave his daughter Ayisha in marriage to Mohammed. Others followed till the number of believers reached forty. However, Mohammed's preaching did not meet with much success among the rich and influential men of Mecca who were financially interested in maintaining the idol worship of the Kaaba.

After several years of quiet preaching, Mohammed began more active and open propaganda. He attacked the national religion of the Arabs, saying that the gods they worshiped were no gods. This charge aroused opposition and the persecution began, but most of Mohammed's followers remained faithful.

In A.D. 620, ten years after Mohammed began his mission, Khadija died and she was greatly missed by her husband. However, Mohammed soon comforted himself by marrying two new wives, one of them being the little daughter of Abu Bakr (the marriage was consummated three years later when she was nine or ten years of age). Mohammed continued to add to his harem till he had twelve wives at the same time, two of whom were slave girls.

The situation in Mecca became so difficult that Mohammed finally decided to leave his native town and go to Madina (Medina) where he had friends. Accordingly in A.D. 622 he took this important step, and some two hundred of his followers migrated with him to Madina, to the north of Mecca. This migration is called the Hijra or Hegira, and Moslem history is dated from it. In Iran the year A.D. 1960 is 1338 A.H. (622 plus 1338 equals 1960).

Mohammed's position in Madina was very different from what it had been in Mecca. There he had been a preacher preaching against idolatry without much success, but in Madina he soon became a ruler and legislator. The people of Madina chose him as their chief and soon most of the population professed Islam. There were many Jews in Madina, and Mohammed tried to win their support by facing Jerusalem as they did when he prayed. But the Jews refused to accept him as a Prophet of God, and one day he suddenly turned his back on Jerusalem as he was leading his followers in the daily worship and completed his prayer with his face toward Mecca, thus attempting to win the allegiance of the people of Mecca by making their Kaaba the center of his religion. Later Mohammed fought the Jews and banished or slaughtered many of them. Being in need of money, he also attacked the rich caravans of the Meccans as they passed Madina and divided the booty among his followers. This led to bloody wars with the people of Mecca in which Mohammed won several victories. Many tribes now came and submitted to him as their ruler and accepted Islam as their religion, and Mohammed gradually became the most powerful chief in all Arabia. He finally marched on Mecca with a large army, and the city submitted in 9 A.H. He and his followers went to the Kaaba and took out the idols and performed the rites of the pilgrimage, just as they had done before Islam. Other tribes quickly submitted, and the Prophet of Islam became the ruler of Arabia. Shortly afterward he died in Madina in 11 A.H. (A.D. 633).

The state which Mohammed founded was a theocracy, a Church—State. He was both prophet and king, and there was no separation of politics and religion. All laws were religious laws and all were enforced by the power of the State. Unbelief was rebellion and was to be punished by death. In Arabia there was no such thing as religious liberty, and for the heathen there was no choice except Islam or the sword. Christians and Jews ("People of the Book") who would not become Moslems were required to pay a special tax to the Moslem State. Even today in the opinion of orthodox Moslems it is impossible to separate Church and State, and the mullas (priests) always insist that they have a political as well as a spiritual role to play. It should not therefore surprise Western diplomats that there are frequent attempts by Moslem religious leaders to control the affairs of government—for this is what their Prophet Mohammed did.

There is no doubt that Mohammed was a most remarkable man. But what is the explanation of his career and influence? Opinions differ widely. Moslems believe that he was indeed the Prophet of Allah who was guided in all he said and did by God, and was without sin. Some Western scholars think he was at first sincere in his efforts to make known the one true God but later made religion a means to political ends. Others hold that his purpose was from the first political, and religion was to him always secondary. Still others think that he was a pathological case. Whatever the explanation may be, it is evident that, although in the early part of his career Mohammed made a courageous effort to destroy idolatry and induce the Arabs to fear and obey Allah, in his later years he used his "divine revelations" to justify him in doing things which were condemned even by the heathen Arabs.

B. The Caliphs

How was the political-religious movement begun by Mohammed to be continued after his death? There was some uncertainty as to who should succeed the Prophet, for it seems that he had not clearly indicated who his successor (khalifa or caliph) should be—or else the majority of his followers were not willing to accept the one appointed by him. Finally the leaders agreed that Abu Bakr should be their chief. The task of the new leader was not easy, for on hearing

of Mohammed's death many of the newly converted tribes revolted,
and it was necessary to conquer them again with the sword. The
second Caliph was Umar, a great warrior. Under his rule the armies
of the Moslem Arabs went forth to Syria, Mesopotamia, Persia and
Egypt, and, with the name of Allah on their lips and a lust for plun-
der in their hearts, defeated the armies of Rome and Persia, now
greatly weakened by years of war with each other, and forced Islam
on the conquered peoples. The third Caliph was Uthman, and during his rule in 30 A.H. the variant versions of the Koran were collected
and a standard version adopted and all others were destroyed. The
fourth Caliph was Ali, the son-in-law of Mohammed. Several Moslem
leaders, aided by Mohammed's widow Ayisha (who entered the battle mounted on a camel) fought against Ali, and it is said that 10,000
Moslems were killed in this family fight. Many Moslems refused to
obey Ali, and he was finally murdered in about 41 A.H. Thus these
four orthodox Caliphs guided the Moslem State for thirty years and
under their rule it spread from Arabia to all parts of the Near East
and became a great world power.

Later the armies of Islam conquered all North Africa, which had
been one of the strongholds of Christianity, and crossed over to
Europe, conquering Spain which was for seven centuries a Moslem
land. They were turned back in France in A.D. 732 by Charles Martel
(who "hammered the Moors at the Battle of Tours"). Had not this
battle been won by the Christians it is possible that all Europe might
have become Moslem. Islam again turned eastward and spread
throughout India and Asia. The Turkish tribes which moved westward out of Central Asia into the Near East were Moslems, and by
conquering Palestine they brought on the Crusades when the Christians of Europe tried to conquer the Moslems with the sword and
failed. In later centuries the Sultan of Turkey was considered the
Caliph by many Moslems, but early in the twentieth century the
Caliphate was abolished, and today there is no one head for the
Moslem State. In fact, the Moslem World is divided into many
states, each one independent or dependent upon some non-Moslem
government, and there is no probability that all will ever again be
united under one Caliph.

Sects of Islam

The followers of Mohammed are divided into two main sects, the Sunnites and the Shi'ites. The great majority of Moslems are Sunnites, that is, they claim to follow the Sunna, which are the practices of Mohammed as handed down by tradition. Each member of the Sunnite sect belongs to one of the four recognized schools of interpretation of Islamic law. These schools do not constitute sects. Sunnites recognize the Caliphs as the rightful successors to Mohammed.

The Shi'ites are so called because they belong to the Shi'a (the Sect). They are found in Iran, Iraq, India, Pakistan and some other lands. The Shi'ite religion is the official religion of Iran, and the Shah must be a follower of this sect. Shi'ites do not accept the Caliphs (except the fourth) and contend that the true successors of the Prophet were Ali, the son-in-law of Mohammed, and Ali's descendants, whom they call "Imams." The Shi'ites have books of traditions different from, and often contradictory to, the traditions of the Sunnites. They accuse the Sunnites of having destroyed a part of the original Koran in which was written God's command that Ali should succeed Mohammed. They show great devotion and honor to the family of Mohammed, commemorating the martyrdoms of the Imams and visiting their tombs, a practice which is hateful to the Sunnites. Their beliefs will be described more fully later on.

Doctrines of Islam

In Islam as in Christianity there are many schools of thought, but all Moslems unite in the following brief expression of their faith: "There is no god but Allah, and Mohammed is his Apostle." The basic doctrines of most of the Moslems of Iran and of many other areas follow.

A. Belief in Allah

As we have seen, the Arabs before the time of Mohammed considered Allah one of their gods, but Mohammed proclaimed that he was the only true God, and all the other gods were idols. Moslems place the greatest importance upon monotheism and think that attributing a "partner" to God is one of the greatest sins. The Christian doctrine of the Trinity is hateful to Moslems because they think it denies the divine unity. Moreover, they understand the unity of God to imply uniqueness, so they assert that God cannot be likened to anyone or anything. Once an illiterate farmer, who was threshing wheat by driving his oxen around a pile of straw, asked a missionary, who was watching him, who God was. The missionary replied that God is our Father. "No," said the farmer, "God is *not* our Father, for He cannot be likened to anything. He is different from anything we can think." Such a God is therefore unknowable, for all that can be said of Him is that He is not this or that. While God's name is often on the lips of Moslems, He is to most of them an Unknown Being.

A devout convert to Christianity once said, "When I was a Moslem I thought I knew God, but I did not—I came to know God only when I knew Christ."

As Raymond Lull, the first great missionary to Moslems, pointed out long ago, the greatest deficiency in the Moslem religion is in its conception of God. Great importance is attached to the power of Allah, but little is said about his holiness and his love. The love of God is mentioned only a few times in the Koran, the most important verse being 3:29: "If ye love God then follow me: God will love you and forgive your sins, for God is Forgiving, Merciful. . . . God loveth not the unbelievers." Allah's acts are arbitrary: "Verily God misleadeth whom He will, and guideth whom He will" (7:178; 35:9). The strong conviction found in all parts of the Moslem World that all things have been determined by the will of Allah very often destroys initiative and the desire for improvement. For instance, parents often neglect to put a fence about the open pool of water which is found in almost every yard; and then when their children fall into the pool and are drowned, as often happens, they say, "It was the will of God." There have been various schools of thought in Islam which have fought against this fatalism (Kismet), but without much success. To guard against the danger of making God an arbitrary despot the Moslems of the Shi'ite sect insist that God is *Just* in all His acts.

How different is Allah from the holy and loving Father of Jesus Christ who so loved the sinners of the world that He gave His Son to die for them and save them! Allah is said to be kind to men, but he does nothing for their salvation that costs him anything. Christians love God because He first loved them when they were sinners and gave Christ for them, but if God had not shown His love in this way, they would never have loved Him as they do. And most Moslems do not love God—though they may fear Him and try to obey Him. So it must not be assumed that since Moslems worship one God they are very close to Christians in their faith. The important thing is not the belief that God is One, but the conception that believers have of God's character. Satan also believes and trembles!

B. Belief in Allah's Prophets

Moslems believe that God has sent many prophets into the world to guide men and speak His Word to them. Members of the Shi'ite sect say that the number of God's prophets is 124,000, but some other sects place the number at 144,000. Twenty-eight of these prophets are mentioned in the Koran, but the names of the rest are unknown. Noah, Abraham, Moses, Jesus and Mohammed are considered the "Great Prophets" in Iran, and it is thought that each of these five brought a law which was for all mankind and which remained in force till it was abrogated by the law brought by a later prophet. Though the Koran refers to the sins of the prophets (with the exception of Jesus), many Moslems believe that all the prophets were sinless, for since they were prophets of God nothing that they did could be considered sinful. But none of the prophets were divine or sons of God, they were rather "supermen." Many of the prophets had books which were given them by divine inspiration, and the Koran attests the truth of these books which are the Scriptures of the Jews and Christians. The earlier prophets foretold the coming of those who would follow, so it is thought that Jesus must have certainly foretold the coming of Mohammed. Mohammed, however, is the last and the greatest of the prophets, and he foretold the coming of no one else, for his law will be in force to the end of the world.

While Mohammed in the Koran claims to be no more than a man, many of his followers hold that he is far greater than man. Some say that the first thing which God created was the Light of Mohammed, and everything else was created for him; he is the most perfect of all God's creatures. It is evident that the Moslem conception of Mohammed has been influenced by the Christian conception of Christ. Mohammed is the Perfect Man, and his example should be followed in everything—in eating, in the use of the tooth-pick, in dress, in the manner of caring for the hair and beard, in marriage and the treatment of wives, in the treatment of friends and enemies, in worship and in government and in war. Thus the example of Mohammed (as he is portrayed correctly or incorrectly in the Koran and in the Traditions) has profoundly influenced the lives of countless millions of people. A stream does not rise higher than its source, and while some Moslems have attained a character holier and lovelier than that of their Prophet, most of those who imitate Mohammed fail to reach even his level of moral and spiritual life. Moslems themselves are often the first to admit that their moral standards are not as high as they should be, and they usually say it is their own fault, not the fault of their religion. However, a better acquaintance with the history of their religion would convince them that the source of weakness is not in them alone but also in their Book and in their Prophet.

C. Belief in the Imams

The great division in the Moslem World is over the question, "Who was the rightful successor to Mohammed?" The majority of Moslems, the Sunnites, have held that the rightful successors of the Prophet were the Four Caliphs who one after another ruled the Moslem State after Mohammed's death. But from early times there has been an active minority who maintained that ordinary men were not worthy to succeed God's Prophet, and that the rightful successor was Mohammed's son-in-law, Ali, the husband of Fatima. They held that Ali was succeeded by certain of his descendents, all of whom have the same spiritual rank as Mohammed and Ali. These successors are called Imams, and those who believe in them are known as Shi'ites (sectarians). Many of the Shi'ites believe that there were twelve Imams; but the Ismailis, of whom the famous Aga Khan of India was chief, accept only seven Imams. The Shi'ites believe that their Imams were sinless, that they all performed wonderful miracles, and that all but one died as martyrs. The tombs of the Imams which are located in Iraq and Iran are visited each year by hundreds of thousands of Shi'ites from various parts of the Moslem World. The most important day in the religious year of the Shi'ites is the tenth of the month Moharram when the martyrdom of Imam Hosein, the son of Ali, is commemorated by processions, weeping, breast-beating and even sometimes by devotees cutting their heads with swords till the blood gushes. Those who believe in twelve Imams say that the twelfth (who is called the "Mahdi" and the "Lord of the Age") did not die but disappeared in 260 A.H. and will one day appear again to set up his kingdom on earth. A carpenter in Iran who later became a Christian used to have two swords, one of which he kept in his home and one in his shop, so that whenever the Lord of the Age should appear he might at once gird on his sword and mount a horse and go forth with him to conquer the world for Islam. This belief in the Imams, which for the Shi'ites is of primary importance, is rejected by the Sunnites.

D. Belief in the Resurrection

The heathen Arabs did not believe in a future life; but Mohammed, influenced by Jewish and Christian teaching, assured them that there would be a resurrection of the dead. Hence the doctrine of the future life came to have great importance in Islam, and many details not found in the Koran have been supplied by tradition. In Iran the popular belief is that after the coming of the twelfth Imam, who will be aided by Jesus in forcing the world to accept Islam, everyone on the earth, including Jesus, will die. Then the trumpet will sound and all will be raised to life. God will weigh men's actions in a great pair of balances to determine whether their good deeds outweigh their evil deeds. Hence it is necessary for sinners who wish to be saved from Hell to perform many good deeds in this world, works of merit, to balance off their evil deeds on the Day of Judgment. If one is 51 per cent good he will go to Heaven. Also there will be a bridge, very narrow and very long, over which all men must pass, and those who are sinners will fall off into Hell. Hell is a place of torment where unbelievers and sinners will burn in the fire, and Heaven is a place of sensuous delight where there is a pool of wine which does not intoxicate, and where in addition to women from the earth there are beautiful females called *huris* who are given to male believers for their enjoyment. No doubt some Moslems interpret these descriptions of the future life in a spiritual sense, but to the majority Heaven and Hell are very material. It is not surprising that this sort of hope for the future gives little comfort when death draws near, as anyone knows who has been in a house of mourning or has visited a Moslem graveyard on a Thursday afternoon when it is the custom to weep over the graves of loved ones. It is the resurrection of Christ which has taken the sting out of death for Christians, but Mohammed and the Imams did not rise from the dead on the third day, and in Moslem lands the grave is still victorious.

Religious Practices in Islam

Moslems put great importance not only on their doctrines, which are called "Foundations" or "Roots," but also on the religious duties which are called "Branches." The practices generally accepted as obligatory are the following:

A. Worship (Namaz)

Wherever one goes throughout the Moslem World, he will see men saying the prayers prescribed by their religion. Every adult believer, both male and female, is duty-bound to perform the ritual of worship five times, or in some localities three times, every day. At the stated times of worship—at daybreak, at noon and in the afternoon, sunset, and evening—the call to prayer is sounded forth from minarets and housetops in thousands of towns and villages, and religious people turn from their ordinary tasks and perform the rite of worship. Some go to the mosque, but most of them say the prayers where they are—in the field, by the roadside (as the bus in which they are traveling waits for them), in the office or the shop, on the housetop or in their homes. The worshiper first makes the ablution with water in the way prescribed by his particular sect, then takes his stand facing the Kaaba in Mecca and recites the appointed prayers in the Arabic language, kneeling several times and touching his forehead to the earth. The prayers consist chiefly of passages or expressions taken from the Koran, and the same words may be repeated as many as ten times in one day's worship. Since it is not lawful to recite the prayers in any language except Arabic, the great majority of Moslems in Iran and other lands where Arabic is not spoken understand no more of what they say than would Americans should they be required to say their prayers in Greek. But according to

Islamic teaching it is not necessary for the worshiper to understand what he says. To repeat the words correctly is sufficient, and saying the prayers is a very valuable work of merit which will atone for many sins. To a few the worship may be a spiritual exercise when God is worshiped in spirit and truth, but for most Moslems it is a mechanical act with almost no moral or spiritual value to the worshiper. Sometimes at the close of the formal Arabic prayer the worshiper makes a brief request of God in his own language for something he needs. But prayer such as a Christian knows, that is, free and joyous intercourse between a child of God and his Heavenly Father, is almost unknown in Islam. It is therefore not strange that many Moslems, especially the educated classes, seldom perform the duty of worship.

B. Fasting

Mohammed commanded the observance of the Arabic month Ramazan (Ramadan) as a month of fasting, and today throughout the Moslem World the fast is observed every year. Since the Moslem calendar is lunar rather than solar, Ramazan comes each year about ten days earlier than it came in the previous year. In 1960 it roughly corresponded with April. It is the custom in many cities and towns during the month of fasting to fire a cannon every morning about four o'clock (when it is too dark to distinguish a black thread from a white one) to warn people that the hour for fasting has arrived. From that time till after sunset all adults, except the sick and travelers, are forbidden to eat or drink, and strict Moslems will not even swallow their saliva. For working people the day is very long, and they may be seen in the afternoons sitting wearily in their shops or their courtyards waiting for the evening gun to give them the signal to take nourishment. And since eating is forbidden in the daytime, night is turned into day; and there is more feasting in the night hours of Ramazan than in any other month of the year. Is it also frequently a time of gambling and drunkenness, for though the use of alcoholic beverages is forbidden by Islamic law, there is in most Moslem lands a great deal of drinking. There is also much illness during this month, as the records of missionary hospitals show; and short tempers often produce quarrels. It is a time of great religious fanaticism, and the police are usually on the alert lest enemies of the

State take advantage of the large nightly gatherings in the mosques to preach sedition or produce riots.

Ramazan is a difficult time for converts from Islam to Christianity, for they are often under great pressure during the fast to deny their faith by word or deed. In Iran the government, for the sake of placating the religious leaders, puts pressure on the people to make them observe the fast, closing teahouses and restaurants during the daytime, and sometimes arresting people seen eating or smoking in public. No doubt Moslem governments in other lands take similar action. Many of the people, especially the educated and well-to-do classes, ignore the religious law and eat and drink as usual during Ramazan—but not in public! There is in some places growing resentment on the part of working people against the enforcement of a practice which from every point of view is harmful to them, but many of the uneducated people through fear of what will happen to them in this world or the next continue to rise at 3 A.M. to eat their breakfast, and then endure the long hours of fasting till night arrives to end their discomfort.

C. Almsgiving

One of the good things commanded in the Koran is the giving of alms and caring for the poor and needy. This has been made one of the chief duties of Moslems, who are supposed to give one-tenth of their income to charity. And because Mohammed ordered that one-fifth of the booty taken in war should be given to him as his share, the Shi'ites say that every Moslem should give one-fifth of his property to the *seyyids,* the descendents of Mohammed now living, who in Iran are numerous and are often recognizable by their green turbans. It is the custom in Moslem lands to give money to beggars; and as such giving is considered a work of merit, the beggar really confers a benefit on the donor by making it possible for him to lay up treasures for himself in Heaven. Perhaps this is one reason why beggars often do not express appreciation for what is given them. No doubt another reason is that the amounts given them are usually too small to deserve an expression of thanks! Probably most Moslems do not give any considerable portion of their capital or their income to charity, but now and then large gifts are made by rich people to build mosques and schools and hospitals and to support shrines.

D. Pilgrimage to Mecca (Hajj)

Mohammed made Mecca, which from ancient times had been a sacred city for the heathen Arabs, the center of the religion of Islam. He himself made the pilgrimage to Mecca and performed the customary rites, and his example has become law for his followers. Every Moslem who has the means to make the journey should visit Mecca at least once in his life. So each year at the appointed time of pilgrimage hundreds of thousands of believers from Algeria and Afghanistan, from Java and Syria, from Pakistan and the Sudan, and even from Europe and America, make their way to Mecca, traveling by ship, plane, train, bus and foot, enduring the terrific heat and all the hardships of the journey in order to gain the title of Hajji and win the heavenly reward which will be given to everyone who visits the Sacred Places. Many pilgrims die on the journey, but those who return home receive a tremendous welcome from their countrymen, who meet the bus or plane on which they are traveling and kiss and embrace them, that they too may have a little share in the merit of the pilgrimage. Unfortunately, the journey to Mecca seems to produce no moral or spiritual results in the lives of the pilgrims; and with the title of Hajji to protect them, they may even devour more widows' houses and swear more false oaths than they did before. In Iran it is well to be on one's guard when he has business dealings with a Hajji. However, the pilgrimage is no doubt of great value in strengthening the bonds of union between Moslems in all parts of the world and in increasing their devotion to their faith. The entrance of non-Moslems to the Sacred City of Islam is forbidden on pain of death.

The Shi'ites visit not only Mecca but also the tombs of the martyred Imams in Iraq and Iran, and the have traditions which assert that a visit to the grave of Imam Hosein in Kerbala (Iraq) or of Imam Reza in Meshed (Iran) is of far more merit than even the pilgrimage to Mecca. Hence great multitudes of people are constantly journeying to these and other shrines, weeping over the graves of the dead saints, kissing the gravestones and giving presents to the keepers of the shrines in the hope that their sicknesses may be healed and their sins forgiven. When asked as they travel back to their homes whether God has accepted their pilgrimage and forgiven them, they always reply, "Only God knows!" And so they go back again and again, never sure whether or not God has forgiven them. It should be remembered that the Sunnites are strongly opposed to this practice of visiting the graves of the Imams.

E. The Holy War (*Jehad*)

Mohammed made war on the heathen of Arabia and forced them at the point of the sword to surrender and accept Allah and his Prophet. The Koran commands: "Kill those who join other gods with God wherever ye shall find them . . . but if they shall convert . . . let them go their way" (9:5). Mohammed's followers used the sword to extend their empire throughout Asia and North Africa, and even today patriotic Iranians deeply resent the fact that their country was conquered by the armies of the Arabs and Islam was forced upon their ancestors. Religious warfare is considered a duty for Moslems, and many of them look forward to the time when they will once more be able to conquer non-Moslems and establish Islam as the religion of the world.

But who has the authority to call them to engage in Holy War? The Shi'ites say that only the twelfth Imam has this authority, and they are waiting for him to return and lead their armies. The Sunnites, not believing in the twelfth Imam, hold that their religious leaders can proclaim a *Jehad*. From time to time an attempt is made by someone to unite Moslems in such a war against non-Moslems, but these attempts are doomed to failure because differences of belief and nationality make it impossible for Moslems to act together in such matters.

F. Miscellaneous Practices

In addition to the duties listed above, there are other practices, not included in the list of essentials, which are generally observed by Moslems. One of these is circumcision; all males are circumcised in infancy or childhood. Another practice to which great importance is attached is the veiling of women. The Koran does not directly command the use of the veil, but Mohammed forbade his wives to appear unveiled, and his example has become law for most of the Moslem World. At present the type of veil differs in different lands. In some places the woman is completely covered from head to foot by a thick cloth, black or white or colored, so that even her husband would not recognize her on the street. In other places only a thin veil is thrown over the head. In recent years strenuous efforts have been made by those concerned about the rights of women to abolish the veil, and in the larger cities of the Moslem World many women may be seen in the streets dressed as Europeans without any veil whatever. A few years ago the veil was officially abolished by the Shah of Iran, and not a veil was to be seen anywhere, but later there was a strong reaction to this innovation, and in many parts of Iran today a woman would not dare to go out of her house unveiled. Another custom widely practiced is that of eating only the foods permitted by the religious law. The Koran follows the Mosaic Law in forbidding the eating of various kinds of meat, particularly swine's flesh, and most Moslems are careful (at least in public) to abstain from the use of forbidden foods and alcoholic drinks. Sad to say, to many Moslems the marks of a Christian are eating pork and drinking wine! Since Christians eat forbidden foods they are considered unclean by the Shi'ites, and are not permitted to enter their mosques or shrines. If they drink tea out of a cup belonging to a Moslem, the cup should be broken, or at least carefully washed, to get rid of pollution. All running water, and water in a tank of a prescribed size or larger, is according to Moslem law, considered pure, no matter how full of germs it may be, and naturally this belief causes a great deal of sickness. Fortunately most of the educated people have now rejected such antiquated and injurious ideas.

G. The Sufis: Opponents of Moslem Externalism

Peter spoke of the Jewish law as "a yoke . . . which neither our fathers nor we were able to bear" (Acts 15:10). In like manner, to many followers of Mohammed the formal laws and practices of Islam as described above have proved intolerable, and in order to find something more satisfying to their souls they have become Sufis. The Sufis are the mystics of Islam. They do not form a separate sect, and are found both among Sunnites and Shi'ites, but chiefly among the latter. They profess to be orthodox Moslems, but they hold secret beliefs which are quite different from those of ordinary believers. They say that some men are carnal and some are spiritual. The laws and practices of religion are for carnal men, but for spiritual men these ablutions and fastings and prayers are unnecessary. Spiritual men are partakers of the life of God, and are People of the Road (Tariqat), not People of the Code (Shari'at). They rise above material things to a spiritual life which ends in union with God. For the spiritual men there is no sin, for whatever they do is of God. Gold is not injured, they say, by falling into the mire—nor is a spiritual man injured by any act which he may commit.

Sufis believe that there must always be someone on earth who is a Manifestation of God, and who is one with God. All the prophets were divine manifestations. When asked what they think of Christ they reply, "He is God!" And then they add, "All the prophets are One Light, all are God." Their belief is really pantheism, which destroys the distinction between false and true, between good and evil. They see no difference between Christ and Moses and Mohammed, "All are One." Henry Martyn, after meeting the Sufis in Shiraz in 1811, predicted that they would be the first people in Persia to become Christians, but this has not been the case. Having blinded their consciences so that they are no longer able to see their own sins, or to distinguish between the holy Christ and sinful men, they are unable to repent and believe on the Saviour.

The Sufis usually unite in fraternities, following different spiritual guides and different rules of spiritual living. They are admitted to membership by secret rites, in which they pledge absolute allegiance to their leader. They attempt by frequent repetition of the names of Allah, or by other practices, to bring on an ecstatic state in which they will attain to union with God. Their "spiritual" experiences seem to have little influence on their moral lives. There is no hope for the betterment of individuals or of the community in Sufism.

MARRIAGE AND DIVORCE

The home is the unit of social life, and the laws and customs which regulate family life are of the utmost importance to society. Mohammed lived in a society in which polygamy was practiced, and he not only did not forbid it, but by his example actually encouraged it. After the death of Khadija he married one wife after another till his wives numbered at least twelve. In the Koran permission is given to men to marry as many as four wives, provided they are able to act equitably toward them (Sura 4:3), and the Shi'ites interpret this verse to mean that in addition to the four regular wives, a man may marry as many concubines as he will. Concubines are legal wives, married for a fixed period of time, be it a day or fifty years, and the marriage tie is dissolved when the time expires. There has been considerable polygamy practiced among Moslems, and it has often been the cause of a great deal of dissention, and the weakening of family life. A student in a Christian school once said to his American teacher, "My father has four wives, and our home is Hell!" Because of the expense involved, and also because of the growing conviction that polygamy is a bad thing, the practice of monogamy is on the increase. However, there is an increasing amount of prostitution.

According to Moslem law, the right of divorce belongs to the man alone, and he is able to exercise this right at will. He can divorce his wife for any cause, or for no cause whatever, and the only legal protection which the wife has is the unpaid sum of money fixed by the marriage contract which the husband must pay his wife before he can divorce her. Educated women have tried to instigate reforms in the marriage and divorce laws of Moslem lands, and in some cases they have met with partial success. Since Mohammed married Ayisha when she was seven years of age, it was formerly possible in Iran for very young girls to be married to men old enough to be their grandfathers, but now the age for the marriage of girls has been set by law at sixteen, provided they have the consent of their parents. One of the things in Christianity which most deeply impresses Moslems is the high standard which Christ has set for marriage, and the love and harmony which is found in true Christian homes.

MODERN CHANGES

Within the past half-century enormous changes have taken place throughout the Moslem World. Millions of young people, both boys and girls, have received a modern education, and as they have studied science and history and have had their eyes opened to the superstitions of their ancestral faith, most of them have become either irreligious or antireligious. Very few of the educated people in Iran say the prayers, or keep the fasts, or attend the services in the mosques, or observe the laws of their religion, and the upper classes are more and more becoming thoroughly secular, with no religion and no faith in anything. Many of them despise the mullas (priests or preachers), whom they rightly consider responsible for many of the evils in their country. Having seen the corruption of one religion they are convinced that all religions are equally corrupt, and hence they will have nothing to do with any religion.

When, therefore, these irreligious intelligentsia see how America and Britain are trying to support "religion" in the Moslem World as a bulwark against Communism, and by Islamic broadcasts over the radio and by various other means are seeking to bring about a revival of Islam, they naturally react against this kind of propaganda. They often throw themselves into the arms of the communists, who assure them that they too are opposed to superstition and corruption, and are the protagonists of freedom and progress. Hence the people in the Near East who have been deceived by the fair promises of Communism usually have not been the ignorant workers but the educated young people. Having lost faith in their old religion, and having found nothing adequate to take its place, they have often accepted the new religion from the North with fanatical zeal. It is therefore entirely incorrect to suppose that all those counted in the almanac as Moslems are really devoted to their religion, for millions of them have no more faith in Islam as a religion than many Americans have in Jesus Christ. A Christian living in the Moslem World must give his message both to devoted believers in Mohammed and also to the enemies of all religion. All will call themselves Moslems, but many of them are such, not in a religious but only in a nationalistic sense.

Little is known of what has happened to the millions of Moslems residing behind the Iron Curtain, but we can be sure that religious faith there has not survived any better than it has among Moslems of other lands who have come into contact with the new religion of Secularism.

As indicated above, efforts are being made today to unite Moslems and Christians in the war against Communism. In order to do so the impression is being given in radio broadcasts and in the press and in conferences between Moslems and Christians that there is little difference between these two great religions, both of which believe in the one true God, and that it is possible for them to recognize one another, and to unite in opposing falsehood and evil. Christians should be ready to recognize and welcome truth and goodness wherever it is found, and in accordance with Christ's command should love even their enemies. But while they are ready to meet Moslems in a friendly fashion and discuss with them matters of common interest, it is impossible for Christians to accept as true a religion which denies that God is our Father, that Jesus Christ is the Son of God, that He died on the cross for our sins, and rose from the dead. From the Christian point of view, Islam is as far from the truth as is Communism.

ISLAM AND THE BIBLE

It is of special interest to Christians to learn what influence the Bible had on Mohammed's religion. Though he was unable himself to read the Jewish and Christian Scriptures, Mohammed learned from Jewish acquaintances a number of the Old Testament stories, and repeated them more or less accurately in the Koran. He considered Abraham, Moses, David, and other prophets of the past to be true prophets of Allah. However, he often mixed Jewish legends with the Bible records. His knowledge of the New Testament was even more limited than that of the Old Testament. The Koran states that Jesus was born of the Virgin Mary (but it confuses Mary with Miriam the sister of Moses), that He spoke as a babe in the cradle, and that as a Prophet of Allah He healed the sick, cleansed lepers, and raised the dead. Jesus is called in the Koran the "Spirit of God" and the "Word of God," but Mohammed was bitterly opposed to the term "Son of God," as he apparently thought it implied physical sonship. Moslems hate this term today, and often ask, "Do you think God took a wife and had a son?"

Mohammed also misunderstood the Christian Trinity, thinking that it consisted of God, Mary, and Jesus, and he condemned Christians for making Jesus and His mother gods along with Allah. The Koran states that Jesus was not crucified, and Moslems believe that He was taken by God to Heaven, and is alive today in the fourth Heaven, and say that one of Jesus' enemies was crucified by mistake in His place. The Koran also states that Jesus foretold the coming of an apostle whose name will be Ahmad, and all Moslems interpret this as a prediction of the coming of Mohammed (which word is from the same Arabic root as Ahmad).

When Christians tell Moslems that the New Testament says that Jesus is the Son of God, that He died on the cross, and rose from the dead, and that He did not predict the coming of another prophet to succeed Him, but promised to be with His followers personally till the end of the world, the reply is frequently given that the Book which the Christians now have is not the true Gospel (called in the Koran "Injeel," from "Evangel") , but a false book which the Christians have forged. Sometimes Moslems refer to the promise of the Comforter (Paraclete) in John 14—16 and say that it is a prediction of Mohammed. Thus while Mohammed in the Koran often refers to the Jewish and Christian Scriptures and attests their truth, he also makes many statements which are contradictory to the teachings of the Bible. When a serious-minded Moslem reads both the Bible and the Koran he is greatly puzzled, and if he carries his study to a conclusion he will either reject the Bible as a forgery, or else will hold to the Bible and reject the Koran. Both cannot be held together.

Missions To Moslems

Since Islam arose after Christianity, and claimed to be superior to Christianity (and something of a culmination of Christianity) , it has always been difficult to convert Moslems to Christ. For many centuries the Church of Christ made almost no effort to preach the Gospel to the followers of Mohammed, and even today a great many Christians think that Moslems cannot be converted, and that it is therefore useless to preach to them. However, there are some Christians who believe that all men need Christ, and that Christ is able to meet the needs of all men, and who are earnestly trying to make Christ known to all men, including the people of the Moslem World. It was at first very difficult to carry on missionary work in Moslem lands where there was no freedom of religion, and where according to Islamic law anyone who left the "true religion" might be put to death. But nothing is too difficult for God, and during the past century there have been thousands of Moslems in many different lands who have professed faith in Christ and have become members of the Church. A number of these have died as martyrs to their faith, but the majority have been able to live and witness to Christ among their own people, and their lives have often made a deep impression on those who know them.

What induces Moslems to become Christians? God uses many different means to draw them to Himself. Often they lose faith in their old religion, and as they are searching for something better, God leads them to Christ. They sometimes find a Bible or a Christian book which impresses them; they compare Christ's teaching with that of the founder of Islam; they realize that while Mohammed is dead Christ is alive, and they come to Him and find rest for their souls. Sometimes they are influenced by the life of a true Christian, sometimes by what they see of Christianity in a missionary school or hospital, sometimes by a dream or vision, sometimes by a sermon or a church service or a Christian film. In a few lands there are whole congregations of Christians who have come out of Islam into the Church, but usually these courageous believers are found in little groups or one by one, scattered far and wide in towns and villages, hidden away in a population of non-Christians, yet letting their light shine quietly before their fellow men as they live the life of Christ in a dark and evil world.

In this new day when tens of thousands of students and travelers from Moslem lands are to be found in Britain and America, many Christians who had never before come in contact with Islam now have the opportunity to make Christ known to these Moslem guests. The question may often arise, How should one present Christianity to a Mohammedan? The Christian who wants to lead Moslems to Christ should remember that they are men, and have the same needs as men who were born in Christian lands. He should talk to them as men rather than as Moslems, telling them what Christ can do for any man anywhere. It is true that there are some misunderstandings which may have to be cleared away, such as the meaning of "Son of God," the fact of Christ's death on the cross, the absence in the Bible of any prediction of Mohammed, etc. However, it is better to avoid controversy and to try in a loving, friendly spirit to acquaint our Moslem friends with Jesus Christ as we know Him. The best way to do this is to read the New Testament with them, first the Gospels and then the Acts and the Epistles, showing them the love and purity of Christ's life on earth, the moral grandeur of His teachings, the divine character of His claims, the wonders of His death and resurrection, and how He is able and ready to help us today.

Then they should be shown the life in Christ as it is lived in true Christian homes, and as it is revealed in sacrificial service to the poor and the fallen. They should be brought into the fellowship of Christians in the churches who will love them and pray for them. No pressure should be brought upon them to force them to become Christians, for accepting baptism may mean that they will be cast off by their families, or deprived of financial support, or even be threatened with death. When God's Spirit gives them the new birth they will themselves ask for baptism, whatever the cost may be. Great patience and faith and humility are needed in the effort to lead Moslems to Christ, and holiness of life is more important than great learning and intellectual skill.

Though the number of foreign missionaries and native evangelists who are devoting their lives to the task of converting Moslems is pitifully small, and though the results of missionary work when measured by the number of converts are disappointing, we should realize that during the past half-century God has mightily shaken the whole Moslem World. Millions of so-called "Moslems" no longer have faith in Islam, and are indeed as sheep without a shepherd. Millions of others have come in contact with Christians and have lost much of their pride and fanaticism, and are now willing to hear the Christian message. The day for making Christ known to these multitudes has come. It is true that the tense political situation in most parts of the Moslem World, and the bitter opposition of both fanatical Moslems and fanatical Communists often makes Christian effort exceedingly difficult; nevertheless the Lord to whom all power in Heaven and on earth belongs is with us, and with Him all things are possible. The day of harvest will surely come. God's appointed time for the ingathering in Moslem lands is drawing near. Then a great multitude which no man can number of those who now pray toward Mecca will bow the knee before Jesus Christ, and millions who repeat the creed, "There is no god but Allah and Mohammed is his Prophet," will joyously confess that Jesus Christ is Lord, to the glory of God the Father.

BIBLIOGRAPHY

The Koran. Rodwell's trans. New York: Everyman's Library, 1918.

ANDERSON, J. N. D. (ed.) *The World's Religions.* London: Inter-Varsity Fellowship, 1950.

BROWNE, LAURENCE E. *The Prospects of Islam.* London: S.C.M. Press, 1944.

CRAGG, KENNETH. *The Call of the Minaret.* New York: Oxford University Press, 1956.

DONALDSON, DWIGHT M. *The Shiite Religion.* London: Luzac and Co., 1933.

———. *Studies in Muslim Ethics.* London: S.P.C.K., 1953.

HARRIS, GEORGE K. *How to Lead Moslems to Christ.* Philadelphia: China Inland Mission, 1953-55.

HARRISON, ANN M. *A Tool in His Hand, The Story of Dr. Paul W. Harrison of Arabia.* New York: Friendship Press, 1958.

HARRISON, DR. PAUL. *Desert Doctor.* New York: John Day Co. (The author tells of his medical work in Arabia.)

JOHNSON, R. PARK. *Middle East Pilgrimage.* New York: Friendship Press, 1958.

JONES, L. BEVAN. *The People of the Mosque.* Calcutta: Y.M.C.A. 1932. (London: Carey-Kingsgate Press.)

———. *Christianity Explained to Muslims.* Calcutta: Y.M.C.A., 1952. (London: Carey-Kingsgate Press.)

JURJI, EDWARD J. *The Christian Interpretation of Religion.* Chapter XII. New York: Macmillan Co., 1952.

———. (ed.) *The Great Religions of the Modern World.* Princeton: Princeton University Press, 1946.

LAMMENS, H. *Islam, Beliefs and Institutions.* New York: Scribner's, 1929.

MACDONALD, D. B. *Development of Muslim Theology, Jurisprudence and Constitutional Theory.* New York: Scribner's, 1903.

———. *Religious Attitude and Life in Islam.* Chicago: University of Chicago, 1905.

MARGOLIOUTH, D. S. *Muhammed and the Rise of Islam.* New York: Putnam's, 1905.

MILLER, W. M., trans. *Ali-Babu 'L-Hadi 'Asher, A Treatise on the Principles of Shi 'ite Theology* by Al-Hilli. London: Luzac and Co., Ltd., 1958.

MUIR, SIR WILLIAM. *The Life of Mohammed.* John Grant, Edinburgh: 1923.

NICHOLSON, R. A. *Mystics of Islam.* London: G. Bell and Son, 1914.

PADWICK, CONSTANCE E. *Temple Gairdner of Cairo.* London: S.P.C.K., 1929.

———. *Henry Martyn.* Chicago: Inter-Varsity Press, 1519 N. Astor, Chicago 10.

PAYNE, GRACE VISHER. *The Unveiling.* Philadelphia: Westminster Press, 1950.

PIGOTT, BLANCHE. *I. Lilias Trotter, Founder of the Algiers Mission Band.* London: Marshall, Morgan and Scott, Ltd.

RASOOLI, JAY M. and CADY, H. ALLEN. *Dr. Sa'eed of Iran.* Grand Rapids: International Publications, 1957.

SELL, EDWARD. *The Faith of Islam.* London: S.P.C.K., 1920.

WILSON, J. CHRISTY. *Introducing Islam.* New York: Friendship Press.

———. *The Christian Message to Islam.* Westwood, N. J.: Revell, 1950.

———. *Apostle to Islam, a Biography of Samuel M. Zwemer.* Grand Rapids: Baker Book House, 1952.

WYSNER, GLORIA M. *Near East Panorama.* New York: Friendship Press, 1950.

ZWEMER, SAMUEL M. *Islam a Challenge to Faith.* New York: S.V.M.F.M., 1907.

FIG. 5.—Shinto shrine, the Heianjingu Shrine, Kyoto, Japan. (Courtesy of the Consulate General of Japan.)

*Shinto means "The Way of the Gods." The word expresses religious
faith about the past of Japan. . . . The Japanese islands are a
special creation of the gods. The leading families of Japan and
the whole Japanese people descended from the minor deities
residing on the islands.*

—Noss

V.

Japan

by William H. Pape

The Place of Religion in Japan

A CLEAR AND SIMPLE PRESENTATION of the religious beliefs of the
Japanese would be misleading. Their beliefs are neither clear
nor simple. Religion, culture, nationalism, traditions, myths, custom,
and feudalism are inextricably tangled. Isolating any one of these
elements creates a false impression, and minimizes the difficulty of
setting at liberty a nation in bondage.

Japanese society is a complex of inescapable obligations that deny
the individual freedom of choice or liberty of action. Speech, behavior, and decisions are all predetermined by tradition. Each new
year in Japan begins with millions of people greeting one another
with set phrases as unchanging as the rising of the sun. Another
year dawns, but as far as it is within the power of men to control
such matters, the pattern of life shall follow the course set in the de-
parting year. The people are bound as no other people on earth

A Canadian, William H. Pape, B.A., is currently on the faculty
of the Japan Bible Seminary and a lecturer at the Japan Christian College. He began his missionary career in China, serving
in Yunnan province for seven years. After leaving China, he ministered as a pastor in Newfoundland. In 1952 he went to Japan.
A member of the Evangelical Alliance Mission, Mr. Pape is
also associate pastor of the Tokyo Overseas Chinese Christian
Church. He is the author of *The Lordship of Jesus Christ*.

are bound. And religion is part of the binding web. Its function has always been to control and restrain rather than to liberate and save. Shinto, for example, has never promised salvation, but only guaranteed that the Japanese shall forever remain Japanese. Religion, often by deliberate design of the State, has helped bind the nation into a compact unit. The people think and act as one. In speaking to Westerners, individuals more often begin their sentences with "We Japanese," than with "I." The opinion of one is the opinion of all. The strength and the bondage of religion in Japan, therefore, is the strength of society. Religion exists as part of Japanese society and consequently must be peculiarly Japanese. Not to be a Buddhist and, if such a thing were possible, not to be a Shintoist, is to be outside of society and outside the nation. Just as Japanese prisoners of war, severed from the society that bred them, found themselves without morality, standards, precedents, or creed, so anyone who dares to break with the religions of Japan finds himself to be a stranger in his own country.

While religion is an integral part of Japanese society, it is not a completely dominant factor. Patriotism and family ties are the controlling interests. Often patriotism has become a religion, and the god of Japan has been Japan. And concern for family interests has been the root of ancestor worship which is the oldest of all Japanese religious forms. These two elements of love of country and love of family form the basis of religion in Japan. Although neither element is necessarily religious, both are expressed in the two religions of Japan. Shinto is an affirmation of the people's passionate love of their nation and faith in their own destiny, while Buddhism demonstrates and preserves the solid unity of the family.

The reason for religion's varying fortunes, and the different ends to which it has been so easily put, is that theory rather than fact fascinates the Japanese. Stubborn, unyielding facts are unwelcome and avoided when possible. The Japanese cultivate a habit of "looking without seeing." By this means the unpleasant part of life can be ignored. Theories are welcome because any adjustment necessary to avoid embarrassment can easily be made. While all heathen religions are theories, some have historical founders. But it is significant that Shinto owes its origin to no particular person, and entirely lacks any historical basis. It is altogether nebulous theory. Buddhism, in its Japanese form, is equally devoid of facts. To a Western mind this is its weakness. To the Oriental, this is its strength.

The place of religion in Japan has been influenced by a long period of feudalism. Like all men everywhere, the Japanese have an instinct to worship and a sense of the supernatural, but during the Middle Ages all such instincts were paralyzed by a feudal system that denied the people liberty of thought or choice. During that period the smallest details of life were regulated. A farmer had no choice as to the type and number of toys that he could buy for his son. His wife had no choice as to the price she could pay for hairpins. Such trivialities were predetermined by laws that regulated the lives of every man, woman, and child throughout the land. For generations the masses became tragically accustomed to a tyranny that denied them the right to think for themselves.

In the years preceding World War II, that tyranny was renewed. Middle-aged people of modern Japan have all been through a period of rigid thought control. Religion was a tool of the State, and all religious beliefs and practices were supervised by the State. With defeat in war came emancipation from that tyranny, but the scars remain on the minds of multitudes. By tradition and training, the people regard personal decisions and freedom of thought as dangerous phenomena. Religion therefore has always lacked a sturdy independence. People have seldom, if ever, had the privilege of a faith based on personal convictions and free choice. Any religion, such as Christianity, that demands individual action is a violent opponent of the Japanese system.

Religion in Japan therefore is a matter of custom and decree rather than conviction. Many modern intellectual atheists continue to bow before their family shrine to accord with custom. In spite of their scientific outlook, their motive for worship remains the same as that of their more ignorant ancestors. They follow Japanese cutom, and to the majority of the people custom is synonymous with religion. The majority of people are not Buddhists because they are convinced that Buddhism is true; nor are they Shintoists primarily because they believe in the Shinto Pantheon. They accept these two religions because every true Japanese is expected to do so out of loyalty to the Emperor, the nation, and the family.

In consequence of a lack of convictions, the Japanese have very vague ideas about their religious beliefs. The majority cannot explain precisely what they believe, or why. Custom is regarded as a good argument. Even a definition of religion is not easy. When the present Minister of Education, for example, was asked what he thought about the Shinto shrines, he replied, "Personally I do not think that the shrines are necessarily religion. I think that shrine worship is but the beautiful expression of the Japanese people's ancestor worship." This distinction between religion and worship is incomprehensible to most Westerners accustomed to think of religion as a system of faith and worship. Vagueness however is characteristic of the Japanese mind. Black and white are seldom presented as alternatives: black and white merge into an uncertain gray that is itself absorbed into a misty cloud, exactly in the manner of the old-fashioned ethereal paintings of Japan. The only test that can be applied to religion is whether or not it is consistent with things Japanese. To a Japanese, any religion is bad that threatens the solidarity of society, or that introduces gods worthy of more respect than the gods of Japan. But any religion is good that can promote the welfare of Japan and strengthen the binding cords of society. Defeat in war and a military occupation have not greatly affected the position of religion in Japan. The end of the Occupation soon proved that the fires of nationalistic religion had been merely smoldering, and not extinguished. New winds of nationalism threaten to fan them into a brightly burning flame. Some changes however certainly took place in the cataclysm of war. National unity survived the shock of defeat, but social pressure was weakened and individual liberty increased. The younger generation, specially in the large cities, are breaking away a little from the old social bondage. Democracy, sometimes misunderstood as the equality of all under the authority of none, and American movies, often understood as advocating a life ruled by sex and guns, are having their strange influence upon a people unaccustomed to make decisions. A few young people are beginning to plan their marriages without reference to their parents' wishes, but fewer have the privilege of making a free choice of religion. In these postwar years two opposite trends are clearly discernible: less religion, and more religion. A skepticism that regards all religions, including the Gospel, as unscientific and superstitious is the fashion for many intellectuals who, unhappily, include a large number of professors and teachers responsible for the education of a new generation. On the other hand, many people who became disillusioned with the failure of traditional forms of religion are turning with pathetic eagerness to the innumerable sects springing up all over the country.

According to the most recent statistics, 340 religious sects are now flourishing in Japan. The majority are brands of Shinto and Buddhism, but the percentage of adherents to the minor sects, many of which are known as "profit giving religions," is steadily increasing and already exceeds that of the Christian Church. Within these new sects every kind of wild fancy is found. Some are moralistic; others are spiritist. Some are exceedingly superstitious; others are grossly immoral.

Typical of the postwar confusion is the "House of Growth" religion which has been called "the department store of religions." With a "bible" that includes plentiful quotations from Genesis and the Gospel of John, a vocabulary that incorporates Christian phraseology, and practices that involve a form of Christian Science, the "House of Growth" has captured the allegiance of about 1½ million people during is short history. It optimistically claims that all men are children of God, and lightheartedly plunders from the best of all religions.

What has been changed by the recent war is much less than what has not been changed. The present Emperor's denial of divinity does not have as much significance to the Japanese as Westerners anticipated. Even before the war many people had ceased to believe that their emperor was a god. The religious system of Japan did not rest upon the concept of a divine emperor. The cornerstone of religion in Japan has always been the concept of a loyalty which was unscathed by war. The household gods have been unshaken by the turbulence of the times. And the pagan beliefs of the people, dating back into the misty beginnings of history and inherited from generations of loyal people, have not been greatly changed by the decade of an unfortunate war. This is especially true in rural areas where "all things continue as they were from the beginning of creation."

Since the Occupation, State and religion have been separated, but the division is technical rather than actual. A divorce has been enforced, but the parties still live together and, finding themselves still very compatible, often talk of remarriage. The great shrine at Ise remains the spiritual capital of the country. Members of the Imperial household, and the Prime Minister of Japan continue to make official reports there to the Sun Goddess. The implication is inescapable that the rulers of Japan have not ceased to feel their responsibility to the ancient gods. The Sun Goddess was not in fact dethroned by MacArthur's decrees, nor indeed could be. A nation's gods cannot be written off by a signature on a piece of paper, even though they themselves are paper gods. They live enshrined in the hearts of the people. If they are ever to be removed it will be by "weapons . . . not carnal but mighty through God to the pulling down of strongholds."

SHINTO—THE HISTORIC FAITH OF JAPAN

Almost all Japan's 89 million people were born into the Shinto faith. To be a Japanese and to be a Shintoist are synonymous. To be a Shintoist and not to be a Japanese is impossible. Unlike Buddhism which is international, Shinto is exclusively nationalistic, offering nothing to the world, but demanding everything of a Japanese. It is not so much a creed to be believed, as a way of life. Shinto means "The way of the gods"; and by tradition, instinct and custom all Japanese tread this path.

Shinto is as old as the nation, with its beginnings in ancient and uncertain legends. Its real origin is accurately described in Romans 1:21 (A.S.V.) : "Knowing God, they glorified him not as God, neither gave thanks; but became vain in their reasonings, and their senseless heart was darkened." Out of those "vain reasonings," fantastic and sometimes filthy tales have appeared to account for the origin of the Japanese people and their islands.

> Izanagi and Izanami stood together on the Floating Bridge of Heaven. With a jeweled spear, Izanagi leisurely stirred the brine until it curdled. On withdrawing the spear, drops of falling brine became the island of Awaji, where Izanagi and his bride went to live. Their children were the gods of wind and fire, trees and mountains, sea and storm. Other children became the islands of Japan.
>
> Izanami was scorched to death by her son the Fire god. Izanagi descended into hell to attempt to rescue her. This nearly cost

him his life, and he returned without her. As he washed from his body the filth accumulated on the fearful journey, it became new divinities, chief of which was the Sun Goddess.

The grandson of the Sun Goddess was Ninigi-no-mikoto, who was commanded to rule all Japan from an eternal throne. His bride was Konohana-sakuya-no-hime, goddess of Mount Fuji. Their grandson was Jimmu Tenno, first historical emperor of Japan, and founder of the Imperial Dynasty that has ruled in unbroken succession from 660 B.C. until now.

So declares the ancient *Kojiki,* the earliest of Shinto's scanty literature. As evidence of these things, the mirror and jewels that once enticed the Sun Goddess from her hiding place when the Rainstorm god was threatening her, and the sword that the same Rainstorm god found in the tail of an eight-headed serpent he slew, are kept as imperial treasures in the great Shrine of Ise.

In modern times, particularly in the postwar period of skepticism, such tales are no longer believed by the younger generation. School textbooks which once taught such fantasy as fact now contain a "scientific" and materialistic account of the origin of the Japanese race. But Shinto, like the Hydra, can survive any number of amputations. Since its nebulous theories never did rest on a factual foundation, the present rejection of its mythical beginnings has not appreciably affected it. Indeed Shinto has never grown out of the misty confusion that makes analysis into a logical system possible. The gods of Shinto cannot be defined, and their character and powers are exceedingly vague. However, three ideas are predominant in Shinto. These are: the worship of the gods of Japan; loyalty to Japan; and the cultivation of a pure Japanese spirit.

A. Ideas Predominant in Shinto

1. The worship of the gods of Japan

Holding a position of uncontested pre-eminence is Amaterasu Omikami, the Sun Goddess, worshiped by all, from the Imperial Family down to the lowliest imperturbable farmer. Japan may be a "man's country" in which women have an inferior position, yet it is before a feminine deity that the nation bows. The Japanese word for *god* is *kami.* It bafflles definition. It is applied to the sun, to mythological creatures, to men, birds, beasts, plants, and trees. Indeed, anyone real or imaginary, and anything true or false, possessing extraordinary power can be *kami.* Soldiers who died in World War II became *kami:* large lakes and rocks were already *kami.* When so much can be included in the term, it is not surprising that the total number of gods is estimated at either 80 or 800 myriads. The only limitation to *kami* is that all must be of Japanese origin.

Shinto blithely ignores the creation of the universe and any nation outside of Japan, and has no place for gods of foreign ancestry. Even the gods of Buddhism cannot be reckoned as *kami.* Having a Japanese nature and possessing supernatural power are the qualifications for deity: character is of no account. The morals of many of the gods are, in fact, lower than any Japanese would accept for himself. The immoral behavior of a few irresponsible American soldiers in Japan is often censured in the press and by public opinion, but the licentious gods of Shinto have never been subject to criticism.

The character of the Shinto gods, their uncertain and changing functions, and their origin are illustrated by three of the most popular deities, Inari, Hachiman and Tenjin. *Inari,* the god of prosperity and good crops, is favored by farmers, shopkeepers, and barren women. Inari, literally "rice-bearer," is associated with a mythical princess called Ugatama-no-Mikoto who is supposed to have first taught the Japanese to grow rice. Every Inari shrine has a pair of foxes before it since these animals are supposed to be the messengers of the god. Inari is also the patron saint of geisha girls and prostitutes, being honored with a shrine in every geisha house and brothel.

The second popular god is *Hachiman* who is identified with Hikohoho-demi, a mythological Imperial ancestor. At first he was regarded as the guardian of fishermen. He was also patron of the forge which, through the making of spears and arrows, brought him to the attention of fighting men who had made him their protector. In the Nara period, Hachiman was made the guardian god of Buddhism, but in recent years he has been transformed into a pacifist and reverted to his original role of god of fishing and agriculture. A pigeon is his messenger.

The third Shinto god, specially popular with students, is *Tenjin.* He began as an historical person, Sugawara Michizane (A.D. 845-903), a minister in the Imperial court. As a result of slander he was sent into exile on the back of a bull. In his lifetime he was a poet and man of letters; after death he was deified to become the "Celestial Deity," or Tenjin. A bull is considered to be his messenger.

2. Loyalty to Japan

As it is true that the gods have no morals, so Shinto, the way of the gods, has no ethics. The Japanese, regarding themselves as descended from the gods, argued not unreasonably that a divine people had no need of ethics, and were inclined to despise the Chinese for their concern with moral issues. The only virtue known to Shinto is loyalty, and even this has a peculiar Japanese twist. It is based upon the feudal relationship between a powerful lord and his dependents. Loyalty is not a virtue for its own sake, but faithfulness to whoever possesses the power to take care of those subordinate to him. Loyalty to the emperor, who at the very least is regarded as ruling by divine right, is an essential Shinto doctrine. To the emperor is entrusted the care of the nation, and in consequence loyalty to him is an obligation upon all. Of all Japanese qualities, this is perhaps the most outstanding. Purified, refined, and directed toward Christ, it could have great possibilities. But in the past it has been this very virtue that has been exploited and debased for ignoble ends.

3. Cultivation of a pure Japanese spirit

Purity is a predominant idea in Shinto. The words must not be understood in a Christian but in a Japanese sense. In Japan, sex gratification is normal, and prostitution organized and legal. Purity is ritualistic. It is seen in the daily bath without which no Japanese is happy; in the washing of hands and mouth at a laver before every Shinto shrine; in the constant sweepings of conspicuous places in home, streets, and shrine approaches; in the curious habit of drawing back "defiling" breath through the teeth before each sentence of a prayer; in the use of unpainted wood for houses; and in the avoidance of contact with death.

The worship of the gods of Japan, loyalty to the emperor and all that he represents, and ritualistic purity are the chief elements that produce the Japanese spirit which appears to be the practical goal of Shinto. This *"Yamato damashii"* is the peculiar possession of every Japanese, and the unique, eternal character of the nation. Although the old myths of Japan's divine origin have been repudiated or challenged, Shinto clings resolutely to its doctrine of the supremacy of the Japanese spirit. The aim of Shinto is to insure that the Japanese remain Japanese.

B. Three Types of Shinto

Although many Japanese themselves are not always aware of the distinction, three types of Shinto have evolved. There is a rough, but not exact, connection between these three types and the three emphases of Shinto. Popular Shinto, which grew up with the people, is concerned with the worship of the gods of Japan. Sect Shinto, which developed from the teaching of individual founders, tends to be concerned with personal progress in living as a true Japanese. This idea crystallized in the seventeeth century as the famous "Bushido," or "Way of the Warrior." And State Shinto, which emerged as part of government policy, has loyalty to the State as its goal. These three forms of Shinto, therefore, are distinct both in origin and in objective.

1. Popular Shinto

Popular Shinto has its strength in the home. A miniature shrine, or *kami-dana* is kept on a high shelf in the principal room of every house. It usually contains a mirror, symbolizing the Sun Goddess, and a small tablet on which is written the name of the god. Paper charms, sold at local or national shrines, are often attached. And before the shrine, vases of flowers and bottles of rice-wine are placed as offerings. The wine is significant since drinking, even to excess, is not uncommon in certain Shinto observances.

Popular Shinto strengthens its hold upon the people by the local shrines of tutelary deities known as "Ujigami." The *kami-dana* in the home welds the family into a tight unit: the local shrines bind the family into the social organism. The basic design of Shinto shrines with an inner and outer section has led to speculation as to whether it might be traced back to the plan of the Hebrew tabernacle. In fact, the shrine is built like a house of the first century. Into the inner part only the priest may enter. There are kept the symbols of *kami*, which may be a mirror, a sword, a spearhead, or even phallic emblems. In the outer part of the shrine, priests meet with representatives of the community on important occasions such as the announcement to the gods of outstanding events, or prayer for a good harvest. The whole shrine area is marked out as sacred by an arch or *torii* which is so often featured in Japanese paintings and pictures.

Whatever changes may have been brought about by war and the military occupation of Japan, it is evident that popular Shinto has been completely unaffected. The family shrine retains its position of eminence in the home and remains the hard core of resolute resistance to the Gospel. In towns and cities, and more particularly in villages and rural areas, little evidence, if any, exists that the local shrine has lost either its popularity or its power.

2. Sect Shinto

Even to enumerate all 142 sects and summarize their teaching would be too long and unnecessary a process. This type of Shinto can best be understood by taking a specific example. Tenrikyo can serve as an illustration. It is the most active of all the Shinto sects. The founder was a woman, Miki Nakayama, who at the age of forty-one claimed to have a divine revelation by which she became a living temple of a god. Giving away all she had inherited from her rich family, she entered a life of utmost poverty, and began to experience the "joyousness" which is characteristic of the sect. Tenrikyo was officially founded in 1838, and from the beginning, Miki Nakayama and her followers were bitterly persecuted and oppressed by civil authorities. Even at the age of eighty, the founder was several times thrown into prison.

The sect worships Tenri-ō-no-mikoto, "the god of divine reason." Salvation ultimately depends on living in accord with true reason. The system depends on a belief in reincarnation. Because of imperfection inherited from a previous existence, and aggravated by present failures, man is contaminated by such evils as greed, hatred, and anger which are called "dusts" of the soul. These dusts can be removed by faith in Tenri-ō-no-mikoto and following the way of reason. The climax is a union with the divine by which healing of the body becomes possible, unhappiness is replaced by joy, and salvation comes to the soul.

Tenrikyo is not however merely concerned with personal salvation, but strives to reform society, and regards service to man as being a service to its god. The sect has established clinics, tuberculosis sanatoria and research institutes, orphanages and day nurseries. The educational program is extensive, including a seminary, a university, a college, and high, middle, and primary schools. On the seventieth anniversary of the death of Miki Nakayama, a five-story ferro-concrete "Parental House" was built containing special training rooms where 10,000 followers at a time can be given a series of nine lectures to prepare them for receiving the Divine Gift, or symbol of the rank of preacher. With such a comprehensive training program, it is not surprising that Tenrikyo has grown rapidly. In 1955, the sect had 11,978 churches, 76,315 trained priests, and 1,158,414 followers; all of these figures being far higher than those for the whole of the Protestant church in Japan. But even these results fall short of Tenrikyo's ultimate aims. In the schools English, French, German, Spanish, Malayan, and Chinese are taught in preparation for world conquest in the name of Tenri-ō-no-mikoto. Already there are 530 churches overseas, and at the headquarters in Nara, the former ancient capital of Japan, a location has been chosen for a "Terrace of nectar," which is to be built on the great day when the whole world is converted. Sect Shinto has awakened, and is lifting up its eyes upon the fields of the world.

In contrast to Popular Shinto, Sect Shinto has historical founders, definite doctrine, a social program, and plans for expansion. The sects, in part, owe their strength to the fact that their followers become members by conviction rather than by birth, as is the case with Popular Shinto. This explains the virile strength of Tenrikyo, and the other sects of Shinto, as well as their fervent efforts to make converts. In addition, Sect Shinto has a big appeal to women, for whom the other forms of Shinto have little to offer.

The effect of the recent war upon Sect Shinto, as well as the subsequent occupation, was to cause a rapid multiplication of the sects. The restless search in the postwar years of disillusionment and the breaking of the power of State Shinto provided the opportunity for the sudden appearance of inventors of new religions.

3. State Shinto

The oldest Shinto writings are the Kojiki, *The Record of Ancient Matters,* and the Nihongi, *The Chronicles of Japan,* both of which were compiled in the eighth century A.D. when Buddhism had become a rival to the historic faith of Japan. Religion was part of political maneuverings, and the Kojiki and Nihongi were compiled to establish the legitimacy of the reigning family and to secure the social position of the court nobles. For the first time the name *Shinto*—"The way of the gods"—was used in distinction to the newly imported Buddhism. It was then that State Shinto's peculiar doctrines began to crystallize. The illusion was created that the Japanese, in virtue of their divine origin, are a race apart, excelling all others in virtue, intelligence, and courage.

In the nineteenth century, the emperor was rescued from the obscurity into which he and the Imperial Family had for generations been driven by military commanders (shōguns), who had virtually ruled the country. Loyalty to the Emperor became the rallying point for the nation. Old Shinto beliefs took a new lease on life, and State Shinto really came into existence. The Sun Goddess, as ancestress of the Imperial Family and founder of the nation, was honored with new fervor. And when a national constitution was written in 1889, it was declared that "the Emperor is sacred and inviolable." The nation began to dream of a divine mission and a great empire.

Shinto gained a grip on the people by three means, a state controlled educational system, national shrines, and prescribed ceremonies in honor of the emperor. A climax was reached in the years immediately before the outbreak of war in Asia. In 1938 an army general was made minister of education, and under him the whole educational system was integrated into the army's indoctrination program. Official-thought supervisors, and Thought Inspection Commissions were set up. Students were trained to accept all they were told without question. The noticeable inability of even well-educated Japanese to think analytically may perhaps be traced to those tragic days when independent thought was a luxury in which no one dare indulge. Certainly the present middle-aged generation have all gone through that stringent process of indoctrination that passed as education, and this is an important factor in considering the impact of the Gospel upon the people. In those days, Shinto myths were the beginning of a child's education, and worship of the Emperor and State the end of the process.

The national shrines claimed to perpetuate the traditional beliefs of the Japanese, and worship at them was the ultimate test of a true Japanese. State Shinto was under the Home Office, and priests were appointed and supported by the government under civil service regulations. Patriotic ritual, such as bowing at the shrines, was required of all Japanese subjects, and in order to avoid antagonizing Christians, Buddhists, and members of other religions, State Shinto was declared not to be a religion. This strategy deceived no one except those ready to be deluded for the sake of avoiding trouble. The shrines were officially known as jinja, which means, "The dwelling place of the gods." Three of these national shrines as especially important.

In a class all by itself is the great shrine of Amaterasu, the Sun Goddess, at Ise. There the Emperor himself performed rituals, and announced events of outstanding moment such as important treaties, war, or earthquakes. Government officials reported on affairs of State to the goddess, and multitudes of ordinary people made an annual pilgrimage.

A second shrine of great note is the Yasukuni shrine on Kudan Hill in Tokyo. Shinto taught Japanese not to fear death on the battlefield by the promise that all who gave their lives for the Emperor would immediately become *kami* (gods), dwelling in eternal honor in this shrine. The *Japan Times,* an English-language newspaper published in Tokyo, in an article dated October 20, 1938, illustrates what was taught in those days.

> Enshrined as *Kami* they [the soldiers] become deities to guard the Empire. They are no longer human. They have become pillars of the Empire. As they are enshrined at Yasukuni, they retain no rank or other distinction. Generals and privates are alike. They are no longer counted as so many military men, but so many "pillars." It is because they are pillars of the nation that they are worshiped by the Emperor and the entire populace.

A tragic little poem, in the form of a farewell between a soldier and his wife, eloquently reveals the feelings of the Japanese people regarding the Yasukuni shrine.

> The cherry blossoms bloom for the Emperor,
> And a storm strikes our country.
> "Fall bravely, O my husband!"
> "Don't cry! I'll certainly return,
> In a little wooden box covered with gold brocade.
> Come to see me at Kudan Hill."

The third great national shrine is the Meiji Shrine, where the soul of the Emperor Meiji and his consort are supposed to dwell. On New Year's morning the shrine is visited by millions of loyal Japanese who wish to begin the year by paying their respects to the Imperial line.

Through control of education, by means of the national shrines, and finally, through ceremonies in honor of the Emperor, Shinto flourished. Students were required to bow before the Emperor's picture which had a place of honor in every school. The twelve national holidays, most of which were concerned with the worship of the Emperor or his ancestors, were kept with meticulous care. February 11, for example celebrated the accession to the throne of Jimmu, the first ruler of Japan, and grandson of the goddess of Mount Fuji. By these means, Japan achieved the goal of State Shinto which was national unity under the rule of a divine emperor.

Defeat in war was defeat for the gods of Japan. A people, who assumed confidently that their divine origin gave them an unquestionable supremacy over other nations, found to their utter dismay that their hopes, like their ruined cities, were but a pile of ashes. Under the Occupation, State Shinto became the target of directives from MacArthur's headquarters. The whole of the complex politico-religious organization was dismembered. Shrine and priests lost all State support. The Emperor disavowed his divine origin. School textbooks were purged of Shinto myths. National holidays ceased to be in honor of the Imperial Family. State and religion were separated. Teaching of any religion in schools was forbidden. State Shinto officially ceased to exist. But if Ichabod were written over the door of every national shrine, memories of an elusive glory remained.

C. Shinto in Korea

The methods, purpose, and essence of Shinto became clearest when it was introduced into Korea after the Japanese invasion of that country. The three methods of enforcing the faith were education, the family altar, and national festivals. School principals, usually Japanese, acted as priests, daily conducting a service at which attendance was compulsory. As the Imperial Rescript on education was read, all students were expected to worship by a dutiful clapping of the hands, and at noon the whole school engaged in silent prayer.

A small book of Shinto doctrine, including the myths of Japan's "divine" origin, was added to the required textbooks for all schools. The god-shelf or *kami-dana* was introduced into every home and constantly checked by local authorities. Failure to possess and use such an altar was punished by denying children of the family admittance to school. Japanese festivals were introduced, such as New Year's Day and the birthdays of the Emperor and Empress, when all *kami-dana* were decorated and duly inspected. Students were given a vacation on those days, but forced to visit school in order to eat rice cake and drink bean soup in honor of the occasion.

Koreans regarded Shinto as having three purposes. The first was to turn all Koreans into Japanese. To them the system appeared to be nationalistic and political rather than religious. The second purpose seemed to be the replacement of Christianity, and the third to be the worship of the Emperor of Japan.

As to the essence of Shinto, Koreans were bewildered by its vague doctrines and empty ritual. Two things only were clear. Shinto was a means of oppression, and the *kami-dana* was the most important part of the religion. That the Japanese themselves regard the god-shelf as the heart of their faith was proved by the penalties inflicted on Koreans who failed to honor it. A farmer, plodding home from a Shinto shrine he had been forced to attend, was unfortunate enough to lose the lucky talisman he had unwillingly bought. Consequently he could not decorate his god-shelf with the little piece of white folded paper given him by the priest. For failing to show proper reverence to the Sun Goddess, whose image the *kami-dana* contained, the hapless farmer was condemned to three days in prison.

At the end of the war, Korean reaction to Shinto was certain and swift. As a man, the nation arose and by ax and fire destroyed every shrine and god-shelf till not one remained. Any buildings too substantial to ruin were plundered and the contents burned. Oppression and Shinto perished together.

BUDDHISM—THE ADOPTED FAITH OF JAPAN

This section will deal only with the peculiar forms of Buddhism found in Japan, which, in the opinion of Buddhists of international repute, are completely different from any other school of Buddhism.

An idol from Korea introduced Buddhism to Japan. It was sent as a present to the Emperor of Japan by the ruler of Pakche in A.D. 552. The new religion found favor, and in 655, by order of the court, every household was required to set up a shrine for worship. This is probably the origin of the *butsudan,* or Buddhist family altar found in almost every home throughout the land today. The vagueness of Shinto, and the excessive tolerance of Buddhism insured that no conflict could arise between the two religions. In fact, from A.D. 800, to A.D. 1700 Buddhism and Shinto were united to form "Ryobu Shinto," or "dual aspect Shinto." Buddha Sakyamuni was identified with the Sun Goddess, and all other Shinto divinities were regarded as Buddhas and Bodisattvas in a different form. The gods of India suddenly found themselves with Japanese nationality. The fact is important, for it vividly illustrates the Japanese attitude toward all religions. Imported beliefs are expected to conform to the Japanese pattern.

The Buddhism that entered Japan was already far different from the original teaching of the founder. In its passage through China, Confucian ethics had been added, Taoism had contributed its mystic teaching, and a multitude of gods had been invented. But Buddhism offered what Shinto lacked. Buddhism could point to an outstanding personality as its founder; could present a philosophical system with a code of ethics; and could promise an easy way of salvation. But, most important of all, Buddhism, in contrast with Shinto's concern with the present life, could promise a Heaven and threaten a Hell. Shinto had always avoided the defiling contact with death, and thus it fell to the lot of Buddhism in Japan to be largely concerned with death. In doctrine, a multitude of contradictions appear. For example, Shinto promises a place of immortality and honor at the Yasukuni shrine for the spirits of all men who give their lives in battle. The ashes of the same solders are buried with a Buddhist ceremony in their home town, where their spirits are supposed to dwell. And at the same time, Buddhism promises them a place in its paradise. It is however no part of either Shinto or Buddhism to be logical. Buddhism succeeded in its gentle penetration of Japan because it offered salvation to all regardless of social status, sex, or age. Shinto had always favored the ruling classes, flourished in a feudal society, and promised nothing to the masses except to keep them in their places. Buddhism conquered by yielding. Bending like the bamboo before the breeze, it caused no offense to Japanese culture. This particular reason for Buddhism's swift victory helps to explain the reason for the slower triumphs of the Gospel which cannot be molded to suit national preferences.

In the nineteenth century, the Japanese rulers tried to disentangle Shinto from Buddhism in order to make Shinto the supreme national cult. This proved impossible. The boundaries of both religions were too loosely defined, and Buddhism was too closely integrated into the social structure. The religious partnership has continued to the present time.

A. General Buddhism

Just as Shinto centers around the shrine and the family god-shelf, so Buddhism centers around the temple and the family altar. The temple, usually built in the ornate Chinese style, is symbolic of Buddhism's place of honor in Japan. Children play in its spacious courtyards, which are often the only sanctuary they know from the noisy crowded streets. Women meet there to gossip; and markets are often held in its precincts. Since the last war, TV sets have been set up in the courtyards beside stone lanterns supposed to guide the spirits home.

In the Tokugawa period, every family in Japan was ordered to belong to a temple, which functioned as a kind of town office as well as a religious center for the community. In modern times, the great majority of people voluntarily register their names at a local Buddhist temple of their choice to insure that they will be buried with appropriate rites. Many temples have an association known as a *danka* which makes all arrangements for funerals. Members of the association rarely attend the temple, but make regular contributions of money or rice. Buddhism therefore has always been more financially independent of the State than Shinto; and since death is their business, the temples are certain of a steady income. Among such nominal Buddhists, women show more interest than men, and engage in charitable work or go on mass pilgrimages which often resemble a picnic.

The real strength of Buddhism is in the home. Most Buddhists, regardless of sect, have a *butsudan* or Buddhist family altar in addition to the Shinto *kami-dana*. The *butsudan* is an ornate box, bought at a department store or local shop, containing a small idol of some Buddhist god and wooden tablets on which are written the Buddhistic names of the deceased members of the family. It symbolizes the rule of the dead over Japan. Here the spirits of departed ancestors are worshiped daily, before the morning and evening meal. The tinkling of a little bell, folding of the hands in prayer, and a respectful bow before this altar marks the beginning of the day for countless Japanese. This is more than a formality. All of the great decisions of life are strongly affected by the tyranny of the dead. A woman has been known, for example, to refuse the offer of eternal life in Christ because she felt that she should not spend eternity in a better place than her dead husband. The *butsudan* and the *kami-dana* are the last strongholds to be surrendered. While many Japanese will agree to certain elements of Christian truth, such as the Sermon on the Mount, their resistance will harden when it becomes evident that "thou shalt have no other gods besides me" (A.S.V., marg.). On this point the battle for the soul of the Japanese rages. Not a few have cherished the illusion that the Gospel could be modified, and the significance of the *butsudan* ignored, so that the one could be reconciled with the other. And in some cases churches have weakened themselves by tacitly tolerating such an arrangement. A crisis for new Christians occurs when there is a death in their family. Interest in the *butsudan,* which may have fallen into a rut of formality immediately revives and becomes vital. Fruit, vegetables, and sweet cakes must be offered, and relatives invited for memorial feasts. The Buddhist priest is invited, and returns on the occasion of subsequent memorial days. To refuse to take any part in such pagan worship not only means breaking with the family, but also with the long line of ancestors extending back into the dim past.

Young people with both parents living find it easier to accept Christ than those who are already in bondage to the worship of a dead father or mother. It is also easier for a second son in the family to receive Christ than the eldest son, who has the responsibility of preserving the family *butusdan* on his father's death. If a full floodtide of blessing is to come to Japan, it will be when the Word of the Lord to Gideon is obeyed: "Throw down the altar of Baal that thy father hath."

Buddhism is sometimes presented to the world as a treasury of truth hidden in deep mysteries. In fact, as a converted Japanese priest has confessed, it contains nothing solid that anyone can lay hold of or even understand. Only by adopting one particular line of teaching and rejecting all other as false can Buddhism be made intelligible. Every sect in Japan is doing exactly that. The two hundred or more sects have been compared with the Christian denominations; but the comparison is not valid, for differences of doctrine among Buddhists are far wider than any that exist, or could exist, among Christians.

While there is a sleepy form of nominal Buddhism that has pervaded most of Japanese life, it is the sects that give Buddhism its virility. Indeed, the story of Japanese Buddhism is the story of the sects, many of which in modern times are not ashamed to copy Christian methods. Sunday schools have been organized where little children learn to sing, "Buddha loves me, this I know, for the Sutra tells me so"; a Young Men's Buddhist Association has been formed; and a social program launched stimulated by Christian example. At the present time, there is even a controversy between Buddhists on the relative merits of "evangelism" and "a social gospel." Buddhism, which pioneered education in Japan, now makes its influence felt at the highest educational levels. In addition to having six universities and sixteen seminaries of their own, Buddhists have contributed professors of renown to some of the greatest secular universities of the land. And by newspapers, magazines, and popular articles, published both in English and Japanese, Buddhism is reaching out to the multitudes. Nominal Buddhism waits till death to claim its victim: the sects are out to make living converts.

Japanese Buddhism is commonly divided into six schools, each of which includes many sects and subsects. The six schools bear the name of Nara, Tendai, Shingon, Amida, Zen, and Nichiren. The first three are the oldest and have become the weakest numerically. The Nara sects, named after the old capital, now only attract those interested in old temples and the art treasures they contain. The Tendai sects have declined from the days of their glory when even emperors sought the peace of the monasteries and now has only a little more than a million followers. Of the old sects, Shingon (taken from a Sanskrit word meaning "magic formula"), has survived the best.

By trading on the credulity of country people, it manages to do a relatively brisk trade in the sale of talismen, incantations of magic, and in healing. But the real strength of Buddhism in Japan is in the later sects of Amida, Zen, and Nichiren. Amida school represents a Buddhism that seeks salvation by faith alone; Zen represents a philosophical type of Buddhism, and Nichiren represents a fanatical and nationalistic Buddhism.

B. Amida Buddhism

No evidence exists to support the claim that Amida was a real historical person. He is probably the personification of infinite benevolence. Amida is supposed to have refused to become a Buddha unless all who had helped him to attain such a position could share his merits. When he finally reached Buddhahood he established a western paradise, called the Pure Land, where he is supposed to preach the law of Buddha to the blessed.

A priest by the name of Hōnen (A.D. 1132-1212), studying the forty-eight vows of Buddha Amida, was fascinated by the eighteenth which reads, "If any sentient being in the ten quarters who wishes to be reborn in my world and meditates on me . . . even no more than ten times in his life . . . should not be reborn in my world, then I will not attain to Buddhahood." Hōnen interpreted this to mean that the mere repetition of the name Amida would guarantee rebirth in the Pure Land. The doctrine, which was slightly altered and developed by Hōnen's disciple Shinran (1173-1262), is concisely stated in the Amida Sutra as follows: "Good men and women, who, on hearing the preaching of the compassion of Buddha Amida, keep the name of the Buddha, heart and soul for one day, two days, three days, four days, five days, six days or seven days, will be visited by Buddha Amida and his attendants on their death beds. They will go instantly to the World of Highest Happiness." Buddhists have a technical word, "Nembutsu," for the formula "O save Amida Buddha," which the devout repeat constantly. A giant rosary of 108 beads, held by a group of kneeling people who each repeat the formula as the rosary is circulated, is sometimes used to increase the efficacy of the words. Group chanting of the *Nembutsu* in this way is said to be equal to a million repetitions of the formula.

Amida Buddhism or Shinshū quickly gained favor. Not the least reason was its offer of salvation to women who previously had all been regarded as impure and unworthy of salvation. The appeal to women was strengthened by having in the temples on one side of the statue of Buddha Amida, an idol of Kannon, the Goddess of Mercy, whose multiple arms and thousand hands not unnaturally fascinated busy mothers. But the easy way of salvation appealed to all. In the Tan-I Sho, Shinran wrote, "It is sufficient to believe the blessed master's words, 'Only call the name Amitabha and attain salvation.' . . . A man who tries to work out his salvation lacks the simple trust in a power without, and the vow is not for him." These sentences illustrate the fact that the Amida Buddhist uses terms that rival the Christian vocabulary. Salvation by faith alone, the useless-ness of works, salvation even for the sinful, a new birth, changed lives, and the equality of all believers, in which no distinction exists between priest and laymen are all found in this school of Buddhism. It would seem as if the Devil succeeded in planting the lie deep in the hearts of the people, even clothing it with Christian terms, before the truth could be brought to them. One sect of Amida Buddhism, the Jodo Shin, even teaches that faith is a gift of Amida.

This school of Buddhism has made a permanent impression upon the people of Japan. From it they have received vivid impressions of a Heaven and Hell that are graphically described in stories taught to children. A yearning has been created in the hearts of many for this imaginary paradise, called the Pure Land, making suicide easy since by it a happy life in another world can be entered. In modern times, the scientific skepticism of a younger generation challenges the reality of the western paradise of Amida, but the older people cling to their faith with pathetic and futile hope.

C. Zen Buddhism

A monk sitting silently, staring at a blank wall for nine years symbolizes Zen Buddhism. The Indian who introduced Zen to China thus spent part of his life. Zen is the exact opposite of Amida Buddhism. It despises a way of salvation through faith in another, and had no time for formula or sacred writings, but believes in salva-tion through self. Amida appeals to the weak and helpless who feel they have no power within themselves to find salvation. Zen appeals to the strong-willed, and searches for reality within the soul. The method used is concentration, meditation, and contemplation. Zen leads men to the ultimate in frustrated thought, promising that this will be the door to liberty. In fact, it is the abandonment of reason. "Professing themselves to be wise, they became fools." The favorite device is the use of the *koan* which is an irrational question to baffle the mind. A well-known *koan* asks, "Two hands when clapped make a sound, what is the sound of one hand clapping." It would be wrong to think that all Zen Buddhists spend time on such empty speculation. Only a minority of specialists, such as the priests, school-teachers, and military men, torture their minds in this fashion, while the majority are content to belong to a Zen temple without being particularly active.

The effect of Zen Buddhism on Japan has however been tre-mendous. This is seen in the three directions of militarism, educa-tion, and the arts. Zen entered Japan just at the beginning of the feudal period. To the military or samurai castes then appearing, Zen with its asceticism and mental discipline, had a strong appeal, and eventually emerged as "The way of the warrior" or "Bushido." This movement inevitably united with Shinto, and came to tragic maturity in a militarism obsessed with the "Japanese spirit." In education, Zen brought real benefits to Japan. Its monks were the first to start schools throughout the land, and for a time all teachers were priests. In the arts, Zen has had a very great influence on architecture, litera-ture, painting, customs, drama, and dances. The famous tea-cere-mony, with its hundreds of minute rules governing every movement in the making and drinking of the tea, and lasting several hours, is a Zen product whose purpose is not to satisfy the thirst, but to practice self-culture. The strange old Noh Plays, which in bygone days were the only plays the samurai warriors were allowed to see, is also a contribution from Zen Buddhism that has survived to the present day.

Since Zen spurns Scriptures and formulae, it has been able to ad-just itself to changing conditions. Some sects of Zen send preachers throughout the country to engage in widespread propaganda. Others are active in social work. Through its abiding contributions to Japa-nese culture, it has a firm place in the life of the people. And with-in the silence of Zen temples, there are still not a few who seek for the mind of Buddha to be transmitted direct to the believer in a sudden flash of enlightment. In this, as in other Japanese religious sects, Satan has produced a seductive and devilish travesty of man's true aim to "let this mind be in you, which was also in Christ Jesus."

D. The Nichiren School of Buddhism

The Nichiren Sect is now 700 years old, but still retains the colorful characteristics of its founder's magnetic personality. Nichiren lived from A.D. 1222-1282. His fiery zeal as a reformer made him one of the most outstanding men in Japanese history. Convinced that the multiplicity of Buddhist sects of his time were evidence that much of the original teaching of Buddha had become perverted, and certain that such divisions would weaken and eventually destroy Buddhism, he set out to rediscover Sakyamuni's true doctrine. In the Sutra of the Lotus of Truth, Nichiren discovered a prediction of the appearance of a second Buddha 2,000 years after the first had died. This would be Kuon Ganjo, the beginning of all activities in the eternal past, coming into the world as Jogyo Bosatsu. As the 2,000 years had nearly expired, Nichiren, never over-burdened with meekness, immediately recognized himself in Jogyo Bosatsu, and with the words, "Glory to the Sutra of the Lotus of the supreme law" began his turbulent career. He attacked every form of Buddhism then current in Japan, singling out Amida Buddhism for his most vicious lashing because it seemed to rob Buddha of his proper glory. He extended his denunciations to the State, threatening destruction if Japan remained divided in religion and administration. His threats were given weight by Japan's narrow escape from defeat by the Mongols, and a subsequent devastation by earthquake, typhoon, famine, and disease. Encouraged by this onslaught, Nichiren promised more of the same if his words were not heeded. For this he was persecuted, and finally sentenced to death. According to tradition his life was spared by the sudden appearance of a giant meteor which terrified the executioners. From this originated the belief that he rose from the dead. He died in 1282 leaving his considerable followers a fanatical example as their inspiration.

Nichiren wrote no less than 430 volumes, all based on the Lotus Sutra. His teaching may be summarized as follows:

1. The cosmos and the lives of men are one.
   This harmony is broken through evil and impurity.

2. The basic cause of all trouble is false religion which would be defined as any religion not in agreement with the Sutra of Lotus of truth.

3. Salvation is only through the Lotus Sutra within which are "Three Secrets." These are, "the great mandala," describing the eternal Buddha; the Secret Formula "Namu Myoho Renge Kyo"—glory to the mysterious Lotus Sutra; and the "Precept Platform," which is the center for the sect at the foot of Mount Fuji, and which it is hoped will become the religious center of the world.

After Nichiren's death his followers organized their sect which in 1321 received official favor. During the turbulent warring years from the fourteenth to the sixteenth centuries, Nichiren Buddhism appealed to the militant spirit of the people, and during the Meiji era was an important factor in expanding the Japanese Empire. Nichiren's glittering personality, by that time deified, attracted the religious, the patriotic, and the intellectual. Many fanatical nationalists have been members of the sect, which may be compared with the order of the Zealots. In modern times, Nichiren members have played an important, and sometimes bloody, part in Japanese politics.

The average believer seeks salvation through the constant repetition of the "sacred formula," which is often repeated at the top of the voice to the accompaniment of a drum. It is not necessary to read or to understand the Sutra in whose honor so much noise is made. The sect survived the test of the war years, and now numbers around two million members. At a rally in Tokyo in 1955, they were able to pack the giant Korakuen stadium with 70,000 people. At their center at the foot of Mount Fuji prayer services and discussion groups are held and are well attended.

Each of these three great schools of Buddhism in Japan has a special characteristic. In Amida Buddhism, the appeal is to faith; in Zen Buddhism the appeal is to the mind; and in Nichiren Buddhism the appeal is to the emotions. These three schools also illustrate the main characteristics of Buddhist sects. They have a creed based on some particular Sutra; they have individual founders or exponents whose personalities have influenced the course of the movement; they usually have a definite membership which is in contrast to nominal Buddhism to which most people vaguely subscribe; and they often have a proselytizing zeal.

THE PRACTICE OF RELIGION IN JAPAN

Nearly all that has been written thus far concerns the history and teaching of Shinto and Buddhism. The doctrines of both religions have great variety, and many contradictions. Buddhism appears to allow a man to believe what he likes, and Shinto seems to allow a man to behave as he likes, at least in morals. The average Japanese is not concerned either with the contradictions of his religions, or the laxity of their teachings. On the whole, his religious life is formal, and fairly simple. He would find it most difficult to give a reason for what he does or believes. If asked to explain the difference between Shinto and Buddhism, he may answer that a Shintoist claps his hands, and a Buddhist rubs his hands together. In which he is referring to the common methods of "prayer" used by the two religions.

In his home, a Japanese prays by clapping, bowing, and offering rice, water, or tea at his little Shinto shrine. Before the adjacent Buddhist altar he rubs the rosary between his hands, bows, and offers food. At times of death, the Shinto *kami-dana* is eclipsed by the worship of the spirits represented by the tablets in his Buddhist *butsudan*.

In his community life, he supports a local temple financially, and feels that his obligations are about ended. His wife takes the babies to the Shinto shrine to be dedicated as soon as they are a month old, and at the ages of three, five and seven, she leads them back to the same shrine for a brief and formal moment of thanksgiving and supplication for further favor.

In school, his children are not taught religion. This is a radical change brought about by the military occupation authorities. Previously all education was based on the famous Imperial Rescript of 1890, which gained the prestige of sacred writing and had a greater influence on modern Japan than any other document. Shinto never did have Scriptures, and Japanese Buddhism has always lacked authoritative holy books. The Imperial Rescript on education, together with a similar document adressed to soldiers and sailors, met that need. The words of the Rescript are simple enough, and in no way extraordinary, but they were used to gear the whole of the educational system into the Shinto machinery of emperor worship. The aim of education was no longer a pursuit of truth, but the service of the State. By a directive from MacArthur's headquarters, State control of education was ended, and a new system, based on the American pattern, introduced. To insure that nationalistic Shinto would not again capture the minds of Japanese students, the teaching of any religion in schools was banned. The only religious influences that remained were the example and personal witness of Christian, Buddhist, Shinto, and atheistic teachers. If a child is sent to a school operated by a Shinto sect, such as the Tenrikyo, or to a Buddhist college, the influence of these religions upon him through personal contact with his teachers will be enormous.

At marriage, the average Japanese again has a fleeting contact with religion. The simplest form is the exchange of a ritualistic drink between the bride and bridegroom before the Buddhist family altar. In recent years a normal Shinto ceremony has been developed, which takes place at the shrine. The white-robed priest first drives away all evil spirits by waving a small branch before the couple who then each take three sips from each of three cups of rice wine. The union of the two in marriage is then announced to the myriad gods of Japan. While many modern Japanese are skeptical about the existence of such gods and regard the Shinto marriage ceremony as ridiculous, their unbelief has not reached the point of being a conviction strong enough to make them break with the custom. Belief in the gods of Japan has gone, but social pressure remains.

The average Japanese has a lighthearted interest in his religions through the yearly festivals. These celebrations all stress the unity of the nation, the community, and the family, as well as mark the changing seasons. The strength of the religious significance of the festivals varies in different communities, and with individual people. Among the important festivals in the Shinto celebration of the New Year when all debts are cleared, houses are decorated, and people take their ceremonial first bath, first food, and first wine. The Buddhist "Obon" festival is also widely celebrated. During the months of July and August, the departed spirits of the dead are believed to return to the home, and the Buddhistic family altar is decorated in their honor. In rural areas, a straw horse is burned before the entrance of the home as a sign of welcome to the spirits, and three days later a straw model of the slow moving cow is burned in the same place to indicate that the family is loath to have the spirits depart. To some Japanese, this festival has no more religious significance than American Hallowe'en, but to others the occasion is nothing but religion. In either case, this festival, like other festivals, binds every individual Japanese more tightly to the whole community and makes a response to the Gospel, with its promised liberty in Christ, the more difficult.

In times of sickness, many Japanese, specially in country areas, seek the help of religion. Miraculous help is sought from shrine or temple. Some Buddhist groups, such as the Tendai sect, concentrate on faith healing. In a hopeless death, the Japanese have a final contact with religion. The multitudes who have lived all their days in these over-crowded islands even in death find no spacious resting place. By law, cremation is required. The ceremony is usually Buddhistic. All that remains are a few ashes in a box, tied with a white ribbon; a new Buddhistic name on a little tablet to be placed in the *butsudan;* and the forlorn assurance that successive generations will remember and worship.

THE HEART OF THE PROBLEM

The religious situation in Japan is exceedingly complex. What then is the heart of the problem? Of all the forces that keep the Japanese in bondage, two are exceedingly strong. These are death and nationalism. A fear of death is the real strength of Buddhism. Nationalism is the real strength of Shinto. The Gospel therefore makes contact with the Japanese on these two points, and here the battle rages. For those in bondage through fear of death, the message is that Christ took part of flesh and blood "that through death he might destroy him that had the power of death, that is the devil, and deliver them who through fear of death were all their lifetime subject to bondage" (Heb. 2:14, 15). This is the hope that the Japanese need, and that Buddhism cannot provide. But Christ's victory over death and the Devil is inseparable from His resurrection, and personal deliverance from fear of death involves "believing in thine heart that God hath raised him from the dead."

The implication is also very clear that no emancipation from fear of death is possible until the worship of the dead, who are the virtual heads of the family, ceases. As might be expected by those who are not ignorant of Satan's devices, all kinds of pressure, chiefly through relatives, is exerted against any who begin to consider throwing out the family altar. And the truth of Christ's resurrection is often unacceptable, even to some who profess a desire to be saved. In contact with nationalism, buttressed and supported by Shinto, the Lordship of Christ and the authority of the inspired Scriptures are the points at issue. To a Japanese who has always regarded the authority of his Emperor as absolute, and the decisions of his own family as binding, it is no light and easy choice "to confess Jesus as Lord." And to a people who have never possessed any book or document that was final and authoritative, except the Imperial Rescript, the dogmatic truth of the uncompromising Word of God is not easy to accept.

Many a Japanese would be quite willing to add a little Christianity to his Buddhistic and Shinto beliefs. Many would be willing to accept Christ if it could be shown that He and His teachings were Japanese. Indeed, this very thing has been attempted. But, in fact, the choice that faces them is whether they will accept a Christ who died for their sins, rose from the dead, and who demands a higher place in their hearts than even the Emperor holds. The choice is between custom, strengthened by generations of observance, and the Scriptures, a divine revelation from God Himself. For these reasons, the ambassador of Christ who comes to Japan with the message of reconciliation must himself have made Christ Lord of all, and be fully assured that "all scripture is given by inspiration of God."

THE PROSPECTS

After World War II ended, wave after wave of missionaries invaded Japan. A religious invasion following military victory was not unexpected since the Japanese themselves had used such a method in Korea. But there was a more practical reason for the enthusiasm with which the Gospel was received. It was the religion of the conquerors. Without ethical standards, Japan could judge only by results. They had seen America, whose trust was in God, gain victory over their own nation which claimed a divine beginning. The logical way, therefore, to rise from the ashes of defeat and find a better way to glory was to accept America's God. Loyalty to those who temporarily held absolute power through military occupation added to the readiness of the multitudes to receive the Gospel. Much of such enthusiasm, however, wilted when it was found that God is exacting in His holy demands, tolerant of no rivals, and demanding everything of His worshipers. More than that, the Japanese learned to their dismay that God had no favors to offer except grace to humble and repentant sinners. To many the price of salvation seemed too high. Not a few who would have accepted God as a patron of Japan, refused to recognize Him as King of kings, and Lord of lords. The Gospel became unpalatable when it was found to be dogmatic, unyielding, and not malleable to Japanese requirements.

At the same time as the Japanese felt the shock of the uncompromising truths of the Gospel and realized the absolute demands of Christ, Shinto tried to regain its lost prestige. Just as centuries earlier, Shinto had reacted sharply against a Buddhism invasion, so the reaction against the coming of the Gospel was swift. Shinto turned again to the methods used in Korea, the family altar, education and the festivals. The god-shelf had not been disturbed by war or the Occupation, and it was therefore to education and the national festivals that Shinto turned its attention. For this reason Japan's new educational system is now the center of much bitter controversy. Since the war, the Minister of Education and lower officials of his department have been elected by popular vote; but strong efforts are now being made to return to the old system whereby all such appointments were by the State which thus had control of the whole educational system. This battle for the minds of young Japanese is being fought out in the Diet where the Right Wing of the Government obviously hopes for a return to Shinto which has always favored the ruling classes and sustained them in power. The Japanese are nearly 100 per cent literate, and therefore if the whole of the educational system can again be brought under tight government supervision, then the way will be wide open for traditional Shinto to recapture the imagination and loyalty of a new generation.

Shinto's second means of promoting a revival is through its national festivals and shrines. As soon as Japan regained her independence, the Emperor himself visited the shrine at Ise to report to the Sun Goddess that the military occupation had ended. Later the same year he attended the autumn festival at the Yasukuni Shrine where the spirits of the dead were honored. Following the Imperial example and their own newly awakened nationalistic emotions, the people began to flock back to the Shinto strongholds. In January, 1955, more than 2,700,000 people visited the Meiji Shrine in Tokyo where the soul of the Emperor Meiji and his consort are supposed to reside. It was the greatest pilgrimage on record in the history of the nation. The shrine is now being reconstructed at a cost of over $1,600,000 (U.S.).

Since nationalism and Shinto are so intimately connected, a revival of the one without a revival of the other is almost impossible. The Japanese are an emotionally tense race, and therefore these fires of nationalism, fanned by the winds of Shinto, are exceedingly dangerous. Already ultranationalism is threatening to overthrow Japan's new constitution. If such were to happen, there is no doubt that Shinto would regain all that it temporarily lost.

The future course of events in Japan cannot be confidently predicted. A Shinto revival is certain for it has already begun. No reason exists to doubt that the Buddhist sects will continue to multiply and divide. Whether these twin forces of evil that have so long held th Land of the Rising Sun in a gross darkness will ever be overcome by persistent prayer and empowered preaching of the Gospel is for the Church of the living God to decide.

BIBLIOGRAPHY

Much of the information presented in this chapter is based on personal interviews with Japanese and articles in Japanese newspapers. This explains the brevity of the following Bibliography.

BUNCE, WILLIAM K. *Religions in Japan*. Rutland, Vt.: Chas. E. Tuttle Co.

EAST, YOUNG. *The Japanese Buddhist Quarterly*.

FRANCIS, J. HORNER. *A Case History of Japan*. New York: Sheed & Ward.

HUMPHREYS, CHRISTMAS. *Buddhism*. Baltimore: Penguin Books Inc.

SAKAI, ATSUHARU. *Japan in a Nutshell*. Rutland, Vt.: Chas. E. Tuttle Co.

FIG. 6.—A Buddhist nun performs her religious exercises at a nunnery just inside the city gate of Peiping, China. (Courtesy of Camera Press, London.)

Tao is all-pervading,
    And its use is inexhaustible,
Fathomless!...
Yet crystal clear like water it seems to remain.
    I do not know whose son it is,
    An image which existed before God.
The thing called Tao is elusive...
    Yet latent in it is the life-force.

                                    —LAO TZU

VI.

China

by DAVID ADENEY

RELIGIONS AND THE REVOLUTION IN CHINA

IN MAY, 1949, one hundred years after Karl Marx issued the famous *Communist Manifesto,* soldiers of the "Army of Liberation" entered Shanghai. As we watched the red flag with its five stars appear in the window of almost every home, we realized that a new era had dawned. We were witnessing a tremendous upheaval in which the social structures of an ancient nation would be shaken to their very foundations. Almost 600 million people were being conquered by a minority of enthusiastic communists devoted to a materialistic ideology which was to transform a pattern of life that had prevailed for thousands of years.

The hundred years following the publication of the *Communist Manifesto* proved also to be the most active period of Protestant missionary advance in China. As the isolation of the past disappeared

Born in England, D. H. ADENEY received his education at Cambridge University (B.A., M.A.) and the London Missionary Training Colony. He served as a missionary to China with the China Inland Mission in Honan Province for eleven years. At the end of that time, he traveled extensively in sixteen provinces of China, visiting colleges and universities. Forced out of China by the Communists, he served for several years on the staff of Inter-Varsity, U.S.A. Now he is Associate General Secretary for the Far East of the International Fellowship of Evangelical Students and lives in Hong Kong. Mr. Adeney is the author of *The Unchanging Commission.*

123

and China became aware of Western educational methods, it seemed obvious that the old ethnic religions could never supply the spiritual needs of the people. But if the ramparts of superstition were crumbling, even more powerful defenses against the spread of the Gospel were being erected. Taking advantage of the natural materialistic outlook of the Chinese, advocates of a materialistic philosophy of "life" were quick to ridicule any belief in the supernatural. Thus they prepared the way for the millions of China to be added to the masses within the Soviet's orbit who have already raised the standard of rebellion against the most High God.

In order to understand the spiritual conflict within China, we must study the religious background of the people. Even though rationalistic materialism is the dominant philosophy of China today, the influence of old religious beliefs continue in the lives of multitudes who pay lip-service to the slogan of the militantly atheistic communist regime, but worship their ancestors in the privacy of their own homes.

The origins of Chinese religions are hidden in antiquity. Some scholars believe that Chinese religious concepts "begin with animism, develop into ancestor worship and the worship of heaven and earth, and culminate in what may be called nature theism."[1] Others feel, however, that there is ample evidence to support the belief that the Chinese were monotheists long before they became polytheists. Dr. John Ross finds no hint in Chinese literature as to the manner how or the time when the idea of God originated in China. The name *Shang-ti* or Supreme Ruler bursts upon us from the first page of history without a note of warning.[2] Although long neglected, an ancient altar of Heaven close to our home in Fangcheng, Honan, bore witness to the time when the chief magistrate of the district offered sacrifice to the Supreme Being.

Confucianism

Confucianism, Buddhism, and Taoism, are often regarded as the three main religions of China, though the term *religion (Chiao)* is misleading. To a Chinese, *Chiao* includes the idea of education, culture, and religion. While Buddhism and Taoism are organized in-

---

[1]Leonard M. Outerbridge, *The Lost Churches of China*, p. 18.
[2]John Ross, *The Original Religion of China*.

stitutions with a hierarchy of priests, Confucianism lacks the marks
of a religion and might more properly be described as a philosophy
of life. Confucius who lived during the sixth century B.C. (551-447),
made no claims to deity. He urged his followers to "respect the
spirits but keep far from them."[3] This does not mean that he in any
way despised the worship of spiritual beings, as is seen from the
following quotation: "How abundantly do spiritual beings display
their power! Invincible to the ear and impalpable to the senses, they
enter into all things. It is this fact that causes all people to fast and
purify themselves, and with solemnity of dress, institute services of
sacrifice and religious worship. Like the rush of mighty waters, they
seem to be about, above us, and around us."[4]

But though Confucius himself recognized the mandate of Heaven,
he was much more concerned about the present than the hereafter.
The people among whom he lived honored the spirits (or gods) of
rivers, mountains, and trees, and worshiped the spirits of dead heroes
and ancestors. The interests of Confucius, however, were "chiefly
those of the statesman and the teacher of ethics."[5] Gathering around
him a group of disciples, he sought in his teaching, writing, and example to demonstrate the principles of the superior man (*chuin-tze*).
He set for his followers very high ideals of personal integrity and
clearly outlined the right relationships between a man and his
sovereign, parents, brothers, sisters, wife, children, and friends. He
emphasized the need for self-examination and taught that the superior man must be true to his own inner nature and apply these
principles of his inner nature to his relationships with others.

Recently a Chinese friend of mine, who is now a principal of a
university in Taiwan, drew my attention to some of the precepts of
Confucius which are very similar to the sayings of our Lord Jesus in
His Sermon on the Mount. Very significantly he pointed out that
China has had good ethical advice for more than two thousand years.
But good advice alone can never satisfy the need of sinful man. The
dynamic necessary for the attainment of such ideals can be found only
through the possession of the new life in Christ. Thus he recognized
as he remarked, "My people need not ethical teaching but the mes-

[3]Anni VI, 60.
[4]*Doctrine of the Mean*, XVI, 1-3.
[5]K. S. Latourette, *The Chinese, Their History and Culture*, Vol. II, p. 73.

sage of the resurrection." The Christian concept of the sinfulness of human nature is of course diametrically opposed to the Confucian belief that man's heart is basically good and needs only self-cultivation.

Some attempts have been made to make Confucianism a national religion. Manchu rulers, in a last effort to salvage a crumbling dynasty, issued an edict, placing sacrifice to Confucius on an equality with those to Heaven. In 1913, Article 19 of the draft Constitution stated that "in the education of a citizen, the doctrines of Confucius shall be regarded as the basis of moral cultivation." Yuan Shih-kai in 1916 officiated at both sacrifices to Heaven and to Confucius. But with his death, opposition to any form of state religion increased, and in 1928, the Nationalist government even banned the sacrifice to Confucius in the Temple of Confucius. But on the birthday of the Sage, the crowds would always flock to the temple of Confucius to present their offerings and joss sticks in honor of his memory.[6]

Even among modern scholars who are ardent followers of Confucius, there is opposition to any suggestion that Confucianism should be regarded as a State religion. Chang T'ai-yen stated that "the greatness of Confucius lies with his preoccupation with social and government affairs."[7] Among other Chinese intellectuals, there have been those who have actively sought to undermine the reverence and honor accorded to the ancient Sage. Dr. Hu Shih, an outstanding modern philosopher, has always been very critical of Confucian teaching, declaring that its emphasis upon the distinction between the superior and the inferior, the noble and the lowly, is contrary to the modern idea of equality. In his criticism of Confucianism, he stated: "In the last two or three decades, we have abolished 3,000 years of foot-binding; 800 years of the eight-legged essay; 4,000 to 5,000 years of male prostitution; and 5,000 years of judicial torture. None of this revolution was aided by Confucianism."[8]

Among the very materialistically-minded students there were even some extremists who went so far as to burn a straw effigy of Confucius, shouting, "Destroy, destroy the Old Curiosity Shop of Confucius!"

It is evident therefore that, even before the triumph of the com-

[6]Wang Tsit Chan, *Religious Trends in Modern China*, pp. 7, 8.
[7]*Ibid.*, p. 12.
[8]*Ibid.*, pp. 17, 18.

munist armies, Confucianism as a religious institution had been practically destroyed. But this did not mean that the fundamental principles of Confucius were discarded. In 1934, Generalissimo Chiang Kai-shek used as the basis of the New Life Movement the four Confucian cardinal virtues of *Li, I, Lien,* and *Ch'ih,* which are: regulated attitude, right conduct, clear discernment, and self-consciousness. But while the New Life Movement was successful in a limited way in certain areas, its reforms were mainly superficial, for high moral principles without a spiritual driving-force would never bring about the radical change that was needed, could never overcome the evil and corruption that was so deeply imbedded in Chinese officialdom.

Under the communist regime, Confucianism is regarded as reactionary, and Mao Tse-tung has likened the teaching of Confucius to medieval medicine—unsuited for modern times. Later, however, in his article, "On Entering the Final Stage," he advised party members to learn from Confucius and Sun Yat-sen as well as Marx and Lenin. Premier Chou En-lai, in speaking to Professor Chakravarty of the China Goodwill Mission, acknowledged that "there may be some elements of value in the philosophy of Confucius, but it was formulated more than 2,000 years ago and is no longer valid."[9]

Even before the revolution in China, the majority of Chinese students knew very little about the writings of Confucius, Mencius, and the other great philosophers of the past. Twenty years ago when we first went to China, we could still visit private schools, which were to be found in many of the country villages. There an old Confucian scholar would do little else but teach the children the classics. From afar off we could hear the children as, in unison at the top of their voices, they repeated their lessons, thus memorizing large sections of the writings of Confucius and the other philosophers of the past. Today the aged schoolmaster would be grieved to see his textbooks being used as wrapping paper.

The very basis of Confucian ethics is benevolence, manifesting itself in the solidarity of the family. This has been strenuously attacked by the communists, who demand a loyalty to the party which transcends all other loyalties. Instead of filial piety, children are now

[9]Sundarlal, *China Today,* quoted by Brandon, *World Communism and the Religions of China.*

taught that they can demonstrate their patriotism by exposing reactionary trends in their parents' thinking and even by demanding
heavy penalties for parents who fail to conform to the party line.

Because respect for parents and close family relationships are built
around ancestor worship, this too is attacked by the communists. It
is regarded as a superstitious practice which should be shunned by
all progressive citizens. However, the ancestral cult is deeply rooted
in the lives of the older people, and is certainly still practiced in multitudes of homes, though any public ceremonies in local or regional
temples would be frowned upon.

TAOISM

About the year 604 B.C., half a century before Confucius was born,
Lao-tsu appeared on the scene. The two men were very different for,
while Confucius was essentially practical in his teaching, Lao-tsu was
a mystic. The very beautiful concept of the "Tao" (The Way),
which is developed in the Tao Teh Ching, provided the name for
Taoism. But Lao-tsu himself would have strongly opposed the association of his name with the hodgepodge of superstition that constitutes the beliefs of the typical Taoist. One cannot but admire some
of the teaching given by the ancient philosopher. He mentions three
distinguishing qualities of the possessor of "The Way." "I have three
precious things which I prize and hold fast. The first is gentleness;
the second is economy; the third is shrinking from taking precedence
of others. With that gentleness, I can be bold; with that economy,
I can be liberal; shrinking from taking precedence of others, I can
become a vessel of the highest honor."[10]

Lao-tsu's whole emphasis was upon a return to the primitive
simplicity of Nature: "To him, the way of nature was to cease from
self-assertion and from fussy attempts to save the world."[11] For this
reason, Lao-tsu objected to the strenuous efforts and discipline required by Confucius in his teaching concerning the cultivation of
character. He opposed the formulation of a way of life and reacted
against the rigidity and absolute nature of Confucian ethical standards. Believing that everything comes from Nature, he considered
that the simpler a man can be the greater he becomes.

The religious system known as Taoism bears little resemblance to

[10]Outerbridge, *op cit.*, p. 25.
[11]Frank Houghton, *China Calling*, p. 75.

the teaching of Lao-tsu. Taoism emphasizes a mystical strain in Chinese religions which undoubtedly existed long before Lao-tsu ever lived. The Taoist thinks of the unseen world as being full of spirits, both good and evil. Trees and stones, mountains and rivers are inhabited by these spirits. The great numbers of shrines, scattered across the countryside, bear witness to the efforts made to placate them. Behind a great deal of the superstitious practices is a belief in the dangerous influence of the evil spirits who are not regarded as a separate race of beings but rather as the spirits of the dead. The Chinese recognized the conflict within Nature. On the one hand, there is the *Yin*, which stands for earth, the moon, darkness, evil, and the female sex. On the other side is the *Yang*, which includes Heaven, the sun, light, fire, goodness, and the male sex. The gods (*Shen*) are also associated with the *Yang* and therefore are in opposition to the evil spirits (*Kkuei*) which are *Yin*.

In order to assure protection against these evil spirits, a great variety of deities may be worshiped; and from time to time, Buddhist monks or Taoist priests will be paid to drive away the spirits that are supposed to be causing some form of sickness or misfortune within the family. Thus a vast system of witchcraft, astrology, and fortune-telling has grown up, much of it really debasing in character. This fear of the spirits and worship of a great variety of deities has led to demon manifestations which are not easy for the Western mind to comprehend. To the Chinese farmer, demon possession is very real. They have seen the ignorant and often immoral Taoist priests, with their long hair, go into trances and become possessed by some outside power. They have witnessed amazing happenings as the result of worship of certain shrines which have gained a reputation of being powerful. They have seen their own relatives or neighbors afflicted by evil spirits. Even missionaries who have been most hesitant to accept stories of supernatural manifestations have been convinced of the activity of demons. In many a church, there are those who were once enslaved by evil spirits, a menace to themselves and the despair of their friends. Now—through faith in Christ—they are active, useful members of the church and society in which they live. Many of the miracles of the Gospel have been enacted again and again in China, as Christians have claimed the promises of our Lord and experienced the power of prayer. Faith in the name of Christ can still bring healing to men and women afflicted by the powers of darkness. The writer has been hailed by a spirit speaking through a man whom he had never seen and has witnessed the power of prayer to liberate people who for years have been subject to attacks of demon possession.

While Taoism consists largely of a vast mass of superstitious practices, and its adherents are mostly illiterate, there are also certain secret societies which emphasize the Five Precepts and Ten Virtues of Taoism. The Five Precepts are: not to kill, drink alcohol, lie, steal, or commit adultery; and the Ten Virtues: filial piety, loyalty, love, patience, remonstration of evil deeds, self-sacrifice, aiding the poor, setting live beings free, planting trees and building roads and digging wells, and teaching the unenlightened and promoting their welfare.[12]

On the whole, however, Taoism has become very decadent, and in recent years there has been no sign of a Taoist renaissance, nor has any Taoist prophet appeared on the scene. The priests and vegetarian women, who may or may not leave home in order to live in a temple spend their time performing superstitious rituals in order to obtain some material blessing for those who seek their help, such as wealth, health, longevity, or children. No wonder that in the eyes of the Chinese literati they have become discredited. Over twenty years ago, Dr. Hu-shih said, "Taoism in China is dead." Communism is likely to make doubly sure that Taoism shall not survive. Itinerating Taoist priests are sure to be condemned as superstitious and unproductive and will probably receive severe treatment from communist officials. In the people's political consultative council, which contains a number of Christians and Buddhist representatives, Taoism is completely ignored. Superstitious practices will be certain to continue—they are to be found even in Western society. Taoism as a religious institution is likely to disappear.

BUDDHISM

To any traveler in China, broken-down temples present a familiar sight. Ardent Buddhists speak of the catastrophe of the last few decades, referring to high taxation making repair of the temples im-

[12]Wang Tsit Chan, *op. cit.*, p. 174.

possible and the confiscation of many of their buildings for barracks, stores, and schools. The country people themselves joke about the idols which, because of fallen temple roofs, have been left to the ravages of wind and weather. Even before the communist revolution, a large percentage of the temples were being used for secular purposes. Not only were the temples in a bad state of repair but the half-million monks and one hundred thousand nuns for the most part showed little signs of vitality. Many of them were illiterate and T'ai Hsu, who sought to bring about a Buddhist revival, charged that "the whole Chinese clergy is interested in self-benefit."[13] Before the revolution, their time was mainly given to earning money through officiating at weddings, funerals, and performing numerous other superstitious ceremonies. It is probable that most of those who shave the head, wear robes opening to the right and not the left, adhere to a vegetarian way of life, and become celibates do so for selfish reasons. Perhaps it is because of sickness or poverty in the family, or possibly to fulfill a parent's vow made when some member of the family was ill. Most of them have little appreciation of spiritual values.

Even though the majority of Buddhist adherents know nothing of the philosophical tenets of their religion, we must not underestimate the very great influence of Buddhism on the religious life of the country. Buddhism originated in India contemporaneous with Confucius and Lao-tsu, among a people who were far more otherworldly and mystical than the Chinese. It was introduced into China probably during the first century A.D. and by A.D. 165 was recognized by the Emperor. Lin Yu T'ang has described Buddhism as "the only important foreign influence that has become part and parcel of Chinese life." "Buddhism," he says, "has affected our language, our food, our arts, our sculpture, and directly inspired the characteristic pagoda."[14]

Originally, Buddhism was a religion of monks and very strict rules controlled the lives of those who entered the sangha, the Buddhist order. Monks clad in yellow robes were regarded as holy men. They supported themselves by begging and spent their lives in medi-

---

[13]Wang Tsit Chan, *op. cit.*, p. 80. Author quotes T'ai Hsu Ta Shih Wen Ch'ao, p. 224.
[14]Frank Houghton, *op. cit.*, p. 95.

tation and study. While Buddhism declined in India, missionaries from that land spread the teaching of Gautama to the lands of Southeast Asia. In its original form Buddhism, known as Theravada (the teaching of the elders) but often referred to as Hinayana, survives in Ceylon, Burma, and Thailand. Hinayana, "the little vehicle," is a disparaging term given by those who feel that it is too difficult a way for the mass of mankind. Mahayana, "the great vehicle," was developed several centuries later and appeals more to the masses. It came to China soon after the time of Christ, to Korea in the fourth century A.D., Japan in the sixth, and Tibet in the seventh.[15]

Great changes have taken place in the Buddhism of China since the first missionaries arrived. To a large extent, the Chinese absorbed Buddhism and accepted parts of its teaching without discarding their other beliefs. A Chinese never regards himself as exclusively a Buddhist, a Taoist, or a Confucianist. Elements of all three may constitute his religion which usually tends to be syncretic in character.

In the Sheng Kung Hwei (Episcopal Cathedral) in Kaifeng, the provincial capital of Honan, there is an interesting relic of the past which symbolizes the syncretic influences to be found in Chinese religion. The font, now used for Christian baptism, was once the laver in an old Jewish synagogue which has now disappeared, though descendants of this ancient Jewish colony can still be recognized by certain customs which remain. The stone font is made in the form of a lotus flower, and it was only after it was installed in the cathedral that someone noticed that it must have been carved by a Buddhist stone mason for the petals formed the face of Buddha.

Because of this syncretic attitude it is not surprising to find that Buddhism has been greatly influenced by the popular religions of the people; and the drastic changes which have taken place have produced a great rift between the original teaching of Gautama and the popular belief of the people. The philosophical ideas of Karma, denoting the law of cause and effect, the result of what has gone before, were far too obtuse for the practical-minded Chinese. With his belief in the spirit world and an existence after death, it became impossible to accept the view of separate individual existence being only an illusion, "for the self has neither beginning nor ending, is

[15]J. N. D. Anderson, *The World's Religions*, p. 118.

eternally changing, and possesses only a phenomenal existence."[16]

The doctrine of Nirvāna, a state of mind in which Karma ceases to take effect, a cessation of all sense of being, was also far too metaphysical to satisfy the Chinese mind. The "Pure Land" school of Buddhism, to which most Chinese Buddhists belonged, proclaimed for those not interested in Nirvāna a release from suffering and rebirth. It was the idea of a paradise, created by Amita Buddha, "out of his infinite compassion and by the power of his accumulated merit, in order that those ensnared by desire, hatred, and ignorance might be reborn there and have transferred to them the results of his excellent Karma." At the same time, vivid portrayals of thirty-three heavens and eighteen hells appealed to the illiterate people.

Gautama himself never made claim to divinity. He regarded himself as a teacher but never instituted a religion in the sense of a belief in God or way of salvation and forgiveness. Philosophical Buddhism is not theistic and denies belief in a personal God. In its Mahayana form, however, a supreme reality is introduced and Gautama is deified. To most who worship at the temples, Buddha and the Bodhisattvas are quite indistinguishable from the pantheon of polytheistic deities worshiped in the popular religion. Salvation now became possible through the help of Buddha; and the Bodhisattvas, being those who having attained to Buddhahood, renounced Nirvana in order to help men. Thus the earnest Buddhist hopes, through the accumulation of merit and faith in the name of Buddha, to reach the "Pure Land." In order to win the illiterate, images were introduced; and idolatrous polytheism completely changed the character of the moral and philosophical system instituted by Gautama.

The tendency of Chinese Buddhism to cater to the popular needs of the people is seen in the development of the Goddess of Mercy cult. One of the most widely revered Bodhisattvas is Analokitesvara, known in Japan as Kwannon. There the saint remains, transcendental and heavenly. But in China, under the name of Kwanyin, the saint assumes female form and has become "mother" to millions of devout Chinese who go to the temple to worship the Goddess of Mercy. Multitudes of devout Chinese women seek her protection and present offerings in gratitude for the gift of children.[17] Watch-

[16]*Ibid.*, p. 124.
[17]Wang Tsit Chan, *op. cit.*, p. 87.

ing the women burning incense to the Goddess of Mercy is a reminder of the adoration of the Virgin Mary in Roman Catholicism. For most Chinese Buddhists, salvation is to be obtained by the accumulation of personal merit; vegetarian vows are taken and long pilgrimages performed to famous shrines on some sacred mountain. Merit is also obtained through the observance of certain rituals and the mechanical recitation of prayers. As he fingers his rosary, the devout Buddhist will constantly repeat the prayer, *"Man, mo a-mi-tofu"* (I honor thee and resort to thee, Amithaba Buddha) with little sense of pietism or true worship but as a means of assuring rebirth in a Buddhist heaven.

In spite of the fact that the philosophical aspects of Buddhism are little understood by the majority of the people, the Buddhist faith in China has during the past century produced a number of intellectual leaders; and in some areas there has been what might be described as a minor renaissance. Under the great Abbot T'ai Hsu, a movement was launched to defend the religion, propagate faith, reform monastic order, and promote education. Yin Kuang (1861-1940) also brought a revival of Buddhism in certain districts as he publicly lectured on the importance of piety, holiness, and faith, in realizing one's Buddha nature and combating evil.[18] The general trend of the teaching seemed to be away from other-worldliness to a much more this-worldly philosophy of life. Salvation is to be achieved in this life by realizing the Buddha nature within. It was, however, only a small minority which was significantly influenced by this renaissance.

It is impossible to generalize when discussing Buddhism, as there are a number of differing sects varying greatly in their practices. Most of the large temples have meditation halls in which the devotees of the Zen, or Meditation Sect, seek enlightenment. The Esoteric Sect, often known as Lamaism, is the national religion of Tibet and Mongolia. This sect places far greater emphasis upon picturesque pagantry and ritual. Through the repetition of secret formulas and thousands of prayers, together with full-length prostrations, offerings, and appropriate ritual, the help of the Bodhissatvas may be obtained in the struggle for enlightenment.

[18]*Ibid.*, pp. 56, 66.

The question is often asked as to the fate of Buddhism after the communist revolution. On the philosophical level, Buddhism may appear to be less obnoxious to Communism than other faiths, for there is no belief in a personal god. And the Buddhist's concept of Karma might be compared with the inevitable outworking of dialectical materialism. The general level of Buddhism in China, however, is not philosophical. It is not surprising, therefore, that we find strong communist opposition to the popular Buddhism of the masses. The Buddhist priesthood is regarded as being unproductive and superstitious. It is claimed that they have robbed the people through their demanding payment for religious ceremonies. Their effort to attain to Nirvāna through meditation and separation from the world is condemned as being an activity possible only for the idle rich.

According to refugee Buddhist monks, five hundred of whom are to be found in Hong Kong, 400,000 out of 700,000 monks and nuns have been forced to return to lay life and 200,000 of the younger monks have been drafted to fight for the New Democracy.[19] Some of the temples have, however, been kept open—perhaps to demonstrate the freedom of religion guaranteed in the constitution. In most cases, however, the monks are forced to take up some form of productive work. In an article published in the Shanghai *China Weekly Review,* entitled "A New Life Begins in the Temples," the earnest propagandist describes the way in which Communism is penetrating every sphere of life. Even the Buddhist monks and nuns have been set to doing useful work for the community. In some places they have opened vegetarian restaurants in which the Buddhist monks cook and serve the meals. Other temples have started small factories for hosiery knitting or the making of towels and in some cases farms have been established. Commenting on this article, U Ohn Ghine, a member of the staff of the National Institute of Buddhist Studies in Rangoon, writing in *The Burma Star,* criticized the author of the article in the Chinese paper as being " a propagandist who had no idea of Buddhism and was evidently a pure materialist, so when I see the official handouts of Buddhist activities, I am entitled to wonder whether it is towel-making or Buddhism, or whether it is just another attempt to use Buddhism for political

[19]*Ibid.,* pp. 90, 91.

propaganda purposes which all Buddhists should strenuously resist if Buddhism is to survive in the world."[20]

The communists certainly have realized the importance of Buddhist thought in Southeast Asia. Evidence of this is seen in the publication of a four-page communist pamphlet written especially for Buddhist priests and delivered to the temples in Bangkok and Southern Thailand. Buddhist thought outside of China, however, seems on the whole to be strongly opposed to Communism. Writing in the *Hindustan Times,* on November 12, 1954, Satya Wati says:

> The philosophy of Communism which is the guiding light for Chinese leaders is the negation of the Buddhist principles of moral objectivity and universal fellowship based on love and non-violence and unending pursuit of knowledge. . . . Under the impact of a vast brain-washing process going on in China, Buddhist elements in Chinese culture are fast vanishing. From 1948 to the end of 1954, 10,000,000 copies of Stalin's works were published in China but not a single edition of the works of Buddha or any of his disciples has been published. . . . Careful observers predict that if the process of destruction of old culture and its replacement by communist culture continues for a few more decades, the younger generation in China will not even know that Lord Buddha ever even existed.[21]

The government leaders in Peking certainly would not admit to any attempt to overthrow Buddhism. They would point out that they had repaired an eighteen-hundred-year-old Buddhist temple in Honan. Their recognition of Buddhism is also indicated by the inclusion of two Buddhist representatives among the delegates attending the People's Political Consultative Conference. One of these two is Chu-Tsan, a monk well-versed in Buddhist philosophy and history and presently Dean of the Wulin Buddhist Institute at Hangchow.

ISLAM

An exception to the Chinese tendency to combine elements of various religions is to be found in the Moslem community. No Moslem can ever tolerate idolatry and there are, therefore, none who are

---

[20]Mission bulletin published by Roman Catholics in Hong Kong, February, 1955, pp. 164, 165.
[21]*Ibid.,* March, 1955, p. 267.

partly Buddhist and partly Taoist. Prof. Latourette says, "Outside the main stream of Chinese religious life forming separate religious communities are the Moslems."[22]

By the year A.D. 651, less than a century after the death of Mohammed, Moslems were to be found in China, but after thirteen centuries they still remain a foreign religion on Chinese soil. Up until modern times, they were largely cut off from the world Islamic community and so have been little affected by intellectual movements in other parts of the Moslem World. Estimates of Moslem population in China have ranged from three to fifty million. One Moslem scholar believes there are between thirty and forty million, but a more conservative estimate would seem to be between fifteen and twenty million. Even so, there are more Moslems in China than in Egypt, Iran, or Turkey. They are to be found in practically every province, though the heaviest concentration is in the northwestern province of Kansu. A large number of Moslems are also located in Yunnan in the southwest.

During the eighth century, Arab traders established themselves on the China coast; and during the Mongol Dynasty sea-borne commerce was largely under their control. They met among themselves for worship but no attempt was made to win others. Not until the Sung Dynasty (960-1279) did they begin to build permanent religious edifices. During the thirteenth century, a number of Moslems attained high positions in government circles and established a reputation for scholarship. Still the atmosphere of foreignness remained, as the Hwei-Hwei—the name given to Moslems throughout China— kept strictly apart from Chinese society.[23]

In the Northwest there were three main groups. First there were the Arab Hwei-Hwei, descendants of merchants and soldiers who entered by the overland route from Central Asia. The Salars, or Turki Hwei-Hwei, migrated from Samarkand in the late fourteenth century. Finally, there were "the Mongol Hwei-Hwei, who comprised descendants of Ouigurs (a tribe which turned from Buddhism to Nestorian Christianity and was partially absorbed by the Mongols and then became Moslem) and of a Tartar tribe which allied itself to the Ouigurs and adopted their religion."[24]

[22]Frank Houghton, *op. cit.*, p. 98.
[23]Wang Tsit Chan, *op. cit.*, pp. 205, 206.
[24]Frank Houghton, *op. cit.*, p. 25.

The Chinese Moslem can be easily distinguished from others. He usually lives with other Moslems for convenience in worship and adherence to the food laws. Greetings are given in Arabic or Persian and he may often wear a distinctive headdress such as the white turban. In the Northwest they practice circumcision. Unlike the Chinese, they do not use coffins for burial and they adhere to a number of unique marriage and funeral ceremonies. Intermarriage with non-Moslems is strictly forbidden. They usually abstain from pork and alcohol, and throughout the country the sign of a teapot or Arabic characters denotes a Moslem eating place.

One reason for the Moslem isolation may be traced to the Manchu Policy of setting Moslems against Chinese. Between 1648 and 1876 there was a series of rebellions in Yunnan and Kansu. But at the beginning of this century the situation improved, and Chinese and Moslems united to overthrow the Manchus. Now the Hwei-Hwei insist that they are not a separate race but are Chinese.

Chinese Moslems are not held together by any central authority but by a community feeling. It is only during this century that national Islamic organizations have appeared and there has never been any form of Islamic hierarchy. Each mosque is autonomous, no one mosque being higher than another. The work of the mosque is very closely related to the community, for the local leaders elect the iman, one chosen because of his scholarship and mature years, to direct the activities of the mosque and lead in prayer. Together with the local leaders, the iman invites an ahung, whose function it is to teach, officiate at funerals and weddings, and arbitrate in disputes.

Chinese Islam belongs to the liberal tradition of the Sunnite, or orthodox, school of law, as such it follows the tradition of the Hanafis, who insisted that the Koran can be applied differently according to different situations. In the seventeenth century some Chinese Moslems went to Mecca and discovered that customs in China were not in accord with those in Arabia. On their return they started a new movement to go back to a literal observance of the Koran. The old sect adhered to Chinese custom and opposed the efforts of the new sect to force conformity with Islamic regulations. Thus there has been considerable conflict between these two parties in Chinese Moslem communities. About eighty years ago, yet another sect appeared called the New New Sect. This sect emphasized that the spirit rather than the letter of the law should be followed. It was the most liberal of all sects and stressed religious ethics rather than knowing Allah.[25]

During the past fifty years efforts have been made to introduce modern practices. The Chinese Moslem Mutual Progress Association, founded in Peking in 1912, established some schools, published a magazine, and undertook the translation of the Koran. By 1923, there were 3,000 branches. Since the war, the Chinese Islamic Association has been active in educational, medical, and relief work. Modern methods, some perhaps copied from the Christian church, have also appeared and numerous organizations such as "Knowing Allah" associations and "Young Moslem" associations are now connected with the mosque, especially in large cities. Originally, the Koran could only be recited in Arabic, and it was not until 1945 that the first translation in colloquial Chinese was published. Some years earlier a translation had been made in classical Chinese.

Progress in education has been slow. By 1950, there were only twenty Moslem high schools, two hundred primary schools, and one Islamic theological college in Chungking, formerly the war-time capital of China. In 1947, there were only nine Moslem periodicals with a small circulation of a few thousand each. A good deal of prejudice has, however, been broken down; for many Chinese Moslems used to believe that the study of Chinese books was to destroy their religion. In those days Moslem students had to spend much time studying Arabic, but now the Chinese language is used both in their schools and literature.[26]

The Moslems of China are, on the whole, more tolerant than their co-religionists in other parts of the world; and those who have become Christians have not, as a rule, faced as violent persecution as has been the lot of converts from Islam in other countries. We have known some extremely fine Christian Moslems actively serving Christ within the Church. In the past, Moslems have often welcomed the missionary, claiming that they are united in their opposition to idolatry. But controversy is soon aroused when the deity of Christ and the mesage of His death and resurrection are presented. They have no conception of the atonement; the idea of Christ dying for the sins of the world is abhorrent to them. When they speak of the

[25]Wang Tsit Chan, *op. cit.*, p. 195.
[26]*Ibid.*, pp. 204, 205.

majesty and glory of the one true and living God, they know nothing of His love; and an intimate personal relationship with Him is impossible because they know not the Saviour. "Is it not enough to say that Allah is merciful" was the question asked by one Moslem who later became a Christian when the need for forgiveness was broached.

After the Communist Revolution, some of the Moslems were intensely interested in Christian literature concerning the existence of God for they too were opposed to the dialectical materialism of Karl Marx. But, while eager to read Christian apologetics relating to the nature and Person of God, they resented the distribution of booklets dealing with the claims of Jesus Christ. They acknowledged Him as a prophet but denied His unique place as Saviour and Mediator between God and man. To argue with a Moslem is futile. He can, however, be reached by a clear witness to the reality of the forgiving love of Christ and the transforming power of His indwelling presence.

The communist government regards the Moslems as a minority ethnic group rather than a religion, and as such have treated them with considerable caution, especially in areas where there is a heavy concentration of Hwei-Hwei. They know that the Moslems of the Northwest are sturdy fighters and not a few communist soldiers have lost their lives at the hands of the Moslems in Kansu. General Pai Chung-Hsi estimates that at least 59,000 Moslems were killed because they resisted communist rule.[27]

Unlike the Buddhists and Taoists, the Moslems are a fairly closely-knit body of believers. The trials through which they have passed in former years have caused them to stand together in times of adversity. Their social and religious life all centers around the mosque. Through regional conferences and a national organization that meets every two years, they maintain contact with groups across the country. In areas where Moslem influence is strong, the communists have frequently made special concessions to the mosques. In other places, however, mosques have been closed and some of the ahungs have suffered because of failure to submit to communist authority.

To the outside world, Chinese communist leaders are most anxious to give the impression that every consideration is given to the

[27]Braden, *War, Communism, and World Religions*, p. 79.

Moslem minority, for Islam is a world religion and China is anxious to win the approval of her Moslem neighbors. The New China News Agency, on November 4, 1954, published an account of Moslem celebrations in Peking: "The 1,427th anniversary of the birth of Mohammed observed by Peking's 78,000 Hwei residents. Four hundred attended the ceremony in the Tungszu Pailou Mosque and services were held in half of the capital's sixty-five mosques. Others will mark the anniversary later in the week."

Efforts to create a favorable impression among the Moslem population in other parts of Asia do not seem to have been eminently successful. A delegation of Chinese Moslems en route to Mecca were delayed in Pakistan. Newspaper reporters, eager to obtain first-hand information from China, were repulsed in every effort to get into communication with the pilgrims, who were only allowed to speak to the newspapermen through an interpreter furnished by the communist diplomatic authorities. Apparently the pilgrims could not be trusted to give an entirely favorable account of religious conditions in China. It is not surprising, therefore, that the editor of *The Gazette,* the leading Moslem paper in Lahore, openly questioned the extent to which there was real religious freedom in China.[28]

Indonesian Moslems have been especially otuspoken in their attacks against Communism. One member of the Moscow 1951 Good Will Mission warned Indonesian Moslems that Communism was antireligious and antidemocratic and its ideals were entirely different from those of Islam. He went on to say that, "The fact that in the Soviet Union there are about 25,000,000 Moslems and in the Republic of China about 80,000,000 does not prove that the communists love and respect religion but only that they are unable to destroy it." Sharif Usman, another leading Indonesian Moslem, stated categorically, "It is impossible for a Moslem to be a communist and it is impossible for a communist to be a Moslem. . . . I appeal to all religions which believe in God to form a front for the defense of Theism."

Undoubtedly, the communist government recognizes the right of the Moslem minority to maintain the life and worship of the mosque. Pilgrimages to Mecca are permitted and every effort will be made to impress the Moslem world with the freedom that is accorded to

[28]*Ibid.,* p. 80.

their co-religionists in China. At the same time, however, every attempt will be made to control Moslem religious activities and to indoctrinate their youth with materialistic teaching.

CHRISTIANITY

If we are to understand the spiritual conflict through which the Christians are passing in China today, we must turn back the pages of history and seek to learn from the record of the many attempts that have been made to establish the Church of our Lord Jesus Christ on Chinese soil.

The history of Protestant Missions covers a period of a little more than a hundred years, but the earliest attempts to establish a Christian witness date back to the seventh century. Strengthened by refugees from persecution in the West, the Nestorian Church in Persia expanded toward the East and emissaries of that church appeared at the court of the emperor in China in A.D. 635. Even before that date Christians had entered China. The first missionaries were traders who carried their faith with them and we have the record of a great Nestorian family, the Mar Sabas, who emigrated from western lands and settled in Lin T'ao, Kansu.[29]

The first missionaries to the imperial court were favorably received for they came at a time when an alliance had been made between China and Persia and just a few years after the suppression of Buddhism. For two hundred years the Nestorian Church, known as the "Luminous Religion," flourished and the Nestorian Tablet, discovered near Sian in 1623, bears witness to its existence. As we looked at the carved inscription on that stone, we wished that a fuller description of the beliefs and practices of that early church had survived. Excavations of Nestorian cemeteries, monasteries, and various monuments indicate the widespread influence of China's first Christian church, but the inscriptions would seem to indicate that something was lacking in the message proclaimed by the Nestorians.

In the ninth century Confucian scholars struck a blow at Buddhism, and the Nestorian Church was also involved in the drive to overthrow all foreign religions. National and cultural pride produced strong opposition to the foreign religious invasion from India, and the fire spread to other religions as well. Evidence of this is

---

[29]Outerbridge, *op. cit.*, pp. 35, 36.

seen in the following decree: "As to monks and nuns who are aliens and who teach the religion of foreign countries, we command that these over 3,000 people of Nestorians, Moslems, and Zoroastrians, return to the secular life and cease to confuse our national customs and manners."[30]

Thus Nestorian Christianity disappeared and we must naturally inquire into the reason for its failure. From the inscription made by a Nestorian priest named Adam (King Tsing), it would appear very possible that some compromise in doctrine had taken place, for in the summary of the message proclaimed by the Nestorians, no mention is made of Christ's atoning death and resurrection. A contemporary Buddhist document also indicates that King Tsing himself collaborated with a Hindu priest in the translation of Buddhist Sutras. The Nestorian Church also depended a great deal upon political favor at court and, instead of spreading the Gospel among the ordinary people, they seemed to have concentrated upon the building up of large monasteries. Parts of the Scriptures may have been translated into Chinese but in those days, before printing was invented, there must have been a great scarcity of written materials and probably study was confined to the monasteries.

In the thirteenth and fourteenth centuries, Nestorian Christians again returned to China, this time in the court of the conquering Mongols. Most of them were from tribes in the North and were looked upon as members of the conquering forces. Nestorian Christians were found in official positions in many parts of China; and edicts have been discovered exempting them from military service and authorizing Christian monks to travel by sedan-chair, thus indicating the special respect that was accorded to them. These privileges, however, may also have earned for them the jealousy of the people.

When Marco Polo visited China, he found many evidences of the work of the Nestorian Christians. He arrived at a time when the Chinese emperor was anxious to have the support of the West against the Moslems and so he carried back with him a request from the emperor to the Pope to send a hundred missionaries. When the Franciscan delegates arrived, however, it became apparent that they were determined to undermine the work of the Nestorians, for Rome was opposed to any thought of reconciliation with them, and

---

[30]P. Y. Saeki, *The Nestorian Documents and Relics in China.*

unlike the Nestorians who used hymns, liturgies, and Scriptures in Chinese, the Franciscans made no attempt to learn the Chinese language and conducted their services in Latin. They too were dependent on the patronage of the Imperial Court, and one traveler reported that a beautiful cathedral had been built near the court and that the clergy had their subsistence from the Emperor's Court. A letter written to Rome about that time indicates that at least some of the Franciscans were conscious of the cultural barriers that hindered their work: "We truly believe that if we had their tongue, wonderful works of God would be seen. The harvest is great but the laborers are few and with no sickle, for we are but a few brothers and very old and unable to learn languages. May God forgive those who hindered brothers from coming."[31]

When the Mongol Dynasty collapsed in 1366, fierce persecution broke out again under the new and completely Chinese dynasty, which was bitterly opposed to all foreign influences, especially those connected with the Mongols. Converts of both the Nestorians and Franciscans, mostly Mongols, were either killed or forced to leave the country.

The next attempt to establish the Church in China was made in the sixteenth century by members of the Society of Jesus. For fifty years all attempts were abortive: "O rock, rock, when wilt thou open to my Lord?" was the cry of the General Superior of Jesuit Missions to the Far East.[32] A great deal of jealous rivalry between orders of the Roman Church and political intrigue also hindered the work. The Portuguese at Macao resented the attempts of missionaries from other countries to enter China, for they felt that the monopoly granted by the Pope to the king of Portugal for trade and political expansion in the Orient, which carried with it an obligation to send out missionaries, gave them the exclusive right to preach the Gospel in China. The church of those days was still imbued with the idea that the way of the cross should be carved out by the sword, and Christianity was identified with European cultural forms and customs. In 1583, the Bishop of Manila wrote to Philip, king of Spain and Portugal, urging him to send an army which would subdue the Chinese and force them to receive the Gospel.[33]

[31]Moule, *Christians in China*, quoted by Outerbridge, *op. cit.*
[32]Houghton, *op. cit.*, p. 64.
[33]Outerbridge, *op. cit.*, p. 73.

Among the Jesuits, however, there were some ardent missionaries who realized that high-handed methods would not succeed. They saw the necessity for an understanding of the language and culture of the people. This devotion is illustrated in a letter written by Matteo Ricci, one of the first Jesuits to gain a foothold in China. In "Senectute Mea," he wrote, "I return as a boy to school. It is not so great a thing inasmuch as I have resolved to do it for love of Him who, though God, became man for love of me."[34] This led to a more successful advance by the Jesuits during the seventeenth century and very large numbers were baptized. Several Jesuits, the most famous of whom was Father Adam Schall who became Director of the Bureau of Astronomy, gained important positions in Peking. Other Catholic religious orders, however, became jealous of the Jesuits and their unwise methods, failure to learn the language, and criticism of the Jesuit policy caused great embarrassment. Palace intrigues also hindered the work, as the Jesuits constantly sought to advance their cause through political alliances and, on more than one occasion, when their enemies gained power, the Christians passed through a period of persecution.

The Emperor, Kang Hsi (1662-1722) was especially interested in Christianity, and the Jesuits had high hopes of converting him and thus making Christianity the official religion of China. It is said that the emperor would have been baptized if it had not been for the fact that the Pope refused to countenance ancestor worship. It was about this time also that the church was shaken by the Rites Controversy upon which succeeding Popes gave opposite verdicts.[35] The Jesuits permitted ancestral rites, maintaining that they had no religious significance. They also used the classical name, *Shand Ti*, for God, while other Catholic religious orders insisted that only the term *Tien Chu* (heavenly Lord) was permissible. The Emperor Kang Hsi supported the Jesuits and was very incensed that a foreign Pope should decide by what name the people of China should worship God. The result of this controversy was that the Pope dissolved the Society of Jesus, and in China an Imperial Edict was issued in 1724 against Roman Catholicism.

Severe persecution then spread throughout China and again all

[34]*Ibid.*
[35]Houghton, *op. cit.*, p. 107.

foreign missionary work ceased. How clearly this indicates the impossibilty of seeking to build the Church of the Lord Jesus upon political influence. For more than one hundred years after the Imperial edict of 1724 permanent residence was denied to foreigners but gradually foreign trade increased and the East India Company established itself as the main European trading agency in China. Perhaps it was the increased knowledge of China resulting from this trade that caused Christians to awake to the responsibility to take the Gospel to the unevangelized millions.

Robert Morrison, the first Protestant missionary, did not wait for open doors. In spite of opposition from the East India Company, and Chinese government orders forbidding their nationals to teach their language to a foreigner, Morrison gained a foothold in Canton and succeeded during his lifetime in publishing a translation of the whole Bible and compiling an Anglo-Chinese dictionary. Although he saw few conversions, he laid the foundation for the preaching of the Gospel throughout China in the years that followed. Eight years after his death, by the Treaty of Nanking, Hong Kong was ceded to Great Britan and five ports opened to foreign trade and residence.

While the opening of these ports enabled missionaries to gain an entrance into the country, it is tragically true that the means used to make possible foreign residence in China provided enemies of the Gospel with a powerful propaganda argument. The opium trade fostered by Great Britain and other Western nations was the immediate cause of the war which led to the Treaty of Nanking. While the missionaries, and many in the British Parliament, were opposed to the opium trade, the fact remains that it continued until 1908 and remains as one of the darkest blots upon the history of Western relations with China. In the second half of the century the Chinese government again became embroiled in a war with Britain and France and the Treaty of Tientsin which ended hostilities led to further concessions and privileges for both Western traders and missionaries.

Resentment against foreign encroachment was partially responsible for the Boxer Uprising in 1901, which resulted in the martyrdom of a large number of missionaries, especially in the province of Shansi. The entry of the soldiers of Western nations into Peking quelled the rebellion, and the Chinese were forced to pay large indemnities. Many of the missionaries displayed the love of Christ by refusing to accept any reparation for the losses they had suffered. Some, however, especially among the Roman Catholics, took advantage of the situation and used political influence to extend their work. Even Protestant missionaries tended to accept a privileged position and sometimes made use of the respect accorded to them to protect the interests of the Chinese Christians. But every effort to increase the prestige of the missionary by political means inevitably hinders the spiritual development of the Church and limits the application of New Testament methods. But in spite of the failures of which we are deeply conscious during the past hundred years, we can also rejoice in the triumphs of faith manifest in the lives of many of the missionaries of an earlier generation. Through the courageous faith of men like James Hudson Taylor of the China Inland Mission and the faithful witness of both missionaries and Chinese, the Gospel was preached in every province of China. In towns and villages throughout the land, groups of believers were gathered out "to the praise of His glory."

World War II brought a period of fresh testing to the Church. The strongest groups of Christians were to be found near the coast, and the life of these churches was disrupted by the Japanese invasion. Suffering for the Church in the East, however, brought blessing to the great western provinces where vast areas were still unevangelized. Among the millions who set out on the long trek to Free China in the mountainous West, were many Christians who brought new life and encouragement to numbers of small churches. Thousands of students congregated in Chungking and Chengtu and other university centers in Free China, and a movement of the Spirit of God resulted in many of them turning to the Lord. After their return to the East an evangelical witness was established in most of the secular universities and colleges.

At the end of World War II, missionary societies, most of them working through the Chinese churches, were operating 13 colleges and universities, 236 middle schools, and a much larger number of primary and grade schools, and 260 hospitals. Unfortunately, however, the majority of graduates from these schools made no profession of Christian faith and on some of the secular campuses there was a stronger Christian fellowship than in many of the mission colleges.[36] It is tragically true that many mission educational institutions failed to lead the students into a personal relationship with Jesus Christ and were content with a purely superficial Christian atmosphere. Much emphasis was placed upon the social benefits of Christianity, but few of the students held personal Christian convictions and too often tended to drift into a religious vacuum. Even at the time of the antiforeign agitation of 1927, in which the students played a leading part, it was estimated that 75 per cent of these students were agnostic or atheistic. While they might observe the religious customs of their parents when at home, few had any real interest in the old religions. In most cases the small Christian fellowship was the only religious organization on the campus.

Long before the triumph of the communist armies, the campus had become a hot-bed for Communism. There was constant underground warfare between the Communist Student Movement and agents of the National Government. In some mission colleges the communists made use of the Christian organizations; and after the defeat of the Nationalists, the communist ranks were strengthened by many who had been trained in mission universities. Many of these graduates of Christian schools renounced any profession of Christian faith and threw themselves wholeheartedly into the work of the Revolution, fully accepting the dialectic materialism of Karl Marx. Others retained some kind of faith in God and sought to serve the Revolution by working within the Church, endeavoring to adapt its teachings so that it would conform to the policy of the new regime.

Even missionaries of a liberal theological background have acknowledged that "Christian liberalism has turned itself easily, too easily, into Christian communist liberalism, at least in China. Where Christianity was too closely identified in the past with projects of social construction, the idea of progress and liberal democratic institutions, this reaction was natural. . . . It is natural also for Christian liberals whose faith has been centered upon institutions and ways of life instead of on personal relations themselves to become revolutionaries in their idealism."[37] The same writer, Barnabas,

[36]Outerbridge, *op. cit.*, p. 25.
[37]Barnabas, *Christian Witness in China*, pp. 63, 64.

went on to criticize what he described as "Christian Apocalypticism" but admitted that it was a powerful factor in the witness of many Christians in China today: "The despair, indeed, the joyful rejection of all earthly hope, because of the coming victory of Christ gives to this theology the morale and courage of a victorious army. . . . Many a communist has been confounded by the vigorous aggressive spirit [not the reasonable argument!] of such enthusiasts. . . . Its centre is the ecstatic experience of common prayer, seeking a special thrill which will be the unmistakable evidence of God's presence in the Spirit."[38] Barnabas describes this hope of the evangelical Christian as "individualistic and divisive—an illusion" but admits that it may today be the predominant influence in Chinese Protestantism. He goes on to say that the majority of Christian students in Shanghai and Peking are organized into fellowships under the inspiration of the Inter-Varsity Fellowship. "The most vigorous Christian life in Peking today lies not in the churches but in those new sects without foreign aid, trained ministry, or any worldly possessions."[39]

COMMUNISM

If we are to understand the nature of the spiritual conflict raging in China today and the type of problems that the Christians are facing, we must realize that Communism is not merely a political and economic system. Its successful conquest of the minds of multitudes of Chinese young people is largely due to the fact that it offers what really amounts to a religious faith and hope for the future. While in China I read letters from students who had been nominally religious and then had experienced what might almost be described as a conversion to Communism. They often claimed that they had become new men and women. Often this has meant that a new element of discipline and self-denial has entered into their lives. They feel that they have discovered a worth-while objective for life and one student actually told a member of an Inter-Varsity group that she had received a new joy greater than anything that they could experience as a result of the filling of the Holy Spirit. Communism has succeeded in creating an enthusiastic core of young people who are prepared if need be to give their lives for the Revolution. So powerful is their propaganda that among those who

[38]*Ibid.*, p. 65.
[39]*Ibid.*, p. 66.

call themselves progressive it has produced a spirit of working together for the common good, of striving toward the new nation which they believe they are destined to create.

Communism claims to be completely materialistic but at the same time it recognizes that it must produce spiritual qualities in its followers. For this reason, Communism seeks to produce a counterfeit for almost every Christian doctrine and thus becomes a kind of pseudoreligion. The marks of religion are usually given as: (1) A doctrine of God; (2) A doctrine of Messiah or chosen revealer of God; (3) A doctrine of man; (4) A doctrine of salvation; (5) A doctrine of last things.

God. The true communist denies the existence of both God and the Devil, although he is not always consistent—like the Shanghai newspaper which came out with a huge headline stating that "MacArthur is the Devil." One Inter-Varsity student, when asked if Communism was the Devil, replied that if they would kindly define the Devil to her, she would be able to answer the question. Children in schools are taught to sing, "There is no God; There is no Devil; So do not be afraid." The communist says that God is not love, God is not personal, but God is the inevitably operating necessity which moves in history to redeem men's bodies and minds from slavery, hunger, and injustice.

The Messiah. The communist equivalent is a composite man—Marx, Lenin, and (before his recent down-grading) Stalin—who is regarded as the Revealer of the Way and the Truth of History and who alone has the words of economic life. To this trio the Chinese would add the name of Mao Tse Tung. For the communist, economic life is the only life. While no worship of God is permitted in Communism, the great teachers of the past and the leaders of today are practically worshiped by the people. This is clearly seen in the hymns which are commonly sung on public occasions containing words such as, "Our eternal liberator; we want no other saviour."

Man. The communist Doctrine of Man is built upon the evolutionary theory. When students in one university asked how human life developed from inorganic matter, the communist replied that there was a directive power inherent in matter. The very first course that every student is required to take deals with the development of human society. It shows how life has developed from the branches of the primeval forest and emphasizes the fact that our present society is entirely the product of man's efforts. The favorite slogan is "Do not worship earth, do not worship Heaven; only worship the effort of the people." Man, therefore, is only a higher, a more intelligent animal, whose actions are guided solely by economic necessity.

Salvation. Communist salvation has no connection with sin as we understand it, for to the communist there is no such thing as sin. He has no absolute moral standards; what is wrong today can be right tomorrow, and always the end justifies the means. To the communist, evil is an accident due to all kinds of causes such as ignorance, social inequalites, and what he describes as "man's animal origin." Communist salvation is concerned with the transformation of man and of the society in which he lives. It is to be brought about purely by human means. Men must be saved from slavery, hunger, and injustice by the rising to absolute power of the *proletariat.* This material salvation is to be brought about by social, psychological, and educational means. The communist, in fact, constantly confuses technical possibilities with moral capacity. While the communist does not believe in sin, as defined by the Christian, he does constantly speak of imperialistic sins. A handbook used in secondary schools in China states that the first virtues of the new democracy are "love of the fatherland, love of labor, love of the people, love of science, and protection of public property." Failure in any of these respects is regarded as sin, and forgiveness is based upon confession of these sins. Some have even infiltrated into the communist-sponsored church and, professing to be Christians, have propagated the communist doctrines. Writing in a magazine called *The New Church,* Prof. Hsieh says, "Whosoever are with the people, they are God's people. Whosoever stands in opposition to the people, whether they stand within the church or without, they are the enemies of God, they are the children of the Devil."[40]

The Doctrine of Last Things. The communists believe that they will "make all things new." They look forward to a new earth in which dwells not Christian righteousness but the social commonwealth. It is to be a completely balanced economic society, free from all injustice and inequality. While claiming to believe in ma-

[40]Rev. Thomas I. Lee, Letters.

terialism, they are in fact idealists, believing that man can eventually, by his own efforts, create a Utopia on earth. This idea is also seen expressed in the writings of some professing Christians. Mr. Ch'eng Ch'u Ku, son of a professor of the Hunan Bible Institute, gives this interpretation of "the new heaven and the new earth." We quote again from the communist church magazine, *The New Church:*

> Dearly beloved fellow-believers. The new heaven and the new earth which we have been constantly yearning for is already here and before our eyes. We ought never again to be confused with the imperialistic, visionary view of the end of the world. The so-called "new heaven and new earth" has suddenly, as if by magic, been placed before our eyes. We need but do one thing. We must arise and work. We must positively enter into and take part in the struggle for the people's liberation and demonstrate that they are the masters of the new heaven and new earth. . . . We must energetically reform our thinking, continuing to purge out the imperialism in our theology.[41]

Communism has taken Christian doctrines and adapted them to further its own ends. The communist seeks to win not souls but the minds of men and women. He believes in conversion through the washing of the brain while the Christian is "saved through the washing of regeneration and the renewing of the Holy Spirit." The communist is "saved" by a process of intense indoctrination.

Many others of their methods are parallel to those used in the church. They too have their pseudoevangelistic meetings with appeals for decisions and dedication to the cause of the Revolution. They place a great stress on singing and even use the tunes of Christian hymns such as "Glory, Glory, Hallelujah" and "God Save our King." Those who accept the communist teaching are called upon to give their testimonies. Often these testimonies appear in the newspapers, and a particularly promising convert may be taken from meeting to meeting to tell of his experience. Great emphasis is placed upon study. Early in the morning I could look out my window and see small groups of communists studying together. The small study group is, in fact, the very center of the whole communist system, for the communists never underestimate the value of theory and the importance of thought. "Study to show thyself approved

⁴¹*Ibid.,* Release 7, p. 10.

unto God," says the apostle and the communist replies, "Study to show thyself approved unto the Revolution." These study groups include the practice of both self and mutual criticism.

In these study groups the first thing that is attempted is a tearing down of the wrong ideas and attitudes of the past. The student is supposed to be kept from complete liberation by the burdens of the past such as his imperialistic outlook, his pride and selfishness, as well as the burdens of private care and responsibility. This burden of sin must be put off by a process of self-criticism. Not only must he criticize himself but he must be willing to be criticized by others. He must come to a place of complete acceptance of communist teaching and a willingness to renounce all self-interest. Second, there is the building up by an intensive study of communist doctrine and practice. Finally, he is tested in order to discover whether every area of his mind is subject to communist belief. At regular intervals he will be asked to write what is known as a "thought examination." This must contain a most detailed account of his thinking and attitude toward the dialectical materialism of Karl Marx.

I well remember a student asking me to pray for him during the week that he had to write his thought examination. In his thought examination he gave a very detailed account of his Christian faith and when he read it to a small group to which he belonged, the members criticized and questioned him for about three hours.

The strength of Communism is to be seen in the degree of consecration found in the lives of many of the young communists. One who later became a Christian described to me the tremendous demands that Communism had made upon him. He was indeed "not his own" and was called upon to glorify the Revolution and the Party with all his being. We watched young communist students give up comfortable homes and go out to join the Propaganda Corps, asking for no salary and content to serve and to "eat bitterness" in order to spread the message of the Revolution. In this connection, Lenin's words are significant. Under the title "Fewer but Better," Lenin says, "We won't accept into membership anyone with any reservations whatsoever. We won't accept into our membership anyone unless he is an active, disciplined, working member in one of our organizations."

For more than seven years the witness of the Church in China has been maintained in this type of communist society. We can now discern the main trends of communist policy in relation to the Church. What is the basic communist attitude to the Christian faith? Perhaps it can best be summed up in the words of a communist leader when replying to a friend of mine who asked the question, "Is there any room for religion in the life of man?" His answer was, "Temporarily, yes; eventually, no." To the communist, "religion is an excusable indulgence, a necessary sedative in an imperfect society; but the need for it will disappear in the coming perfected world order. Therefore, do not persecute it but allow it to die a lingering death."[42]

But if religion is not to be persecuted, it must be controlled, and communist leaders soon devised a plan designed to force the Church to co-operate in the great task of establishing the communist regime in China. Their aim was to make sure that the main energies of the possibly 1,000,000 Protestants and 4,000,000 (including infants baptized) Roman Catholics should be harnessed to the work of opposing imperialism. Almost all of the 4,200 Protestant missionaries present in China in 1948 were forced to withdraw and only a handful of the 6,475 Catholic missionaries have been able to remain. All Christian literature has been examined and as much as 40 per cent destroyed. The government policy is to seek to eradicate religious beliefs by indoctrinating the youth of the country with Marxist teaching and emphasizing the fact that Christian belief is reactionary and hinders true development in the service of the Revolution. But although pressure is brought to bear upon students as individuals in order to persuade them to give up religious belief, the Church itself is not persecuted provided it co-operates with the government. Whenever a Christian suffers imprisonment or even death, the reason given is never religious; some political charge is always preferred against him.

Those who bear the name of *Christian* today in China may be divided into three categories: First, there are those professing Christians who in reality are opposed to the truth of the Gospel, but they remain within the Church. To them the communists have entrusted the task of reforming the Church that it may be brought into line with communist policy. The wedding of the Church and the Communist State took place in a conference between Christian leaders

[42]Quoted by Leslie Lyall, *The Inextinguishable Light.*

and government officials in Peking April 16-21, 1951. At that conference a New Church Movement was established, "The Oppose-America, Aid-Korea, Three-Self Reformed Church of Christ in China." The name of this organization was later changed to "The Chinese Christian Three-Self Patriotic Movement." The chief leaders in this group have been two YMCA secretaries, Mr. Wu Yao Tsong (chairman) and Mr. Liu Liang Mo (secretary). Following the conference, the Accusation Movement was launched. Mr. Wu Yao Tsong intended to use this movement to uproot what is described as the "Spiritual Party"—the true evangelicals within the Church—who were accused of being "above politics; they have a 'holier than thou' attitude; they twist Scripture; they proclaim the superiority of the Church above the government; they oppose Russian Communism and the People—they spread poisonous thinking." The official magazine of the new church, *Tien Feng*, stated in its editorial: "Our Chinese Christian Church has received harmful influences of American imperialism for over a hundred years. We want to purge out that evil influence but it cannot be done with the power of only one accusation meeting."

The communist government is quite prepared to support a church that will fully co-operate with its politics. Premier Chou En Lai said to an anti-Christian official who pressed for a more severe treatment of the Church, "You cannot destroy religion over night. That is a peurile thought. We must mobilize all forces in China, including religion."[43] For this reason, the government may even give financial help to the official church. Some of its leaders are members of the People's Political Council and have attended international conferences, such as the meeting of the council for World Peace which was held in Stockholm.

The second category is made up of true Christians who believe that they can best serve the cause of Christ by co-operating with the government. Some of them even hold influential positions in the Chinese Christian Three-Self Patriotic Movement. The Rev. Marcus Chen, formerly president of the Chungking Theological Seminary, is now one of the vice-presidents of this movement. All pastors connected with this movement have been thoroughly indoctrinated. In order to preach it is now necessary to obtain "a certificate of permis-

[43]Lee, *op. cit.*, Release 6, p. 2.

sion to preach" which is only given to those who have attended a
full course of political instruction. Some pastors connected with the
movement undoubtedly continue faithfully to proclaim the Gospel,
but others refrain from preaching certain truths, realizing that they
are not popular in communist circles. All of them are certainly
forced to include government propaganda in their sermons. It is
probable that many evangelical pastors are extremely unhappy in
this situation and have lost the confidence of many of the Christians
because they have become enmeshed in the government-sponsored
church organization and have been forced to conform to current
political thinking.

A large proportion of the true Christians are to be found in the
third category which is composed of those who have refused active
co-operation with the "Three-Self Patriotic Movement." At the end
of May, 1954, only 414,389 Protestants out of a possible 700,000 to
1,000,000 members had signed a government *Manifesto* denouncing
imperialism in the church. The most outstanding among those who
have refused to compromise is Pastor Wang Ming Tao, the pastor
of an Independent church in Peking. For six years, under the communist regime, he faithfully proclaimed the Gospel and opposed
those who spread false doctrine within the Church. He also rebuked
those who, through fear of men, "watered down" their preaching.
He wrote in his *Spiritual Food Quarterly:*

> There are some evangelists who, though they clearly know
> what they believe and teach is the Word of God, dare not preach
> for fear that others will condemn them for spreading imperialist,
> poisonous thinking. The result is that what they preach is empty
> words, without content and without power.

He went on to point out that "what the 'leaders of the church'
speak of as poisonous, imperialistic thinking is nothing else but the
truth of the Word."

Mr. Wang's ministry in Peking was greatly blessed of God. One
of the latest reports written on May 18, 1955, says:

> In the three months since our last issue, we have continued
> to see the grace and glory of God. Believers are being confirmed
> in grace and truth and the number coming to our services is
> constantly increasing. Even in the coldest weather, many peo-

ple sit in the courtyard because the church is full, and they are able to follow the service by means of a loud-speaker. January 24 to 30 we had seven days of special evangelistic meetings. ... The number [at least 1,000] who came to these meetings was the largest we have ever had at our New Year's evangelistic meetings.

Even after vacation days were over and students had to go back to their classes, the numbers remained as large as ever. During the last three days many signified their intentions of becoming Christians.

Naturally, a great deal of opposition was aroused against Mr. Wang, and violent attacks against him were published in the official church magazines. Finally, on August 8, 1955, he and his wife and eighteen leaders of the Church, including a number of students, were arrested. The following day a letter was mailed from Peking with this message:

Within the nation the spiritual warfare against the evangelical elements of the Church have risen to an unprecedented intensity against the faithful servant of the Lord Jesus, Mr. Wang Ming Tao, and his wife, and also his helpers and his deacons. Eighteen young Christians of college and university age who, according to my knowledge, had participated in communion in Wang Ming Tao's place have been arrested by the government up to yesterday, charged with resistance to the Revolution. Praise God that they love their Lord, they are pleasing in His sight. God has permitted this thing to come to pass.

If one with spiritual insight would understand this thing, please read Luke 23:2. Today it is definitely evident that there are false prophets and false Christians. Under the banner of sins against the government, they have come forth to accuse Mr. Wang Ming Tao. Because they hate Jesus, they naturally hate His servant and those who love Jesus.

Mr. Wang Ming Tao was arrested about one o'clock in the morning of August the 8th. On August the 7th Mr. Wang Ming Tao had given his last message. It was entitled, "They in this manner betrayed Jesus." The Spirit of Jesus made him understand the things that were coming to pass. His spirit would be faithful unto Jesus, even unto death. Mr. Wang Ming Tao gave out his last little booklet, "We, Because of Our Faith." ... Peking has other servants of the Lord and believers who are already prepared to meet persecution. One can believe that in other places throughout the nation there will be true and faithful followers of the Lord who will be preparing to receive this grace.

About the same time a Chinese pastor's daughter wrote from China,

> Do not try to contact me. We are walking the road from Gethsemane to Calvary.

These messages from China show very clearly that the communist government has sought to divide the Church. Its policy is to use the official church to persecute those who are described as "belonging to the Spiritual Party." The whole situation is greatly complicated by the fact that within the official church there are also many true Christians. It is not for us to criticize them, for we cannot fully understand the tremendous pressure that is brought to bear upon them and the temptations which they face. It does seem, however, that within that official organization their testimony is compromised. Often they find themselves forced to accuse and attack fellow believers in Christ who would rather suffer imprisonment and death than be disloyal to the truth of the Word of God and to the Saviour whom they love and serve. God has His own witnesses in China today and though they may pass through the fires of testing, we believe that a testimony to the honor and glory of our Lord Jesus Christ will be maintained.

*　　*　　*

NOTE: After this chapter was written we received news that Mr. Wang Ming Tao had been released from prison. We have just been reading in Chinese the very complete confession of his "sins" against the government, the people, and the church which he has been compelled to issue as a result of the indoctrination and pressure exerted upon him during his year's imprisonment. He has also expressed his willingness to "repent" and enter the Three-Self Patriotic Movement which he formerly so strongly opposed. Some idea of the methods used to produce a "change of mind" can be obtained from reading Geoffrey Bull's account of his imprisonment in *When Iron Gates Yield.*

Mr. Wang Ming Tao has had a complete mental breakdown; and it is said that he sits and weeps, fearing that he may have in some way denied his Lord under the tremendously rigorous course of brain washing which he underwent in prison. He had two men in the cell with him all the time while in prison, and one realizes that with modern psychological methods it is possible to produce almost any kind of confession.

It is very evident that Mr. and Mrs. Wang Ming Tao have maintained a faithful witness to the Lord Jesus. When Mr. Wang was sufficiently recovered, he and his wife went to the authorities after his first imprisonment, and renounced the confession that he signed at the time of his release. It is said that because of this they were both imprisoned again. Recent reports indicate that both have suffered mentally.

Post Script. December 1960

From letters received, and from talks with Christians who have come to Hong Kong from the mainland, we gain the impression that the Church of the Lord Jesus is indeed being sorely tested and many are discouraged. Some churches are still open—four out of the original 65 in Peking, while in Shanghai, a city with ten or eleven million people, there are still twenty churches. One special theological seminary is allowed to train pastors in Peking, but, undoubtedly, a great part of this training will consist of political indoctrination. It would seem that in the country many of the churches have been closed. The widow of a Lutheran pastor told how her husband and a China Inland Mission pastor both died as a result of treatment received when they were arrested and accused of being rightists. Undoubtedly, many of the keenest Christians are now in prison or in labor camps.

There are, of course, many true Christians in the churches which remain open, but they are so saturated with government propaganda that it must be hard to satisfy the spiritual needs of those who attend them. In a recent issue of the one official church magazine only six or seven pages out of a total of twenty-eight were written by Christians, and most of the material was political propaganda.

No one can deny that very great material progress has been made in China during the past ten years, and there have also been striking improvements in some aspects of the social life of the country. Many of the young people are enthusiastic about the transformation of China into a growing world power, united, disciplined and progressive. Christians find themselves a tiny minority caught up in this great incoming tide of the revolution, which seems to carry everything before it. The young people are so occupied by work and political meetings that there is practically no time for attending meetings or having fellowship with other Christians. A young Christian teacher told me how she had to be at school at 7 o'clock in the morning and was busy with her work at school until 6 P.M. After that there were political meetings, so that she usually did not get home till midnight. Insisting that she must be in church to play the organ, she managed to avoid most of the Sunday engagements which prevented many Christian teachers from attending Church Services. The development of the commune system, which has now spread to the cities, increases the general regimentation of life which is aimed at preventing the individual from engaging in any activity which does not conform to the general Communist plan and philosophy of life. There is not necessarily complete segregation of the sexes in the commune. Families may continue to sleep under the same roof, but they eat in communal dining halls, and the children are cared for in nurseries and schools, and may be separated from their parents for the whole week. Every detail of life is so organized that there is no privacy, and it must be extraordinarily hard for Christians to have any fellowship together.

The Church in China has now existed for ten years under Communist rule, practically cut off from contact with Christians in other lands. There are certainly many who have remained true to the faith, but the pressure from every side is very great and we need to pray much that through the miraculous working of the Holy Spirit our brothers and sisters in Christ may have the faith which overcomes the world so that the seed of life in Christ may be sown in the hearts of others and bear fruit to the glory of God.

*　　*　　*

We watch the spiritual conflict in China from afar and there is much which we cannot understand. Certainly we cannot expect the church in China to develop in the same pattern as that of the West. We have much to learn from the experiences of our brothers and sisters in China, and we shall do well to seek humbly forgiveness for our prayerlessness and lack of fellowship with them in these days of testing.

BIBLIOGRAPHY

ANDERSON, J. N. D. (ed.) *The World's Religions*. Grand Rapids: Wm. B. Eerdmans, August, 1955 and London: Inter-Varsity Fellowship, 1950.

BARNABAS. *Christian Witness in Communist China*. New York: Morehouse-Gorham Co., 1951.

BRADEN, CHARLES SAMUEL. *War, Communism, and World Religions*. New York: Harper & Bros., 1953.

HOUGHTON, BISHOP FRANK. *China Calling*. London: China Inland Mission (printed by Canelot Press). London & Southampton, First ed. 1936; second, 1948.

LAUTOURETTE, K. S. *The Chinese; Their History and Culture.* New York: Macmillan, 1938.

LEE, REV. THOMAS I. Letters.

LYALL, LESLIE. *The Inextinguishable Light.* Philadelphia: China Inland Mission.

OUTERBRIDGE, L. *The Lost Churches of China.* Philadelphia: Westminster Press, 1952.

KUO, PIN-CHIA. *China: New Age and New Outlook.* New York: Knopf, 1956.

ROSS, JOHN. *The Original Religion of China.* New York: Eaton & Mains, n.d.

SAEKI, P. YOSHIA. *The Nestorian Documents and Relics in China.* Tokyo: The Academy of Oriental Culture, Tokyo Institute, 1937.

SUNDARLAL. *China Today,* quoted by Brandon, *World Communism and the Religions of Today.*

CHAN, WANG TSIT. *Religious Trends in Modern China.* New York: Columbia U. Press, 1953.

WALKER, RICHARD L. *China Under Communism, The First Five Years.* New Haven: Yale University Press, 1955.

FIG. 7.—Decorative group in front of Wat Phra Keo, Temple of the Emerald Buddha. The Emerald Buddha is carved from one huge jaspar stone twenty inches high. (Courtesy of Waagenaar—PIX.)

Birth is suffering; Decay is suffering; Death is suffering; Sorrow,
Lamentation, Pain, Grief and Despair are suffering; not to get
what one desires is suffering; in short: The Five Aggregates of
Existence are Suffering.

The Noble Truth of Suffering; Digha-Nikaya 22

VII.

Southeast Asian

by RAYMOND BUKER

Buddhism

HISTORY

BUDDHISM IS THE RELIGION, Buddha an honorific title meaning "the Enlightened One." The real name of the founder was Siddhartha Gautama (Pali, Gotama). His given name, Siddhartha, significantly means "the completion of purposes." Siddhartha Gautama was born about 560 B.C. in the village of Lumbini near the city of Kapilavastu, just south of the present Nepalese border and 130 miles north of Benares. His father, Suddhodana, was a raja and the family belonged to the Kshatriya or warrior caste of Hinduism. His mother's name was Maya. Gautama is sometimes called Sakayamuni, the sage of the Sakyas. Another title sometimes given him is Tathagata, meaning "he who has come thus."[1]

RAYMOND BUKER, B.A. (Bates College), S.T.B. (Boston University), S.T.M. (Andover-Newton Theological School), D.D. (Eastern Baptist Theological Seminary), is chairman of the Department of Missions at the Conservative Baptist Theological Seminary in Denver. For fifteen years he served as a missionary to India and Burma. In 1945 he was named foreign secretary of the Conservative Baptist Foreign Missionary Society and in 1956 assumed his present post.

[1]Other titles include Sarvartharsiddha, Mahasamana (the great ascetic), Bodhisatta (destined for enlightenment), Bhagara (Lord).

At his birth there was a prophecy that the child would either renounce the worldly life and become a religious teacher or he would
become a great king, conquering all of India. To keep him from
the former, his father purposely gave him ease and luxury, surrounding him with a beautiful and pleasant environment.

When Gautama was nineteen years of age (some say sixteen), he
married his cousin Yasodhara (Bimba). Ten years later she gave
birth to his son, symbolically named Rahula, "the fetter." Near the
time of the birth of his son, he saw for the first time an old man reduced to physical degeneracy by reason of his age. A few days later
he saw for the first time a man suffering from a loathsome disease,
and some months after this, for the first time, a dead man. On each
occasion he asked his *charioteer*, Channu, for an explanation. Channu told him that each of these was the fate of all living beings. Later,
Gautama saw a calm ascetic religious teacher. Channu explained to
the prince the function of the monk.

A careful consideration of these incidents brought Gautama to
the conclusion of the vainness of worldly, fleshly pursuits and the
decision to follow the life of renunciation. That night at the age of
twenty-nine years, after one final look at his sleeping wife and infant
son, he left the palace luxury, deserting his former pursuits and
associates. For six or seven years he followed the way of extreme
asceticism. Realizing that excessive self-mortification itself was a
delusion, he gave up this way of seeking the answer to life. He then
devoted himself to simple living and concentrated meditation. Finally, after a prolonged period of meditation, one day under a peepul
tree (*fiscus religiosa specia* of the fig), he received the revelation
which became the core of a new religion. His experience gave him
spiritual and mental enlightenment; and he has been known ever
since as Buddha, the Enlightened One. The tree under which he
sat has from that time been called the tree of wisdom—the Maha
Bodhi Tree (Bo-wisdom). The place, Uruvela, has become a shrine
and is now called Bodhi Gaya.

The enlightenment (525 B.C.) was followed by forty-five years of
peripatetic ministry some 250 miles along the Ganges Valley from
Benares. Dialectic teaching and dynamic preaching resulted in a
steady but nominal growth of the order within the kingdoms of
Magadha and Kosala by the addition of disciples, monks, nuns, and

devout laymen. Gautama died at the age of eighty in the village
of Pawa (Kusinara) about 483 (477) B.C. The body was burned,
a rite usually reserved for royalty and the ashes divided and sent to
eight kingdoms, where monuments were erected over the holy relics.

The next two centuries following the death of Gautama witnessed
only a gradual development of Buddhism, predominantly in northwest India. In the third century B.C. (264 B.C.) Asoka Vardhana
ascended the throne of Magadha (Modern Bihār). Shortly after
this he came into contact with Buddhism and accepted its teaching.
Expanding his interest from a personal religion to a national one,
Asoka became the Constantine of Buddhism.

Buddhism became the dominant religion of India. It spread with
royal favor and encouragement throughout India. A third Buddhist
Council was called, and at that time the decision was made to send
missionaries to other lands. So it was that 200 years after the death
of its founder, Buddhism first appeared in other lands. The countries of Kashmir and Ghandara, West of the Punjab, Deccan, Bactria,
the territory of the Central Himalayas, the west coast of farther India
and Ceylon were selected for this missionary invasion. During the
mid-third century B.C. missionaries went forth to the lands listed
above. Ceylon was entered under the son of Asoka, Mahendra; and
the brotherhood or Samgha was established. During the third century B.C., Buddhist influence entered Syria and West Asia in the era
of Magos, Epirus in the era of Alexander II, and Macedonia in the
era of Antigonus Gonatas. This obscure religious sect was in the
process of becoming a world religion.

Not until four centuries after Gautama's death was the canon of
Buddhism committed to writing. It consists of Tripitaka (Tipitaka),
the Three Baskets, from Pali manuscripts; namely:

1. The Vinaya-pitaka, the Discipline Basket, being the equivalent
of Leviticus, Numbers, and Deuteronomy of the Old Testament,
involves the giving of the law, rules, and orders of the faith.

2. The Sutta-pitaka, the Discourse Basket, which is the sermons
and general discussions of Buddha and his disciples.

3. The Abhidhamma-pitaka, a later philosophical development
and interpretation of the teachings of Buddha.

Another Canon based on Sanskrit texts is used extensively among
the followers of the Mahayana (Northern) form of Buddhism and is

called the Mahayana Canon. It is very voluminous, the Chinese alone having some 1,500 works in more than 5,000 volumes.

The saffron robe continued its world conquest. The Indian Peninsula containing Burma, Thailand, Cambodia, Annam, followed Ceylon; and the races of the Himalayas and Central Asia as far as Tien-Shan, Tibet, China, Mongolia, Korea, and Japan all became adherents of Buddhism in the one thousand years following the third Council held during Asoka's reign.

Buddhism itself lost out in India proper in the struggle with Brahmanism at the end of the first thousand years. Peculiarly enough, in Cambodia, another area where Buddhism and Brahmanism struggled for two centuries, Buddhism won out by the twelfth century A.D.

Twenty-five hundred years have passed since Gautama received his enlightenment under the Maha Bodhi Tree. During that period Buddhism has developed into one of the three great missionary religions of the world. Its spread has been limited for the most part to the Continent of Asia and the related islands. In the middle of the twentieth century its adherents are counted at about 200,000,000 (authorities vary from 100,000,000 to 600,000,000).

The Buddhistic movement has been characterized by Councils, sometimes called Buddhist World Councils. The First Council was held in 483 B.C., six months after the death of Gautama at Rajagaha, for the purpose of collecting and reciting the doctrines.

The Second Council was held at Vesali in 383 B.C., a hundred years after Gautama's death for the purpose of dealing with disciplinary matters.

The Third Council was held in 247 B.C. at Patalipatta, during the reign of Asoka. It was decided at this Council to send missionaries beyond the dominion of Asoka into foreign lands.

The Fourth Council was held around A.D. 100 at Jalandhara in Kashmir under King Kanishka of the Dushana realm. At this time the official division of Hinayana and Mahayana was established.

The Fifth Council was held in 1871 in Mandalay, Burma.

The Sixth Council, Chatta Sangayana, was held in 1955-56 in Rangoon, Burma. By some this is called the tenth Council by using additional councils as follows: 1, 2 and 3 as given above; 4. Matele, Ceylon, 29 B.C. Kavihara Council; 5. Jalandhara, Kashmir, A.D. 100; 6.

Chiengmai, Thailand, 1477; 7. Bangkok, Thailand, 1788; 8. Ratna-pua, Ceylon, 1865; 9. Mandalay, Burma, 1871; 10. Rangoon, Burma, 1955-56.

DOCTRINE

The enlightenment of Gautama constituted a revelation from which he evolved his simple doctrines. Basic to his doctrinal system were the Four Noble Truths:

1. The Noble Truth of Suffering
2. The Noble Truth of the Cause of Suffering
   a. Desire for pleasure
   b. Desire for existence
   c. Desire for prosperity
3. The Noble Truth of the Cessation of Suffering—eradicate desire and suffering ceases
4. The Noble Truth of the Path that Leads to the Cessation of Suffering, which is the Holy Eightfold Path (sometimes called the Middle Path), consisting of:

   a. Right views
   b. Right aspirations
   c. Right speech
   d. Right conduct

   e. Right livelihood
   f. Right endeavor
   g. Right awareness
   h. Right meditation

Buddha, from the beginning, formed his followers into an order or Sangha (Samgha). Each new recruit is required to affirm the formula of the Three Refuges:

1. I take refuge in the Buddha
2. I take refuge in the Doctrine (Dharma)
3. I take refuge in the Order (Sangha)

The followers who come into the order are to observe ten precepts:

1. Not to kill
2. Not to steal
3. Not to lie
4. Not to commit adultery
5. Not to drink intoxicants
6. Not to eat at forbidden times
7. Not to indulge in dancing and theatricals
8. Not to use any form of personal adornment
9. Not to use a broad or high bed

10. Not to receive gold or silver

Some monasteries follow only the first five percepts. The last five are to be observed during certain holy seasons.

The goal of the Buddhist is nirvāna (Neikban, Nibbana). Gautama's original concept of nirvāna was the extinction of all desire and the final release from all suffering (definitely not annihilation). This is accomplished over a period of numberless rebirths. The possibilities for the next life are boundless. Your rebirth will be determined according to how much merit your present existence (life) accumulates. An evil or bad life may accrue a debit balance which will result in a rebirth lower in the scale toward the desired Buddhahood or complete elimination of all desire. (One manuscript claims that Gautama Buddha had already lived 550 previous lives.) [2]

In the seeking to achieve the attainment of nirvāna, it is necessary to overcome five mental hazards and to break away from ten fetters as follows:

The five mental hazards:

1. Sensual Desire (*kamacchanda*)
2. Ill-will (*vyapada*)
3. Sloth and Torpor (*thinamiddha*)
4. Agitation and Worry (*uddhaccakukkucca*)
5. Doubt (*vicikiccha*)

The ten fetters:

1. Belief in a self
2. Uncertainty
3. Belief in efficacy of good works as practiced by Brahmans
4. Evil thirst
5. Evil attitudes
6. Desire to live on earth
7. Desire for future life in Heaven
8. Pride
9. Self-righteousness
10. Ignorance

One writer has said,

> In its expansion Buddhism underwent great changes, sometimes even in the fundamentals of religion, so that Buddhism is

---

[2] A Pakistani Buddhist, *Buddhism in Pakistan*, p. 23.

really a family of religions rather than just a single religion.[3]

Actually, this concept is not quite accurate, as we look upon Christianity as a single religion with many forms, so we should look upon Buddhism. It is a common procedure to speak of Burmese Buddhism, Siamese Buddhism, Japanese Buddhism, etc. In each of these countries, moreover, there is a variety of Buddhist sects. Buddhism itself, however, since the Fourth Council in A.D. 100 has recognized the two major divisions of Hinayana, the Lesser Vehicle or Vessel, and Mahayana the Greater Vehicle or Vessel.

Hinayana or Theravada Buddhism, or simply Southern Buddhism, is the philosophical or metaphysical branch. It follows close to the original teachings of Gautama himself. The original concepts of life as outlined in the Four Noble Truths and the Eightfold Path with the goal of the extermination or elimination of desire and self as the achievement of nirvāna, a condition rather than a place, represent Hinayana. The accomplishing of this objective is considered possible or likely by only a few—hence, the title Hinayana or Lesser Vehicle, for only a limited number will attain its final end. It is well to bear in mind that in the original doctrine as given by Gautama, no mention was made of God. He himself avoided any claim to divinity. The Pali Canon of the Tripitaka provides the basic scriptures for the Theravadin Buddhist. The followers of Hinayana Buddhism are found largely in Ceylon, Burma, and Thailand.

Buddhism in its Mahayana form has a dominant characteristic of adaptability to new situations in different countries and in a changing social environment. Perhaps one of its most significant changes is its concept of Gautama as a deified Buddha. R. L. Slater has well described the change.

> In Mahayana Buddha is deified. He is no longer simply a human voice announcing the Way to the Beyond, but the Beyond itself—the Absolute, the eternal Buddha Essence, Dharmakaya, the noumenal, abiding Reality underlying all phenomenal existence, transcending all apparent distinctions.[4]

The ramifications of the deified Buddha as other cultures and re-

---

[3]A. K. Reischauer, *The Great Religions of the Modern World*, ed. E. J. Jurji, Buddhism, p. 90.
[4]R. L. Slater, *Paradox and Nirvāna*, p. 84.

ligions are contacted are partially comprehended by Charles S. Braden:

> Gautama became but one in a great line of Buddhas, back of whom stood the eternal Buddha—the Dharmakaya—a conception similar to the old Hindu Brahma manifest in Vishnu or Siva. There were five principal Buddhas, of whom Gautama was one. One Buddha, Maitreya, was yet to come. Attempted identification of Jesus as the one to come has sometimes been made where Buddhism and Christianity have touched. Thus could Buddhism without any serious difficulty enwrap Christianity within its ample fold—if only Christianity would cease to make its exclusive claims.[5]

This Greater Vessel, Mahayana, or Northern Buddhism, opened the way of salvation to the multiudes. Its deviations from the original form are well described by David Bently-Taylor:

> The more striking innovations of Mahayana Buddhism are the following:
> 1. The introduction of a supreme Reality from which the universe emanated.
> 2. The deification of Gautama himself, regarded as a transitory manifestation of that Reality. Some would go to the length of denying that he was really human at all.
> 3. The ideal of actually attaining full Enlightenment gave way to another in which the element of Compassion for humanity predominated. Those who might have attained Buddhahood, but voluntarily abstained from nirvāna in order to help in the deliverance of erring men, are known as Bodhisattvas. A vast number of such Wisdom Beings constitutes the pantheon of Mahayana Buddhism.
> 4. The way of salvation became faith in Gautama and the Bodhisattvas. The repetition of their names was inculcated to an extreme degree. Of this salvation the lotus flower, rising pure and white from the muddy pool, became the emblem.
> 5. Vivid portrayals of Heaven and Hell were given and individual immortality was the hope set before the devotee.
> 6. Images were introduced to aid the illiterate, and idolatrous polytheism supplanted Gautama's original atheism. In some

[5]C. S. Braden, *The World's Religions*, p. 123 f.

lands the Goddess of Mercy, the Hearer of the World's Prayers, came to hold a place akin to that occupied by the Virgin Mary in Roman Catholicism.

Mahayana Buddhism is subdivided into many sects and movements, comprising a gigantic syncretism of Philosophy and popular superstition.[6]

Mahayana Buddhism has made its way and found a large following across Central Asia, Nepal, Northern Burma, Tibet, Mongolia, Korea, China, Japan, Annam, Java, and Sumatra. If we wish to assign a very general date, we would say that it reached China soon after the time of Christ, Korea in the fourth century A.D., Japan in the sixth, and Tibet, Java, and Sumatra in the seventh. With the Muslim invasion of the fifteenth century, Buddhism was largely displaced in Java and Sumatra. The original Mahayana scriptures are found in an extensive set of uncodified Sanskrit documents.

MODERN CONDITIONS

Twenty-five centuries have passed since the doctrine of Buddhism was first enunciated. The growth or spread was slow during the first three centuries. During the next three centuries, however, under the impact of the royal initiative of Asoka, it attained far-reaching international development. This attained its major geographical limits by the eighth century A.D. By the time Buddhism reached its greatest extent however, it had declined at the source of its origin, India. Today Buddhism is considered only as a vestigial religion both in Pakistan and Hindustan and has no influence within the countries themselves. The other lands where Buddhism is a dominant religious force disclose a present-day activity.

Reports received by the World Council of Churches in the summer of 1953 indicated a general renaissance of world religions, especially of Hinduism, Buddhism and Mohammedanism.[7]

The renaissance of Buddhism has been a combination of "keeping in step" with the trend of international and national events and an adjustment within to meet the situation without. Dr. Landon in his book on southeast Asia says,

[6]David Bentley-Taylor, "Buddhism," J. N. D. Anderson, ed., *The World's Religions*, pp. 130, 131.
[7]*Britannica Book of the Year*, 1954, p. 605.

Westernized persons in Southeast Asia in some instances have simply discarded their old religious attitudes and have accepted the humanism of the West. Many of them, however, carry their eggs in two baskets between which there are no exchanges.[8]

Dr. Reischauer points out this dominant trend to relate the religious life with the secular world.

To be a loyal Ceylonese, Burmese, or Siamese, Buddhist monks, especially in the larger centers, are taking more and more interest in politics and in the affairs of the modern world. So much is this the case that older and more conservative monks are expressing concern lest "true Buddhism" will not survive.[9]

One of the major interests of the world is Communism. In the consideration of Buddhism as it functions today, one seeks with much interest the influence of Communism upon Buddhism or Buddhists and vice versa. Approaching the matter via the angle of pure metaphysics and blunt facts, it would seem that Communism and Buddhism are not compatible. In the theoretical realm of the equality of all peoples, these ideologies seem to be similar. Beyond this, however, there is little, if any, semblance. The philosophy of Buddhism is far from the ideology of Cummunism. The pragmatic implementations of either design are very different.

Dr. Charles S. Braden traveled extensively in Buddhist countries in 1952, making a special investigation as to the effect Communism has had in these countries. His findings are of real interest. It will be valuable to note his comments, country by country.

Ceylon:

At present Buddhist leaders of Ceylon lag well behind those of either Thailand or Burma in their concern about Communism.[10]

As in the other Buddhist countries, there are those who do not find it incompatible with their Buddhism to embrace Communism. I was told that there were several Buddhist monks who were Communists.[11]

Burma:

Dr. Braden based his initial investigation of Communism in

[8]Kenneth Landon, *Southeast Asia*, Preface VI.
[9]A. K. Reischauer, *op. cit.*, p. 121.
[10]C. S. Braden, *War, Communism and World Religions*, p. 123.
[11]*Ibid.*, p. 117.

Burma published in 1951 on a speech of U Ba Shwe, the socialist leader. Dr. Braden writes:

U Ba Shwe hopes that the revolution may proceed by democratic rather than dictatorial methods. But if it cannot be thus won, what then? "We Socialists and Marxists are not blood-thirsty. We are fighting for world peace. If a problem can be solved by peaceful negotiation, we shall certainly solve it in a peaceful way. But if it can be solved only by force, we do not have any qualms about using it." But this could hardly be squared with Lord Buddha's teaching. What then of his claim?

Do Buddhists generally accept U Ba Shwe's contention? I inquired diligently among both laymen and priests, some of them of highest rank in either the government or religious life of Burma. I found none of them agreed with him. One distinguished priest did refuse to condemn Marxist philosophy wholly, saying that there might be some value in it. But most were quite definite in declaring that the two were incompatible, and most of them refused to distinguish between Marxism and Communism. One pamphlet is being circulated under the title "Marxism and Buddhism" in which it is shown quite clearly that simply on the philosophical basis alone the two are in violent contradiction.

Francis Story, an English Buddhist, founder of the Burma Buddhist World Mission and very highly respected among leading Buddhists with whom I talked, has been publishing serially, in one of the Rangoon English dailies, a study of Buddhism. In it, while admitting certain superficial similarities between Buddhism and Communism, such as nonbelief in a creator god and the fact that the "Sangha" or monastic order is a kind of communism, he affirms categorically that the two look in quite different directions. There is, he asserts, a basic philosophical difference between the two that makes them impossible to mix. If one is a Buddhist in the true philosophical sense, then he is not a Marxist, dialectical materialist. On the more practical plane, the distinction between the communism of the "Sangha" and that of Marxism is very obvious. The former is wholly voluntary, and designed to aid in the extinction of craving; that of Marxism is one of compulsion. One may leave the "Sangha" at will; one may not escape the imposed Communism of Marx with impunity. Furthermore, the idea of a classless society, the

Marxist ideal, he asserts, imposes an artificial limitation on the living and developing organism which is in opposition to its function as an instrument of evolution.

Can Buddhism serve as a major deterrent to the growth of Communism? I asked numerous leaders, lay and priestly. Almost all of them said yes. But the difficulty is that Communism wins, usually not at the ideological level, but by promising the poor and the exploited a better life, not in another world which religions may assure them exists, but here and now. They are not acting primarily as Buddhists, but as hungry, oppressed people whose eyes have been opened through propaganda, whether false or true, to a possible better existence than they now enjoy. Unless it comes to them in the form of an overt attack upon their religion, they are not likely to consider religion one way or another.

What were they doing about it? The first part of the reply was the promotion of a revival of Buddhism, an awakening of Burmans to a conscious recognition of the values that lie in their historic faith.[12]

A government-stimulated revival has been in evidence during the years since 1950, through a group called the Buddha Sasana Council. This Council working through four committees, sponsors a Pali university with twenty-two constituent colleges and more than 500 students throughout Burma. The main purpose of the government support of this program is to oppose and offset communist ideologies.

Buddhism and the Personal Life, edited by U. Thittila, was written as an anit-communist pamphlet.

Thailand:

There is a greater awareness of Communism among the students of Thailand than in some other Buddhist countries, such as Japan.[13] The communists have used two approaches in Thailand.[14] One has been a frontal attack that belittled the religion that sought the heavenly condition of nirvāna by withdrawal from the world and its reality. Such a withdrawal is possible for the idle parasite who exploits the people. Therupon the virtues of Communism, the way for the great good of the peoples, are greatly extolled. The great and high regard for the priests has brought this approach into much dis-

[12]*Ibid.,* p. 110 f.
[13]*Ibid.,* p. 97.
[14]*Ibid.,* p. 99 ff.

favor. A leading paper that followed this propaganda was reduced in patronage until it rated only fifth or sixth place.

Another approach, however, has been more subtle and indirect. The similarities of Communism and Buddhism have been emphasized. Specifically, there are many, including no class distinctions, no personal deity in Hinayana, and salvation through social forces. This method also has failed to achieve its goal.

An abbot of one of the large Buddhist temples in Bangkok contrasted Buddhism and Communism as follows:

> "Communism is only capable of appealing to the basic instincts and sentiments of man. It encourages immorality and animalism. It levels down, not up. It incites hatred, greed and jealousy, and aims at a revolutionary overthrow of all the moral values of mankind and of justice. It is indeed a destructive force."

In contrast to this he presents Buddha, who renounced kingship, etc., to become a humble monk. By his sacrifice and pure life, and through insight, he attained Supreme Wisdom and freedom from all sufferings, eternal peace and happiness, and for forty-five years taught his doctrine, "Seeking to lift up men from ignorance and evil to goodness and enlightenment towards a freer life on earth, full of compassion to all sentient beings, full of happiness and lasting peace."[15]

Indochina:

Buddhism is not too active in Indochina. One of the associations in the South has become quite alive in social activities. The reason seems to be because the refugees from communist areas have required help. Indeed some have considered the communist example as the incentive for this social service.[16]

Tibet:

An example of communist adaptation to Mahayana Buddhism comes from Tibet. Geoffrey Bull from his intimate acquaintance with the lamas and his experience as a prisoner of the communists for three years gives this illustration:

> The allusion to the "millennial" kingdom of Buddhist mythology was a clever point in their propaganda. According to the lamas, salvation was to come out of the north country, and was not the name of Stalin and the hope of the Communist Era as

[15]*Ibid.*, p. 104.
[16]*Ibid.*, p. 90.

a beacon shining to all the oppressed peoples of the earth sitting in the shadows of reaction and tyranny? The policies of Mao Tse Tung, faithful disciple of Marx, Engels, Lenin and Stalin, would fulfill the highest aspirations of Buddhism. For the Tibetan people it would mean autonomous government, religious freedom, and protection from aggression.[17]

The mid-twentieth century has produced interesting changes in the Buddhist world. These manifestations may be in the form of revivals, modifications, new societies or orders, and virile activities. A brief review of these manifestations will indicate the present status of Buddhism in Central and Southeast Asia.

Two new religions, Hoa-Hao and Caodai, in Indochina have a Buddhist background.[18] Hoa-Hao aims to reform Buddhism by centering interest in (1) the ancestors; (2) the fatherland; (3) the Buddha, law, and community; (4) one's compatriots and the whole human race. After a decade of activity this movement is becoming more political and less and less religious. Caodai is a syncretized faith, honoring the religious and political leaders of many movments and lands. Although somewhat disrupted by war conditions, it continues to grow and even has a missionary in California.

Buddhism in Thailand during the last three decades has adapted itself to modern educational and political changes. Such organizations as the Supreme Council of the Order, the Young Buddhist Association, the Buddha Dharma Association and the more than 800,000 residents of monasteries keep this religious approach active and virile for all the land, both in the cities and in the out-of-way villages. Some of these groups have served to keep up a continual contact with other Buddhist countries such as Ceylon, Burma, and Japan.

There are several potent causes for the vitality of Buddhism in Thailand. It is as well organized as in any country. Decisions and programs work smoothly from the Supreme Council down through to the local village committees. The Tripitaka is versatile because of its extensive size. Something is found to appeal to every type of man and condition of society in these efficacious tomes. Action helps to offset lethargy. Buddhist monks teach and preach the wholesale participation of achieving merit by giving. Monks and monasteries

[17]Geoffrey Bull, *When Iron Gates Yield*, p. 116.
[18]C. S. Braden, *op. cit.*, p. 91f.

are everywhere. The follower of Buddha will receive merit by giving. Therefore, *all* are exhorted to give and to give daily. With expression comes impression and Buddhism is strong in Thailand.

The training of *every* boy for a shorter or longer period within a Buddhist monastery is one of the strongest assets in keeping Buddhism nationally alive in the countries of Ceylon, Burma, and Thailand.

The sending forth of missionaries to America, to the hill tribes of the Burma borders, and to other non-Buddhist areas is an indication of new life in Buddhism since the turn of the mid-twentieth century.

The organization of a Burma Buddhist World Mission is resulting in the production and distribution of hundreds of books, tracts, and pamphlets. In Siam a single decade saw an increase of Buddhist literature circulation of some 300 per cent. There is a demand for reprinting. A beginner's manual for novices that used to sell approximately 5,000 copies each year is now selling some 50,000 copies yearly. Buddhists also are making use of the radio. Sermons and lectures in behalf of the faith are a common program in the three Hinayana countries of Ceylon, Burma, and Thailand.

The sixth Buddhist World Council (Chatta Sangayana) held in Rangoon, Burma, over the two-year period of 1955 and 1956 marks the milestone of twenty-five centuries of Buddhism. This Council was officially carried on by the five Southern or Hinayana Buddhist countries—Ceylon, Burma, Thailand, Cambodia, and Laos. There were five sessions of the council, and a leading monk from each of these countries presided in turn over a session. The Northern or Mahayana Buddhist countries sent fraternal delegates to Rangoon. The leadership of this Rangoon World Council was vested in the celibate saffron-robed monks. All scripture recitation was from the Pali. This would rule out lay leadership as scripture recitation was the main activity of the Council.

The Pali title of the Council, Sangayana, is the key for the main purpose of the meeting. This word may be translated "to compare the texts with each other and to recite them together." Thus, through a process of lower criticism, the Buddhist monks are attempting a revision of their Tripitaka texts, similar to the work of a group of Biblical scholars in revising the King James Version of the

Christian Bible. Thus far, there has been no evidence that this great Buddhist World Council has made any attempt to analyze its need to adjust its approach on the level of the people with a social program to meet the world's requisites in the face of the changes of life today.

Dr. Reischauer has predicted a possible trend for Buddhism in his analysis of the situation.

> It is quite likely that in the immediate future the next development in the Buddhist world will be along two main lines. One will be the acceleration of the present trend toward the secularization of the masses who in the past sought the "good things of life"—largely material blessings—through religion but who will look more and more to modern science and technology for such gifts. The other is the semi-Christianization of Buddhism itself, a trend already seen in the Amida sects of Japan.[19]

There is no doubt that there are indications in various countries, such as Thailand, Japan, and Burma, where this trend is developing. It is coming, however, from a combined effort of laymen and monk. The urge of nationalism is forcing the devout layman to reinterpret his religion in terms of the political situation. The priest or monk feels the pressure of his supporters. A superficial adjustment is evolving by which the religious will keep step with the steadily marching unswerving, secular forces of history.

Buddhism has not been considered as a religion in India during the last thousand years. Recently (1956) a remarkable thing has happened which may result in the renewal of Buddhism as a dominant religion in the land of its origin. Dr. Ambedkar, the highest government representative of the outcastes (nonscheduled groups) of India, has for several decades been considering how to combat Hinduism's treatment of the outcasts. For years he has seriously considered advocating Christianity for all outcastes; Dr. Ambedkar took the vow of Buddhism for himself on October 14, 1956. He died the following month. This move has had a strong influence to encourage all scheduled classes to accept Buddhism.

Dr. Radhakrishnan, vice-president of India, philosopher and teacher of Hinduism, is currently speaking highly of Buddhism.

[19]A. K. Reischauer, *op. cit.*, p. 140.

These factors would seem to indicate a great possibility of widespread growth of Buddhism in India during the next decade.

CHRISTIAN APPROACH

The procedure of presenting Christ to a Buddhist should include several factors. The primary feature should be a Holy Spirit-filled and a Holy Spirit-led worker. Given this factor, the Lord's servant may well include several other elements. The missionary should be well informed. Naturally the information will involve a thorough and complete book knowledge. In addition to this, however, the Lord's agent will do well to have a good understanding of the form of Buddhism practiced by the person being presented the claims of the Gospel. Is this Buddhist of the Hinayana or Mahayana persuasion? What are the local customs of the temple worship and the habits of the priests or monks of that locality? A firsthand knowledge of these things will often keep the Christian from making references to Buddhist practices and beliefs that are not apropos to the given case.

An essential characteristic is friendliness. If there has been opportunity to develop a friendship whereby a certain rapport has been established and wherein barriers have been broken down and confidence is present between the Buddhist and the Christian, the vital presentation of Gospel truths will have a much better reception. Wisdom alone is not enough to gain a hearing. If one can show an understanding of the background and environment of the hearer, he will increase the chances of his message being listened to and considered. It is not wise to emphasize the negative parts of Buddhism; it is better to mention the good points of their religion. Of course, one should be careful not to overdo this, lest they receive the impression that we think Buddhism is satisfactory. Say only enough to have them realize that we do know and appreciate their viewpoint. Thus, any resentment they may have will be much reduced. In areas where the discussions could be quite controversial, we will be diplomatic. If possible, we will do well to bring the conversation to the point where the Buddhist is induced to bring out the weaknesses of his own religion. He will, therefore, by his own initiative suggest the differences.

The conversational, rather than the preaching, approach is usually the better way to present the claims of the Gospel over Buddhism. Through this method the Buddhist is encouraged to reveal his own religious state. Thus, we can build on an actual rather than a theoretical foundation. Starting along lines where the seeker is desirous of having more light, we can lead him out for further discussions on varied angles.

A good and understanding knowledge of the doctrines of Buddhism will be of great value to the Christian worker among the Buddhists. Some of the doctrines which should be well known come under the following categories:

Salvation	The soul and the spirit
Future life	God
Sin	Morality
Merit	Worship
Suffering	Sacred Writings
Prayer	

Although the purpose of this chapter does not include a lengthy philosophical discussion of the doctrines of Buddhism, it may be well to give a brief statement about these we have listed here. We recognize that in most cases the Hinayana and Mahayana definitions are quite different. In general we are giving the Hinayana approach.

Salvation is elimination of all desire, the arriving at or achieving the state of nirvāna. Nirvāna is the word with which we would equate our "Future Life," and yet it is quite different from what is usually considered as the Christian Heaven. Nirvāna is arriving at nonexistence, but definitely not annihilation. The goal of all the rebirths is to become nothing and, therefore, to have no existence. Existence is an evil to be overcome. We are quite sure that very few Buddhists really conceive nirvāna in the true sense of their philosophy. As human beings, they introduce different degrees of reality into nirvāna. This in turn provides more incentive to follow their Dharma or Law.

Sin is a social matter. It has no direct relation to a deity, for there is not supposed to be a deified personality in the system. Sin is the violation of the Eightfold Path of the Noble Truth that leads to the cessation of suffering. Sin is associated with the five mental hindrances and the ten fetters as enunciated in the Dharma.

Merit gained in one existence determines whether the individual will advance or retrogress in the next rebirth. Dr. Wells in his exhaustive study of Buddhism in Thailand has given a suggestive list of ways to achieve merit.

Merit is acquired by making pilgrimages to shrines or temples, by assisting monks in various ways such as by carrying their bags and umbrellas, by copying Buddhist scriptures on palm leaves and presenting them to the temple, by listening to the reading of the Tripitaka in Pali or Siamese in a respectful attitude— seated on the floor with hands upraised and palms together, by repeating Pali sutras in worship or by preaching the Dharma. The most common way of making merit is by some form of giving such as alms to the needy; gold leaf for temples and images; flowers, candles and incense for altars and shrines; books, money, building materials and labor for a monastery; food for the monks, and latterly, gifts of money to hospitals and to new schools. In a published list of ways of making merit, a list by no means exhaustive, there were forty-four different methods specified, most of them involving the presentation of offerings of some kind. The practice of giving is fostered by the use at services of worship of such books as the Vessantara and Unahisavijaya Jatakas which teach the benefits derived from benevolence.[20]

The Buddhist concept of suffering is found in the four Noble Truths. The first defines suffering as birth, decay, illness, death, presence of hated objects, separation from loved objects, and failure to obtain one's desires. Desire is the cause of suffering. When desire ceases, then suffering ends. The road that leads to cessation of desire is the following of the Eightfold Path.

The Buddhists recognize a soul but have no place for a spirit in their doctrines.

There is no god, deity, or divinity in the Hinayana doctrine, but Mahayana makes a god of Buddha and deities of the Bodhisattvas, later followers about to achieve Buddhahood.

Morality in Buddhism is a by-product. In the desire to achieve nirvāna, the Eightfold Path is followed. The observance of the Dharma or Law does produce a rather high standard of morality.

[20]K. E. Wells, *Thai Buddhism: Its Rites and Activities.*

This morality, however, is not a goal per se of Buddhism. Violation of the moral code only diminishes the merits acquired.

Worship in Buddhism becomes the rituals in the monasteries, the proper observance of festivals and the reciting of the Dharma.

A knowledge of the Buddhist concept of these and other doctrines will help the Christian evangelist to understand as the Buddhist presents his views. The presentation of the Christian Biblical viewpoint will not be modified but may be adjusted in the light of this knowledge.

The Christian worker will study in books and in life, i.e., through theory and through actual contact, to understand the Buddhist's concept of his doctrines. By this means one will try not to interpret a Buddhist doctrine in terms of our Christian and Occidental way of thinking. One will first endeavor to see, to understand, and to feel the doctrine as does the Buddhist and the Oriental. This is not an easy thing. It requires the individual acquaintanceship with the people of the country where the Christian work is being done. It means that the worker will learn the language, not only to speak it, but to use it by reading its religious books and to comprehend its religious conversations. It means living with the people to learn through the avenue of their habits and customs until the unique colloquialisms and particular language forms will become natural to the foreigner.

Indeed, the foreigner will so adapt himself to the new environment that he will be able to think and act according to the land of his adoption. Verbal phrases, prepositions, and conjunctions will be understood in terms of the thinking of the people. Then it will be possible to comprehend the doctrinal fine points, the shaded differences and the acute emphasis that the Buddhist has in his own thinking. Then one can understand the differences and the otherwise unrecognizable gaps between Buddhism and Christianity. This detailed knowledge and comprehension is not for the purpose of argument. Normally, argument in religion, especially when one is trying to win another to a new faith, is of very little value. It may have its place at times. It could help to sharpen the wits and clarify many points. Perhaps it has a comparable part that playing scales does for a musician. It will help to keep the mind keen and fresh. The real task of winning souls to Christ, however, is not one of argument. One must present a positive message. The method of presentation, however, cannot be purely Occidental; it must be as far as possible Oriental. The message should be couched in terms and word forms that are as similar as possible to those used in the religious books and conversations of the Buddhists.

Starting with a complete knowledge of the counterpart in Christian doctrine, the evangelist will present the apologetic for the Christian doctrine with as little mention of the Buddhist doctrine as possible. Comparisons are very apt to be odious. Yet a thorough knowledge of the Buddhist belief is necessary in order that we may be sure that the listener is not confusing his concept with ours. For instance, to equate our concept of Heaven with the Buddhist nirvāna (Nibbana, Neikban) would be quite wrong. Salvation by works is not the same as the Buddhist concept of achieving a higher rebirth by reason of earned merit. In fact, the Buddhist concept of merit can be quite different from ours. Only a careful study and a personal sharing of life will give one the appreciation of the shades of differences. From time to time it will be possible to point out the similarities of certain phases of any given doctrine. One should not, however, be too eager to claim unity and oneness lest the main point of difference, the goal of allegiance to Jesus Christ, be lost. The writer remembers a Moslem trader in his town of Kengtung, Burma, who insisted upon being the same, like-minded, etc., because neither of us had idols like the Buddhist. The fact that we had this belief in common formed a barrier of satisfaction which the trader would never hurdle in order to consider the claims of Christ over Mohammed.

Some of the difficulties which one faces in presenting the Gospel to a Buddhist may be illustrated in our familiar text, John 3:16. Let us take only the first clause, "For God so loved the world. . . ." The Buddhist does not understand the term *God* as we do. The Hinayana form of Buddhism repudiates the concept that Gautama, the Buddha, is a god. In fact, in Hinayana Buddhism there is no god as we conceive of God. The followers of Mahayana Buddhism tend to deify Buddha. Their idea of God, however, has no such comprehensive attributes as has the Christian God. He is a great being with power to influence the lives of human beings and perhaps nature, but he is not conceived of as the creator, without beginning or end or as an entity with a very personal relationship to human beings. It is a long process to build in their minds and hearts the concept and understanding of God as Christians know Him.

The next barrier is found in the word *love*. The Buddhist does not have the concept of love that we have. The word is rarely used. They, of course, understand the relationship of passion between sexes, but the greater concept of love as an idealistic soul relationship is indeed far from their normal mode of thinking. It is the responsibility of the missionary somehow to reveal to the prospective convert a true comprehension of love in its divine aspect. To do this requires a good knowledge of the language and a deep understanding of the thinking processes of the people. Nor should we ever neglect the effectiveness of living a life of love before them.

The third word of importance in this text is *world*. The missionary is dealing with a person whose knowledge of geography is most likely nil. Usually he knows it only in the perverted, weird form that is taught in the Buddhist monastery. It is a real challenge to enlarge the horizons of the inquirer until he comprehends the greatness of the *world,* especially in its relation to its Creator.

In peroration, the Christian missionary faces tremendous barriers as he endeavors to show a Buddhist that God, whom he does not comprehend, loves—a relationship he never thinks about in this sense—the world, an area he has not known. To go on to the vital part of the reason for and result of God's love for us as is developed in the full text requires long and careful explanation. This explanation, let us again emphasize, must be couched in Oriental words and concepts.

Lest one, however, become discouraged, it should be pointed out that our Bible is in itself an Oriental Book. Most of it in its original form is more adapted to and comprehended by an Oriental than by an Occidental. It is our English or Western phraseology and thinking that confuses the process.

Having reached the stage of a tolerable acquaintance with Buddhist doctrine and with a thorough understanding of our Christian doctrine, the missionary is ready to evangelize the Buddhist. The approach should be positive. Very, very little will be accomplished in trying to persuade the prospect that his doctrine is wrong. By knowing the opponent's position in detail, the missionary can present the

Christian doctrine, emphasizing those points that refute the Buddhist position. The presentation will be simple. Those who know our doctrines well can best simplify them. Jesus said: "Except ye be converted, and become as little children, ye shall not enter into the kingdom." This may well mean to "present the Gospel so that a child may understand." No matter how wise and learned the inquirer may be, the simple Gospel will be the most effective.

It will be well to remember the simple adage, "A man calls the doctor when he is sick." Negatively interpreted this will explain why the majority of those to whom the Gospel is presented, not sensing their need of salvation as the Christian conceives it, do not respond to the life-giving message. Whenever the opportunity presents itself, the evangelist will endeavor through the processes suggested above to sow the seed, not only of John 3:16 but also of the true sinful nature of man, his need of salvation, and the remedy as in John 3:16. As this is faithfully done again and again to as many as possible, as frequently as possible, and over as large an area as possible, there will come a day when through a series of circumstances that only God can predict and arrange, the individual Buddhist will reach a crisis, a place of need, or a peculiar circumstance that will make him a seeker for a solution. Then he will remember the one who preached or taught a new and strange doctrine and he will wonder if that one will not have an answer to his predicament and need. He is now sick and needs the healer. The evangelist will recognize the initial opening, this opportune moment, and will with the guidance of the Holy Spirit develop the advantage, cultivating the spark of interest. The actual difficulty that brought the inquirer may be something for which no direct solution can be found. It does provide the occasion for the presentation of the Gospel and the Buddhist will now begin a serious consideration of the Christian way of salvation. The following steps may be rapid and an acceptance of Christ quickly arrived at. More likely, however, the growth of the soul and the comprehension of God's appointed deliverance will come very slowly. It is the Christian evangelist's responsibility to cultivate and nourish the growing plant until it is a ripened fruit. Although we fully realize how marvelously God works to fulfill His plan of salvation in a soul where the Seed-word has been sown, the teacher-evangelist must be patient and enduring to feed the soul as the work of grace comes to its fruition.

Finally, it should be always remembered that it is the function of the Holy Spirit to bring conviction and conversion in the heart of an inquirer. The power of the Holy Spirit will enable the Lord Christ's servant to present the Gospel message. He, the Holy Spirit, will do the work in the heart. We sow the seed. He causes the seed to grow and bring forth fruit. The writer knows well the indifference, the self-satisfaction, the contentment, the ignorance and the antagonism within the heart of the Buddhist. It was declared by Karen Christian leaders that a Tai Buddhist would not become a Christian unless he were brought up as a child in the home or institution of the Christians. And yet, it was our privilege to see Tai Buddhists accept the Lord by ones and twos, until they reached one hundred a year for five years. It has been done. It can be done. God's arm is not shortened. His promises remain true. The need is for laborers who will faithfully sow the Word and persistently claim His promises. He will not be unfaithful to Himself, to His Son, and to His Word. "Pray ye therefore the Lord of the harvest."

BIBLIOGRAPHY

ANDERSON, J. N. D. *The World's Religions*. London: Inter-Varsity Fellowship, 1950.

BRADEN, CHARLES S. *The World Religions*. New York: Abingdon Press, 1934.

———. *War, Communism, and World Religions*. New York: Harper & Brothers, 1953.

Britannica Book of the Year, 1954.

BROWN, BRIAN. *Story of Buddha and Buddhism*. Philadelphia: David McKay Co., 1927.

BULL, GEOFFREY. *When Iron Gates Yield*. Chicago: Moody Press, 1955.

FINEGAN, JACK. *Archeology of World Religions*. Princeton: Princeton Univ. Press, 1952.

HACKMANN, H. *Buddhism as a Religion*. London: Probsthain & Co., 1910.

HAMILTON, C. H. *Buddhism in India, Ceylon, China and Japan* (A Reading Guide), Chicago: Univ. of Chicago Press, 1931.

JURJI, E. J., (Ed.). *The Great Religions of the Modern World*. Princeton: Princeton Univ. Press, 1947.

KELLETT, F. E. *A Short History of Religions.* London: Victor Gollancz Ltd., 1949.

LANDON, KENNETH. *Southeast Asia.* Chicago: Univ. of Chicago Press, 1947.

MENDE, TIBOR. *Southeast Asia Between Two Worlds.* London: Turstile Press, 1956.

A PAKISTANI BUDDHIST. *Buddhism in Pakistan.* Karachi: Pakistani Publications, 195.....

SLATER, R. L. *Paradox and Nirvāna.* Chicago: Univ. of Chicago Press, 1951.

SMITH, F. H. *The Buddhist Way of Life.* London: Hutchinson's Univ. Library, 1951.

WELLS, K. E. *Thai Buddhism: Its Rites and Activities.* Bangkok: Bangkok Times Press, Ltd., 1939.

Magazine Articles

CADY, J. R. "Religion and Politics in Modern Burma," *Far Eastern Quarterly,* 12:149-62, February, 1953.

EADIE, D. G. "Twenty-Five Centuries of Buddhism," *The Christian Century,* March 28, 1956.

EASTMAN, M. "Under the Bo Tree," *American Mercury,* 72:477-8, April, 1951.

MACKLE, E. J. "Hinayana and Religious Paradox," *Review of Religion,* 17:23-8, November, 1952.

ROSAN, L. J. "Desirelessness and the Good," *Philosophy East and West,* April, 1955, Vol. V, No. 1.

Fig. 8.—Symbol of the new India is Mahatma Gandhi. After decorating the Gandhi Memorial, Marian Anderson sang before a crowd of 10,000.
(Courtesy of World Wide Photos.)

I cannot set him (Christ) on a solitary throne, because I believe
God has been incarnate again and again. In my religion there is
room for Krishna, for Buddha, for Christ and Mohammed.

—GANDHI

VIII.

Hinduism

by EVERETT L. CATTELL

HINDUS IN THE WORLD number some 300,000,000 and are found mostly in India. Hinduism in its orthodox form is not a missionary religion, and no one can be a Hindu except by natural birth. Under the stimulus of Christian missions recent reform sects have taken to proselytization with special emphasis on recovery to the fold of those who have gone over to Christianity or Islam.

ORIGIN

The most ancient civilization known in India is that which has been revealed by the archaeological discoveries at Mohenjo-Daro in the Indus Valley. This civilization was closely akin to that of Mesopotamia with which it was contemporaneous. Religion in the Indus Valley civilization like that in Mesopotamia was polytheistic and idolatrous with heavy emphasis on the Mother Goddess and Siva worshiped as phallic symbols.

The memory of monotheism seems to have survived in the world

EVERETT L. CATTELL, A.B. (Marion College), M.A. (Ohio State University), D.D. (Cleveland Bible College), is now General Superintendent of the Ohio Yearly Meeting of Friends. After ten years of pastoral work in Ohio, Dr. Cattell went to India as a missionary. There he served for twenty years, returning to this country to take up his present post in September, 1957. While in India, he was Superintendent of the American Friends Mission and Executive Secretary of the Evangelical Fellowship of India, of which he was one of the founders. He has authored *The Self Giving Missionary*, *Christ Prayed for You*, and *The Spirit of Holiness*.

189

despite the growing polytheism, and Abraham set out from Meso-potamia to be true to the vision. At about the same time a great people known as Aryans left Central Asia and, flowing through the Khyber Pass, invaded India. They were high-minded and hardy, and brought to India the Vedic civilization. While they were not mono-theistic, with Indra, Varuna, and Mitra as their chief deities, yet they did not worship images but turned to supernal phases of nature such as the heavenly bodies and natural phenomena like fire, wind, and storms. Moreover, they condemned phallic worship.[1]

While Abraham was recovering the light of the one true God, the Vedic civilization demonstrated the inevitable development which takes place where monotheism is not held inviolate. The Dravidians whom the Aryans found peopling India were, like the Indus Valley folk (who may or may not have been of the same race) animist in faith. Gradually the Aryans absorbed most of the Dravidian pan-theon, and this accounts for both the multiplicity of gods and god-desses in India today and the difficulty of putting them together in some semblance of logical order.[2]

It is interesting to find that in the folk songs of southern tribal peoples who use Dravidic languages, there persists a sense of morality and the hideousness of sin. Vedic thought, on the other hand, tends to deify man and minimize sin.[3] As a result, the sense of morality and the hideousness of sin have faded out of the Sanskrit-based lan-guages.

Another contrast between Vedic and Dravidian religion appeared in the area of sacrifice. Animal sacrifices offered by the Aryans seemed unnecessary to the Dravidians, a fact reminiscent to Chris-tians of the conflict between Cain and Abel. This emphasis on sacrifice gave rise to a priestly class whose task was to perform the sacrifice with appropriate and exact ritual. Thus originated Brah-manism (the priestly control of Hinduism). The Vedas as such have little to say about caste although there is recognition of the four di-visions of society into priests, warriors, merchants, and servants.

[1]Majumdar, R. C. and others. An Advanced History of India, p. 22.

[2]The best and most graphic arrangement of Hindu gods and goddesses will be found on a three-page spread in the special issue of *Life Magazine*, Feb. 7, 1955, de-voted to Hinduism.

[3]*Orient Review and Literary Digest*, Aug. 1956, "Extracts from Charles Gover's Folk Songs of Southern India: Badaga Songs," pp. 19-23.

This division carried no prohibition of intermarriage, interdining, or change of occupation, and no ceremonial defilement by touching lower castes. Probably the idea of racial superiority and color distinction helped to crystalize the caste system as the light-skinned Aryans mingled with the dark-skinned Dravidians.

Scriptures

The Brahmanical schools passed down from memory a voluminous literature which, together with the much later Bhagavad Gita, is today considered canonical scripture (Sruti) in distinction from later additions which are only semicanonical (Smriti). The former is regarded as eternal revelation while the latter is recorded tradition. The revelation was put in writing around the time Moses was leading the children of Israel out of Egypt.

A. The Vedas

The canonical or revelatory scriptures are known as the Vedas, and comprise four categories:

1. The Mantras (about 1200 B.C.) consisting of four collections:
    a. The Rig-Veda claims to be the oldest religious book in the world, consisting of hymns to various gods recited by the priests.
    b. The Sama-Veda, mostly taken from the Rig-Veda and used as chants at the Soma (an intoxicating drink) sacrifice.
    c. The Yajur-Veda, book of sacrificial prayers and formulas.
    d. The Atharva-Veda, much later than the foregoing consisting of songs, spells, and incantations for healing disease, and exorcising evil spirits.

2. The Brahmanas (1000-600 B.C.), mostly prose expansion of and commentary on each of the Mantras, with observations on sacrifice, myths, and legends.

3. The Aranyakas (1000-600 B.C.), appendices to the Brahmanas, meant as instruction for forest dwelling hermits and concerned with the allegorical and mystic meaning of the texts rather than sacrificial ritual.

4. The Upanishads (about 600 B.C.), some imbedded in the Aranyakas, some appended to them and some independent,

specializing in speculative philosophy, and especially concerned with the universal soul, the Absolute, and the individual self. They also emphasize meditation, the ways of knowledge and devotion as against the Brahmanical emphasis upon correct works. Of some 113 Upanishads, twelve are considered important.

To the above Vedas should be added a book of late composition (A.D. 350) the third and final part of the Mahabharata, called the Bhagavad Gita, or Song of the Lord, which is included by modern Hindus in the canon of revelation. To the modern Hindu the Bhagavad Gita stands like the Sermon on the Mount to Christians.

B. The Vedanga

After the Vedas come the Vedanga, or limbs of the Vedas, known as memory or tradition which, while not classed as revelation, are nevertheless closely connected in an auxiliary sense and regarded as sacred. Principal among them are the following:

1. The Sūtras (600-200 B.C.). Vedic materials reduced to aphoristic form for easy memorization. Manuals of pronunciation, grammar, ritual, etymology, metrics, astronomy, etc., as related to Vedic worship.

2. Codes of Law (600 B.C.-A.D. 300) the most important of which is that of Manu.

3. The Agamas (about 250 B.C.) or sectarian scriptures. Jainism and Buddhism arose as reform sects reacting against Brahmanic evils such as caste, idolatry, ritual, and sacrifice without regard to morality, and the subordination of individual reason to the teachings of the Vedas. They also gave personal saviors to fill the vacuum left by Vedantic emphasis on the impersonal Absolute. But Brahmanism won the victory at last by popularizing personal gods by manifesting the Impersonal Absolute, Brahmana in a triad of limited beings known as Brahma, the creator; Vishnu, the Preserver; and Siva, the destroyer. To popularize these deities, cults sprang up around them producing a quantity of sectarian scripture.

4. Epics

    a. The Mahabharata. (Parts I and II 400 B.C.; Part III, The Bhagavad Gita A.D. 350). This is the story of a great war between two rival groups of princes, the Kauravas and the Pandavas, the latter winning. Krishna joins the Pandavas and advises Arjun, their leader, who has doubts about fighting his relatives, to go ahead and do his duty and thus in the Bhagavad Gita finds occasion to set forth the philosophy of Vedant with special emphasis on Karma Yoga.

    b. The Ramayana (A.D. 250). The story of how Ram recovered his wife Sita from her kidnaper Ravana, the king of Ceylon by the help of Laxman his brother and Hanuman, now the monkey god. Ram is the ideal king, Sita the ideal wife, Laxman and Hanuman the ideal brother and friend.

5. The Darshanas (250 B.C.-A.D. 200). These are books of six schools of theological philosophy:

    a. Nyaya founded by Gautama. Hindu science of logic.

    b. Vaishesika, founded by Kanada. Materialistic.

    c. Samkhya founded by Kapila. Atheistic.

    d. Yoga founded by Patanjali. Systematized discipline.

    e. Mimansa. Stresses salvation by works.

    f. Vedanta, founded by Badrayana. Systematized the Upanishads and stresses salvation by knowledge.

6. The Puranas (edited about A.D. 650). Eighteen volumes of old tales of gods and goddesses, mostly mythological, some beautiful, but mostly vulgar. Popular with the masses who practice popular Hinduism without knowing much of the philosophical side.

7. The Commentators. Three great men write on the Vedanta Sūtra but arrive at different conclusions:

    a. Sankara. Emphasizes the Impersonal Absolute and the illusoriness of the world and of the individual soul, setting forth a pure monism but favors worship of Siva as the best medium for ordinary minds to approach the Absolute. His is the way of knowledge.

    b. Ramanuja. Holds modified monism in which the soul is in

God but yet remains individually distinct and it and the world are real. Worships Vishnu by the way of devotion.

c. Madhava. God, world, and soul are distinct realities. Dualism. Worships Vishnu.

We have now pretty well moved out of the realm of scripture but it should be noted that a huge devotional literature has grown up about the Hindu Triad. Vaishnavism and Saivism have already been noted. Saktism, or the worship of Kali, still carries on animal sacrifice and huge superstition, and in its lower forms encourages license and immorality, its five elements being flesh, wine, women, fish, and finger.

A curious discussion among Vaishnavites about A.D. 1200 is of interest to those who are acquainted with the arguments of Calvin and Arminius. As the two parties discussed the grace of Vishnu they divided into two parties championing respectively the cat and the monkey views. Some said God picks us up by grace like a cat takes its kitten by the neck without regard to the kitten's will. Others held that like the baby monkey all depends on whether we take hold as to whether God saves.

POPULAR HINDUISM

Roughly speaking there are two dominant types of Hinduism implicit in the scriptural development and explicit on today's scene. One is popular and the other philosophical. For the masses popular Hinduism centers in (1) the observance of caste, (2) the worship of the idols of popular gods with observance of rites and customs and vast superstition, and (3) immersion in the folklore and stories of the gods contained in the Puranas, the Mahabharata and the Ramayana.

Caste, more than any other thing, is the one feature universally true of popular Hinduism everywhere. What started with the four occupational groups has divided into some 3000 subcastes. These divisions carry with them severe restrictions which include the prohibition of intermarriage, interdining, and change of occupation. The practice of "untouchability," (a rather euphonious translation of the emotionally charged Hindi word *achhut*) which is applied to the so-called outcastes, has been the darkest blot on India's social structure. The impact of Western civilization and particularly of the Christian Gospel has brought this evil into focus and started large-scale reform movements. Change of occupation is now commonly accepted, and among the advanced, interdining is practiced. But even this is not done by the masses. The new Constitution and the laws passed for its implementation now make it a criminal offense to practice any kind of discrimination on the basis of caste or untouchability. But actual practice is a very different thing. Mahatma Gandhi waged a relentless warfare against untouchability but it must be noted that he did not subscribe to the destruction of the caste structure. This distinction is important. In the exigencies of modern modes of travel many old caste restrictions have broken down but the major points are still intact. The acid test is intermarriage and at this point caste is just about as rigid today as ever.

Idolatry and religious ritual are part of the whole day's work for the ordinary person. Breakfast is late for it must be preceded by a bath and worship for the upperclassman. The day's work is punctuated with little acts of worship. For instance, the bus driver starts his day's driving with an act of reverence for the steering wheel—or more accurately for the god in the steering wheel—thus hoping for safety on the road. Likewise others worship the implements of their trade. The housewife has sacred spots built into her stove, and anything that has to do with food or its preparation for eating comes under the minutiae of caste regulation, touchability or untouchability, and has religious significance. No one of different caste dare come too near the cooking place. At a railway station someone left his drinking glass on top of a big storage box. A mechanic wanted to open the lid but he must not touch the glass for fear of defilement. So he gingerly lifted it off with his pliers. Women, near midday, go for their bath. Conveniently an idol has been placed at the edge of every well, river bank, or reservoir where people bathe, for after the bath a jar of water must be poured over the idol in worship. The bath need not involve soap or even get the whole body wet but without the idol worship it is an incomplete bath. The day ends with more worship. At least incense should be lighted before the household gods; more elaborate ritual may be practiced.

When one hears about the "great spiritual East" he may properly raise questions; first, about the definition of *spiritual* where it really

means merely a mystic mind; and second, as to whether it has anything to do with the masses who are as earthly as one ever finds
anywhere in the world. But of the "religiousness" of Hindus there
can be no question.

The number of religious holidays is great, and the observance of
the principal ones, together with the religious fairs or melas, add
much color and brightness to otherwise drab lives. Pilgrimages to
sacred spots, religious bathing, visits of wandering bards and sadhus
with their recitals of the old stories, all add to the filling of life with
the externals of religion. This is the Hinduism of the masses. The
knowledge of the detailed lore which makes it up must largely be
learned by living among the people, especially since it varies greatly
from place to place in its detail and according to the influence of
prevailing local sects.

Essential to this popular worship is the pantheon of popular gods.
No one knows the number of gods but some ancient book facetiously
remarked that the original 33 gods had become now 33 crores
(330,000,000). Roughly they may be grouped in three levels. At
the lowest level stands Varuna, the god of cosmic order, and a host
of demigods and demons. Ravana the demon king who abducted
Sita, Manu the great lawgiver, Soma, and Yama are included here.
Above this is a second level where one finds the old Aryan supernal
nature gods, such as Ushas, dawn; Surya, sun; Agni, fire; Indra, stars;
Chandra, moon; Vayu, wind; and Maruts, storm. These are rarely
made into images or worshiped directly but are part of the pantheon and people the stories of the gods. The top level contains the
gods which have come forward to make concrete Vedantic philosophy.
They account for the popular idols and devotion of today. Supreme
among this group is the triad: Brahma, Vishnu, and Siva. Brahma
is the Creator, Vishnu is the Preserver who has manifested himself
on earth in nine avatars or incarnations, chief among which are
Rama and Krishna, and a promised tenth to come after 425,000
years, called Kalki. Siva is the Creator and Destroyer, whose helper
is the genial Ganesh or elephant god. Each god has a consort. That
of Brahma is Sarasvati, the goddess of learning. Visnu has Lakshmi,
the goddess of wealth, who had an incarnation in Sita the wife of
Rama. The wife of Krishna is Radha who is an ordinary mortal.
Shiva's consort is Parvati who is pictured and worshiped according

to her mood as Uma the beautiful and lovely, Durga the fierce, and Kali the bloodthirsty.

PHILOSOPHICAL HINDUISM

Underlying popular Hinduism are a few doctrines which are held dogmatically by the masses but which are part of a larger philosophical whole characterized by the utmost subtlety.

The philosophy known as Vedanta, which means the end or fruition of the Vedas, as we have already seen, was set forth among the Darshanas by Badrayana who systematized the Upanishads. Many things which lay in the Vedas in germ form he declared with system and clarity. Later the Bhagavad Gita sets forth the same views in a form which is accepted as canonical revelation, and perhaps its greatest commentator (about A.D. 800) is Sankara. If the numbers by which a doctrine is accepted should be the criteria, then this is historically the main line of Hinduism which is flowering into the great revival movements of today. These we shall note later.

Some of the chief views of Vedanta are as follows. First is the view of god who is called Brahmana,[4] the Absolute, than which (not whom) there is nothing else. He is without qualities and unknowable. It is best to speak of God as *It* for Brahmana is impersonal. *It* is beyond all appearances, changes, differences. *It* is the Reality, the Unchangeable, and the One. Positively *It* is spoken of as Satchitananda—absolute existence, consciousness, and bliss. Negatively *It* cannot be mentally comprehended, is qualityless, causeless, energyless, indescribable, limitless, above good and evil, personality and gender, distinction, and difference. It is difficult to be consistent here, for in reality not a single thing can be said about such a god. Yet Hindus do talk about Brahmana and even assign attributes to that which is attributeless. Sometimes all that can be said is the scriptural negative: "He is not this; He is not that." And yet another equally common quotation from scripture is: "Thou art that." The basis of this concept is the understanding that Brahmana is Paramatman (the great Soul), Paramapurusha (the great Person), or Atman (Soul). This soul or self which pervades our lives is the same as the great Self or Soul of Brahmana, and the final act of

---

[4]Three similar words must be distinguished: Brahmana (pronounced Brŭhm), the Absolute. Brahma (pronounced Brŭhmah), one member of the Triad who manifest the Absolute. Brahman (pronounced Brahmin) the highest caste.

salvation is a mystic experience which blanks out all sense impression and releases one into a sense of identity with the great All.

To secure the experience of "realization" requires years of hard discipline according to rules and practices called Yoga. Through intensity of devotional worship of particular gods as representing Brahmana, and through austerities by which trance-like escape from the world of sense is achieved, one may hope at the end of years of struggle to attain salvation through the experience of finding oneself the same as god, the all pervading Soul of the universe. Sri Ramakrishna was able to get this experience repeatedly by various paths. He started with Kali as the Mother Goddess and through intensity of devotion to her and after years of effort finally got beyond her to the All. He then tried to lay aside Hindu ways and practiced Christian and Muslim devotions and claimed to come out to the same experience. He thus proved to his own satisfaction what every Vedantist believes, that all religions are equally good and equally false and every man should therefore remain in the one of his birth without bigotry and without claiming exclusiveness for a particular religion.

The new Constitution of India guarantees freedom to "profess, practice, and propagate religion," not "our religion"—in other words no particular religion—but just "religion," by which is meant this Vedantic view of the inadequacy of any particular religion to make exclusive claims. All are but varying and inadequate ways through to the all-pervading All, or One. This is the most significant fact in today's meeting of Hindu and Christian thought. Christians are despised for their seeming intransigence in making exclusive claims for Christ. The simple positive proclamation of Christ is fine, but one has to go beyond this and emphasize the uniqueness of Christ. Otherwise Hindus simply add Christ to their pantheon. Of course Christians are quick to point out that the inclusivistic view of God and religion presented by modern Vedanta is likewise but a particular religion and therefore likewise bigoted in not studying the exclusive claims of Christ.

There are also three ways outlined in the Gita by which one can come to the mystic realization that he is one with Brahmana. The first is Jnana-Yoga (pronounced gyan) or the path of knowledge. The second is Karma-Yoga or the way of right action. And the third is Bhakti-Yoga or the path of devotion. In all of these, great renunciation is called for.

The way of knowledge is largely philosophical and centers in grasping the principles of Vedant, especially its view of the nature of God and our being a part of Him, so that eventually this knowledge of a rational sort turns into a mystic insight and the experience of "realization." Renunciation here largely consists of enormous concentration of mind. Yogis are instructed to sit cross-legged and to concentrate on one spot of their bodies such as the navel or the spot on the nose between the eyes and through intense mental effort to shut out all thoughts but those of God. Years of practice precede the final state of realization which usually leaves one apparently unconscious. This is the way for those of philosophical temperament.

The way of works is for those of activist temperament. It is intended to enable one to work his way to realization. The way of action then becomes hedged about with rules of conduct, but this must not be confused with Western ideas of ethics. The core of this exercise is to renounce the fruits of action. Evil inheres in our desires—in wanting things which come by striving. Therefore one must attain a state where action is done as a fulfillment of duty but with complete disinterestedness and detachment from the results. Final realization is accompanied by wanting nothing but union with God.

The path of devotion is the way for emotional temperaments. The exercises all center in a chosen deity. By song, meditation, and worship, with the utmost of feeling, devotion, and love, and renunciation of everything that distracts from these, one hopes to come to the place of realization where through the particular deity he sees beyond to the all-embracing All and merges himself into It. The saints of Hinduism have left intricate instructions for following these paths.

But what of the phenomenal world we see around us, consisting of a multitude of particular details? To the Vedantist this is Maya or illusion. It is just the dramatic play of Brahmana when known in his creative aspect as Ishwar. The world then is really not real. It only seems. But philosophers differ in their explanations of this subtlety ranging from a denial of the reality of the world to a dualism in which Brahmana and matter are separate and eternally co-existent. Vedanta however in its main stream tends to the former.

Two other essential concepts are the doctrines of karma (works) and transmigration. The laws of moral action are immutable. Wrong actions inevitably produce punishment, and good actions their reward. This is inescapable in an almost fatalistic sense, and to talk of forgiveness or the canceling of sin is completely unrealistic and does injustice to the noble moral law of cause and effect essential in the universe. Whatever of ill one bears in this life is the product of wrong action in a previous existence, and life's blessings come from the good that was done. Our works set off reactions as cause and effect and they must work themselves out to the bitter end. Salvation consists, not of having this canceled or interfered with, but through doing enough good gradually to evolve toward the highest, where one may then experience the enlightenment that we are essentially God. In Him there are no distinctions, even of good and evil, and thus one escapes from the ceaseless round of rebirths. One would think that this emphasis on the harvest of evil deeds would act as a great deterrent to evil. But it does not seem to act that way. Perhaps one hopes to balance his evil with good deeds. And anyway there are many more lives in which to put things right. Actually it seems that the only religion which really puts a deterrent on evil is the doctrine of forgiveness through grace and atonement.

In spite of this heavy emphasis on the inexorable harvest from deeds good and bad, the difference between them is not to be called sin. We are not sinners—we are God. And while actions may be labeled good or bad according to whether they are productive of good or evil circumstances in life, still this does not involve sin in the sense of a broken relationship with God, for we *are* God in spite of our illusion of being separate entities. Therefore the evil is only seeming. There can be no broken relations where there is no relationship but only oneness. Swami Vivekananda used to preach most eloquently about the great disservice done by Christian missionaries in India through giving the people a sense of sin. It was weakness to feel guilty and we should throw this off and realize our strength. These then are the leading ideas of Vedanta.

MODERN HINDUISM

When modern Christian missionaries first came to India about 150 years ago, their preaching of Christ together with the impact of the newly arrived Western civilization began to make a tremendous impression. The first impulse was to accept Western civilization wholesale and many became Christians. This produced a strong reaction. First came reform movements which tried to wipe out the social evils which had grown up in Hinduism. The Brahmo Samaj founded by Ram Mohan Roy started with a strong Christian content but became syncretistic. The Arya Samaj was started by Swami Dayanand who knew no English and was less influenced by Westernism. He advocated cleansing of Hinduism by returning to the Vedas which alone he regarded as infallible scripture. The movement is a most militant and even violent champion of Hinduism against all enemies. It is also strongly opposed to idolatry and caste distinction and other evils within Hinduism.

Following the reform movements came what is known as the Renaissance of Hinduism. It starts with the spiritual experience of the unschooled but mystic saint known as Sri Ramakrishna (1836-1886). His brilliant disciple, Swami Vivekananda (1863-1902) organized the other disciples into the Ramakrishna Mission which carries on an immense social service today, obviously inspired by Christian missions. Swami Vivekananda was a brilliant graduate who longed for peace. A Christian professor recommended that he visit Sri Ramakrishna. He was so impressed that he became his disciple. With his outstanding mentality and personality, he reacted against the tendency to Westernism and became the most eloquent apostle of modern Hinduism, bringing about a tremendous revival. He taught his people not to be ashamed but proud of Hinduism and proclaimed its superiority over all religions. As the Hindu representative at the Parliament of Religions held in the United States in 1893, his eloquence swayed many Americans and opened for him long lectureships abroad. It led to the establishment of the Ramakrishna Mission in New York and some ten other centers in the United States which carry on a vigorous propaganda today. His was the most outstanding advocacy of modern Vedanta coupled with a sense of nationalism based on pride of ancient culture.

Following Vivekananda came a galaxy of famous names who have

given great weight to modern Vedanta. Rabindranath Tagore was
its poet and artist, Mahatma Ghandhi and Rajagopalacharya its poli-
ticians. Sri Aurobindo its philosopher, nationalist, and mystic, and Sir
S. Radhakrishnan its best-known philosopher, now the vice-president
of India. All these have proclaimed Vedantism in a subtly altered
form which shows absorption of Christian ideas and trying to make
them appear a part of basic Hinduism. This requires juggling of
thought and allegorizing or spiritualizing of their scriptures, reading
meanings into them which are not really there.

IMPACT OF CHRISTIANITY

Christianity made its first impact on Hinduism through the Syrian
Christian Church of Malabar, possibly starting with the ministry of
Thomas who is alleged to have gone to India. These Christians however soon became satisfied to develop into a respectable caste, living
peaceably alongside Hindus with never a thought for evangelism.
This was true until late in the last century when under the stimulus
of modern Christian missions a reform movement comparable with
a combination of Luther and Wesley sprang up and led to the forming of the Mar Thoma Syrian Christian Church which has shown a
commendable and fruitful zeal for evangelism.

With the coming of Ziegenbalg in 1706 and Carey in 1793 commenced the era of modern missions. The impact of these missions
had two phases. At first there were notable high-class converts. This
produced the reaction noted above. But during the last half of the
last century the impact of Christianity gave hope to the multitudes of
oppressed, downtrodden, and exploited outcastes. Great mass movements occurred which have raised the total Christian population
today to nearly 9,000,000, of which 5,000,000 are Protestant and the
rest Catholic. The record of Christian missions in having a heart
that cared for, and a plan of action which relieved, these outcastes
can never be offset by the objections of modern Hindus who resent
the loss of the outcastes from their fold. All kinds of charges of using
improper and material inducements are being made against missionaries. But the record is there for all to see as a monument to the
constraining love of Christ. Missionaries loved and helped. Hindus
only talked.

Today the mass movements have subsided, although ingathering still goes on at a rapid pace in Assam and Andhra. New mass movements are not likely to occur now as the government is spending huge sums of money on removing the disabilities of the outcastes. The offering of material inducements is regarded as a crime for missionaries who want to make Christians, but a virtue when done by the government to keep them in the Hindu fold. The Constitution now makes the practice of untouchability a criminal offense but its enforcement is negligible.

Christian missions under fire, having a very precarious future, are turning to the strengthening of the existing church and devolving upon it the burden of the evangelization of India. At present the church is in need of spiritual revival before this can be effective, but there are indications that such an awakening is beginning.

Hinduism has entrenched itself in the subtleties of Vedanta into which have been imported many Christian ideas and from which have been theoretically renounced many of the evils of Hinduism. Hinduism and nationalism have been equated (even in a secular state) and set forth as vastly superior to Christianity (whose professed followers have produced two world wars) and thus brought the Christian movement to a near stalemate. It is unlikely that large accessions from among the upper classes of Hindus will come until disillusionment sets in. At present India through neutrality is living in a vacuum and is easily satisfied with patriotic fervor for the ancient culture.

We Christians can afford to be patient and we must not lose hope. That day of disillusionment is bound to come and then Christ may have His day. We await some new order to advance. The chief problem is to find a satisfactory way of meeting and offsetting the specious argument of Hindus that all religions are the same. We are still under the spell of preaching Christ and Him crucified, but it does not penetrate this Vedantic armor. Either Christian Indian preachers must make a more powerful frontal attack which will somehow crack the defenses or we shall be obliged to wait for those defenses to distinegrate. Below is listed a number of books nearly all written by living Hindus of this vigorous revival movement. Its basic premise must be shown false. Otherwise we get nowhere. In preaching the Gospel one learns that because of this basic premise nearly every religious word used by the preacher has another meaning to the Hindu than it has to the Christian. He is obliged to build new concepts into nearly every word. Much of our frustration grows out of a failure to find a way to break through the complacency of this ultrabroad philosophy. The Hindu feels vastly superior because he tolerates and incorporates with his own all other religions. He looks down upon those who seem so unenlightened and bigoted as to insist that their religion is exclusively true. It is hard to see how this can be changed until God works something new in affairs whereby this complacency is shattered.

Among the intelligentsia this disillusionment has begun and some are being converted. Likewise the common people still listen gladly, lifted for the moment by the ray of hope which Christ gives, but only too often to shrink back from fear of persecution and go away sorrowing. Hinduism is vastly tolerant of ideas—but socially through its caste sytem which still dominates all but a tiny fraction of Hindus, it is one of the most intolerant systems on earth. Yet the present response is such as to make us know that the Gospel of Jesus Christ is still "the power of God unto salvation." After years of opposition, great disillusionment came in China; and before the communists took over students were turning to Christ in masses. May God hasten such a day in India.

BIBLIOGRAPHY

(All, with the exception of Max Müller's work, have been written by Hindus and are therefore primary source works.)

ATHALYE, D. V. *Quintessence of Yoga Philosophy,* based on the Teachings of Swami Vivekananda. D. B. Taraporevala Sons & Co., Ltd., 210 Hornby Rd., Bombay 1.

DIWAKAR, R. R. *Mahayogi (Life of Sri Aurobindo).* Bharatiya Vidya Bhavan, Chaupatty, Bombay.

MÜLLER, MAX. *The Vedas.* Calcutta 12: Susil Gupta (India) Ltd., 35 Chittaranjan Ave.

MAJAMDAR, R. C. and others. *An Advanced History of India.* Macmillan & Co., New York and London.

NEHRU, JAWAHARLAL. *The Discovery of India.* Meridian Books, Ltd., 8 Garrick St., London W.C. 2.

NIRVEDANANDA, SWAMI. *Hinduism at a Glance.* Bengal Vidyamandira, Dhakuria, Bengal, India.

PARAMPANTHI, SRIMAT PURAGRA. *The Cardinal Doctrines of Hinduism.* Published by the Author, "Viraj," Dr. Basu's Road, Dibrugarh, Assam, India.

RADHAKRISHNAN, SIR S. *The Heart of Hindusthan.* Madras: G. A. Natesan & Co., George Town.

RAJAGOPALACHARYA. *Hinduism, Doctrine and Way of Life.* The Hindustan Times, New Delhi.

SARMA, D. S. *Hinduism Through the Ages.* Bombay: Bharatiya Vidya Bhavan, Chaupatty.

A Wedding Ceremony

The ceremony of initiation into the Zoroastrian Faith. Usually performed at seven years of age, the ceremony involves investiture with the sacred thread and sacred shirt.

A Worship Ceremony

Fig. 9.—The Parsee or Zoroastrian faith is the least known of the living monotheistic religions of the world. Here three of their basic religious ceremonies are portrayed. (Courtesy of F. V. Wallin.)

*My first (duty) on earth is to confess the Religion, to practice it,
and to take part in its worship and to be steadfast in it, to keep
the Faith in the Good Religion of the worshippers of Ohrmazd
ever in my mind, and to distinguish profit from loss, sin from good
works, goodness from evil, light from darkness, and the worship of
Ohrmazd from the worship of the demons.*

Zoroastrian Catechism

IX.

Lesser Living Religions of India

by PAUL C. HAAGEN

PART ONE—ZOROASTRIANISM

INTRODUCTION

OF THE MANY FOREIGN RELIGIONS referred to in the pages of Holy
Writ, Zoroastrianism is the only one that has survived to the
present day. Of all non-Biblical systems it bears the closest resemblance to revealed truth, while among nonbelievers its adherents
alone receive commendation within the sacred pages.

The Zorastrian king, Cyrus, conquered Media in 559 B.C. and
Babylon in 539 B.C. Tradition asserts that the Jews, who were then
captives in Babylon, showed Cyrus the prophecy of Isaiah in which
he is addressed by Jehovah as "his Messiah" (45:1-7) and ascribed
the title "My Shepherd" (44:28). Whether this world-conquering
Zorastrian ever read the 200-year-old prophecy or not, history assures
us that he fulfilled it. Many other Zoroastrian kings are mentioned

PAUL C. HAAGEN, A.B. (Franklin and Marshall College), graduate
of Nyack Missionary College, is a missionary to India with the
Christian and Missionary Alliance. He is stationed at Dholka,
Bombay State. Before sailing for India in 1945, Mr. Haagen held
Alliance pastorates in the United States.

207

in the books of the Old Testament (II Chron. 36:22, 23; Ezra 1:1; 8:1; Neh. 2:1; Esther 1:3; 10:2; Dan. 9:1; 10:1; 11:1; Haggai 1:1; Zech. 1:1). Although Zoroastrianism as a religion is not mentioned in the Bible, it has a close historical connection with it. Some scholars even mistakenly ascribe Zoroastrian sources to certain Biblical concepts.

Among the first persons we meet in the New Testament are Zoroastrian priests, Magi from the East, who inquire: "Where is he that is born King of the Jews? for we have seen his star in the east, and are come to worship him" (Matt. 2:1, 2). These Magi believed, as do Zoroastrians today, that every good man has a fravashi or double in Heaven. This guardian angel or guiding star appears in the sky when the individual is born. The greater the person, the brighter shines his star. As he matures on earth, the fravashi grows in Heaven, being united with him finally at death. Some scholars would read this Zoroastrian idea into Jesus' own words when He said: "Take heed that ye despise not one of these little ones; for I say unto you, That in heaven their angels do always behold the face of my Father which is in heaven" (Matt. 18:10). While hanging on the cross, Jesus promised the penitent thief: "Today shalt thou be with me in paradise" (Luke 23:43). Ignoring the Hebrew word for the place of departed souls (Sheol), Jesus used a word etymologically derived from the Avestan of the Zoroastrian scriptures. In birth, in life, and in death, Jesus Himself was closely associated with the followers and teachings of Zoroaster.

Although we repudiate the claim that the Jews adopted religious ideas from Zoroastrianism, ideas which were later taken over by Christianity, we do acknowledge that these two peoples arrived at similar ideas by different roads and that some of the great truths of the Bible were likewise voiced in rudimentary and independent form by Zoroaster.[1] "Outside of Judaism and Christianity it is impossible to find in antiquity so true, so noble, so ideal a belief in the resurrection of the body, the life everlasting, the coming of a Saviour, and the rewards and punishments for the immortal soul as is to be found in the scriptures of ancient Iran which are illumined by the spirit of the great teacher Zoroaster."[2] These facts add to the stature and

[1]Max Müller, *Chips from a German Worship* (New York: 1881) I, 140-157.
[2]A. V. W. Jackson, *Zoroastrian Studies*, p. 3.

respectability of this ancient religion, which, of all the great living religions, has the fewest adherents today.

If a religion is to be evaluated by its glorious past or by the quality rather than the quantity of its present-day followers, then Zoroastrianism deserves still to be numbered among the great religions. It has brought inspiration to ages gone by, and is producing among the Parsis of India and their coreligionists of Persia as fine a type of character as can be found outside Christianity. They are a people of industry, charity, peacefulness, and love of truth. The esteem in which they are held is indicated by the proverb: "As binding as the word of a Parsi." They actually practice the four virtues of liberality, justice, friendliness, and sincerity in which they profess to believe, for their philanthropic gifts average higher per person than those of any other faith. Neither are they unmindful of the threefold duty laid upon them: "To make him who is an enemy, a friend. To make him who is wicked, righteous. To make him who is ignorant, learned."[3] They also have the distinction of being the most advanced people in India in education, in wealth, in their treatment of women, and in their general culture. Truly their influence goes far beyond anything their numbers would warrant, especially in India but also in other places.

Zoroastrianism has an interest and attractiveness derived from the high moral dignity of its founder. Unlike Hinduism, it is not the thought of many men throughout many ages but it is the vision and clear-cut conviction of one man—he whom the Greeks admired as Zoroaster, but who was known to his own people as Zarathustra in his own Avestan language or as Zaratusht in later Pahlavī or as Zardusht in Modern Persian.

ZARATHUSTRA'S LIFE

(660-583 B.C.)

Although legend and fable have so encrusted the figure of the great religious reformer as to obscure his real personality, yet he was without doubt a historical character whose individuality can be discerned from the Gāthās, the seventeen chapters of the Zoroastrian scriptures that claim to be his spiritual experiences.

His birth date is a subject of much dispute. The traditional dates,

[3]W. Durant, *The Story of Civilization, Our Oriental Heritage,* p. 369.

which would make him a contemporary of the Seven Sages of classical antiquity and of Jeremiah—660-583 B.C.—are generally accepted as the latest possible. Some scholars with good reason place him about 1000 B.C., others at 1400 B.C., or even 6000 B.C.[4] The student's choice from among these dates takes on great significance, for with it goes the dating of the Gāthās.

The place of Zarathustra's birth seems to the region west of Media in Azerbijan near Lake Urumiah. His mother was said to come from the Median Raga or Rai. As a young boy he was unusually astute in conversation (S.B.E., 47:43, 45). At the age of twenty he departed from his parental home to give himself entirely to a religious life. He inquired as he went: "Who is most desirous of righteousness and most nourishing the poor?" Upon receiving the answer, he went "to that place" and assisted in serving the poor with food (Zat-sparam 20:8-9).

The turning point of Zarathustra's life came at the age of thirty when he received his divine call. This summons came through "the wail of the kine" who demanded protection for themselves such as the introduction of agriculture alone could secure. Zarathustra envisioned himself selected as teacher and protector, although the cattle wept because a priest rather than a warrior was chosen (Yasna 29). This vision which came through the Immortal Holy One, Good Mind (Vohu Man), was followed by another through the Immortal Holy One, Justice (Asha), and later by a vision or conference with Ahura Mazda himself. These three experiences recorded in the Gāthās are evidently the basis for the traditional seven questions he is supposed to have addressed to seven divinities in seven different places during the five-month winters of the ten-year period that followed (Zāt-sparam 22:13).

Before going out to preach, Zarathustra meditated on the revealed message that initiated him into the mysteries of morality and agriculture (Yasna 31:5) and prayed that universal conversion might improve contemporary conditions (Yasna 33:8, 9, 10). He then gave himself as a sacrifice to his god, asking for eternal reward in the life to come (Yasna 33:14, 11). For a long time his preaching was without success (Yasna 46:1, 2). Finally after ten years he won a solitary

[4]For a critical study of this problem see A. V. W. Jackson, *Zoroaster, the Prophet of Ancient Iran*, pp. 150-178.

convert. This was Maidhyōi-Māonha, his own cousin, who became the St. John of Zoroastrianism (Yasna 51:19).

At forty-two years of age he reached a second turning point in his life with the conversion of the Magian chieftain, Kavi Vishtāspa, the Constantine of the Zoroastrian faith (Yasna 28:7; 46:14; 51:16; 53:2). Thereafter his message attracted many converts including the king's brother, his son, a counselor, and even the grand vizier of the realm. Yasna 53, the last of those written by Zarathustra, is a bridal hymn celebrating the marriage of Zarathustra's daughter, Pournchista, to this grand vizier, who is promised happiness if he remains faithful to the Cause, but woe if he abandons it.

The death of Zarathustra, as well as the final twenty years of his life, is not mentioned in the Avesta. These were years of Holy Wars when his religion was spread widely throughout Iran and to foreign lands as well. Extracanonical documents record that he died at seventy-seven years of age during an attack of the Turanians on the City of Balkh. His was a violent death at the hands of a priest of the old religion, as he performed a ceremony before the altar fire of Ahura Mazda for victory in the Holy War he had directly or indirectly started. Although we cannot with assurance impute militaristic nationalism to Zarathustra himself, yet it appears from his frantic appeals to force (Yasna 31:18; 12:9; 57:1) that his unnatural end was a fitting reward, for a more perfect revelation than his own declares: "All they that take the sword shall perish with the sword" (Matt. 26:52). Although Isfendiār, the great crusader, won a victory that established the Faith on a firm international basis, yet Zarathustra was no longer alive to enjoy the fruits thereof. Unlike the prophets of Israel he had no successor in the prophetic tradition to inspire faithfulness to his highly abstract monotheism, with the result that the old polytheism soon returned under the guise of angel worship.

Later Zoroastrian documents represent the founder as the most adorable personage of history—the very acme of humanity—one of supernatural origin who was deserving of worship along with the deity. The following statements concerning him are mostly found in the Gāthās, the Little Avesta, or in the still later Pahlavī literature based on the lost Spend Nask of the Avesta:

1. He was prophesied as "The Saviour" 3000 years and 300 years before his birth (*Sacred Books of the East*, 5:21; 47:31-34).

2. He was virgin born (S.B.E. 47:17-20).
3. He was visited by adoring Magi.
4. He was miraculously saved in infancy from the treachery of a jealous ruler (S.B.E., 47:175).
5. He was found disputing with the theologians of his day, and confounding them with his precocious wisdom (Dinkart 73:34-43; Zāt-sparam 17:1-6; 18:5-7; 19:8).
6. He began his prophetic ministry at the age of thirty (Dīnkart 73:51; 8:14).
7. He was tempted by the Devil (the demon Būiti sent by Ahriman) in the wilderness. At that time he answered his tempter thus: "No. I shall not renounce the good religion of the worshippers of Mazda, not though life, and limb, and soul should part asunder" (Vendidad 19:8).
8. He gave sight to a blind man.[5]
9. He cast out demons.
10. He performed miracles by the score.
11. He preached the gospel of a Supreme God of goodness and truth.
12. He was transported to Heaven by angels without having to await the Day of Judgment.

Although tradition has fancifully colored a series of miraculous events around the truly unusual life of the greatest of all Gentile prophets, and the reader with a Christian background reads Christian connotations into the ideas and terms of Zarathustra which they did not contain for their originator, nevertheless one is struck by the remarkable parallels between the lives of the founders of Christianity and Zoroastrianism. No other religion so nearly approaches Christianity in this as in many other similarities. When the dross of Oriental fantasy and unmitigated absurdity are removed, choice grains of enduring gold are undoubtedly to be found. Closing our eyes to much that strikes us as mere nonsense, let us note the outstanding aspects of the prophet's message.

ZARATHUSTRA'S MESSAGE

Zarathustra was the pioneer among the prophets of living faiths in founding a religion that was universal in its appeal. Of all teachers, he was the first to address his message to all men irrespective of the

[5]A. V. W. Jackson, *Zoroastrianism*, pp. 94, 95.

distance of time or space. He did not guard his revelation for himself nor for his clan with miserly fear lest it be exhausted or contaminated. Rather, he envisioned the truth he received as something to be shared with all men—a light to unite those far and near. It is one of the contradictions of history that in modern times the followers of Zarathustra have lost their founder's vision and are now perpetuating a religion that is more narrowly hereditary and exclusive than any other in the world today. Thus the first religion to be emancipated from the concept of the tribal God and to be offered to universal man has degenerated into the peculiar possession of a chosen people, the Parsis.

Zarathustra also founded the first religion to be voluntarily and individually accepted. He was emphatically the prophet of free moral choice. Free will was the pivot of his whole theology. He showed men the path of freedom—freedom from the multiplicity of shrines that make a travesty of devotion, freedom from blind observance of meaningless ceremonies, freedom to choose truth and justice. His written teachings are almost devoid of any mention of the ritualism of worship. He places almost sole emphasis upon conduct and the moral motives that prompt it. When we consider the great number of men who even today follow the path of blind formalism which is completely devoid of any moral content, we begin to appreciate the greatness of this prophet. Though surrounded by witchcraft and magical rites, he declared that religion is truth only to the extent of its moral significance. For him the value of religion was its ability to sustain mankind in a life of good thoughts, good words, and good deeds. Here again the distance between the founder and his modern disciples is vividly displayed in the ceremonialism that is the characteristic of Parsiism.

Zarathustra was likewise the first religious leader to teach belief in an abstract god who could neither be seen nor touched by the worshiper. This one, wholly spiritual deity was to be worshiped supremely. His name was Ahura Mazda, Lord of Wisdom, or Auharmazd, or Ormazd as abbreviated in the Pahlavī and Persian of later Zoroastrianism. He is "creator of all things through the holy spirit" (Yasna 44:7). Although surrounded by personified attributes, he reigns alone without equal or second. The proclamation of his supremacy was the central tenet of Zarathustra's reform.

The prophet's profound instinct not only grasped the primary truth of the oneness of God, but went on to establish its necessary corollary—diversity *within* the godhead. (For lack of this conception the monotheism of Islam is barren.) This diversity is expressed by common nouns that represent divine attributes within the hypostasis of deity, but which were incorrectly designated as archangels by later Zoroastrianism. Of these abstractions those most frequently associated with Ahura Mazda (Lord of Wisdom) are Asha (Right, Order, Justice) and Vohu Man (Good Mind, Thought, Disposition). Other attributes are Kshathra (Power, Dominion), Armaiti (Piety, Pity, Love), Haurvatat (Wholeness, Welfare, Health), and Ameretat (Immortality, Eternal Life).

Putting all these attributes together in a unity that represents deity, we are astonished at the maturity of Zarathustra's omniscient and omnipotent god. Although frequent reference to these six attributes is contained in the Gāthās, yet the complete hexad appears but once in association with Ahura Mazda: "By his holy Spirit and by Best Thought, deed, and word, in accordance with Right, Mazda Ahura with Dominion and Pity shall give to us Welfare and Immortality" (Yasna 47:1). It should be noted that some of these attributes are also bestowed upon man as divine gifts.

The most distinctive feature of Zoroastrianism is usually represented as its doctrine of a fundamental cosmological dualism in which a good god and a lying devil are constantly fighting against one another. Yasna 45:2 seems to state this doctrine explicitly: "I will speak of the Spirits twain at the first beginning of the world, of whom the holier thus spake to the enemy: 'Neither thought nor teachings nor wills nor beliefs nor words nor deeds nor selves nor souls of us twain agree.' " This statement is substantiated by a longer passage in Yasna 30:3-6:

> Now the two primal spirits, who revealed themselves in vision as Twins, are the Better and the Bad in thought, word, and action. And between these two the wise once chose aright, the foolish not so. (4) And when these twain Spirits came together in the beginning, they established Life and Not-Life, and that at the last the Worst Existence shall be to the followers of the Lie, but the Best Thought to him that follows Right. (5) Of these twain Spirits he that followed the Lie chose doing the

worst things; the holiest Spirit chose Right, he that clothes him with the massy heavens as a garment. So likewise they that are fain to please Ahura Mazda by dutiful actions. (6) Between these twain the demons also chose not aright, for infatuation came upon them as they took counsel together, so that they chose the Worst Thought. Then they rushed together to violence, that they might enfeeble the world of man.

The exact meaning of these passages is much in dispute. Moulton says: "The whole ring of the passage forbids the recognition of mere metaphysics. If the prophet gives a thought to the origin of evil, it is just as the doctor searches for the cause of his patient's malady: both are thinking only of the problem of a cure. . . . He is simply hammering home his fundamental precept, that right and wrong have no concord, that compromise is impossible, and we must make our choice knowing that all eternity depends upon it."[6] On the other hand, Jackson[7] believes Zarathustra made dualism "in its moral and ethical aspects . . . a typical unit in his great system." At the same time he recognizes that "Zarathustra's dualism is monotheistic and optimistic," for it prophesies the ultimate triumph of good. (The Zervānites who made the two Spirits twins of Eternity never were accepted within Parsi orthodoxy. Isaiah 45:7, addressed to Cyrus, the Zoroastrian king, seems to be a rebuke of dualism and would thus indicate its prevalence before the time of that historic conqueror.) Whatever metaphysical conclusions you may arrive at, all pain, suffering, disease, pestilence, injustice, and war—in short all evil—are due to the existence of the implacable devil, Angra Mainyu, the unrelenting enemy of the human soul who, with his retinue of inferior demons,[8] must be constantly and openly resisted.

Zarathustra's concept of the duty of man could almost be summed up in the Biblical phrase, "Fight the good fight of faith." This view of life as a colossal moral battle with the outcome dependent upon man's own courageous efforts is certainly more ennobling than the doctrine of karma, in which man is the helpless plaything of fate. Thus Zarathustra's ideal is that of the fighter. Paradise must be gained through conquest. It can only be won by those who choose the right side and employ the proper spiritual weapons. Man's hope

---

[6]Moulton, *The Treasure of the Magi*, p. 28.
[7]Jackson, *Zoroastrian Studies*, p. 30.
[8]Cf. Asmodaeus in Hastings *Dictionary of the Bible*.

lies in the fact that the beneficent Ahura Mazda is on the side of those who choose right. For them the conflict will terminate in a symphony of spiritual union at the House of Songs (Heaven).

The pure spiritual character of Ahura Mazda demands inward spiritual and outward ethical qualities from his worshipers such as few other religions have exacted. Temporal blessings there are for the faithful, but the attention of man is primarily directed beyond the passing rewards of this life to the judgment that will follow death. Here the injustices of life will be redressed :"In immortality shall the soul of the righteous be joyful, in perpetuity shall be the torments of the Liars" (Yasna 45:7). Indeed Zarathustra's whole system of theology seems to be rooted and grounded in eschatology, for one of his earliest and most frequently repeated messages concerns a future judgment in which the wicked are punished in Hell and the righteous rewarded in Heaven. This Heaven is devoid of sensual features, but is rather "the glorious heritage of good thought" (Yasna 53:4). It is both the "House of Songs" and the dwelling place of Ahura Mazda. There he rules from a throne of gold surrounded by the righteous. Hell is conversely described as "the House of Demons" —a place of torment, the age-long, lonely punishment provided for liars. Situated in the north under the earth, it is full of darkness and horror. In it the wicked are confined along with the poets and rishis of the Vedas (Yasna 46:11). A third destination called the "separate place" is distinguished for men whose deeds are a hopeless mixture of evil and good.

The process of differentiating good from bad souls is accomplished on the narrow Cinvant bridge that stretches between Heaven and Hell (frequently mentioned in the Gāthās and later literature). Three days after death each soul comes to this Bridge of the Decider. There good and evil forces contend for permanent possession of the soul. If the Better wins the tug-of-war, the soul then meets his conscience or self in the guise of a fair lady—fairer by every good thought, word, and deed of his earthly life. She leads him safely across the Bridge to Paradise, where he is received by Vohu Man with these words: "How hast thou come up here? O righteous one! tasting immortality, from that perishable world which is afflicted, unto this imperishable world which is unafflicted" (Mēnōk i Khrat 1:95). Without this escort the soul topples from the narrow bridge into

Hell, although it is really the man's own Self that determines his future destiny, for if the Hand points downward for the quaking soul at the Bridge, it is but the final endorsement of a doom the Self has determined in life. (Some authorities on folklore see in the universally played children's game called "London Bridge," a dramatization of the Zoroastrian Bridge of the Judge. The prisoner's choice, the tug-of-war, the phrase "off to prison you must go," and the constantly repeated appeal to "My fair lady" are all ingredients of this long-held but vanishing belief.)

Zarathustra's most fundamental precept in his meager doctrine of sin takes us back to the source of action—the thought. (Cf. Matt. 5:21, 22, 27, 28.) For him Thought is of more importance than Word or Deed, for Good Mind is constantly associated with Ahura Mazda while the others but infrequently appear. Good Thought eventually leads to the accomplisment of Good Word and Good Action. This triad appears so frequently in the sacred scriptures and in religious conversations with Zoroastrians as to warrant its recognition as the formula on which their ethics are based. To cleanse oneself with pure thoughts, words, and deeds is true religion that leads to salvation for the Zoroastrian. "He needs no other rosary whose life is strung with beads of loving thought." This precludes the fact that violence and cruelty, arrogance and especially falsehood stand condemned as the outworking of the Lie. Thus Zoroastrian salvation is one of good works that have their source in the individual's free choice of Good Mind rather than the Lie *(Druj)*. When his soul is weighed, he will be saved if his whole record shows a balance of meritorious works.

The hamartialogical emphasis in the Gāthās is upon the punishment of sin in the hereafter. This emphasis is probably a deliberate attempt to turn sinners from their wicked ways. Not only are there many references pertaining to the individual's destiny as indicated above, but there is likewise a vast imagery attached to a general judgment when souls will pass through an ordeal by fire. At the end of time, a flood of molten metal will be poured forth over the earth to destroy all evil (Yasna 30:7). The righteous will pass through this fiery stream as though it were warm, soothing milk, but the wicked and all their wickedness will be burned up thereby. Thus the fire itself shall declare every man's work.

Many other apocalyptic figures are used which do not readily lend themselves to forming a consistent picture of future events. A later document delineates the events following the general bodily resurrection of the dead when Mazda, the Lord of the Resurrection, appoints Zarathustra as judge at the final tribunal to separate the righteous from the wicked. These two groups are then sent to their appointed places. Before this climatic event takes place, three saviours (Aushedar, Aushedar-Mah, and Sōshyant, all virgin-born descendants of Zarathustra) will appear on the earth at intervals of a millennium. However, the central fact of Zarathustra's eschatology lies in the certainty of victory for the forces of Good. This salvation of the whole world, like the salvation of the individual, depends upon the collective accumulation of enough merits to outweigh all the demerits of life. The "life-work" and thoughts "that from Good Thought arise" (cf. the Honover) are the assets of the pious presented to Ahura Mazda for safe keeping until his storehouse is full enough to usher in the promised Kingdom of Righteousness (Yasna 49:10).

The contrast between the above spiritual message of ancient Iran and that of ancient India, which had roots in a common source, could hardly be more extreme. The almost Semitic monotheism of Zarathustra is poles removed from the pantheistic speculations of the Upanishads. Zoroastrianism commends a life of lofty moral responsibility and of simple everyday labor on behalf of the dependent cattle. Hinduism commends a life of speculative knowledge and planned austerities for personal gain. How Zarathustra derived his exalted views from a nature worship, that must have been very much like the Vedic hymns, is impossible to comprehend. The explanation must lie in Zarathustra himself, for none of the elements of Zoroastrianism were ideas derived from books or received through religious teachers. Zarathustra did not arrive at them by a disciplined system of thought, or by following a prescribed school of tradition. They were inspirations which were out of context with their surroundings. They came as illuminations, as communications from without, as revelations from a god. Among the Gentile prophets Zarathustra holds a singularly exalted place. And among the ancient scriptures of non-Biblical origin those written by him and his immediate successors hold a fragrance not shared by others. Certainly the Avesta deserves to be better known.

ZOROASTRIAN SCRIPTURES

Avesta (knowledge) is the inclusive name for the Zoroastrian scriptures. Avestan, the language in which they have been written, is cognate and contemporary with Sanskrit, the two being sister languages. It was Sir William Jones who first pointed out the resemblances between them: Both have three numbers, eight cases, and harmonize even in the grammatical irregularities. The differences are chiefly in sound. Even the casual observer notices how the Sanskrit *asura* (lord) becomes *ahura; soma* (juice) *haoma;* and *ā* (chapter) *hā.* Just as later Sanskrit differs from that of the Veda, so later Avestan differs radically in sound and grammar from that of the Gāthās. Still later the infusion of Chaldean words changed the language into Pahlavī. This in turn has a close connection with modern Persian into which the Avesta has been translated.

The scriptures as used by the Parsis today are generally known to Europeans as the Zend-Avesta—the extant remnants of the original Avesta with commentary (Zend). The larger and more important of the two parts is called the Great Avesta. It contains three divisions:

1. THE YASNA (Sacrifice), consisting mostly of miscellaneous prayers offered at the sacrificial rites, has embedded within it seventeen chapters by Zarathustra written in a dialect distinct from the rest of the Avesta. These seventeen chapters are arranged into five Gāthās or Psalms as follows: (1) Gāthā Ahuna-vaiti, Yasnas 28-34; (2) Gāthā Ushtavaiti, Yasnas 43-46; (3) Gāthā Spenta Mainyu, Yasna 47-50; (4) Gāthā Vohu Xshath-rem, Yasna 51; and (5) Gāthā Vahishta Istish, Yasna 53. (Chapters 35-42 are written in prose rather than verse and belong to a different period.)

2. THE VISPARAD (All the Lords), containing twenty-four prayers in honor of the heavenly "authorities" similar to those in the Yasna, is used with it in priestly worship.

3. THE VENDIDAD (Law Against Demons) including ceremonial law, cosmology, history, and eschatology, is the Leviticus of the Avesta.

The smaller second part of the Avesta is not reserved for the use of the priests as is the Great Avesta, but is the prayer book of the layman, called the Small Avesta. It contains:

1. THE YASHTS, twenty-one prayers and hymns in adoration of specific deities or angels as Parsi theology terms them.

2. THE AFRINGAN, miscellaneous rituals.

3. THE SIROZAH, a devotional calendar with invocations to the beings that preside over the thirty days of the month.

4. THE GAHS, prayers to be used in the five divisions of the day.

5. THE NYAYISH, petitions to the powers of nature.

In addition to the above, there is an extensive literature produced by later authors in Pahlavī, which has little value except insofar as it has preserved otherwise lost Avestan texts. The most recent body of literature records rituals written in modern Persian. The Avestan and Pahlavī are dead languages known to a very small group of Western Orientalists and Parsi Dasturs (High Priests), who are far from agreement on their correct translation. Therefore, the average student is limited to such translations as the three volumes on the Avesta and the five volumes of Pahlavī selections contained in the forty-nine volumes of *Sacred Books of the East* edited by Max Müller.

HISTORY OF ZOROASTRIANISM

Zoroastrianism did not die with its founder, but lived on reanimating the life of ancient Iran. For one hundred years (583-480 B.C.) the national revival it produced developed unchecked until finally stopped in Europe by the Greeks at the battle of Salamis. For Biblical students the most important event of this century of expansion was the conquest in 539 B.C. of its western neighbor, Babylonia, thus bringing the Jews into contact with Cyrus and the great empire which Darius later ruled.

For two centuries, from the Persian conquest of Babylon to the invasion of Persia by Alexander the Great in 331 B.C., Zoroastrianism was the dominant faith of a vast empire stretching from the Indian Ocean to the Mediterranean Sea. Though the Greeks vanquished the Persians on the battlefield, yet they were deeply impressed by their religion, so that we find many references in Greek literature to Magian wisdom and philosophy. Zoroastrian tradition also asserts that the sacred writings of Iran were translated into Greek. During this Greek period, however, the monotheistic religion degenerated into polytheism. Ahura Mazda came first to be known as Ormuzd, and still later as Mithra, the half-god-half-man symbolized by the sun. Aingra Mainyu came to be called Ahriman, and later Beelzebub. Until the time of Constantine, a corrupted form of Zoroastrianism dominated the Eastern Mediterranean world under the name of Mithraism. The Neo-Platonic school was greatly influenced by this altered Zoroastrianism, and the doctrines of Zoroastrian Manicheism greatly disturbed Christianity for a time.

In A.D. 220 the Avesta was translated into Greek and Latin and an explanation or commentary called the Zend was added. Taken together they are now known as the Zend-Avesta. For about 400 years from this epochal event there was substantial ecclesiastical activity with a vigorous and successful attempt at restoring the religion to the purity of its original faith. Following this temporary revival under the Sassanid Dynasty that re-established Persian independence after 550 years of subjugation, a definite decline set in with the spread of Christianity under Constantine. This diminution of Zoroastrianism was forever sealed by the rise of Mohammedanism as a military power. Even the pages of the Koran, however, are not free from the influence of the faith it all but extinguished. The flickering light of the sacred fire still burns today in the Fire Temples and in the hearts of a mere remnant of Zoroastrians, the so-called Parsis of India—the people from Pars, that is Persia.

After the Battle of Nihavand and the downfall of the mighty Sassanid Empire (A.D. 651), the victorious Moslems gave the defeated Zoroastrians the usual categorical alternative—either the Koran or the sword. Many cast the promise of easy emancipation to the winds and chose rather to die as true Zoroastrians. Some took the verses of the Koran on their tongues—*La ilaha illa-l-lah! Muhammadur-Rasul-elah*—but kept the old Zoroastrian doctrine enshrined in their hearts—*humat, hūkhat,* and *huvarsht* (good thoughts, good words, and good deeds). Still others fled the country to Ormuz where they suffered unbelievable hardships. Finally in A.D. 717 the banished people arrived at the little port of Sanjan, sixty miles north of Bombay, where in Jadav Rana, the Indian monarch, they found a kind-hearted friend. There they re-established the sacred fire brought with them from Persia and there a hereditary priesthood kept up the traditional interpretation of such scriptures as they were able to preserve. These priests were the backbone of the community, preventing them from assimilating with the masses by emphasizing their national characteristics. At first their own weakness and the enervating nature of the Hindu environment in which they were immersed reacted on their faith until their creed was hardly outwardly distinguishable from lower forms of Hinduism. Their sacred canon had long since been closed and their isolation checked the normal development of their religion. Their prosperity and freedom, however, attracted other immigrants from Moslem-held Iran, whose more orthodox devotion infused new interest into the old faith. More recently the sacred languages have been studied, the sacred books edited and translated, and European savants have performed the great task of interpreting the Zoroastrian faith to the world. The foundation for the labors of these European philologists was prepared by the great Neriyosang Dhawal and his followers, who set up a school of Avestan and Pahlavī studies at Sanjan, where translations of the old texts were made into Sanskrit. With this religious revival, initiated in 1770 by the translations of the French scholar Anquetil du Perron, has come a fraternal interest on the part of prosperous Indian Parsis in the even smaller remnant (about 10,000) still seeking out an existence in their ancient fatherland.[9]

Although the fortunes of history placed the Parsis at the very bottom so far as worldly circumstances were concerned, yet these monotheistic agriculturalists early displayed their adaptability and were soon pioneering every field afforded by their adopted land. Until the end of the eighteenth century, Sūrat, Navsāri, and the neighboring area of Gujarāt were their only abode. Later the commercial predominance of Bombay attracted many to that city. From there they have spread thinly over all India and the centers of commerce throughout the East. They have often been called the Jews of India, for they display unusual industry and intellect as they mingle intimately and successfully in the trade of the land but ever retain their

[9]Cf. H. D. Dārukhānawāla, *Parsi Lustre on Indian Soil*, Intro. by J. R. B. Jeejeebhoy.

distinctiveness and the iconoclastic tenets of their faith. Some students have attempted to identify them with the ten tribes of Israel lost to history in the cities of Media. With the advent of the British in India these representatives of the laws of the Medes and Persians made themselves indispensable as the middlemen between the East and the West, a position they still retain, even if somewhat precariously, within the new Republic of India.

There are many similarities in the tragic history of the Zoroastrian people to the history of Israel. Both were crushed by conquerors. Both suffered exile. Both are "a people scattered and peeled." Until recently both were and even now the Zoroastrians are, a people without a national homeland. Yet both these people held tenaciously to the faith of their fathers and to their national identity. The superior strength of the Jewish faith is displayed in its more successful maintenance of pure monotheism and an unwavering sense of its divine election and mission. Having lost both these qualities, the Parsis have become an exclusive "caste"—a museum piece among the religions of the world.

OUTWORKING OF THE PARSI INHERITANCE

We have seen that traditional Zoroastrianism is a religion productive of action, hope, and morale. We have been told that the modern Parsi holds tenaciously to his ancient faith. Now let us examine to what extent he practices his heritage as an everyday, living faith.

The spiritual life of the Parsi community centers around three buildings: the home where he is born, the Fire-temple (Atash Bahram) where he worships, and the Tower of Silence (Dākhma) in which his body is exposed after death. In the first two all ceremony centers about the tending of the sacred fire. The third owes its existence to the necessity of keeping the element of fire, along with earth, and water, free from contamination. This has led some to call the Parsis, "fire-worshipers." This accusation they vehemently deny. They claim that fire to them is no more than a symbol of the purity and righteousness of Ahura Mazda, just as the cross symbolizes for Christians the sacrifice of their Saviour.

The spiritual life of the individual Parsi begins with the impressive ceremony known as the Navjote (New Priest). This ceremony may take place at the early age of seven or as late as eleven. It cannot be postponed beyond puberty for the child would then be guilty of "running about uncovered" and would therefore be claimed by Angra Mainyu. The protective covering provided in this induction of the novice consists of the sacred shirt (*sudra*) and the sacred cord (*kusti*). The investiture may take place in the child's home or in one of the assembly halls that usually adjoin a Fire-temple. After the preliminary bath, the one to be initiated sits before the officiating priest naked to the waist under his shawl. A new set of clothes lies before the priest.

The ceremony begins as the priest recites a prayer (the Patet, or confession) and the child responds with the Honover (short for "*Ahura vairo*"), the "Pater Noster" or "Our Father" of Zoroastrianism. Then both stand and recite in the original unknown tongue a creed praising the Mazdāyāsnian Law as given by Mazda through Zarathustra. Following this, the priest invests the child with the sacred shirt in the prescribed manner, and after the recitation of another creed winds the sacred cord three times about the child's waist. As this is done there is a chanting of prayers and a reciting of scripture portions. The ceremony finally terminates in a benediction, after which the priest takes the child for his first visit to the Fire-temple.[10]

The sacred shirt is made of choice white muslin symbolizing innocence, light, and purity. It is made of many pieces stitched together under the arms. The front half represents the future, the back half the past, with the wearer in between. Thus the Parsi always symbolically has his back turned to the past as he faces the future. The most important part of the shirt, however, is its solitary pocket located below the collar in the front. This is called the "purse of righteousness" (*gariyan*). The Parsi is expected to examine it daily to see if it is filled with the monetary rewards of industry as well as righteous deeds of mercy.

The sacred cord symbolizes the three basic principles of Zoroastrianism: good thoughts, good words, good deeds. It is tied with two relief knots in front and two in back. These knots represent the four elements—fire, earth, air, and water. At each end of the cord are three tassels typifying the six sacred festivals which must be ob-

[10]Cf. J. H. Moulton, *op. cit.*, pp. 160-164.

served every year. Furthermore the cord itself is made of seventy-two threads just as the Yasna consists of seventy-two chapters. The *kusti* like the *sudra* is worn by women as well as men. It is believed to preserve both body and soul from the power of the evil spirit. Instead of being worn over the shoulder as is the sacred cord of the Hindus, it is used as a girdle around the waist. Even reformed and agnostic Parsis who have discontinued the use of the *sudra* generally continue to wear the *kusti* under their street clothes.

Both the sacred shirt and the sacred cord are worn at all times by the orthodox. The only exception is the time of bathing. The *kusti* must be ceremonially untied and retied upon getting out of bed, before each meal, before prayers, after bathing, and when visiting the water closet. It must be tied in the prescribed manner along with the recitation of the last two prayers used in the initiation ceremony. Thus the devout Parsi repeats these formulas seven or eight times a day year in and year out with his face toward the light—either that of sun, moon, sacred fire, or lamp. This does not, however, comprise the sum total of his daily prayers. He may add those prescribed for the five Gāhs (the five divisions of the twenty-four-hour day), those for the dead, those for the festivals of the new moon and the full moon, those at the autumnal equinox, and the many other holy days, each one of which is sacred to some specific divinity. Outwardly the Parsis are certainly a religious people. Public and private prayer occupies a prominent place in their lives. But these prayers for many have become a dead form, the intonation of meaningless syllables in a dead language they do not understand. Even worse they are generally regarded as *mantras* or spells having an inherent potency if pronounced correctly. When any religious system lays its principal emphasis upon a punctilious performance of ceremony, and attributes occult power to prayers correctly chanted, it makes of sin an inconsequential thing that can be blotted out by mere mechanical processes. It is at this very point that Parsiism especially offends.

Space does not permit the detailed recitation of ceremonies connected with marriage, the purification of the mother after childbirth, the monthly feasts (Fasans), the seven high days, and other special holy days. All of these lay great emphasis on purity, for ceremonial purity is the most highly prized virtue in Zoroastrianism. This almost absurd devotion to ritualistic purity accounts for their unusual method of disposing of the dead. Their doctrine of the sacredness of the four elements forbids burial or cremation, for a dead body to them is unclean; therefore, the body is exposed in a Tower of Silence from the parapet of which scores of vultures watch the funeral cortege as it slowly winds its way up the hill. The mourners walk two by two behind the iron bier carried by inferior priests permanently set aside for this unclean service. Arriving before the Tower the procession halts. The priests carrying the body of the deceased up the flight of steps alone enter the enclosure where they lay their burden in one of the three sections reserved for men, women, and children. The waiting scavengers eagerly pounce upon the body as soon as the priests withdraw and clap their hands. In Bombay where a large Parsi population assures constant use of the Towers, a bare ten minutes elapses before the flesh is consumed to the last shred. Twice a year the bleached bones are pushed into the central well of the Dākhma where they are reduced to powder by the action of the elements. For the Parsi our burial customs appear exceedingly wicked, since burying of the dead according to his sacred books is an unpardonable sin. Zoroastrianism challenged the widely held view that the future life was dependent upon the preservation of the human body. Instead of doing everything possible to delay the disintegration of the body, it advocates that the process be hastened. Thus it teaches that there need be no concern as to what happens to the physical remains after death. In the words of the Vendidad it would be a small task for the Creator, who had originally created all out of nothing to reassemble the disembodied frame of man. The questions: "Whence does a body form again, which the wind has carried and the water conveyed?", "And how does the resurrection occur?", are answered as follows: "Observe that when that which was not was then produced why is it not possible to produce again that which was? For at that time one will demand the bone from the spirit of earth, the blood from the water, the hair from the plants, and the life from fire, since they were delivered to them in the original creation." Yet with this advanced enlightenment is mixed many superstitions from nature worship, such as the four-eyed dog (*sag-dīd*) which is supposed to be able to frighten away the demon of the dead by its mere glance.

Many educated Parsis are in revolt against the crude and meaningless ritual that circumscribes their lives, and are seeking to purge it from such revolting practices as the washing of a corpse in *gomez* (bull's urine) or the setting apart of a mother as unclean until the fortieth day. These reform efforts are almost entirely negative and have therefore been doomed from the start. Until the Parsi Reformation includes a positive affirmation of basic religious principles, its denunciation of apparent error will have little appeal to the spiritually starved of the Parsi community. Today the Parsis are divided into a credulous orthodox portion and a reforming section that renounce everything that does not stand their test of pure reason. Far worse than either of these extreme groups is the religious indifference and apathy of the majority, who have lost all consciousness of the unseen and even shrink from discussing the good in their own religion lest they should be constrained to share it with others.

Thus we see that the Parsi inheritance of high religious ideals through the Gāthās has not made of them a religious people. For all the superiority of their religion to that of their Indian neighbors, it seems to be disintegrating and to be unable to command earnestness and reality in its own community. The Parsi Society as a whole is moving rapidly toward unbelief and an unrestrained materialistic pursuit of wealth and pleasure. The failure of this ancient religion of noble precepts illustrates dramatically wherein the supreme need of man lies. Man needs not a teacher, nor even a living example, but life—eternal life. This, and much more besides, is precisely what our Lord Jesus Christ gives. Zarathustra led the Zoroastrians a long way from the barbarisms of his day; in the fullness of time the incarnate Son of God came into this world to fulfill and provide that salvation concerning which the prophets could only foretell. Only through the cross of Christ is the power of sin canceled; only through the incarnate Word is eternal life imparted. The Parsis must be led on from all that is best in their religion to say with Christ's disciples: "Lord, to whom shall we go? thou hast the words of eternal life" (John 6:68).

THE PARSI AND MISSIONS

From all that has been written concerning the nearness of Zarathustra's message to that of Christ's, one would naturally surmise that the road from Zoroastrianism to Christianity would be a short and easy one. Nothing could be farther from the truth. For the Parsi the good of his own religion is the bitter enemy of the best as found in Christ. Like the Jew, whom he resembles in so many ways, the Parsi stubbornly resists the claims of Christ. Like the Jew, with unmovable assurance and unlimited pride, he points back to an outstanding prophet who established his faith in the very dawn of history. Like the Jew, he is too self-satisfied with the splendor of the past and the prosperity of the present to heed that founder's prophecy concerning the coming of a greater Prophet who would be the future Saviour. Like the Jew, he has added ritualistic accretions and traditions of less inspired men until the original spiritual beliefs have been made of noneffect. Like the Jew, he gives more attention to his Vendidad (which corresponds to the Talmud) than to his more spiritual writings. Like the Jew, he finds the cross of Christ an offense; his proud Asiatic heart stubbornly rebels at accepting salvation as a free gift like the alms of a beggar. He insists it must be purchased by exhausting works. Like the rich young ruler of Jewish extraction, the Parsi has a yearning for eternal life that leads him to ask: "What must I do?" But having received the divine answer he turns away sorrowfully, for he has great riches of spiritual tradition as well as worldly acquisitions with which he is unwilling to part in order to follow Christ.

To interest a Parsi in Christianity one must approach him as an equal. His religious heritage, although inadequate, is truly great. If ever the methods used by the apostle Paul on Mars' Hill are to be adopted in the proclamation of the Gospel to unbelievers, they should be used in dealing with the Parsi. His inordinate pride demands that you begin with his own neglected and little understood but prized religious forms. Only then can he be led on from their emptiness to fullness of salvation in the Lord Jesus Christ.

Remembering the above it is quite understandable that little missionary work has been done among the Parsis. Dr. John Wilson, founder of the Christian college of Bombay that still bears his name, was probably the first and most illustrious missionary to devote himself especially to a ministry among these people. The earliest Parsi converts were two youths baptized by him in 1839. One of these boys later became the greatly admired minister, Dhanjibhai Navrojji.

Missionaries who have labored among the Parsis exclusively have been a very small, choice group. One of the most faithful of these was Miss Mary Dobson who on August 22, 1923, by death terminated twenty-three years of consecrated service in the Missionary Settlement for University Women in Bombay. Like the number of missionaries, the number of Parsi converts has been exceedingly small, yet their spiritual quality and outstanding natural gifts have been most extraordinary. The mere mention of such names as those of Miss Susie Sarabji, the Poona educationalist; Miss Gulbai Vakil, the convert who published an open letter to the Parsi High Priest on the occasion of her baptism; Rev. Darashaw, pastor of the Union Church in Ootacamund, where many of us missionaries worship during our hot-season leave, will serve to illustrate this fact. Like the Jews of Paul's day, the Parsis once converted are divinely prepared by ages of moral training to go forth immediately into the Master's vineyard in effectual service for Him. And yet the Christian Church today is carrying out its missionary program almost as if the 100,000 and more Indian Parsis did not exist. Certainly this blind-spot in missionary statesmanship should be diagnosed for what it is—failure to carry out the divine commission of our ascended Lord. Even as the great apostle to the Gentiles continued going first to the synagogue of the Jews for the difficult ministry of recruiting ready-made workers for the missionary task, ought not Christ's ambassadors in western India go constantly to those people whose prophet predicted a coming Saviour and whose priests were the first Gentiles to worship the Babe of whom it was prophesied: "Thou shalt call his name Jesus: for he shall save his people from their sins"? (Matt. 1:21). Then will the descendants of the Magi offer unto Him not only "gold, frankincense, and myrrh," but also their own hearts as altars aflame with the holy fire of divine love.

BIBLIOGRAPHY
BOOKS NOT MENTIONED IN THE TEXT

CASARTELLI, L. C. *The Philosophy of the Mazdayasnian Religion under the Sassanids* (tr.) Bombay: 1889.

CROOKE, W. *Imperial Gazetter of India.* Vol. I, pp. 439, 440, Oxford: 1907.

DHALLA, M. N. *Zoroastrian Theology from the Earliest Times to the Present Time.* New York: 1914.

230   *Religions in a Changing World*

French Views on Zoroastrianism Translated from the Texts of M. Adolphe Franck and M. Jules Oppert, Bombay: 1868.

GRAY, L. H. *The Foundations of the Iranian Religions.* Bombay: 1925.

GUTHRIE, K. S. *The Life of Zoroaster in the Words of His Own Hymns.* Brooklyn: 1914.

HAUG, M. *Essays on the Sacred Language Writings and Religion of the Parsis* (3rd ed., ed. and enlarged by E. W. West). London: 1884. (Esp. Essay IV.)

HENNING, W. B. *Zoroaster, Politician or Witch-Doctor?* Oxford: 1951.

J. M. *The Parsis and Their Religion* (Christian Literature Society for India). Madras: 1900.

MACNICOL, N. *The Living Religions of the Indian People.* Edinburgh: 1934, pp. 233-266.

"A Missionary." *Comparison of Zoroastrianism and Christianity.* Surat, B. S., India: 1886.

MODI, J.J. *The Religious Ceremonies and Customs of the Parsees* (2nd ed.). Bombay: 1937.

MOULTON, J. H. *Early Zoroastrianism.* London: 1913.

———. *The Teaching of Zarathushtra* (Eight Lectures Delivered to Parsis in Bombay). Bombay: 1919.

PARKS, L. *His Star in the East* (*A Study in the Early Aryan Religions*). Cambridge, 1887, pp. 201-242.

ZAEHNER, R. C. *Zurvan* (*A Zoroastrian Dilemma*). Oxford: 1955.

———. *The Teachings of the Magi.* London: 1956.

TRANSLATIONS OF ZOROASTRIAN LITERATURE

MILLS, L. H. *Sacred Books of the East* (Yasna) Vol. 31:1-332 pp. 1-194 cover the 17 chapters of the Yasna known as the Gāthās).

DARMSTETER, J. *Sacred Books of the East* (Vendidad) Vol. 4:1-240.

———. *Sacred Books of the East* (Yashts) Vol. 23-21-345.

WEST, E. W. *Sacred Books of the East* (Pahlavī Texts). Vol. 5, 18, 24, 37 and 47.

GUTHRIE, K. S. *The Hymns of Zoroaster.* Brooklyn: 1914 (Transliterated text, translation, concordance and dictionary with brief notes).

BODE, DASTUR FRAMROZE ARDESHIR and NANAVUTTY, PILOO. *Songs and Zarathushtra* (*The Gāthās*). London: 1952.

BLEECK, A. H. *Avesta: The Religious Books of the Parsees, Spiegel's German Trans.,* 1884. (3 vol.).

WORKS QUOTED IN TEXT

DARUKHANAWALA, H. D. *Parsi Lustre on Indian Soil.* Bombay: 1939.

DURANT, W. *The Story of Civilization, Our Oriental Heritage.* New York: 1935.

JACKSON, A. V. W. *Zoroaster, the Prophet of Ancient Iran.* London: 1889.
———. *Zoroastrian Studies.*
MOULTON, J. H. *The Treasure of the Magi.* Oxford: 1917.
MÜLLER, M. *Chips from a German Worship.* New York: 1881.

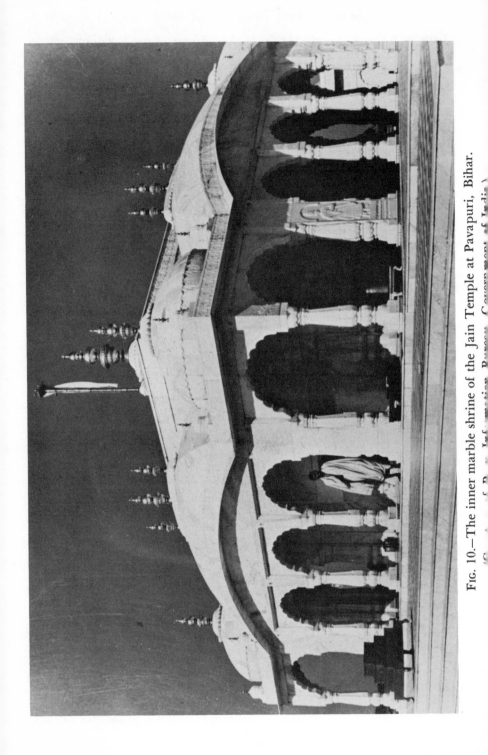

Fig. 10.—The inner marble shrine of the Jain Temple at Pavapuri, Bihar.
(Courtesy of Bureau Information Bureau, Government of India.)

This is the quintessence of wisdom: not to kill anything. Know
this to be the legitimate conclusion from the principle of the
reciprocity with regard to non-killing.
Sutrakritango.

Book 1, Lecture 1, Chapter 4, verse 10.

X.

Lesser Living Religions of India

by PAUL C. HAAGEN *

PART TWO—JAINISM

INTRODUCTION

J AINISM IS PROBABLY THE LEAST-KNOWN among the living religions
of the world. This is possibly due to the lack of interest displayed by European scholars in this quiescent faith. No scientific or
comprehensive account of the religion was available until Buhler
prepared a treatise in 1877 entitled *On The Indian Sect of the Jains
(Uber Die Indiscae Secte Der Jaina),* and Jacobi edited the *Kalpa-
Sūtra of Bhadrabāhu* (1879) and published his article on "Mahāvīra
and His Predecessors" (1880). With some notable exceptions, Jainism has fared little better at the hands of Indian scholars. Even today Jainism offers more unexplored historical problems and a larger
volume of untranslated literature than any other Indological study.
So eminent and learned an Orientalist as Dr. E. W. Hopkins in his
book entitled *The Religions of India* states the following concerning Jainism: "A religion in which the chief points insisted upon are
that one should deny God, worship man and nourish vermin has
indeed no right to exist, nor has it had as a system much influence
on the history of thought."[1] Dr. Hopkins later acknowledged the
unfairness of this judgment. Yet to this day, in spite of the great

*For biographical statement, see Chapter IX.

[1]E. W. Hopkins, *The Religions of India,* p. 297.

corrective work accomplished by scholars of East and West, Jainism still suffers more fantastic and unfounded conclusions than any other religion that has produced a high standard of character and morality in its people.

Jainism does hold a notable place among the religions and philosophical systems of its native India. It is the oldest personally founded religion of that land of religions. It was the earlier of two contemporary reform movements within Hinduism. Thirty-two years later Buddhism arose to exercise with Jainism a democratic and corrective influence over caste-ridden, animal-sacrificing Brahmanism. The primary result of both reform efforts was the founding of separate religions. These two religions, widely as they differ, yet had much in common.

Like Buddhism, Jainism had its rise in Magadha (modern Bihār), opposed the caste system by which it was surrounded, and inspired for a time a missionary spirit in its adherents. Like Buddhism it was a philosophical religion based primarily on the Sānkhya system. Like Buddhism its metaphysical speculations occupied a subordinate place to its high development of moral principles, in contrast with the orthodox systems of Indian philosophy. It differed from Brahmanism, even as Christianity from Judaism, in rejecting outward ceremonies and theological knowledge as evidence of holiness, and in its insistence on purity of heart and life displayed in relation to one's neighbors, both animal and human.

Buddhism and Jainism also agree in opposing Brahman claims of exclusive right to monastic orders and spiritual leadership. Both were heretical movements to establish non-Brahmanic orders and are therefore monastic in character and outlook. Both may be described as atheistic, for they agree in denying the existence of a personal, supreme Spirit. The fundamental doctrine of both is that life is characterized by suffering. To redeem mankind from the miseries of this mundane existence through the annihilation of desire is the chief pursuit of both religions. This is accomplished by the renunciation of the world and by the practice of kindness to all creatures. Thus both are pessimistic religions facing toward nirvāna as their supreme goal of deliverance from endless rebirths, although for each this final goal has a different content and meaning.

Jainism resembles Buddhism: (1) in rejecting animal sacrifices;

(2) in renunciation of the Vedic scriptures that prescribe these sacrifices; (3) in repudiation of a Supreme Deity; and (4) in utilization of the vernaculars for religious teaching and sacred writings.

These two religions are so similar that Jainism was long considered to be only a sect of Buddhism. Research has established them as distinct systems founded by the two foremost teachers of many who opposed Brahmanism in the sixth century B.C. For all their similarity of background, they are in fundamental variance in some essential respects.

The most outstanding difference between these two sister religions is in regard to their teaching concerning the soul. While Jainism retains belief in the existence of the human soul, Buddhism denies its existence and thus makes salvation the annihilation of the self. Thus the way of salvation and its final goal must differ. Unlike Buddhism Jainism admits of no rivalry between its ascetic members and the laity, for it accepts lay-brothers and lay-sisters, as well as monks and nuns, into full relationship in the congregation (sangh). Thus it does not deprive itself of the support of large groups of adherents. This strength enables it to maintain and also to build some of the finest architectural specimens to be seen in India today. Note, for example, The Dilwārā and other more modern temples on Mount Ābu. Unlike Buddhism, Jainism never completely severed itself from Brahmanism. Neither did it adopt an active missionary program but practiced its peculiar rites in unobtrusive quiet. Accordingly it has never disappeared from the land of its birth as Buddhism did almost 1,000 years ago. Neither has it become a world religion like Buddhism but has remained confined to the land of its inception with its chief influence restricted to the trading centers of western India. Today the order is largely recruited from the merchants and bankers of Gujarāt, Mārwār, and Rājputāna, and from the agriculturalists of Karnataka District near Belgaum, but not from among the natives of Bihār where the religion had its beginning.

Jainism differs from Buddhism: (1) in recognizing permanent entities like soul (*jiva*) and matter (*ajiva*); (2) in a positive rather than a negative interpretation of nirvāna; (3) in its close integration of clergy and laity; (4) in the exercise of severe austerities; (5) in identifying itself with Hindu customs, manners, and rituals; and (6) in its provincialism.

Jainism is indigenous to India. It is a creation of the Indian spirit and genius, and is accordingly impregnated to a large degree with its peculiarities. These will be examined later. As a system it is closely akin to Hinduism, sharing with it many of its basic beliefs, notably the dogma of the transmigration of souls. It is clearly differentiated from Hinduism by other contradicting tenets and is distinct in its origin, its history, and its organization. After all it is but a phase, even if a heretical one, in the long development of Hinduism. It naturally absorbed elements from the complexity that exists under that name. Even now it responds to and reflects the spirit of Hinduism to a marked degree. Accordingly Jainism has little in common with Christianity. Comparison of the two religions yields striking contrasts as we shall presently note.

Unlike other religions Jainism does not derive its name from its founder (as was the case in Zoroastrianism) nor yet from the people who espouse it (as we shall see in the case of Sikhism), but from the ideal entertained by each votary. The Jains are those who aspire to be Jinas (Victors), like Mahāvīra, the Jina par excellence, the twenty-fourth Thirthankara (he who shows the fording-place of virtue) in the long succession of emancipated souls venerated by the Jains. Its very name indicates the ethical nature of this faith. The central fact in this system, determining its discipline and establishing its goal, is the all-absorbing desire for deliverance from rebirth—the emancipation known only to Conquerors (Jinas).

MAHAVIRA

599 (?) -527 B.C. (?)

As in many other countries, the sixth century B.C. witnessed a revival of religious activity and heightened spiritual aspirations in India. This movement centered in Bihār, and was led by such bold reformers as Mahāvīra, Buddha, Goshāla, and Jamāli, all founders of heretical sects. Yet of the many ancient orders then established only one has survived to the present day in India—that one is Jainism, founded by Mahāvīra or his master, Pārshvanātha.

The historical dates of Mahāvīra, the last of the recognized Thirthankaras, is a subject of debate, but it seems to be established that he was a contemporary of Zoroaster, Confucius, Lao-tze, Jeremiah,

Ezekiel, and Buddha. In the Buddhist scriptures he is called Nāta-putta. Some biographical material is found in three of the canonical books translated into English, but no attempt has been made to furnish a continuous biography of the founder. Even these scattered references were written 1,000 years after Mahāvīra's death and are a chronicle of purported miracles connected with his birth.

Mahāvīra is believed to have been born the second son of a petty rajah named Siddhārtha, a Kshatriya by caste. His mother was Princess Trishalā. He was named Vardhamāna by his royal parents but has become known to posterity by the title Mahāvīra (Great Hero). His parents, according to Jain tradition, were followers of Pārshvanātha, the twenty-third Thirthankara, believed to have lived 250 years before Mahāvīra. Some scholars consider Mahāvīra's teachings little more than a codification of this little-known predecessor's creed. It is probably true that he was no innovator, yet his strict reforms set his imprint so deeply on the Jain congregation that later ages look to him as the outstanding teacher and example.

Like Gautama he was not only born into the warrior caste but also into luxurious surroundings (*Sacred Books of the East*,[2] 22:192-193). He married Yashodā of the Koundinya Gotra princely family and had one daughter, Anojjā by this marriage. Upon the death of his parents, Mahāvīra, who was about thirty years of age, renounced his duties as a householder, and left Vaishali to become a sādhu (ascetic), in an effort to obtain salvation (S.B.E., 22:200). After twelve years of meditation and self-mortification so profound as to destroy the last of all karma (the cause of rebirth), he is reported to have received that which he sought: "During the thirteenth year, in a squatting position, with joined heels, exposing himself to the heat of the sun, with the knees high and the head low, in deep meditation, in the midst of abstract meditation, he reached nirvāna, the complete and full, the unobstructed, unimpeded, infinite and supreme, best knowledge and intuition, called Absolute [Kevala]. When the Venerable One had become an *Arhata* [one worthy of veneration] and Jina [Conqueror of the eight karma] he was a Kevalīn, omniscient and comprehending all objects" (S.B.E., 22:201). This was not the final nirvāna reached at the dissolution of the body, for he spent thirty more years upon this earth instructing his followers, but was

[2]Hereinafter designated S.B.E.

rather that state of god-like omniscience unhampered by worldly connections, a state called by orthodox philosophers *jivanmukt*.

Having become a *kevali* (omniscient being) at forty-two years of age at Jrimbhikagrāma on the Rijupālikā River, Mahāvīra wandered over a wide area teaching his religious system, organizing groups of ascetics, and making converts of high and low, among whom were four kings. He apparently visited all the principal towns of Bihār. The rainy seasons were spent in accordance with his own precept at his home town and at Rājagriha, the old capital of Magadha. "When the rainy season has come . . . many living beings are originated and many seeds just spring up. . . . Knowing this one should not wander from village to village, but remain during the rainy season in one place" (S.B.E., 22:136).

At the time of his death at seventy-two years of age, Mahāvīra had succeeded in establishing a community of 14,000 monks, 36,000 nuns, 159,000 lay-brothers, 358,000 lay-sisters, and about 5,400 *kevali* (S.B.E., 22:267). His death occurred in the house of the scribe of King Hastipāla, ruler of Pāpa (modern Pāvāpurī), where he was spending the Pajjusana (principal Jain festival held at the close of the Jain year). Several Jain temples in an enclosure mark the site, which is still visited by thousands of Jain pilgrims especially at Divālī time. It is incorrectly claimed that Divālī (Festival of Lamps), the most universally celebrated religious holiday in India, observed by Jains and Hindus alike, was instituted to commemorate Mahāvīra's death. According to Jain chronology this event took place in 527 B.C.

HISTORY AND SECTS

Mahāvīra organized monastic groups which he placed under the supervision of his disciples. All these orders perished with the passage of time except that of the five hundred monks under Suddharma, the converted Brahman. All present-day sects trace their spiritual descent through him.

Two centuries after the death of Mahāvīra the great Maurya Emperor Chandragupta (322-298 B.C.) is reputed to have embraced the faith. A devastating famine during the closing years of his reign made it impossible for the starving population to support the large body of monks then in eastern India. Abdicating his throne he led a group of monks to southern India, where they established a famous center of Jainism at Shravana Belgōla in Mysore.

This new center in the south observed a stricter asceticism than that commonly practiced in the north. Their distinguishing conduct gradually produced contending parties. Sometime in the first century of the Christian era these differences produced the great schism within Jainism which persists to this day. The Digambara (sky-clad) separated from the Shvetāmbara (white-clad) over the troublesome issue of clothing. The former rejected all clothing as harmful to the spiritual life, whereas the latter, on the authority of Pārshvanātha, maintained that white clothes do not impede the spirit. Although with the coming of the Mohammedans the Digambara Jains were compelled to wear a minimal loincloth, yet their ascetics continue to practice what they profess. When they are compelled to move from place to place an obliging cordon of Digambara householders surround them in order that the stark-naked sight of these holy men on their way to nirvāna might not bring public offense. Since it is impossible for women to go about nude, they are excluded from the monastic orders of the Digambara and cannot on that account attain to salvation. Their only hope lies in being reborn as a man who can become a naked monk. The Shvetāmbara practice no such inequality of the sexes but maintain separate nunneries for the white-clad women who aspire to the bliss of doing nothing forever and ever (nirvāna). The chief difference of worship between the two sects lies in their representations of the twenty-four Thirthankaras. Whereas the Shvetāmbara clothe their idols, the Digambara worship images as naked as the munis who adore them. The literature of the two factions is also distinct. Although the differences between the two sects are not great, the feeling is.

With the conversion of the missionary-minded Samprati, grandson of the Buddhist Emperor Asōka, Jainism began to spread throughout India and even into Afghanistan. Owing to this and the subsequent patronage of the princess of Gujarāt and Mārwār, the center of Jainism shifted from its Holy Land of Bihār to its mission field in Gujarāt. When the historic conference to determine the canon of the Jain scriptures was called in A.D. 514 (?), it met at Vallabhi near present-day Bhāvnagar in the new Bombay State.

The golden period of Jain prosperity extended from this Council

of Vallabhi to the thirteenth century. Throughout the medieval period its political influence was considerable. Its adherents held high
offices such as that of prime minister in most of the courts of western,
central, and southern India. Under King Kumārapāla (1125-1159),
who was a convert of the celebrated Jain scholar Hemachandra,
Jainism became the State religion of Gujarāt, building artistic Jain
temples, prohibiting the killing of animals, and establishing Gujarāt
as the permanent stronghold of Jainism.

Although by making concessions to Brahmanism, Jainism was able
to survive the revival of Hinduism that swept Buddhism from India,
yet it had fallen on evil days which worsened into the horrible devas-
tations wrought by the Mohammedan conqueror, Ala-ud-dīn. During 1297 and 1298 he demolished many stately shrines, destroyed
irreplaceable libraries, and massacred large communities throughout
Gujarāt. Jainism has never recovered its temporal power and to this
day displays consequences of that conquest in its close union with
Hinduism and in its underground Treasure Houses (for the storage
of sacred books) to which no unbeliever is admitted.

The third principal group among the Jains arose as a reform movement of the earlier (1474) Lonkā Shā reforming sect. The Sthānakavāsī Reformation was contemporaneous with Martin Luther and
temporarily accomplished for Jainism what the Protestant Reformation achieved for Christianity. This nonidolatrous sect stresses the
fact that idol worship is not once mentioned in their original scriptures. Except on this very crucial point they differ little from the
Shvetāmbara group from which they indirectly sprang. They are
subdivided into eleven bodies, whereas the older sect is made up of
eighty-four subsects.[3]

SCRIPTURES AND LITERATURE

Jain literature is rich, extensive, and linguistically varied. In addition to the present-day vernacular of western India, it encompasses
languages nowhere else preserved. All the books of the canon are
written in Ardha-Māgadhī, the Prākrit vernacular current in north-

[3]C. J. Shah, Jainism in North India, 1932; C. B. Sheth, *Jainism in Gujarāt* (A.D.
1100-1600). Dr. B. S. Saletore has written a treatise on medieval Jainism dealing
with the religion in Kārnataka with special reference to the Vijayanāgara Empire. The
author has not been able to secure a copy of this book.

central India at the time of Mahāvīra. Later commentaries and poetry are written in an early Marāthī known as Jain-Mahārāstrī. After the turn of the century Sanskrit was used in the north while the early Tamil, Telugu, and Kanarese literatures of the south were predominantly Jain. Hemachandra, the greatest of all Jain writers, was a native of Dhandhukā, a small town in the heart of Gujarāt. Most modern literature is written in Gujarāti although books in English and Hindī are constantly appearing.

Each Jain sect holds a different list of books as comprising the correct canon. The Digambara Canon differs so completely from the others that the student is inclined to conclude the sect was not present at the codifying Council of Vallabhi in A.D. 514 (?). The Shvetāmbara and Sthānakavāsī agree on eleven Anga (limbs, or principal members of the body of scripture), twelve Upānga (inferior limbs), and six Chedagrantha. Some groups add certain of the eight Mūlagrantha or some of the thirty Payannā, twelve Niryukti, or nine miscellaneous works, of which the Kalpa-Sūtra is by far the most honored and used. Thus the total number of books in the canon is thirty-three, forty-five, or eighty-four according to the sect. The Shvetāmbara and Sthānakavāsī also agree that there were originally twelve Anga. The missing Anga consisted of fourteen books recording the utterances of Mahāvīra himself. The inclusive name for the whole body of sacred writings for which no special inspiration is claimed is Agamas (precepts). The books of the sacred canon were probably composed sometime before the beginning of the Christian era, but were not reduced to permanent written form until the fifth century. The Jain community generally leave the study of their scriptures to the scholars of their religion and content themselves with books of choice quotations gleaned from them and with the recital of the mere names of those books they hold sacred, in the same manner as Christian children are taught to chant "Genesis, Exodus, Leviticus . . ." all the way through to Revelation.[4]

---

[4]An exhaustive treatment of this subject down to the writings of the past century will be found in the following publications:
J. N. Farquhar, *An Outline of the Religious Literature of India*, 1920, pp. 73-77; 119-121; 162-166; 213-219; 228; 277-283; 359-361.
H. R. Kapadia, *A History of the Canonical Literature of the Jains*, 1941.
H. A. Popley, *The Sacred Kural, or The Tamil Veda of Tiruvalluvar*, 1931.
A. Weber, "Sacred Literature of the Jains," *Indian Antiquary*, 1888-1892.

PHILOSOPHY AND DOCTRINE

Jainism was not a wholly new religious discovery. It was rather a new beginning. Mahāvīra lent the power of his gifts to strengthen, purify, and deepen a tradition from the dark ages of unrecorded history. This popular but unorganized philosophy passed through the cataloguing mind of Mahāvīra essentially unchanged. Thus Jainism attributes its own origin not to Mahāvīra, the twenty-fourth and last Thirthankara, but to Rishabha the first, a figure of remote antiquity, who, if he ever had any existence, lived ages before Mahāvīra. The Veda records this name, and the *Vishnu Purāna* and the *Bhagavata Purāna* relate stories about Rishabha that tally with Jain tradition. The Jains firmly believe their religion is the oldest in India and take great delight in quoting passages from the Hindu scriptures and especially the Veda which prove to them the existence of Jainism when the Veda were being written. Thus we see that Mahāvīra was not a prophet as was Zoroaster, but a reformer who brought religion back from the involved speculations of the rishis, who had made it a system for Brahmans only, to the ideas implicit within early animistic Hinduism. Accordingly the doctrines of Jainism come within the salient features of the Hindu tradition. Neither did Mahāvīra possess the personal charm of Buddha. To a remarkable degree his great powers lay in his unusual gift for organization that displays itself both in his teachings and in the formation of his four orders or *tīrtha*. The existence of Jainism today is due largely to its historical founder's faculty for systematization.

Jainism begins by denying the existence of an eternal Supreme Being, Creator, or Lord, who is the mainstay of the universe. For these nontheistic humanists there is no need to assume a first cause (S.B.E., 45:245). They flatly deny the whole Hindu polytheistic belief in supernatural powers (S.B.E. 22:152), yet they accept most of the gods and demigods of Hindu mythology as little different from man. Accordingly Jains are incensed when their religion is referred to as atheistic. But within the whole of Jainism theistic elements of any sort are few, feeble, and far between, for they believe rather in the eternity of existence, in the universality of life, in the individuality and indestructibility of the human soul, in the immutability of the law of karma, and in human intelligence and self-reliance as the means of liberation (moksha). Deified liberated souls take the place of God. Consequently the practice of prayer was condemned by Mahāvīra (S.B.E., 22:33), although he himself was apotheosized after his death and is now worshiped and prayed to along with twenty-three other Victors or Saints (Thirthankara) despite his own atheistic beliefs. Two modern expositors of Jainism[5] explain: "We worship the Thirthankaras . . . merely for the sake of their purity and perfection, but not for the expectation of any reward in return." The aim of such devotion is to inspire in the devotee a desire to follow in the footsteps of the liberated. It is like the Asiatic giving of alms which has no particular concern with the beggar, but is given in the belief that the exercise of charity is beneficial to the giver. The Jains pray on the assumption that all forms of true worship possess inherent power to advance the spiritual liberation of the worshiper. Help comes not from the gods, nor yet from the liberated Thirthankaras, but from the inherent goodness of prayer and the resourcefulness of man himself. The individual soul can attain godhood by its own continuous efforts. In what is probably his most familiar text, Mahāvīra states: "Man! Thou are thine own friend! Why wishest thou for a friend beyond thyself?" (S.B.E., 22:33).

Shri Jawāharlāl Nehru was voicing the Jain point of view when he wrote: "It has always seemed to me a much more magnificent and impressive thing that a human being should rise to great heights, mentally and spiritually, and should then seek to raise others up, rather than that he should be the mouthpiece of a divine or superior power. Some of the founders of religions were astonishing individuals, but all their glory vanishes in my eyes when I cease to think of them as human beings."[6]

The uncreated universe, according to Jain metaphysics, is divided into two independent, coexisting, everlasting categories. These two realities are the living (*jīva*) and the nonliving (*ajīva*), the finer and the grosser realities. This is considered to be a basic, perfect, and unassailable division. Philosophically speaking this recognition of soul (*purusha*) and matter (*prakriti*) is called dualism. Around this belief the whole religion centers. Thus everything that is, was, or shall be, has been classified as either animate or inanimate. The

---

[5]P. C. Nahar and K. Ghosh, *An Epitome of Jainism*, p. 260.
[6]Shri Jawāharlāl Nehru, *The Discovery of India*, p. 61.

classifications are somewhat surprising to the Westerner for almost everything—insects, plants, fire, water, wind, and even earth—possesses a *jīva* (vital force or soul). Each of these numberless *jīvas* has an entity of its own. The *ajīva* (without soul) is further divided into helping conduct (*dharma*), hindering conduct (*adharma*), space (*ākāsha*), indivisible time (*kāla*), and matter (*pudgala*). This last-named division (*pudgala*) includes the five senses, things enjoyed by the five senses, mind, and all material objects as well as karmas. It is through *jīva* and these five divisions of *ajīva* that the creatorless universe exists. Except in final liberation (nirvāna) the *jīva* is constantly in combination with the *ajīva*. How the *jīva* is fettered without an intervening cause is the unexplained flaw in this elaborate philosophic system. The fact of this bondage is taken as self-evident. The imperative demand is not to discover the means of bondage but of liberation. The matter which keeps the soul in bondage and prevents final liberation is known as karma. It is viewed as material of very subtle form. Every action, every word, every thought, besides its obvious visible effect, produces an invisible transcendental one. Under certain conditions this invisible effect may materialize as rewards or punishments. However this may be, the deeds of the soul, combining with matter (*pudgala*), take on moral distinctions of good or evil and so account for all the suffering in this world. To understand *jīva* and *ajīva* thoroughly in their inherent properties and mutual connections is to understand the source of all our woes and to be prepared for salvation therefrom. Accordingly the Jain theologians (*sāstrakāras*) have formulated nine categories (*nava tattva*) as the foundation of their philosophy. Belief in these nine categories is the doorway to salvation: "He who truly believes the true teaching of the fundamental truths possesses righteousness" (S.B.E., 45:154).

In addition to *jīva* and *ajīva* these nine categories include *punya, pāpa, āshrava, samvara, bandha, nirjarā,* and *moksha*. We agree with Nical Macnicol that "the elaboration of [these] classification [s] of physical and mental states and attitudes does a certain amount of credit to [Jain] ingenuity but has very little relation to the facts either of human intelligence or of religious experience."[7] We will not exhaust the reader by pursuing the elaborate details and sub-

---

[7]Nical Macnicol, *The Living Religions of the Indian People*, p. 180.

divisions of each classification. We must recognize, however, that these concepts, together with the doctrines of karma and transmigration, are the fundamental elements of which Jainism is made.

All the characteristics of the nine categories are connected in one way or another with the soul until it attains release, or *moksha*. *Moksha* is the state in which the soul is entirely free from kārmic forces such as weal (*punya*) and woe (*pāpa*). This is no divine substitution of one thing for another but is the soul coming into its own potential by the removal of obstructing forces. The soul has an upward tendency but it is kept down by the weight of adhering karma like a balloon is held down by its ballast.[8] It is karma that holds the *jīva* in bondage, for it not only determines the kind of birth the *jīva* shall receive but also causes it to be reborn. Only when all deeds—good as well as bad (*punya* as well as *pāpa*) —are exhausted will deliverance be attained. This involves the stoppage or impeding of new karma (*samvara*) through control of the mind, body, and speech, as well as the expulsion of existing karma (*nirjarā*). The whole monastic system with its austerities (*tapas*) is designed to accomplish this end. The human activity that causes the inflow of new kārmic matter into the soul is called *āshrava*. These channels (*āshrava*) through which karma enters a *jīva* are catalogued under forty-two heads, chief of which are the five senses. The activities of body and mind that prevent such an inflow are called *samvara*. The investiture of the soul with karma-matter makes for bondage (*bandha*). Thus man is himself responsible for his own condition of freedom or bondage, weal or woe. Although karma is immutable and cannot be changed by prayer or by worship, yet it is not fatalistic. Man is free to exercise his capacity for right action (*ananta-vīrya*). The Jain scriptures assert that through a religious life of austerities, all karma can be destroyed and moksha attained. The doctrine that salvation is secured through human works arrives at its most extreme form in Jainism. We could almost sum up its beliefs in the well-known expression "lifting yourself by your own boot straps." Many Jains daily quote the following Māgadhī *shloka* (stanza of scripture) listed by Mrs. S. Stevenson in her classic on Jainism: "The soul is the maker and the non-maker, and itself makes happiness and misery,

[8]Hermann Jacobi, Encyclopaedia of Religion and Ethics, IV, p. 484.

is its own friend and its own foe, decides its own condition good or evil. . . ."[9]

ETHICS AND DISCIPLINE

The Jain scriptures declare: "This is the quintessence of wisdom; not to kill anything" (S.B.E., 45:247). The duty of noninjury (*ahimsā*) is therefore basic alike for Jain theology and Jain ethics. It occupies the foremost place in Jain thinking as in Hindu ethics generally. It is fundamentally a metaphysical concept devoid of compassion and only becomes a moral principle in the later development of Jainism. Today it is the most dominating characteristic of this religion. The Jains even call their faith, "The Nonkilling Religion" (*Ahimsā Dharma*). Although the Jains are not the originators of ahimsā (it is as old as history), yet they are the present-day specialists of this virtue. The Chhandogya Upanishad of the Hindus teaches nonviolence toward all creatures except at sacrifices. The Sūtras of Gautama give a prominent place to this doctrine. It is Jainism, however, that enthrones this merit as the cardinal basis for a whole system of teaching and conduct.

Modern Jains say *ahimsā* is grounded on the maxim: "Look upon other beings as you would look upon yourself." This is the Golden Rule of Jainism. As an ideal it has been given a prominent place in the discipline of confession used in the Jain faith. Injury (*himsā*) is unavoidable and inevitable. Therefore a daily confession is necessary, for *himsā* is the greatest of all sins, just as abstaining from the taking of life is the most important of all moral obligations.

Jain teachers classify *himsā* under four categories—accidental, occupational, self-defensive, and intentional. A layman is expected to abstain fully from the latter and, as far as possible, from the other three. Stricter observance of the ideal is required of the monk who may not take life of any sort, by any means, at any time, or for any reason. He must not injure any living thing in thought, word, or deed—not even to save his own life. Accordingly a Jain monk carries a broom of peacock feathers as a regular part of his equipment. This he uses to sweep away small unseen insects from the places he intends to sit or walk. Desire to avoid inadvertent destruction of life also explains the rule prohibiting the partaking of food or drink after

[9]Mrs. S. Stevenson, The Heart of Jainism, p. 192.

dark as well as the practice of straining every cup of fluid drink and the habit of carefully examining every mouthful of food eaten. For the same reason the monk does not light a fire but does wear a cloth mask over his mouth. Even the eating of certain vegetables thought to be "alive" is prohibited (e.g., potatoes). Jains admit that the grains, vegetables, fruits, and nuts they do eat, also have life. Since *himsā* cannot fully be avoided they choose to eat forms of life having the fewest sense organs, so that their sin may be the least possible. Hence the greatest possible virtue is to sit still and fast. In the final stages of spiritual attainment this means a fast unto death.

The Jains further distinguish between spiritual murder and actual murder. Both are condemned. Even the wish that death or harm might befall some other living object is considered unworthy of a Jain. Moreover Jain ethics condemn indirect injury just as vehemently as it does direct injury. It is no less a sin to cause injury through an agent or to approve in any way of injury caused by others. This is an advance over Buddhist teaching, which, repudiating injury, nevertheless allows the purchase of meat from a butcher who is an occupational killer. In following this principle to its rationalistic end the Jains bind themselves to be strict vegetarians. In fact, vegetarianism becomes the outward badge of their creed. Wherever Jainism flourishes, as in Gujarāt and Kārnataka, it makes the gastronomic life of the nonvegetarian vexatious and gives practical help to the vegetarian who finds the strict daily practice of his beliefs difficult if not impossible in most societies. The Jains are probably the only people in the world who take the law prohibiting destruction of life so seriously. These beliefs make it impossible for the Jains to countenance war or to condone capital punishment. They are vocal against animal sacrifices in religious ceremonies and vivisection for scientific or medical purposes. The hunting of animals and birds, and the catching of fish for sport or food is anathema to them. Their strict espousal of *ahimsā* has also closed most forms of occupational employment to them. They do not ordinarily engage in agriculture for it necessitates plowing which destroys earthworms and other forms of life. They cannot engage in large-scale industry for it involves the use of machinery that by its operation would destroy lower forms of being. They could not be confectioners for the bakery ovens would cremate insects and vermin. So the conscientious Jain is restricted to becoming a monk, a teacher, an artist, a trader, a clerk or a banker. Nor will he indulge indiscriminate trade. For example, he could never deal in firearms, fishing tackle, or traps. The commodities that give full scope to his talents are gold, silver, precious stones, textiles, insurance, etc. Entering high finance and banking has brought him both wealth and the ill-will of his neighbors.

According to present-day adherents of Jainism, *ahimsā* is not a negative principle but has a positive foundation—that of universal love. The believer in *ahimsā* will extend a loving hand to remove pain and alleviate misery wherever such woes are found. He will be compassionate toward all creatures, benevolent, self-sacrificing. This modern twist to an ancient doctrine seems to indicate the influence of Christianity even upon those who have chosen to reject it. Such allegations are found only in the modern writings of those conversant with the tenets of Christianity.[10] Most Jain writers admit that a spirit of renunciation and resignation characterizes Jainism, and that all its spiritual injunctions are negative. They do insist, however, that positive aspects are deducible from Mahāvīra's teachings, although specific statements expressing the positive implications are wholly lacking. In actual practice active support of living creatures is restricted largely to animals and insects. Throughout the length and breadth of Jain territory the traveler can see that distinctly Jain institution, the animal asylum (*pānjarāpola*). Stray dogs and cats, maimed and half-starved cattle, decrepit and unwanted animals of all kinds and descriptions are sought out and kept in these establishments by the munificence of the Jain laity. The visitor, traveling by public conveyance, is often apprized of their existence by being handed a neatly printed card requesting a donation. It is not an uncommon sight to see devout Jains in earnest search of ants that cannot be institutionalized to feed them sugar. Having completed this prescribed act of religious duty, it is not uncommon for the zealot to return to his creed-determined occupation to "devour widows' houses" without compunction in the normal course of the day's work. It is said that wealthy Jains hire men to sleep on their bug-ridden cots until the multitude of permanent occupants have their fill. When the employee leaves, the master sleeps peacefully on the bed

[10]Shri A. Chakravarthy, M.A., I.E.S., "Jain Ideas in the Modern World," *The Aryan Path*, October, 1954.

so full of undesirable life he may not decimate. Without fear of contradiction it can be stated that the central thought of this unique order is not so much the saving or preserving of life as it is the avoiding of its destruction.

Modern writers also call attention to the implications of the principle of *ahimsā* to the self as well as to other living things: "The strict observance of *ahimsā* forms the main factor in spiritual development. A person trying to observe this principle must adopt a psychological attitude conducive to its observance. He must rid himself completely of all the gross emotions, such as hatred and anger. He must put himself mentally in the place of the suffering beings."[11]

Here again the emphasis is selfish rather than philanthropic. Unlike the Parsis, Jain charity, which is considerable, is largely restricted to animal asylums, the building of temples and the alleviation of distressed members of its own community.

Next to the practice of *ahimsā*, the practice of *tapas* (austerities including fasting) is most important. The object of these austerities is to combat desire, since karma enters man's soul primarily by this avenue. Austerities bring the body under control and thus develop the psychic powers directing the attention to the inner self. By delving deep into the subconscious, self-knowledge superior to sense perception can be gained through telepathy and clairvoyance. This development of soul force is an essential characteristic of Jainism. Thus Jain renunciation and penance has two aspects: one pertaining to externals, and the other to the thought activity of the human soul. The first seeks the abandonment of worldly objects that cause passions to be generated in the soul. The second, or internal penance, involves the destruction of the passions that already exist. External penance is of six kinds: fasting, eating less than appetite demands, total abstinence from delicious foods, minimizing thirst, mortification of the body, and solitude. Internal penance also consists of six kinds: courtesy, service to one's religious teacher (*Guru*), abandonment of the possessive feeling expressed in "I" and "mine," study, meditation, and expiation of sins. The external aspects of penance are intended to bring about internal changes. In actual practice the internal aspects tend to be ignored in preoccupation with superficialities.

Four other ethical maxims spring from the fundamental principle

[11]*Aspects of Jainism*, reprints by The Jain Mission Society, 1955.

of *ahimsā*. They are *satya, astheya, brahmacharya,* and *aparigraha.* These are the principles of truthfulness, nonstealing, chastity, and nonattachment, respectively. They could almost be stated in Biblical commandments: Thou shalt not speak falsehood. Thou shalt not steal. Thou shalt not covet thy neighbor's wife. Thou shalt not set thy heart on material possessions. When put into personal form, these four rules, together with the fundamental one (*ahimsā*), constitute the five vows (*pancha vrata*) of Jainism, the practice of which is incumbent upon all true adherents. These four subsidiary vows are only maintained, however, as long as they do not conflict with the primary one. Thus if the practice of truth results in cruelty to any living thing, it becomes evil, and must give way to the overriding principle of *ahimsā*. As lesser or partial vows (*anuvrata*) these five principles are practiced by all householders and together constitute "right conduct," one of "the three jewels of religion." But the householder's life is only a preparation for the life of a monk. The five lesser vows are but a prerequisite to the five greater or complete vows (*mahāvrata*). The lesser and greater vows are identical in substance but diverse in degree. No concessions are allowed or any limits set for the monk. Let us illustrate with the last two vows: For the householder the fourth vow means chastity, while for the monk it means absolute celibacy. For the layman the fifth vow means nonattachment to material things, while for his spiritual teacher it means total renunciation—a renunciation which according to one sect (Digambara) includes even his clothing.

The *summum bonum* of the Jain religion is the attainment of salvation (moksha). For the Jain it means freedom from an endless cycle of births and deaths in the varying forms of infernal beings, animals, human beings, and gods. This freedom is the result of man's own strenuous efforts in a long series of advancing states. The way to final liberation (nirvāna) is attained by a threefold path: This consists of (1) right knowledge (*samyak-jnāna*), (2) right faith or vision (*samyak-darshana*), and (3) right conduct (*samyak-chāritra*). These virtues constitute the three jewels of religion (*ratnatraya*) essential to a victorious religious life. "Knowledge, faith and right conduct are the true causes of final liberation" (S.B.E., 45:123). Right knowledge is the understanding of Jain philosophy. Right vision may be defined as faith in the Jain scriptures. Right conduct is the day-by-day practice of the first two jewels. It is interesting to compare the Parsi triad of Good Thoughts, Good Words, Good Deeds and the Christian trio of faith, hope, and love with this Jain summation of virtue. Mahātma Gāndhi synthesized them into his own triology of truth, love, and *ahimsā.*

For the ascetic member of the Jain community generally distinguished by the name "continent" (jati), right conduct consists in scrupulous observance of the greater vows described above. After twelve years of progressive austerities following the example of Mahāvīra, the *muni* eventually becomes eligible for the crowning penance of such a life. Over and above the many vows of abstinence he has taken, there remains the greatest vow—to abstain from food and drink for the remainder of life. In the sight of a non-Jain this amounts to suicide by self-starvation. My friend, Sant Bālji, a well-known Jain *muni* of Gujarāt, made this characteristic Jain distinction when discussing this matter with the writer recently: "If a man gives up his life because of weariness of the world, that is suicide. But if he gives up his life voluntarily for some moral principle as Christ did, that is not suicide, but penance." Indiscriminate self-destruction is not encouraged. Only those who are looking upon all things equally and seeking nirvāna with a pure motive after the manner of Pārshvanātha, Mahāvīra, Hemachandra, and the long line of Jain examples that reaches down to our own day, can hope for liberation by such a death (*santhāro*). Even for such a zealot moksha is not a certainty. All depends upon the nature of the seeker's vow and of his mind, or in other words on his karma. To the very end the monk pursues a rigid system of self-help. His religious search, that began and continued with minute regulations to avoid the taking of lower forms of life, ends in giving up its own life that this ideal of noninjury might be fully attained. According to the Uttarādhyayana Sūtra *santhāro* can be practiced in three ways: If at the time of natural death man vows to abstain from food and water, his penance is called *bhakta pratyākhyān.* If in the prime of life a man decides voluntarily to divest himself of all karma and searches out a place devoid of life where he can do so, his penance unto death is known as *ingit maran.* If a man at any time remaining right where he happens to be, closes all his sense organs to the world and sits like a tree without moving until death overtakes him, his penance is called *pādopgamana maran.*

For the lay-brother generally designated a "hearer" (shrāvaka; lay-sister: shrāvikā), right conduct means the observance of the lesser vows and the support of those devoted to the ascetic life. Only ascetics can hope for immediate release. Faithful laymen can entertain no hope beyond that of becoming ascetics in a future life. Yet the house-holder too hopes for *samādhi.* When he knows that death is imminent he cheats the grim reaper of his sovereignty by taking the same terrible vow the ascetic espouses when in the best of health. The way of salvation preached by Mahāvīra and his followers is indeed an arduous one open only to those willing to endure the cruelest of austerities. Nevertheless, in contrast to exclusive Brahmanism, it is open to all who care to tread its rugged path. Even Americans, who have never so much as heard of Jainism, may attain salvation if they unconsciously keep the above vows with their thirty-five karma-destroying rules.

FESTIVALS AND PILGRIMAGE

Of the many holy days observed by the Jains, Pajjusana, the solemn fast that closes the Jain year, is by far the most important. It is almost entirely a spiritual observance. Many Jain laymen fast for the eight days of the celebration while attending the special prayer services and lectures conducted throughout this period. The program is designed so as to cover the entire field of Jain belief and practice during the eight days. The final day is called Samvantsarī. It is a day of fasting, meditation, and confession. Every Jain observes this day even if he neglects all others.

Jainism encourages its laymen to vow performance of a fortnightly repentance (*pashadha*). Thus twice a month the householder temporarily becomes a monk and seeks to balance his spiritual account by payments in the coin of asceticism. If he cannot do this fortnightly, then he should do so at the end of each season—every four months. The majority of Jains, however, perform only the minimum requirement by doing *pashadha* once a year on Samvantsarī. It is an odd coincidence that the writer is penning these lines on the eve of Samvantsarī (September 7, 1956) after returning from the morning lecture covering the two cardinal doctrines of chastity and nonviolence. Tomorrow will be the last day, the great day of the fast. At the close of the meeting those present will ask forgiveness of one another so that no quarrels will be carried over into the new year. Some will go home to write letters to distant acquaintances and non-Jains, asking forgiveness for misdeeds and inadvertent vexations. During the entire period that the sun is in the constellation of Leo the scriptures are read persistently. The Shvetāmbaras concentrate on the Kalph Sūtra; the Digambaras on the Samaysar and the Stānakvāsis on the Uttarādhyayana.

Pilgrimage to the five holy hills (Satrunjaya, Girnār, Ābu, Ashtāpada, and Sameta Sikara) forms an integral part of practical Jainism. Satrunjaya, holiest of the five, about thirty-four miles from Bhāvnagar, is sacred to Ādinātha (also called Rishabhadeva), the first of the Thirthankaras, who is said to have performed penance here. Orthodox Jains from all parts of India make a pilgrimage to this main *tīrtha* (community) where they climb the 1,977-foot mountain, eat once a day, practice strict self-control, and observe personal religious vows. A special religious fair (*yātra*) is held on the full-moon days of the months of Kartik and Chaitra. The most rewarding form of pilgrimage practiced here is called the "ninety and nine." This consists of ninety-nine separate ascents from the bottom of the hill to the principal temple which is encircled in worship. The last few days of climbing are made more difficult by abstinence from food and water. After all ninety-nine ascents have been accomplished, the image of a Thirthankara is installed under a canopy in the main temple court for a special service in which the triumphant pilgrim eleven times performs the eightfold worship: *Fala pūjā*—washing the idol; *Candana pūjā*—marking the idol with auspicious yellow powder; *Puspa pūjā*—the offering of flowers to the idol; *Dhupa pūjā*—the waving of incense before the idol; *Dīpa pūjā*—the waving of a lamp; *Aksata pūjā*—the offering of rice to the idol; *Naivedya pūjā* and *Phala pūjā*—the offering of sweetmeats and of fruits.

The hill of Satrunjaya is unique in that it is reserved for gods alone. It is not used by the people for any purpose other than worship. Apart from the more than 860 temples containing over 11,000 images, the pilgrim finds nothing else on the hillside. All is kept meticulously clean as no one is permitted to reside here or to prepare food on the hillside. The whole area is surrounded by walls and gates that are closed each evening. Perhaps there is no other city of temples in the world like this.

PRESENT STATE OF JAINISM

According to *The Hindustan Year Book of 1956*[12] the Jain community numbers just over one and a half million, or less than one-half of one per cent of the population of India. Due to their great wealth and generally superior education, the Jains occupy a place of greater importance and yield a greater political influence than would naturally be expected from their small numbers. Jainism definitely is a religion of the upper classes, having little appeal to the masses. That it has never been a popular religion is proved by archaeological inscriptions, indicating its present distribution to be practically the same as that of the fourth century. Census reports would seem to indicate a steady decrease in numbers. This may be more apparent than real since there is a growing tendency among the Jains to list themselves as Hindus. The line that divides them from practical Hinduism is indeed a narrow one. They follow the Hindu law of inheritance, except that heirship is not dependent upon the performance of the funeral rites. (The Jains do not practice these rites.) Although repudiating the exclusiveness of caste they are stricter in its observance than most Hindus. They do indulge connubial relationships with corresponding Hindu castes. They visit the Hindu places of pilgrimage and often worship in Hindu temples as well as in their own. They venerate the cow, and call upon Brahman priests (*pujārīs*) to conduct their domestic rites. Many Hindu sects differ more widely from the accepted orthodox tenets than do the Jains and still remain within the fold of Hinduism. More and more Jainism seems to be coming under the great assimilative powers of Hinduism. Less and less is it resisting the almost suffocating embrace of this environing religion.

Many younger Jains are more disturbed by the old ascetic ideal set before them than by the pressures of Hinduism from without. They have observed the hollowness and hypocrisy of much that is maintained in the name of their religion. They are bewildered by the conflict between the tenets of the faith taught in their home and the principles of modern science taught them at school. They are averse, even when they cannot explain why, to the negation of personality

[12]p. 430.

so central to their way of life. In their perplexity they take the easiest course open to them—indifference to the religious system within which they remain nominal adherents. But if the generality of monks as well as householders are superficial in their observance of Jain precepts, performing but conventional ceremonies and outward rites, yet, as in days gone by, there is still a vitality in the ancient system that produces exemplary householders and princely ascetics. Perhaps Jainism's present state of health can best be ascertained by noting the unusual life of one of its recent *munis*.

On September 18, 1955, the Jain world was informed that Shānti Sāgar Mahārāj, head of the Digambar community, had attained nirvāna. Dr. Sarvapalli Rādhākrishnan, India's vice-president and Hinduism's foremost philosopher, paid this tribute: "Shānti Sāgar Mahārāj is one of those exceptional human beings whose spiritual greatness fashions bricks and mortar for the tall edifice of human civilization. He has been a superman, a prince among ascetics. His passing away is a loss to the human race."

Shānti Sāgar had been called the St. Francis of modern India. Like the Christian saint this Jain *muni* lived a life of poverty, chastity, and penance but with a characteristic Jain emphasis. At eighteen years of age he had made up his mind to become an ascetic, but in deference to his parents he refrained from doing so until after their decease. At the age of forty-one, he, like St. Francis, distributed his earthly possessions to the needy. Then he prostrated himself as a disciple at the feet of Sādhu Devinder Kīrti who initiated him into the order of monks as a common sādhu. After a probationary period of four years he was ordained an *upādhāya* (instructor). Five years later he was elected *āchārya* (Superior of an organization of monks).

For almost half a century Shānti Sāgar devoted himself to a life of mortifying the flesh. A whisk of peacock feathers for clearing his path of insects, and a small wooden bowl that would hold a pint of tepid water, constituted his earthly belongings. Of clothing he was entirely lacking. Not even a scant loincloth was retained. The hard earth was his bed and the arching vault of the sky his roof. Once in twenty-four hours he partook of a few morsels of food, eaten in a standing position, and a little water whenever a charitable householder was present to proffer such a gift. But suitable donors were not always at hand and even this daily pittance often went unclaimed. Periodically he pulled out by the root the hair of his head and face.

Most of his time was spent in forest and mountain retreats, fasting, praying, and meditating. From 1928 through 1933, however, with six of his chief disciples, Shānti Sāgar journeyed throughout northern India. This retinue of seven sky-clad *munis* were dubbed Sapta-Rishi (Seven *Rishis*) in allusion to the constellation by the same Indian name. Later they toured through the Gujarāt and Kāthiawār areas of western India. In Dholkā, where the writer has been stationed for some years, the group were compelled by the municipal fathers to leave at 4 A.M. before the town awoke. In spite of many similar rebuffs, Shānti Sāgar and his group traveled over 3,500 miles on foot, led approximately 700 men and women to renounce the world for an ascetic life and greatly increased the interest of believers and nonbelievers in the Jain philosophy and religion.

Shānti Sāgar is also credited with the discovery of two long-lost scriptures reputed to have been written by the founder, Lord Mahāvīra. These scriptures are known as *Jai Dhavala,* and *Maha Dhavala.* They were discovered in the cellar of an ancient temple at Mudbidri. Time had played such havoc with these palm-leaf texts that they disintegrated when touched. Therefore, they were transcribed and later translated into Hindi and English. Their discoverer thought them of sufficient importance to direct their being engraved on copper plates. Prof. Hiralāl, the well-known Sanskrit scholar of Madhyā Pradesh, remarks concerning these texts: "It is a pity the book lay dormant for so many years. Had it been discovered earlier, many an aspiring soul would have been freed and have attained to nirvāna."

So at the age of eighty-four, full of years, works, and austerities, the Jain saint decided to crown his career through engaging in religious suicide (*santhāro*), the time-honored Jain practice of giving up the ghost at will. For thirty-five fateful days he observed a complete fast while he kept to his daily schedule of austerities. Addressing the thousands who came to have a look (*darshan*) at this fearless *yogi* who dared to challenge the dreaded god of death (Yāma), Shānti Sāgar advised: "Leave the easy path. Enter the order of renunciation. Give up all attachment to things which are today, and after a short time cease to be. Think of your soul first and last."

After a final sermon, he asked forgiveness of the multitudes gathered as eyewitnesses to the triumph of the human spirit over the weakness of the flesh. Then he blessed them. Retiring, he uttered a verse from the sacred writings of Mahāvīra and lay down to eternal rest. On the morning of September 18, 1955, the whole world knew that Shānti Sāgar Mahārāj was no more and that Jainism, hoary with age, was still one of the living religions of the world.

The strength of Jainism lies in just such outstanding examples of noble earnestness and utter devotion to religious ideals, however inadequate. These examples although uncommon are by no means rare. While the *ingit sanlakhana* of Shānti Sāgar was being proclaimed in nation-wide headlines, an ordinary Jain laywoman of Kāthiawār espoused the same road to liberation. Her death on a much more limited scale brought new life to Jainism. Organizationally, the lay-members of the order are united by close ties of mutual support to their ascetic leaders, forming an integrated congregation (sangh) —the oldest among the voluntarily entered religious organizations of the world. Coupled with scrupulous care for ancient customs, institutions, and doctrines this system constitutes a "threefold cord not quickly broken." Yet it is a shorn strength. Its impotence can be seen especially in its inability to solve the several problems that have plagued it through its long history. It has had power enough to lessen for a time but not permanently to break the obnoxious shackles of caste. More significant than this social failure is its basic spiritual one. It has never been able thoroughly to purge itself nor its temples of the polytheism and idolatry which it denounces.

JAINISM AND CHRISTIANITY

Jainism and Christianity have many superficial resemblances. Both had their origin in the East and are imbued with an Oriental spirit. Both founders were of royal birth but renounced their high estate to espouse a life of poverty, affliction, and effrontery. Both chose twelve disciples (*ganadhara*). Both suffered at the hands of a wayward disciple (Judas and Goshāla). Both preached meekness, mercy, and salvation from worldly miseries, using the vernacular of the common people and illustrating their teaching from the commonplace objects of everyday life. Here ends abruptly the similarity between the author of fruitless regulations and dead laws and the Giver of life and immortality.

Having noted these superficialities we now turn to fundamentals. Here there is intrinsic divergence. It is well-nigh impossible to conceive of religious systems more dissimilar, giving rise to spiritual effects more opposite in their character and value.

Whereas Christianity is Christ the divine Son of the living God, Jainism is the personal faith of those aspiring to be overcomers (*jinas*) through their own efforts. In place of a supreme God, Jainism has outstanding men of like passions, successful in attaining their own salvation, yet uninterested in the efforts of those still climbing the well-nigh inaccessible heights to nirvāna. Without a deity the religious ideal becomes ritualistic rather than personal holiness. Without a God the Jain desires to be freed from the all-but-endless cycle of births rather than to be freed from sin. Without a Supreme Being the goal of Jainism becomes an unethical attempt at escape from the bondage of existence, rather than a positive effort to attain righteousness by divine help. Personality is suppressed into a deathlike trance rather than being developed into "abundant life" ever unfolding in fuller growth "unto the measure of the stature of the fullness of Christ." Its nontheistic foundations are the basis for the paradox so unaccountable to Westerners—a people intensely religious and yet a people half-hearted in their religion.

Christianity postulates a personal God who desires fellowship with man. It also recognizes a capacity in man to respond to such fellowship. This exalted privilege is realized by faith. It is not beyond the most degraded human being. Such a democratic element is not found in Jainism. Those who have no fellowship with a heavenly Father have no inspiration to look upon fellow human beings as brothers. Jainism is limited to a small company who can indulge asceticism. It has no place for the weak, the halt, and the blind. Babes cannot endure its discipline. Faith has no place here. The spoils go to the strong.

Christianity is characteristically a religion of hope. It is the glad tidings of great joy that God has come down to earth and tabernacled among us. Jainism does not have this message, this Gospel, to relieve its night of despondency. It is characterized by pessimism, the result of intellectualism and austerity.

Not only does humanism rob the Jain of faith and hope but also of love. Love of a personal God would be an attachment binding him the more securely to the cycle of rebirth. Love which is the fulfillment of the law of Christ must, therefore, be rooted out of the heart. All attachments, good as well as bad, must be abandoned.

The apostle Paul, in summing up the Christian graces that have their origin and meaning in Christ, wrote: "And now abideth faith, hope, charity [love], these three; but the greatest of these is charity [love]." Jainism also has its triad of essential graces. On the surface the "three jewels of religion" are not dissimilar: They are "right faith, right knowledge, and right conduct." Here again the emphasis is on the last member of the trio. The intellectual perception is superb; the lyconic style is effective; but the content is defective, for right faith, right knowledge, and right conduct refer to an impersonal system of metaphysics and not to a personal, loving Redeemer.

There is justice (karma) in the Jain system and indeed a certain amount of help for those who help themselves. But man needs more than justice! Man needs divine mercy of which Jainism has no knowledge! It is starkly lacking in even the faintest glimmer of grace, for it is without the gracious One. It is a way, but it knows not The Way, The Truth, and The Life. While it seems to have considerable respect and even love of law, yet it misses the mark because it knows not the law of love personified in the Lord Jesus Christ. Jainism's rigid laws of asceticism, along with all other man-made rules, are peremptorily unmasked by the apostle Paul in Colossians 2:23: "These regulations look wise . . . but in actual practice they do honour . . . to man's own pride" (Phillips). Since Jainism is the very antithesis of a theocratic system it of necessity becomes an egocentric one. Christianity is theistic; Jainism cannot discover any place for God in so mechanical a system as that of karma.

Having examined but one substantial difference with a few of its many, many ramifications, we are at once struck by the pathetic, legalistic emptiness of Jainism. This note is best expressed in the words of an old patriarch of the faith: "It is a terrible thing to a Jain to grow old. We may have tried all our lives to keep our innumerable laws, but we know the awful doom that awaits us if we have broken one of them. For us there is no forgiveness."[13] This will ever

---

[13]Mrs. S. Stevenson, The Heart of Jainism, p. 290.

be the plight of those who trust in the self-sufficiency and self-right-eousness of any system of laws and ordinances. Contrast these fearful forebodings with the triumphant assurance of "such a one as Paul the aged": "I have fought a good fight, I have finished my course, I have kept the faith: henceforth there is laid up for me a crown of righteousness, which the Lord, the righteous judge, shall give me at that day: and not to me only, but unto all them also that love his appearing" (II Tim. 4:7, 8).

It is interesting to note that the disciples of this divergent rite have adopted the methods of Christian missionaries for the advance-ment of their faith. In these days when Christian missions are being Easternized, Orientalized, and Indianized, the Jains have deliberately chosen many of the Western methods of European missionaries for the promulgation of their Oriental religion in an Eastern land. They have organized societies for the propagation of the faith such as The Jain Mission Society of Bangalore City. Such groups print tracts and booklets for free distribution. They publish Jain newspapers. They establish Jain schools, and they operate Jain hospitals. The many sects are organized into Conferences that promote their beliefs among the young by Youth Groups and through Young Men's Jain Associations. A special "Ladies' Day" solicits the devotion of half of the Jain community.

The Sermon on the Mount and especially the Beatitudes has a special appeal and built-to-order message for the Jains. In the spirit and genius of Jainism, they corroborate the ancient faith at its very highest mark and still lead on to a higher way. It will probably take a life regenerated from the tradition of Jainism to expound fully this passage of Scripture and to appraise adequately the humility of our Lord Jesus Christ and assess for us the great depths of His gen-tle, long-suffering, loving nature. As Jain converts with a capacity for self-discipline and self-denial lay their treasure at His feet in worship and adoration, the Christian Church too will receive a much needed corrective and be enriched by the exaltation of the spiritual over the natural comforts of life.

How to reach the Jain for Christ is, however, an unsolved prob-lem. Suggestions are not lacking. Theories are plentiful. Yet the fact remains that of all the organized living religions of our day, Jainism has yielded fewer of its sons and daughters to the superior claims of Christ than has any other. Outstanding converts have been won from almost every caste and subcaste of Hinduism. Islam has yielded its Maulvi Safdar Alī, Imām Masīh of Calcutta, and Bishop John A. Subhān of Gujarāt; Parsiism its Rev. Dhanjibhai Navrojji, Rev. Mr. Darashaw, and Mrs. F. J. Anklesaria; Sikhism its Sādhu Sūndar Singh, Kartār Singh, and Rev. Bakht Singh. What are the comparable names of converts from Jainism? Indeed there are none. After living for over a decade in the very heart of Jainism in Gujarāt the author numbers many Jains among his friends and acquaintances, but he cannot report a single Jain convert. At the present time there is but one Jain inquirer requesting baptism through the total efforts of our mission society. Other societies have not been more successful. Certainly Jainism remains a missionary frontier and one of the foremost challenges to the Christian Church.

The Jain is constantly asking not *who* but *what* "shall deliver me from the body of this death?" Unfortunately he never attains to the joyous utterance of praise: "I thank God through Jesus Christ our Lord." In his static universe there is no dawn of hope to inspire his soul, nor will there be until you and I announce the Good News of God's redeeming grace in such wholehearted, self-sacrificial terms that even the followers of graceless Jainism will be drawn to the God of all grace.

BIBLIOGRAPHY

TRANSLATIONS OF JAIN SCRIPTURES

Sacred Books of the East, Vol. 222: Achārānga Sūtra and Kalpa Sūtra. Oxford: 1900.

Sacred Books of the East, Vol. 45: Uttarādhyayana Sūtra and Sūtrakritānga Sūtra. Oxford: 1900.

Bibliotheca Indica, "Uvasagadaso, Text and Translation" by R. Hoernle.

BARNETT, L. D. "Antagadadaso and Anuttaravovaiyadasao," London: 1907.

GENERAL STUDY OF JAINISM

(Some of the more important books not mentioned in the text and obtainable in English are given below) :

BUHLER, J. G. *On the Indian Sect of the Jains.* London: 1903.

CHANDRA, M. *Jain Miniature Paintings from Western India.* Ahmedabad: 1949.

CHAKRAVARTHY, S. A. *The Aryan Path.*

CROOKE, W. *Imperial Gazetteer of India.* Vol. I, pp. 414-417, Oxford: 1907.

FARQUHAR, J. N. *An Outline of the Religious Literature of India.* Oxford: 1920.

GAER, J. *How the Great Religions Began.* New York (3rd ed.) , 1955.

HASTINGS, J. *Encyclopaedia of Religion and Ethics,* articles on Jainism and Ajivakas. New York: 1928.

HOPKINS, E. W. *The Religions of India.* London: 1910.

Hindustan Year Book, 1956.

Jain Mission Society. *Aspects of Jainism.* Bangalore, 1955.

JAINI, J. *Outlines of Jainism.* Cambridge: 1916.

———. *Life in Ancient India* (As Depicted in the Jain Canons) . Bombay: 1947.

JAINI, M. C. *Life of Mahāvīra.* Allahabad: 1908.

KAPADIA, H. R. *A History of the Canonical Literature of the Jains.* Bombay: 1941.

MACNICOL, N. *The Living Religions of the Indian People,* pp. 171-202, Edinburgh: 1934.

MEHTA, M. L. *Outlines of Jaina Philosophy* (the essentials of Jaina Ontology, Epistemology and Ethics) . Bangalore: 1954.

———. *Outlines of Karma in Jainism.* Bangalore: 1954.

MUNI, JAINA VIJAYA (Editor) . *Studies in Jainism.* A collection of three articles on Jainism by Dr. Hermann Jacobi, Ahmedabad: 1946.

NAHAR, P. C., and GHOSH, K. *An Epitome of Jainism.* Calcutta: 1917.

NEHRU, S. J. *The Discovery of India.* London: 1951.

POPLEY, H. A. *The Sacred Kural, or the Tamil Veda of Tiruvalluvar.* London: 1931.

SHAH, C. S. *Jainism in North India.* London: 1932.

SHETH, C. B. *Jainism in Gujarat.* Bhavnagar: 1953.

SMITH, V. A. *A History of Fine Arts in India and Ceylon.* Oxford: 1911.

———. *The Early History of India* (3rd ed.) ; Oxford: 1914.

STEVENSON, MRS. S. *Notes on Modern Jainism with Special Reference to the Shvetāmbara, Digambara and Sthānakvāsi Sects,* Oxford: 1910.

TATIA, N. *Nayas—Ways of Approach and Observation.* Bangalore: n.d.

THOMAS, P. *Hindu Religion, Customs and Manners.* Bombay: n.d.

———. *Epics, Myths and Legends of India* (ninth edition) . Bombay: 1956. (ill.) , pp. 126-137.

VASUDEVA, P. L. *200 Great Indians,* pp. 138 and 9. Delhi: n.d.

WEBER, A. *Indian Antiquary.*

FIG. 11.—The Golden Temple at Amritsar. In the Foreground a Sikh prays.

Wisdom comes and understanding by reflection,
By reflection comes the knowledge of creation,
Slights and slaps are nothing by reflection,
Death's ties are cut asunder by reflection.

The Japjuri

XI.

Lesser Living Religions of India

by PAUL C. HAAGEN *

PART THREE—SIKHISM

INTRODUCTION

SIKHISM, FOUNDED BY GURU NĀNAK (1469-1538 A.D.), a contemporary of Christopher Columbus and Martin Luther, is the most recently developed of the world's major religions. Like Jainism it is closely affiliated with Hinduism. Of the six living religions of modern India, these three are indigenous and closely related historically and culturally. They all exemplify the peculiar temper and thought of India. But of the many reform movements within Hinduism, Sikhism has been one of the most influential. Unlike most other reforming agencies, it has achieved an independent existence and is maintaining its distinctiveness in spite of great pressures that would bring it back into the fold of Hinduism.

The Sikhs are the continuing product of the Hindu renaissance initiated by the alien influence of Islam upon complacent Brahmanism. Espousing the best of Islamic beliefs and practices to resist Muslim intransigence, Sikhism became an adventure in the reconciliation of religions that issued finally in the establishment of a new faith and a distinct community. Unlike many reforms in the long history of Hinduism it formally separated itself from its background. Due to

*For biographical statement, see Chapter IX.

the unusual characteristics of its restricted racial heritage, Sikhism has been able to maintain its religious independence, although its political independence has long since been destroyed. Even so, its chief significance for the non-Sikh has been political rather than religious. With the exception of Judaism, Sikhism is the only profession of faith that has fathered the founding of a new nation. Accordingly this comparatively recent religion is of more interest for the significant place it has held in Indian history than for its rather heterogeneous theology.

This religious and military community is native to the Punjāb, land of the five rivers in northwestern India. To this day its adherents are almost exclusively restricted to this area, which in days gone by suffered continual invasion and consequently developed a frontier complex. Most Sikhs living outside the Punjāb are engaged in temporary police patrols, military missions or as engineers on construction projects. With the exception of groups living in Stockton, Vancouver, London, Singapore, and Hong Kong they regard the Punjāb and its immediate surroundings as their home to which they expect to return when their assignments are completed.

This provincial faith is one of the smaller ethnic religions, having only 6,200,000 devotees, as compared with 303 million Hindus, and more than 500 million Christians. It does outnumber the 100,000 followers of Zoroaster and the 1,500,000 Jains. Like all the minority religions, its importance and worth cannot be gauged by its small numbers—one per cent of the total population of India,[1] but must be reckoned in the light of its tradition of sacrifice and suffering for the faith, which still inspires to daring deeds. It must be remembered that this community is the fastest growing in India at the present time. Their preachers employed by the S.G.P.C. (Shiromani Gurdwara Prabandhak Committee—a Central Board elected by all classes of Sikhs as their statutory body) not only recite their sacred texts but are probably India's most effective propagandists. In addition to propagating their religious views, these ministers consolidate the community by giving direction to its social and political interests. In spite of acute differences among their present leaders, the Sikhs are the best organized community in India. They also are alive to the importance of modern education, having established high schools

[1] S. C. Sarkar, *Hindustan Year Book* and *Who's Who*, 1957, p. 5.

throughout the Punjāb that prepare students for several degree colleges under their direction. Their influence is felt in every department of life and acknowledged by the general public, especially in their traditional role as defenders of the Indian subcontinent.

The Golden Temple at Amritsar—called Darbār Sahib by the Sikhs —is Sikhism's central shrine and is generally considered, next to the Tāj Mahāl, the most striking architectural sight in India. Sir Monier-Williams remarks that it is "one of those rare sights seen at intervals during life which fix themselves indelibly on the memory."[2] This small building (only 53′ square) of white marble, roofed with gilded copper plates and situated in the midst of the Pool of Immortality (a-mrits-ar—un-dying-waters), is the center of the Sikh community and inspiration of the Sikh religion. Here in the place of supreme importance is housed the Ādi Granth, the Sikh Bible.

NĀNAK'S LIFE AND TIMES (1469-1539)

The founder of Sikhism was born the son of the village accountant of Talvandi, thirty miles from Lahore. This little village on the Rāvi River has since been renamed Nankāna Sahib, in honor of its most illustrious son. His father, Mēhta Kālurām, was a Hindu cultivator of the Ksatrīya caste. From boyhood Nānak was interested in religious matters, and according to the extracanonical "Life Stories" (Janam-sākhīs), he spent most of his time discussing spiritual issues with itinerant holy men who brought the insight, inspiration, and emotion of both Hinduism and Mohammedanism to even the smallest villages. Foremost among these traveling holy men who spread their spiritual culture throughout North India were Rāmānanda, Pīpā, Sādhanā, and Tulsīdās. All these belonged to the Bhakti school of Hinduism. Sufi proselytists, although less well known by name, were as numerous as those of the Bhakti movement. Sufi Shaikh Ībrahīm Farīd (1450-1535) is known to have exercised considerable influence over Nānak, for the writings (more than 100 verses) of his master Sufi Farīdūdin Shakargunj were incorporated in the Granth. Nānak was probably even more influenced by the sayings and by the disciples of Kabīr who died in 1398. Although a Moslem, Kabīr was a disciple of the Hindu Rāmānanda. His teachings combined the be-

[2]Sir Monier-Williams, *Brahmanism and Hinduism, or Religious Thought and Life in India*, pp. 175, 176.

liefs of his own faith with those of his teacher. Like the teachings of Kabīr, Nānak's religion is a synthesis of the Hindu Bhakti and Moslem Sufi schools of thought prevalent throughout North India in his day.

Because of his aversion to secular activities Nānak's relatives despaired of him. They thought that he was suffering from some mental disease. Nānak told them he was suffering from "the pain of separation from God." When the urge to find spiritual truth finally became too great to endure, Nānak abandoned his family to espouse the life of a mendicant. Wandering in solitary places, he spent his time in fasting, praying, and religious contemplation until he finally felt qualified to adopt the garb of a religious ascetic and proclaim his conclusions to the world. His first pronouncement was the provocative statement: "There is no Hindu and no Musalman!"[3]

Like the apostle Paul, Nānak is reputed to have made several long missionary journeys. The first one, of twelve years duration, included most of the famous pilgrimage sites of northern India and the Himalaya Mountains. The second journey was even more extensive, taking Nānak and his companions through Madras to the island of Ceylon. The third traversed the extreme northwest of India, and the final journey carried the intrepid prophet to Baghdad and even Mecca, the citadel of Islam.

Nānak's missionary methods were simple but effective. Taking a Hindu peasant and a Mohammedan musician as his traveling companions, he went preaching from village to village. He further exemplified his teaching in his own person by arraying himself in an arresting combination of Hindu and Mohammedan religious garbs. On entering a village, Mardana, the Muslim musician, would attract a crowd by playing his rebab (an oriental stringed instrument antecedent to the violin). Then Nānak proclaimed his principal text: "There is no Hindu and no Musalman." Someone in the crowd would be sure to ask the meaning of this statement. He then took great delight in telling them. Throughout the length and breadth of India and beyond, he taught the followers of all religions that Allah and the many gods of the Hindus were actually but one great God. He called this God Sat Nām or True Name. He insisted that

---

[3]Max Arthur Macauliffe, *The Sikh Religion: Its Gurus, Sacred Writings, and Authors*, p. 37.

Sat Nām was a loving Guru or Teacher. His preaching was essentially a crusade against formalism and cant in religion. It was unusually effective because of its timeliness and because of the preacher's sincerity and humor—a sincerity that made him pattern his own life in accordance with his teachings, and a humor that enabled him to display the ridiculousness of outworn religious usages without ridiculing them.

Several interesting tales concerning his action-teaching methods are related in other connections: At Hārdwār he bathed with the devout Hindus who threw water toward the rising sun as an offering to their ancestors. Nānak threw water toward the West. When fellow worshipers remonstrated with him he replied: "I am watering my fields in the Punjāb. If you can throw water to the dead in heaven, it should be easier to send it to another place on earth."

While disguised as a Moslem at Mecca Nānak slept with his feet toward the Kaaba (the Holy of Holies of Islam). An infuriated mulla (Moslem priest) woke him rudely with the command that he move his feet in another direction. Guru Nānak replied: "Turn my feet toward the place where God does not dwell." Although this statement is also attributed to the Marāthī poet Nāmdev, and raises serious questions concerning the authenticity of Nānak's pilgrimage to Mecca, yet it is symbolic of his method and attitude. Wherever he went he denounced the ascetic practices and ritual of Hinduism as well as the hypocritical humbug of Islam. For the follower of Mohammed he reinterpreted Mohammedanism; for the Hindu, Hinduism. To all he repeatedly affirmed faith in the one true God.

When Bābā Guru Nānak died at Kartarpur in the Punjāb in 1538, both the Hindus and the Muslims claimed his body for disposal according to their respective rites. The sheet covering the body was finally lifted, revealing only a heap of flowers. Thereupon the contending parties cut the sheet into two parts. The Hindus erected a *samādhi* over their half of the sheet and the Moslems a mausoleum over theirs. Both of these were later washed away by the Rāvi River, signifying, as the story goes, the Guru's dislike of material worship. Although an identical legend is told concerning the death of Kabīr, yet the story illustrates the Guru's relationship to the two contending religions of his time. His life was devoted to the task of bringing Hindus and Muslims together. His death was mourned by both communities, His name even today is the most powerful catalytic agent for harmony between these two divergent faiths.

NĀNAK'S MESSAGE

The fundamental content of Nānak's message has been preserved in a book of psalms entitled *Japjī* (Praise). In its traditional form the *Japjī* includes thirty-eight psalms introduced by a preamble called the Mul Mantra (theme verse) and summarized by an epilogue. The whole composition is officially delineated in 375 lines, whereas the 150 Psalms of the Old Testament run to approximately 7,000 lines. The average psalm is about equal to the size of Psalm 23 in length. The essence of Sikhism can be ascertained from the simple expressions of this one small book, for it is an epitome of the voluminous Granth Sāhīb. It is Nānak's own contribution to religious literature and set the standard and supplied the inspiration for all subsequent Sikh writings.

An idea of Nānak's concept of God can be obtained from the Mul Mantra, the essence of the prescribed morning prayer of every Sikh:

> There is One God.
> He is the supreme truth.
> He, The Creator,
> Is without fear and without hate.
> He, The Omnipresent,
> Pervades the universe.
> He is not born,
> Nor does He die to be born again,
> By His grace shalt thou worship Him.
>
> Before time itself
> There was truth.
> When time began to run its course
> He was the truth.
> Even now, He is the truth
> And
> Evermore shall truth prevail.[4]

Thus we see that Nānak's views of God involved two basic factors —oneness and truth. Other complementary attributes are mentioned

[4]All quotations of the *Japjī* have been taken from Khushwant Singh's translation in the appendix of *The Sikhs*, pp. 188-207.

here and in succeeding lines, and some of these (e.g., timelessness) were subsequently given great prominence by Guru Gobind Singh; but these two essentials remain unchanged. The Sikhs to this day stress the unity of God and equate Him with truth.

Leaving the prose of the Mul Mantra, let us note the rhymed verse of Psalm 1:

> Not by thought alone
> Can He be known,
> Though one think a hundred thousand times,
> Not in solemn silence,
> Nor in deep meditation.
> Though fasting yields an abundance of virtue,
> It cannot appease the hunger for truth.
> No! by none of these
> Nor by a hundred thousand other devices
> Can God be reached.
> How then shall truth be known?
> How the veil of false illusion torn?
> O Nānak: thus runneth the writ divine.
> The righteous path let it be thine.

Although stressing the transcendence and essential unknowableness of the God who is pre-eminently the Formless One (Nirākāra), yet the above lines hold out the promise that by a righteous life man can invoke His grace.

The Psalms that follow set forth spiritual and social truths in the name of Sat Nām (True Name), who as Creator of high and low makes no discriminations among them (Ps. 2), whose loving-kindness is infinite (Ps. 4), and who recognizes the potential goodness of man. Nānak's tendency to syncretize Hindu and Islamic beliefs can be seen in the view that God may be called by any name so long as the worshiper recognizes He is more than any one of these names can convey. "Thou, O Lord, art One. But many are Thy manifestations."[5] Yet the principal and proper designation for deity is Sat Nām, the opening words of Nānak's *Japjī*. This name reappears in every psalm and is repeated by the Sikhs as a formula for obtaining salvation. The name is considered to be the mysterious concrete embodiment of the deity and as such is itself efficacious. As a means of salvation repeti-

[5]Rag Asa, Mahala of Guru Arjun, as quoted in *Treasure-House of the Living Religions*, by R. E. Hume, p. 5, stanza 28.

tion of the name supersedes the performance of sacrifices, the giving
of alms, and the acquistion of knowledge.

Sikhism is further unique in designating the Supreme as Guru
(Teacher). This term is also ascribed to *avatāras* and to religious
leaders who are thought to be one in spirit with the deity. Since Sat
Nām is conceived as an abstraction, holiness becomes an attribute
rather than an acquisition. The way to godliness is through obedience
to the divine Guru. The unspecified divine will is ascertained
through association with the human guru. "For though it be the
Guru's word God Himself speaks therein" (Ps. 5). Thus the religious teacher is essential for salvation and every Sikh becomes a
disciple. (The word *Sikh* is a corruption of the Sanskrit word *Shish*
or *Shīshya* meaning "disciple"). In Psalm 6 we read:

> Thy mind, wherein buried lie
> Precious stones, jewels, gems,
> Shall opened be if thou but try
> And hearken to the Guru's word.
> This is the Guru my teacher taught,
> There is but one Lord of all creation,
> Forget Him not.

Thus Nānak's psalms repudiate the loose popular ideas of Hinduism concerning the Supreme Being while at the same time they soften
the starkness of Islamic theism. Yet they are not free from implications of pantheism, for the whole Hindu pantheon is given a place
beneath Sat Nām (Ps. 26, 27, 30, 35). The only pronouncement we
can unequivocally make is that Sikhism is theistically inclined with
a single abstract God behind its varied worship and devious practices.

In contrast to the eternal, inscrutable Sat Nām, Nānak viewed the
world as ephemeral, illusory, and worthless, and man as helplessly
dependent:

> He bestows the virtue in whose hand the power lies,
> And men are nothing, O Nānak, be they low or high.
> —Psalm 33

Escape from this worthless world cannot be effected by ritual, by
pilgrimages, nor yet by austerities. Salvation can only be grasped
by comprehension of the True Name which is superior to even a

Benares pilgrimage. By speaking the Name and comprehending its love, the defilement and sin of the world is removed; for there is no sin or sorrow within the True Name:

> Pilgrimage, austerity, mercy, almsgiving and charity
> Bring merit, be it as little as the mustard seed;
> But he who hears, believes and cherishes the word,
> An inner pilgrimage and cleansing is his meed.
> —Psalm 21

> The Name is such to him devoid of passion,
> Who knows him in his heart by due reflection.
> —Psalm 15

> As hands or feet besmirched with slime,
> Water washes white;
> As garments dark with grime
> Rinsed with soap are made light;
> So when sin befouls the soul
> The Name alone shall make it whole.
> —Psalm 20

> Salvation comes at last to those whose thought rests on its Name,
> Their faces glow; O Nānak, and they have become immortal.
> —Epilogue of the *Japjī*

Thus Nānak teaches that salvation comprises a knowledge of God and ultimate absorption into God accomplished through meditation on and repetition of the mystical name, Sat Nām. This pantheistic merging of the human self with the divine is the same method of salvation that is taught in the Upanishads of the Hindus. Yet the accompanying idea of complete submission to God is definitely the Mohammedan method of salvation and foreign to Hindu thought, as is also the Sikh emphasis on action as a means of salvation. Like Allah who is under no constraint outside himself, Sat Nām acts independently.

> What He wills He ordains,
> To Him no one can an order give,
> For He, O Nānak, is the King of Kings,
> As He wills so we must live.
> —Psalm 27

Whatever be Thy wish, I say Amen.
        —Psalm 16

Like all other Indian reformers Nānak was unable to rid himself
of the indigenous twin theories of karma and transmigration. Traces
of these mar the quaint lines of his *Japjī*:

> Words do not the saint or sinner make,
> Action alone is written in the book of fate,
> What we sow that alone we reap;
> O Nānak, be saved or forever transmigrate.
>   —Psalm 20

> By His writ some have pleasure, others pain;
> By His grace some are saved,
> Others doomed to die, re-live, and die again.
>   —Psalm 2

> Though action determine how thou be born,
> Through grace alone comes salvation.
>   —Psalm 4

Nānak reveled in the loving-kindness of Sat Nām (Ps. 4 and 25)
and believed that he gives liberally to those who ask him (Ps. 3). Although he does not distinguish the relationship between Sat Nām
and karma, still it is Sat Nām who frees the believer from the all-
embracing control of karma and thus breaks the unending cycle of
transmigration. By righteous living on the part of man and through
the grace of Sat Nām, it is possible to escape the vicious circle and
attain salvation. Unlike the Hindu theory of karma the Sikh version
is not independent of human volition. The later writings of Guru
Arjun would seem to limit transmigration to human forms: "Thou
hast the body of man, now is thy turn to meet God."[6]

The most used theological word in the *Japjī* as in the Ādi Granth
(636 times) is the word *grace* (*parshad*). It is in this conception of
the love of Sat Nām expressing itself toward his people that Sikhism
comes closest to Christianity. Yet there is a vital difference in the
two Scriptures on this all-important theme. While the Ādi Granth
modifies grace by works (karma) so that it operates only after the
mechanical system of retribution has run its course, the New Testament proclaims a grace that is full, free, and unrestricted—grace not

[6]Rahiras (Rag Asa) as quoted in Macauliffe, Vol. I, p. 257.

based on works, but works resulting from grace (Eph. 2:3-10). Since grace is the distinctive watchword of the Sikh scriptures, as of the Christian, its weakness even in the area of its greatest strength would seem to indicate that Sikhism can be no more than a schoolmaster to bring its followers to Christ. Thus they too may come to know the grace of the Lord Jesus Christ, who being rich, for the sake of all mankind became poor, that through His poverty all men—Sikhs included—might become rich as inheritors of eternal salvation (II Cor. 8:9).

Macauliffe opines[7] that "it would be difficult to point to a religion of greater originality." The present writer considers the very opposite to be true. Sikhism is largely an unsavory hash of Hindu and Moslem ideas, sentiments, and theology. It continually speaks with a double voice. The student finds it well-nigh impossible to reduce its doctrines to consistency. On the one hand, the personalized faith of Mohammed can be seen in its worship of the Guru. On the other hand, its worship of the Granth reminds us of the impersonal Vedānta. At times the goal of blessedness is represented as a paradise called Sāch Khand. At other times the goal is absorption into the divine. According to one account, the recording angels take with them a record of man's acts in order to determine his fate by his own deeds. Yet this same passage goes on to assert: "Nānak, man suffereth transmigration by God's order." These are but a few of Sikhism's unresolved Hindu-Moslem combinations. At least to the Western mind, Sikhism is made up of elements that are incompatible.

If Sikh theology is indefinite and inconclusive, Nānak's statements regarding social and religious practices do not lack conviction. Believing in the unity and formlessness of God, Nānak and his successors even more strongly forbid the worship of idols and emblems. God alone is to be worshiped. He is not to be degraded through the use of images. He is rather to be worshiped in the spirit by meditation on His name. Nānak also denounced religious rites, ceremonies, sacrifices, austerities, and pilgrimages, declaring that truth was greater than them all. He likewise attacked such entrenched Hindu practices as child marriage, infanticide, suttee (self-immolation by widows), and caste. He did much to ennoble the position of woman. Although these subjects are not discussed in his *Japjī*, yet the under-

[7]Macauliffe, *op. cit.*, p. 55 of Introduction.

lying beliefs in the unity of God and the brotherhood of man do appear. All human beings without regard of race, or sex, or caste are equal in the world of Sat Nām. The sacerdotal classes of both communities came under his censure. Nānak refused to recognize any supremacy on the part of the Brahmans. His disciples, unlike Hindus, do not believe in ceremonial impurity at birth and death, and so repudiate Brahmanical usages in the ceremonies of birth, and marriage, and death.

Yet here again in the social sphere, as in the theological, we meet with inconsistency. While caste is vigorously denounced, karma and transmigration, the philosophical bases of caste, are constantly maintained. It is probably for this reason that Sikhism has not been successful even within its own structure in eliminating the evils of caste distinction.

Thus we see that Nānak was not a systematic thinker but was rather an eclectic teacher motivated by intuition and impulse. He does not bother to construct a considered system of theology, nor does he regard a metaphysical basis necessary for the establishment of his doctrine. His rejection of Hinduism is superficial, for he does not disavow many of its doctrines nor break with most of its practices. There is no tangible evidence that the Guru planned to found a new community. Like his predecessors he sought to reform Hinduism. Unlike most of his predecessors he tried to do this by borrowing ideas from the only other religion immediately accessible to him. He himself was a Hindu. His inspiration was Hindu. Although he borrowed basic ideas such as the unity of God, the equality of man, and the futility of asceticism from Islam—yet the following he commanded by his powerful personality was essentially a reformed sect of Hindu dissenters who only subsequently became a distinct religious community. It is the opinion of the writer that most Western scholars tend to read a synthesizing purposefulness into Nānak's teachings which did not exist for the founder of Sikhism.

Sikh Scriptures

Although Nānak had founded the Sikh faith about 1500, it was not until the year 1604 that Arjun, the fifth Guru, finished the compilation of an authentic Sikh bible known as the Ādi Granth (The Original Book). The hymns of the first four Gurus had previously been collected. Using these as the nucleus for his compilation, Guru Arjun invited suggestions of suitable hymns for the contemplated scriptures. As this method would suggest, the resultant volume is a miscellaneous collection of meditations on God and human life written by fifteen different Hindu and Mohammedan *bhagats* (devotees), as well as by seven of the ten Gurus and the bards who accompanied them. Selections by the Ninth and Tenth Gurus now included in the sacred writings were obviously not a part of this original compilation. The non-Sikh authors were chosen from the low as well as the high castes. The total number of writers as now constituted is 37, and the seven principal parts are as follows: (1) the *Japjī* of Guru Nānak, regularly recited as the morning prayer; (2) *So-daru* (that door), extracts from the main body of the book recited with the evening prayer; (3) *So-purkh* (that Supreme Being), used with the evening prayer; (4) *Sohīla* (song of praise) recited at bedtime; (5) the main body of the scripture classified according to the tunes to which each is chanted; (6) the *Bhōg* (epilogue or conclusion) made up of miscellaneous selections by Kabīr, Farīd, the Brahman bards, and the Gurus; (7) the *Rāg Māla,* enumerating all the rags and their raginis.

After the selections were made, Guru Arjun dictated them to his disciple Gudās who wrote them by hand in the Gurumukhi script invented by Guru Angad. When the whole was complete in a stupendous tome of 1500 pages, it ran to almost a million undivided words. This authorized bible was then signed and sealed by the Guru himself, and as the Kartarpur edition (the first of three) remains today the official edition of the Granth. The Sikhs claim for it the distinction of being the only scripture preserved without embellishment or misconstruction. It is interesting to note that this alleged original copy, housed in the Shīsh Mahāl at Kartarpur, does not, according to C. H. Loehlin, contain either the signature nor the seal claimed as marks of that original work.[8] It does contain several blank pages which Guru Arjun prophesied would later be filled by a martyred Guru. This is the authorization for the inclusion in the current text of hymns by the Ninth Guru, Tegh Bahadur as well as a couplet by Guru Gobind Singh.

The reading of this sacred book is complicated by the six distinct

[8]C. H. Loehlin, *The Sikhs and Their Book,* pp. 44, 45.

languages in which it is written. These in turn contain many dialectic variations. Even the Punjābī portions are written in the all but obsolete language of the fifteenth and sixteenth centuries. Added to these linguistic problems is the difficulty of the poetic form in which normal word order is inverted and syllables contracted or dropped to fit the meter of the stanza. The entire work is set to classical Indian music and is better sung than read. In fact, the whole of the Granth is organized according to its tunes (rāgs), rather than to the content of its message. Prose teaching, historical narrative, and epistolary exhortation such as the New Testament contains is wholly lacking. In form it most resembles the allegorical poetry of The Song of Solomon.

These characteristics make the Ādi Granth the most difficult of all sacred books to read. It is therefore the least read. Indeed, probably less than a dozen scholars are capable of intelligent reading of the entire original. Few Sikhs actually enjoy reading it. Their attitude to Gurbāni (the poetic utterances of the Gurus, i.e., the Granth) is simply that of indifference. Only a tithe of the Sikh community are indirectly acquainted with the contents of this book they revere. Few European scholars have devoted time and energy to deciphering the riddles of its pages. Among misisonaries to India there are no authorities on Sikhism as there are on Hinduism, Buddhism, and Islam. The Granth is probably the most neglected of the sacred writings of the world's living religions.

Yet at the same time the Granth is ascribed absolute authority and held in a reverence that is actual idolatry, for the Sikhs give it a dignity and a personality unique among religions. They believe that the Granth Sāhib (The Lord Book), as they generally call it, is the present embodiment of the Lord—their visible Guru. The Granth is treated as though it were a person. It is the central object of all worship. No Sikh ceremony can take place except in the presence of Guru Granth Sāhib. It is dressed in costly embroidered silks and brocade. It is opened with a prayer ceremonial each morning and closed in like manner each evening. It is enthroned under a canopy and is attended by devotees who stand behind waving a yak's tail as do the servants of an Indian prince. Worshipers approach it barefooted with covered heads and make obeisance by touching their foreheads to the ground. They place offerings of food and money on the drapings of the volume. Copies at some *gurdwaras* are even laid to rest in beds at night. Thus Sikhism, with all its ignorance and neglect of its written message, is essentially a book religion which has degenerated into the world's foremost example of bibliolatry. The Sikhs generally repudiate this allegation, contending that they are commanded to worship nothing but Sat Nām. In this, as in many other aspects of Sikhism, precept and practice are quite divergent. Yet present-day Sikhism is characterized by a healthy literary revival that is making strides in translating the neglected Scriptures into forms intelligible to the ordinary worshiper. This is largely being accomplished through commentaries on the Granth, similar in form to our devotional commentaries on the Bible. Foremost in this field is the four volume commentary of Sardar Teja Singh, which carries the text divided into words and stanzas on one page with comments and helps on the opposite page. Even English translations of the more important parts of the Granth are being made by Sikh scholars, thus putting aside the long held superstition that the very sound of the sacred language promotes holiness and fellowship with Sat Nām and obeying the long neglected command of Guru Arjun that the Granth be translated into foreign languages for all to hear. These translations, however, are even more voluminous and costly than the original and accordingly are not available to the average individual.

Most Sikhs also recognize as authoritative and secondary only to the Ādi Granth, a second Granth called Dasam Granth (The Granth of the Tenth). This is a compilation of the works of Gobind Singh, the Tenth Guru, together with translations and varied compositions by his employees. The compilation was made by his disciple, Mani Singh, subsequent to his death, approximately one hundred years after the writing of the Ādi Granth. Unlike the Ādi Granth it is not used for religious purposes, except at the ceremony of baptism, but is employed by the followers of Gobind Singh to promote valor and inculcate warlike virtues necessary to a Singh (lion) but unknown to the pacifist who founded the faith.

History of Sikhism

Although Sikhism started as a religious reform, it developed into a political organization of considerable historical importance. For the world at large its history has more significance than its theology.

This history is closely associated with the lives of Sikhism's succeeding Gurus. Each Guru was thought to be possesed of the same divine spirit that endued the founder, and was thus empowered to give leadership that molded the entire community from generation to generation.

Before his death Nānak appointed a married disciple rather than one of his well-qualified ascetic sons as his successor. By this decision he demonstrated his disapproval of asceticism and made the Sikhs a community of householders freed from many of the social abuses of Hinduism. This successor, Guru Angad (1538-1552) sometimes referred to as Nānak II, consolidated the work of the founder and furthered the separation of Sikhism from Hinduism by revising the old Punjābī alphabet and by establishing the vernacular as the sacred language in which the words of the Guru would be preserved. This script was called Gurumukhi (Guru's language) and is to this very day the vehicle for writing Punjābī. Hereafter the Sikhs used their own sacred tongue instead of the Sanskrit of the Hindu scriptures.

It was largely through the organizational and administrative abilities of Guru Amardās (1552-1574) Nānak III, that the Sikh sect was developed into a church. He organized the Sikhs into parishes with teaching centers presided over by devout laymen. To this day there is no ordained priesthood within the community. Any pious "learner" may perform the prescribed duties of the religious leader. He united these local *gurdwaras* (Sikh temples) through the establishment of a central shrine and place of pilgrimage at what is now Amritsar. He cut the Gordian knot of Brahmanism by devising Punjābī initiation, marriage, and death ceremonies to replace the Sanskrit ones. He furthered the break with Hinduism by substituting Sikh religious holidays for the Hindu festivals. He also strengthened these ritualistic innovations by corresponding social reforms, such as his stand against the old Jāt practice of infanticide and the Hindu custom of suttee (self-immolation by the widow). His establishment of the free kitchen (*langar*) where anyone could receive a gratuitous meal without social discrimination has become an integral part of Sikhism and has been a potent factor in the suppression of caste distinctions and in the fostering of Sikh charity. His vigorous stand against the other-worldly Udāsī sect (founded by Bābā Srī

Chand, elder son of Guru Nānak) was instrumental in keeping the new faith from relapsing into Hinduism.

Guru Rāmdās or Nānak IV (1574-1581) was the son-in-law of Amardās. He introduced the principle of hereditary succession by selecting his own son Arjun to follow him. His most lasting contribution to Sikh solidarity was made through the acquisition of land from the tolerant Mohammedan Emperor Akbar. On this tract he founded the religious capital of Sikhism, first known as Rāmdāspur, but later rechristened Amritsar. In the midst of this city, at the central shrine established by Amardās, he excavated a large bathing pool for ceremonial ablutions, which are such an integral part of all religions indigenous to India. In the midst of this pool he made preparations to build the Hari-mandīr (temple of God). Like King David he was denied the actual building of the sanctuary, which was completed by his son.

With Guru Arjun (1581-1606) the Sikh community took its first steps toward statehood. Needing money to complete the Golden Temple, he appointed taxgatherers (*masands*) in each district to supply revenue for the religious capital and its Guru. He also carried forward other building projects that resulted in the founding of Tarn Tarn and Kartarpur, cities of present-day importance. His supreme project in establishing lasting foundations for Sikhism was, however, made in an entirely different sphere. As mentioned above, it was through Guru Arjun that the sources of Sikh inspiration were gathered together into an authentic body of scripture. This scripture has fixed the beliefs of Sikhism and given it a standard to which reformers have recalled it from its many backslidings into Hinduism. Arjun was likewise able to make the Sikh community conscious of those outside its embrace and with the services of the tolerant Akbar was able through missionary activities and by his own preaching tours to greatly extend the Sikh faith. During his Guruship, the Sikh church reached its maturity and the community a substantial degree of wealth and organization. As numbers, wealth, and influence increased, Guru Arjun was tempted to dabble in political intrigue. As long as Sikhism had remained a purely religious movement, it flourished unmolested; but as soon as it showed signs of becoming a social and political organization it brought persecution upon itself. By aiding the rebellious son of Emperor Jehangir, Guru Arjun incurred the emperor's disfavor, was arrested and tortured to death, thus providing Sikhism with its first martyr and bringing it to a turning point in history. The first five Gurus had been religious reformers. The next five Gurus were destined to be warriors.

In order to fight against the Moghul rulers of Delhi, Guru Har Govind (1606-1638) built the first Sikh fort and transformed the community of devotees into a band of soldiers by raising a standing army and ruling over his people as a priest-king. He was the first of the Gurus to espouse the sword and to make it the badge of his leadership.

Guru Har Rāi (1638-1660) and Guru Har Kīshan (1660-1664) continued military operations against the bigoted Aurangzeb, creating circumstances that converted the farming brotherhood into a military confederacy. The Ninth Guru, Tegh Bahadur (1664-1675) was a warrior of unusual ability, whose successes against the Mohammedans spread his fame throughout all India and established Sikhism as a formidable force. His martyrdom at the hands of Aurangzeb inspired his son, Guru Gobind Singh (1675-1708), to life-long revenge, making him the most intrepid warrior of them all. Thus did outward forces and the natural inclination of the Jāts (racial group from which the majority of Sikhs have come) drive the followers of a tolerant reformer to become more and more aggressive until they were at last molded into a machine of war.

Gobind Singh was also the greatest organizer among the Gurus. He created within Sikhism a military theocracy known as the Khālsā (purified) by inaugurating a baptismal ceremony (*khanda-ki-pahul*) that converted the Sikhs (learners) into Singhs (lions) while conferring ceremonial purity upon them. In order to keep his followers ever conscious of this change, he prescribed five distinctive marks by which a Singh could easily be recognized and distinguished from the uninitiated Sikhs and Hindus among whom he lived. These five marks (*kakkas*), all beginning with the letter *k* are each of military significance: uncut hair (*kes*), comb (*kangha*), shorts (*kach*), iron bangle (*kartha*), and sword (*kirpan*). By binding each disciple to wear these five articles and by other solemn vows to abstain from tobacco, intoxicants, all meat except that of animals decapitated by a single blow, idolatry, distinctions of caste, the Brahman thread, Hindu pilgrimages, suttee, etc., Gobind Singh sought to give his warriors strength through their religion. He also passed special legislation to consolidate the theocracy and wrote a second Granth to inspire the feeble-hearted to exploits. By his distinctive initiation rite and peculiar rules of conduct, Gobind Singh made Sikhism a separate religion, while at the same time entirely eclipsing the religious spirit by the military. Guru Nānak had called into being small bands of pious men to recognize truth and resist evil. Gobind Singh staked his all in resisting political oppression. Dr. G. C. Narang has well said that the sword was forged by Guru Gobind Singh but the steel prepared by Guru Nānak. After two centuries under ten successive Gurus, Sikhism had through many changes and developments attained its permanent characteristics. "Thus for the second time in history, a religion became a military power, and for the first time in India a nation arose, embracing all races and all classes and grades of society and banded together in the face of a foreign foe."[9]

This transmutation of a church into an army was accompanied by many unhealthy developments: Preaching all but ceased. Idols were installed in many homes and even in some *gurdwaras*. The Granth which had been appointed the Guru of the Sikhs by Gobind Singh before his death was given divine honors. Many disciples of high caste drifted back into Hinduism, while there was an influx of members from the lower castes, especially from the Jāts. The establishment of the Khālsā divided the community into two principal parts—the Keshdhāri militant Singhs, and the excluded Sahijdhāri (Easy Goer) civilian Sikhs who followed Nānak closely and resisted the innovations of Gobind Singh. The Khālsā, Nirmalas, and Akālīs, all founded in 1690 by Guru Gobind Singh, Bīr Singh, and Mān Singh respectively, are sects of the first-named division. In the second group are the Nānakpanthīs (founded in 1500), the Udāsīs (1538), the Handalīs (1570), the Minas (1581), the Rām Ranjas (1656), and the Sewapantīs (1700). In all there are more than a score of orthodox sects besides those regarded as heretical. The Akālīs (Timeless) represent the militant ambitions of the Sikhs in their most virulent form. Whenever the passions of the Sikhs are aroused for the defense of their faith, the leadership of the Khālsā passes largely into the hands of these extreme zealots. For a long period of time they exercised the right to call the Gurumatā—the Council of the Guru in

[9]Sir Denzil Ibbetson, article on the Punjab in *Census of India Report*, p. 135.

which the secular authority (*amiri*) of the brotherhood was vested after the Garnth Sāhib was given the permanent position of spiritual Guru. Today they are led by the able by unpredictable Master Tārā Singh. To all intents and purposes he is the leader of the Sikhs, for orthodox Sikhs acknowledge that "the Khālsā is the Guru, and the Guru is the Khālsā."

Shortly after the death of Gobind Singh the Sikhs were scattered and hunted like wild animals. Their struggle for existence only made them more militant. The subsequent overthrow of the Moghul Empire gave the Sikhs territorial power, as they remained the only political force in the Punjāb. With the Marāthās in Central India they partitioned the remains of the great Moghul Empire. It was left, however, to Mahārāja Ranjīt Singh, "Lion of the Punjāb" (1780-1839) to establish the Sikh kingdom in 1800. For continuity of purpose and religious fervor history had not known his equal since Cromwell. From Lahore he ruled not only the whole of the Punjāb but a vast territory from Kashmir in the north to Multān in the south, and from Peshāwar in the west to the Sutlej River in the east. At his death there was no strong ruler to take his place. Military leadership fell into the hands of an elected committee—the *panchāyat* of the Khālsā. Even though Sikh individualism divided the Sikh State into warring factions, this committee was always eager to match its strength with the British across the Sutlej River. This led to the first Sikh War in 1845 and to the extinction of the Church-State with the second Sikh War of 1848-49. A the end of this war, Mahārāja Dhulip Singh made a complete surrender to the British, thus fulfilling the prophecy of Guru Tegh Bahadur that Europeans would destroy his empire. It was this prophecy that bound the Sikhs to the British in a loyalty that saved the day for the latter during the Indian Mutiny of 1857 and continued in helpful service until August 15, 1947. Today the Sikhs form the backbone of the small army of the Republic of India.

With the transfer of British power into Indian hands and the consequent partitioning of India into two separate nations, the Sikhs again came into mortal conflict with their traditional foes, the Mohammedans. A Boundary Commission was constituted (June 26, 1947) to make this division on the basis of contiguous majority areas of Muslims and non-Muslims. When the boundary decision was finally publicized on August 18, 1947, the Sikhs accepted with resignation the fact that 150 of their historic shrines and the most fertile of their lands, including the Canal Colonies were awarded to Pakistan. But it soon became apparent that Sikh landowners were not wanted in Pakistan. If the new Muslim state was to provide economic freedom for the Muslim middle-class who tilled the farms of Sikh owners, the Sikhs must go. Within a few days of the boundary award, there began a drive to dispossess Sikh farmers of their holdings. Those who resisted were murdered. Almost immediately millions of Sikhs, together with their terrified Hindu neighbors, were filling the roads to India with unbroken columns of refugees. Some of them came from as far as 200 miles within Pakistan. All of them suffered untold hardships. Their bitterness often expressed itself in anti-Muslim riots upon the refugee columns headed toward Pakistan, the special refugee trains of Mohammedans, and throughout the whole of East Punjāb. The atrocities on both sides assumed diabolic characteristics and gigantic proportions. No quarter was given to the aged, the weak, or the infirm. Men, women, and children met their death by the hundred thousands on the routes of this great migration. Estimates of the victims range from several hundred thousand to two million. By the spring of 1948 almost every Sikh to the last man had been evacuated from Pakistan, as over ten million people changed homes in the greatest population transfer in modern times. Ten years after this momentous event, the approximately five million Muslim refugees are resettled in West Punjāb and the five million Sikhs in East Punjāb. The population change has been almost equal, but the material turnover has left the Sikhs with less than a tithe of their original holdings. This blow of fortune has humbled the Sikh community and has caused many to speak of Sikh decline. With the merger of Pepsu and the Punjāb on November 1, 1956, the Rājpramukhship of Pepsu came to an end and with it the last vestiges of Sikh rule. His Highness Mahārāja Yādvendra Singh, last ruler of Patiala and incumbent of the Rājpramukhship of Pepsu at the time of its dissolution, abdicated the limited powers left to him in favor of the elected representatives of the people. Thus the ancient Phul Dynasty founded by Chaudhri Phul, a devoted disciple of Guru Har Rāi, came to an inglorious end. It is unthinkable that the theocracy could ever be revived nor that the Akālī demand for

Sikhistān could materialize in the present political setting. Although Prof. Ōm Prakāsha Kahol states[10] that "Sikhism cannot be separated from politics; it is fifty percent politics and fifty percent religion," yet the future of Sikhism would seem to lie in religious and social rather than political spheres. Even Master Tārā Singh, the seventy-one-year-old white-bearded leader of the Akālī sect within Sikhism, seems to have realized this, for in October, 1956, he abandoned his long-waged battle for the creation of a separate Sikh state and admonished his followers to join the Congress Party. By this pronouncement he indicated that the most militant segment of Sikhism would henceforth confine its activities to cultural, economic, and religious matters. This indeed was a tremendously historic event. If truly followed, it will make Sahijdhāri Sikhs, if not Hindus, of the most stalwart Keshdhāri Singhs.

PRESENT-DAY PRACTICES

A religion that primarily consists of group loyalty and a call to battle against its opponents does not find the same scope in twentieth-century India that it did in Moghul India. The Sikh religion notoriously flourishes in times of persecution and languishes during days of prosperity. Strict adherence to the tenets of Guru Gobind Singh are today the exception rather than the rule. Most of the present-day descendants of former Sikh rulers are only nominal adherents of the Sikh faith. Among the peasantry the defection is even more pronounced. Most Jāts of Ambāla, Ludhiāna, and Jullundur Districts not only trim their beards but also commit the serious Sikh offense of smoking the *hookah* or cigarettes. Although smoking is uncommon in the chief city and its environs, yet trimmed beards are often seen. Only in the northern part of the Punjāb do the middle-class Sikhs adhere strictly to the insignia and forms of Sikhism. The magnitude of the trend is all but unbelievable and unless halted by some unforeseen force will bring about the disappearance within our century of Sikhism as we know it.

For the average Sikh, the observance of a few rites and the celebration of special days constitutes the extent of his religion. The first of these is the Initiation Ceremony and naming of the child which may take place at any time convenient to the parents. The child is

[10]*Spokesman*, weekly paper, Guru Nānak number, p. 34.

brought before Guru Granth Sāhib, and the *granthi* (layman who handles the Granth) prepares *amrit* by mixing sugar in water while reading five stanzas from the *Japjī* Sāhib. After the reciting of prescribed prayers, drops of the *amrit* are placed on the child's lips and the mother given the remainder to drink. The Granth is then opened and the child given a name beginning with the first letter of the first hymn on that particular page. Holy food (*karah parshād* —equal parts of wheat flour, sugar, and clarified butter) is then distributed to all present and the congregation dismissed.

The next ceremony the Sikh will probably undergo is that of baptism (*pahul*). If he is a Sahijdhāri, *amrit* will be prepared and given in a simple ceremony as above. If he is a Keshdhāri, he will appear before Guru Granth Sāhib, bearing the five symbols on his person, and with folded hands request admission to the Khālsā. With the assent of the congregation, five Sikh laymen are chosen to administer the ceremony. The senior brother or leader of the five then reminds the candidate of sixteen duties of the Singhs and asks the candidate if he is prepared to observe them. *Amrit* is then mixed in an iron pot. Kneeling on the left knee (*vir asan*) each of the five stir the elixir in turn with double-edged daggers, as they each breathe into the mixture the magic of the Guru's message by reciting one of the Five Words (*Pānch Bānia*) over it. The senior brother first recites the whole of the *Japjī*. Then the second brother reads the Jap Sāhib of Guru Gobind Singh. The third continues with the Ten Swayas by the same Guru, while the fourth reads the Chaupai of the Evening Prayer and fifth concludes with the Ānand Sāhib or Song of Bliss from the same prayer. This takes considerable time to accomplish. The candidate then sitting in *vir asan* repeats, "The Khālsā is of God and to God is the victory." *Amrit* is poured into his cupped hands for him to drink. This is repeated five times. *Amrit* is then sprinkled with force from a dagger by each of the five into his open eyes as he unwinkingly repeats the same phrase five more times. Finally each of the five administer *amrit* to his topknot (*kes*) through his parted turban. As before he repeats five times, "The Khālsā is of God and to God is the victory." Any remaining *amrit* is drunk by the candidate who then chooses a new name which is written down in the official book of the *gurdwara*. *Karah parshād* is then distributed to all and the congregation disbands.

At the time of marriage the bride and groom appear at the place where the Granth Sāhib has been installed for the occasion. Appropriate scriptures are read and prayer offered. The *granthi* then questions the bride and groom as to whether they are prepared for the duties of married life in the light of these scriptures. When they bow their heads to Guru Granth Sāhib in assent, the relative of the bride who is to give her away ties the edge of her sari to the groom's waistband as a symbol that they are husband and wife. The couple then walk four times around the Granth Sāhib as the Four Marriage Hymns (Lavans) are sung. The singing of the Ānand (Song of Bliss) concludes the ceremony.

At death it is customary to arrange for the reading of the entire Granth Sāhib at the home of the bereaved. This is called *"pāth."* Friends and relatives come to the home to listen to the *Bhōg* or concluding portion of the scripture reading. Selections from the Granth are sung as the body is cremated. This last of all ceremonies in the life of a Sikh then concludes with the distribution of *karah parshād*.

The Christian visitor to the *gurdwara* finds many features of the regular worship service, as of these special ceremonies, reminiscent of his own faith and practice. Yet the Sikh actually lives close to Hinduism with few distinguishing beliefs and fewer distinguishing practices. In doctrine the chief difference lies in the Sikh belief in one Supreme Being, with its practical prohibition of idol worship. Yet in spite of these tenets, the same routine of worship is indulged in many Sikh homes and places of worship as is followed at Mathura or Brindaban or Benares. The festivals of the Sikhs, with the exception of the birth and death anniversaries of their Gurus, are almost the same as those observed by the Hindus. In social polity the differences are also so slight that social intercourse between orthodox Sikhs and Hindus, even to the extent of intermarriage between the two communities, is common. The chief peculiarity of the Sikh lies in his military spirit and in his soldierly appearance.

THE FUTURE

Sikhism is today undergoing a profound process of change. In this respect it differs greatly from the more static minority religions of India. The outcome of these changes is as yet uncertain, but elements in the shifting picture can be recognized. The foremost factor making for the dissolution of Sikhism is the growing indifference to forms and symbols mentioned above. This apathy is accelerating reabsorption into Hinduism. The declension is further quickened by Sikh self-centeredness. Despising the missionary-mindedness of their First and Fifth Gurus, Sikhism has become a vested institution bent on self-preservation. Recent proselytizing efforts among untouchables bear suspicious political characteristics and do not seem to indicate a revived missionary spirit. Except in theory, Sikhism is not a missionary religion. Factionalism is the third factor making for the extinction of the Sikhs as a separate community in India. Having arisen as a revolt against caste, Sikhism has within the last half century produced a caste system of its own with a new economic basis, dividing Jāt agriculturalists from non-Jāt urbanites. This is a very fruitful and potent source of internal trouble.

Counteracting the above forces is a new emphasis on the necessity of independence from all Hindu associations. Since the partition of the Punjāb, the orthodox elements within Sikhism have been attempting to stage a revival similar to that which revitalized dormant Sikhism at the close of the last century, when it produced an educational system, purified *gurdwaras,* and a momentum that brought about adaptation of time-worn institutions to modern conditions. This present-day movement includes a new political bias emphasizing Sikh nationality, race, language, and culture. A new economic element has also entered the picture. With partitioning of the Punjāb, the Sikhs have been thrown for the first time into keen economic competition with Hindus for government jobs, Muslim refugee property, and for the necessities of livelihood. Although the Hindu-Sikh riots of post-partition days are a thing of the past, social intercourse between the two communities received a blow from which it will not soon recover. The old fear of the common Muslim enemy no longer serves to unify the two communities in the new India. All these factors tend to keep the two communities apart and to lessen defections to Hinduism. Moreover, the Sikh tendency to factionalism has somewhat been arrested by the national abolition of communal and caste privileges, which has a tendency to lessen the Jāt non-Jāt rift.

In spite of the above cited influences, Khushwant Singh predicts[11]

[11]Khushwant Singh, *The Sikhs,* p. 185.

that "if the present pace of amalgamation continues, there is little doubt that before the century has run its course Sikh religion will have become a branch of Hinduism and the Sikhs a part of the Hindu social system." This reminds us of a similar prophecy made in 1896 by J. N. Bhattacharya: "In the course of a few more generations it [Sikhism] is likely to be superseded by one of those forms of Vaishnavism which alone have the best chance of success among a subject nation in times of profound and undisturbed peace."[12] The present writer is inclined to believe that the prophecy of Khushwant Singh will prove to be as inept as that of the Hindu scholar who preceded him. Conditions will not continue as they are. Some unknown factor will appear to stir the blood of this militant people. This call to battle will unite their factions. The messages of Nānak and Gobind Singh will again be the banners about which they will rally, and Sikhism will be revitalized.

SIKHISM AND CHRISTIAN MISSIONS

The same reforming and supplanting effect which Sikhism produced in a limited measure upon Hinduism, is now being exercised more extensively and to a higher degree by Christianity. Both Hinduism and Sikhism have been forced to re-examine their tenets and practices in the brighter light of the teachings of the Lord Jesus Christ.

Although Christianity numbers its converts in the Punjāb in the hundreds of thousands, most of these Punjābī Christians have been won from the lowest strata of society—from among the Chuhras, the Chamārs, the Bhangīs, and the Doms. In the matter of recruits, both Christianity and Sikhism have much in common, for both have attracted large numbers of untouchables. The present-day Christian gains among these depressed classes have undoubtedly caused a diminution of growth in Sikhism. Although Sikh gains in the Punjāb still exceed Christian gains, yet both are in excess of the total population percentage increase for the nation. Relatively few converts to Christianity have come, however, from among the Sikhs, and even fewer from the sect of Keshdhāri Singhs. Although there are no accurate figures available for the number of Christians who have been Sikhs, the figure probably does not exceed ten thousand. We must

[12]J. N. Bhattacharya, *Hindu Castes and Sects.*

in all fairness admit that while Sikhism has yielded a great host of devotees to Hinduism, it has yielded but a few to Christianity. It has yielded absolutely none to Islam.

Granting that Christianity has not recruited large numbers from the fold of Sikhism, the quality of those it has recruited must not be overlooked. The only world-wide personality produced by the Sikh community in the twentieth century was a Keshdhāri Khālsā Singh who became India's foremost convert to Christianity. Without controversy Sādhu Sūndar Singh has been the subcontinent's most outstanding national Christian. His retention of Sikh ideals made it impossible for him to become an ordained minister of any church but made him the servant and inspiration of the Church universal. His rejection of ecclesiastical Christianity enabled him through the time-honored traditions of the sādhu virtually to become a *bhagat* of Christ—a saint of Christianity who conveyed the message of Christ to the people of India in a language and through forms familiar to them. Probably more than any other Indian convert, Sādhu Sūndar Singh has given the Indian church a challenge to wholehearted consecration of mind as well as body and spirit. Using the worth-while elements of Sikhism, so familiar to him, he explored new methods for representing Christ to the needy of the East. His presentation of the message was sometimes daring in the originality of its approach. It was always Indian and effective. It is for lack of just such creative thinkers as Sādhu Sūndar Singh that the church of India is making so little progress in the urgent need of the day—an indigenous church. Acceptance of the Sikh ideal of martyrdom, ennobled by Christian example, lifted this Christian Sādhu from the confines of his own generation and made of him an example and inspiration for all time.

In the field of present-day Indian evangelism, the most gifted and God-honored national is a Sikh named Bhakt Singh, who reflects his Sikh background in his protest against ecclesiasticism and through the organization of independent groups of Christians led by laymen. Others like Daud Singh and Kharak Singh have taken ordination and have served in the established church. Perhaps Līlavatī Singh has been the best known lady among Sikh converts. After observing that India has produced Christian scholars who rank with the best in the field of Christian philosophy and theology, Willis Church Lamott illustrates his contention by specifying the contributions of a Sikh: "The approach of Surjīt Singh to the problems of theology is from the personality of the God-man, Jesus Christ, rather than from the conventional pattern long adopted by Western theologians. In all of his writing and teaching there is a vital, creative element which augurs well for the emergence of future revolutionary insights."[13] As it has done for the whole of India, Sikhism has brought to the Church of Christ in India a much-needed individualism, leadership, and vitality. During the recent antimissionary agitation engendered by the Nīyōgī Committee investigations, foreign Christian missionaries received unexpected support from the foremost political party among the Sikhs, the Akālī Dāl. Is it not possible that the greatest contribution of Sikhism through converts to Christianity may yet be future?

EPILOGUE

Neither Communism nor Nationalism has had any appreciable effect upon Parsiism or Jainism so far as the writer can discern. A few intellectuals belonging to these faiths have espoused a watered-down brand of Communism consistent with their religious beliefs. A larger number from these minority religions have been swept along in the movement for Indian independence. The part they played in these movements was unrelated to their religion. Parsiism, the museum piece among the religions of the world, does not have vitality enough to cope with Communism, nor is it alive enough to be affected by Nationalism. Jainism is too monastic and withdrawing to influence or be influenced by either of these powers in the new India.

With Sikhism the very reverse is true. The Sikhs both individually and as a religious community have been in the very forefront of the nationalist movement. The fortunes of the Sikh community and Sikhism as a result have been discussed in the manuscript. Their part in Indian Communism has also been a large one. They made up the greater part of the Communist Party in the prepartitioned Punjab. In 1942 these Punjab communists broke with the congress party and their fellow Sikhs of the Akali Party over the war issue. After the war, the congress used this severance to squelch the com-

[13]Willis Church Lamott, *Revolution in Missions*, pp. 108, 109.

munist. This automatically helped the old line orthodox Akali group to power. Not one communist was successful in the election race for seats in the Punjab Legislative Assembly in 1946. This setback was accentuated the following year by partition, with its communal massacres. Although the Akalis took a more active part in the killings, the communists, because of their support of the Muslim League, came in for the preponderance of blame from the anti-Muslim majority. Thus the Communist Party of the Punjab disintegrated and went underground. They re-emerged in the elections of 1952 and have been gaining ground ever since. Sikhism is undoubtedly being affected by the espousal of Communism by so many of its followers. At the present juncture this effect is scarcely demonstrable.

BIBLIOGRAPHY

TRANSLATIONS OF SIKH SCRIPTURES

HUME, ROBERT ERNEST. *Treasure House of the Living Religions* (Topical Selections), New York: 1933.

SINGH, PROF. TEJA. *The Japji or Guru Nanak's Meditations* (rendered into English and Annotated). Amritsar: 1930.

MACAULIFFE, MAX ARTHUR. *The Sikh Religion: Its Gurus, Sacred Writings, and Authors,* (6 Vol.). Oxford: 1909.

SINGH, HARBANS. *Something About Sikhism* (chosen sayings from the Granth). Amritsar: 1929.

SINGH, PROFESSOR PURAN. *A Peep into Sikhism* (Translation of the Watch —Cry of Guru Nānak). Amritsar: n.d.

SINGH, KHUSHWANT. *The Sikhs* (Trans. of Jupji in Appendix). London: 1953.

TRUMPP, ERNST. *The Adi Granth, or Holy Scriptures of the Sikhs.* London: 1877.

BOOKS AND ARTICLES NOT MENTIONED IN THE TEXT

ARCHER, JOHN CLARK. *The Sikhs.* Princeton: 1946.

CAVEESHAR, SARDUL SINGH. *The Sikh Studies.* Lahore: 1937.

CROOKE, W., *Imperial Gazetteer of India* (Vol. I, pp. 426-427). Oxford: 1907.

FARQUHAR, J. N. *An Outline of the Religious Literature of India* (pp. 330-346). Oxford: 1920.

GARRETT. *Cunningham's History of the Sikhs.* Oxford: 1918.

MACNICOL, NICOL. *The Living Religions of the Indian People* (pp. 203-233). London: 1934.

———. *Indian Theism*. From the Vedic to the Muhammadan Period (pp. 135-159). Oxford: 1915.

NARANG, SIR GOKUL CHAND. Transformation of Sikhism, Third edition. Lahore: 1946.

PARRY, R. E. *The Sikhs of the Punjab*. London: 1921.

SINGH, KARTAR. *Sikh Gurus and Untouchability*. Amritsar: 1936.

SINGH, KHAZAN. *History and Philosophy of the Sikh Religion* (2 Vol., first History, second Philosophy). Lahore: 1914.

SINGH, PROF. PURAN. *Guru Nanak's Rebab* (Sikh Tract Published by The Chief Khalsa Diwan). Amritsar: n.d.

SINGH, SIRDAR SIR JOGENDRA. *Sikh Ceremonies*. Bombay: 1941.

———. *Sikhism—Today and Tomorrow*. Lahore: 1945.

SINGH, PROF. TEJA. *Sikhs and Organization*. Lahore: n.d.

———. *The Growth of Responsibility in Sikhism*. Lahore: n.d.

VASUDEVA, P. L. *200 Great Indians*. Delhi: n.d., Article on Nānak. (Reference Works and Periodicals not mentioned in the text)

Encyclopaedia Britannica. Articles: India, Hindustan, Punjab.

HASTINGS, JAMES. *Encyclopaedia of Religion and Ethics*. Articles: Nānak, Granth, Sikhs. New York: 1928.

The Illustrated Weekly of India, June 24, 1956. Illustrated Article: A Sikh Pilgrim Centre. Bombay.

The Sikh Review (November, 1954) Vol. 2, No. 11 (Guru Birthday Number). Calcutta.

Spokesman (November, 1955) Vol. 5, Number 45 (Guru Nanak Number), 56 pages, New Delhi and Jullundur.

Spokesman (November, 1956) Vol. 6, Number 46 (Guru Nanak Number), 72 pages, New Delhi and Jullundur.

Spokesman (January, 1957) Vol. 7, Number 1 (Guru Gobind Singh Issue), 32 pages, New Delhi and Jullundur.

GENERAL STUDIES

ANDREWS, C. F. *Sadhu Sundar Singh*. New York. 1934.

CHAND, PREM (translator). *Kabir's Bijak*. Calcutta: n.d.

WESTCOTT, G. H. *Kabir and the Kabir Panth*. Cawnpore, n.d.

BOOKS QUOTED IN THE TEXT

BHATTACHARYA, J. N. *Hindu Castes and Sects*. Calcutta: 1896.

IBBETSON, D. *Census of India Report*. 1881.

LAMOTT, W. C. *Revolution in Missions.* New York: 1954.
LOEHLIN, C. H. *The Sikhs and Their Book.* Lucknow: 1946.
MONIER-WILLIAMS. *Brahmanism and Hinduism.* London: n.d.
SARKAR, S. C. *Hindustan Year Book and Who's Who.* Calcutta: 1957.

Fig. 12.—The Kremlin in winter. The hub of world Communism. (Courtesy of United Press International.)

*The Communists disdain to conceal their views and aims. They
openly declare that their ends can be attained only by the forcible
overthrow of all existing social conditions. Let the ruling classes
tremble at a Communistic revolution. The proletarians have
nothing to lose but their chains. They have a world to win.
Working men of all countries, unite!*

The Communist Manifesto

XII.

Communism

by ARTHUR F. GLASSER

The Secular Religion of the Twentieth Century

A SPECTRE IS HAUNTING EUROPE—the spectre of Communism. All
the powers of old Europe have entered into a holy alliance to
exorcise this spectre: Pope and Tsar, Metternich and Guizot, French
Radicals and German police-spies." With these portentous words
the *Manifesto* of the Communist Party begins. Then follows a moving exposition of the thesis that the capitalistic system was doomed:
it contained "its own grave-diggers." Its fall and the victory of a
highly desirable communist revolution are "equally inevitable."

Written in 1848, this *Communist Manifesto* soon became the
creed of a revolutionary movement that in the present day is not
only haunting Europe but the whole world, challenging every aspect
of human society and seemingly moving inexorably to the prophesied
victory which its authors, Karl Marx and Friedrich Engels, so spe-

ARTHUR F. GLASSER, B.C.E. (Cornell University), graduate of
Moody Bible Institute, B.D. (Faith Theological Seminary), is Assistant Home Director for North America of the China Inland
Mission. Mr. Glasser served as a Navy chaplain in World War II
and in 1946 went to China as a missionary with the C.I.M. There
he ministered in Yunnan Province until forced out by the Communists in 1951. He taught at Columbia Bible College, 1951-1955,
and then assumed his present position with the C.I.M. In 1956-
57 Mr. Glasser served at the mission headquarters in Singapore
in connection with administration of work in Malaya, Thailand,
and Laos.

297

cifically delineated: the victory of proletarian revolution throughout the earth. Inasmuch as Communism is not only challenging Western civilization but organized religion, especially Christianity, as well, it behooves the evangelical Christian to be informed about this formidable adversary.

Biblical Relevance of This Investigation

Human history is replete with the records of philosophers, reformers, and agitators who have sought to deal with the basic problems surrounding man and society. Plato, the monastic movements, More in his *Utopia,* and many since—all have sought to describe or create ideal communities in which human affairs would be so perfectly organized that the emergence of destructive, degrading inequalities, and rivalries would be impossible. And yet, in age after age, these same unresolved tensions have destroyed society after society.

It is felt by many that among the social panaceas Marxism is but the latest, most thoroughly worked-out, most radical, and most widely applied expression of this timeless desire for an adequate solution to mankind's inherent problems. That it claims to be "scientific" is further alleged as evidence of its being most in harmony with the mood of the twentieth-century world.

But the underlying philosophy of Communism embraces so comprehensive and unified a "world-view," that there are those who feel that its total concept of life warrants its being classified as a religious system. At least, they would argue, it appears to fill the place of religion in the lives of those who embrace it.

However, when the evangelical Christian ponders the essential characteristics and direction of the communist movement from Karl Marx onward—its philosophy and political program—he feels that he is examining something unique in all world history. Its militant atheistic base is strikingly unusual. It is a more thorough expression of man's hunger for social justice than ever before voiced. It is a philosophical movement more peculiarly suited to the modern "scientific materialist." Communism appears to have great relevance when considered in the light of the over-all panorama of the ages as revealed in the Bible, the Word of God.

Scripture reveals God as the God of the personal and social ethic

—the moral Arbiter of the universe. But it also reveals Him as the God of history. As Creator He originated history. By His redemptive work He has provided Himself as the key to history's ultimate triumph. And as omnipotent Providence He is constantly at work, unfolding His eternal purpose and superintending the movements of nations and individuals that in the end "all human history shall be consummated in Christ, that everything that exists in Heaven or earth shall find its perfection and fulfillment in Him" (Eph. 1:10, Phillips' trans.).

And yet Scripture nowhere teaches that the onward march of history to this certain goal will proceed irresistibly upward so that in the end the Lord Jesus Christ will be received and enthroned by an enlightened, willing mankind. In contrast, it reveals that just before the Day of God there shall emerge in the earth the final expression of mankind's age-long revolt against God (II Thess. 2:3-8; Rev. 13). It will be the ultimate Day of Man; the glittering system of the Antichrist which in its outward aspects and early stages will appear to solve all the complex problems of society. But this system will in the end be revealed as an utter failure—the ultimate in human failure and human corruption, because God will have been so completely and deliberately excluded. Though one should not automatically equate the present communist movement with the beginnings of mankind's final political entity—Antichrist's kingdom—such striking parallels exist between them that it is not hard to conceive of the one setting the stage and climate for the other.

MISSIONARY RELEVANCE OF THIS INVESTIGATION

Communism must be faced as a missionary problem. It stands in the way of the completion of "the unfinished task," of the fulfillment of the Great Commission (Matt. 28:19, 20; Mark 16:15). By the mid-twentieth century the Church became painfully aware of Communism. Here was a savage competitor, another crusade likewise world-wide in scope. Within the preceding four decades this adversary had gained control of one-third of the world's population. Never had the Church faced so baffling, so formidable an opponent. Here was a program for world evangelization skillfully integrated to a ruthless center of terrific imperialistic power, the Soviet Union. From whence had it come? Why was it so peculiarly hostile to evangelical

Christianity? Was there significance to the fact that when the communists gained political control, aggressive Gospel evangelism was soon throttled, then expressly forbidden? Is there some dark, menacing force, implacable in its hostility to Christ that is determined to prosper this communist movement so that His missionary purpose shall never be realized? Is Satan involved? What alternative is there to the proposition that he is using the communist movement as a chief weapon in his ceaseless, truceless warfare against Christ? These questions arouse curiosity as to the historical origins of the communist movement.

Historical Origins

It is rather striking to find that the communist movement of today can be traced back to the same period which witnessed the beginnings of the evangelical awakening of the Wesleys. Is it a case of God's attack challenged by Satan's counterattack? The French philosophers of the eighteenth century popularized the thesis that man by nature is a rational being, essentially good, though corrupted by society with its bad political institutions. If society could be reformed by changing drastically its political structure, especially by eliminating the monarchy and authoritative church, man would be liberated to regain his primitive nobility. "Liberty, equality, and fraternity" was one of their slogans. They taught that man must be free; the restraints of society and religious superstitions only produce slavery. Robespierre and his associates imbibed these thoughts deeply, and the French Revolution was an effort to translate them into political action.

Although traceable to this smallest rill, communist dogma as developed by Marx was a confluence of many streams of philosophical and political thought emerging from the eighteenth and early nineteenth centuries. Lenin commences his authoritative work on Marx's teachings by confirming this thesis: "Marx was the genius who continued and completed the three chief ideological currents of the nineteenth century, represented respectively by the three most advanced countries of humanity: classical German philosophy, classical English political economy, and French socialism combined with French revolutionary doctrines.[1] But before one can appreciate the dogma of Marxism he must first understand Marx, the man.

[1]Lenin, *The Teachings of Karl Marx*, p. 10.

A. Karl Marx (1818-1883) —Biographical Sketch

Karl Marx has been regarded as "one of the most influential figures in human history." And yet the record of his life is surprisingly dull. He was born in Trier in Rhenish Prussia in 1818. For many generations all his forebears, both paternal and maternal, had been Jewish rabbis. His father, however, was not a rabbi but a prosperous, highly respected lawyer. For social and business reasons he registered the family as Protestant in 1824. From his ancestors young Karl inherited a mind that was "theoretical, analytical, speculative, rabbinical." From his father he acquired an appetite for Rousseau, Voltaire, Locke, and Diderot. Although he felt keenly the stigma and disadvantage of his Jewish background, many of his biographers attribute his overwhelming sense of authority and Messianic urge to his racial origins. Strangely, he was bitterly anti-Semitic and caustic in the extreme in his correspondence with Jews, or in his writing about them. His solution to the Jewish question was most violent: "The social emanicipation of the Jews is the emancipation of the society from the Jew.[2] During his life he kept himself entirely aloof from anything even remotely connected with his race.

Karl was a boy of books, shunning other children and spending hours questioning his father and a Prussian Privy Councillor, Ludwig von Westphalen, who lived nearby. Intellectually he made rapid progress, but socially he remained aloof from his classmates, manifesting a stubbornness and hardness that made his parents uneasy. Hardly had he begun to study law at the University of Bonn when he became clandestinely engaged to his aristocratic neighbor's daughter, Jenny von Westphalen, "the most beautiful girl in Trier." To discourage what he regarded as an infatuation, his father abruptly transferred his son to the University of Berlin. Marx soon "slipped into the bohemian life of a coffee-house intellectual." Since studying law seemed too confining, he began to read widely and soon was accused by his father of a "lack of order, a brooding prowling around in all the fields of science, a stuffy brooding under a dismal oil lamp."[3]

With his father's death in 1836 he was free to abandon his studies

[2]In an essay on the Jewish question, quoted by Wilhelm Liebknecht, in *Karl Marx Biographical Memories*, p. 21.

[3]F. Nehring (trans. by E. Fitzgerald) *Karl Marx, the Story of His Life*, p. 120.

in law and concentrate on philosophy, history, and political economy. He soon became deeply involved in the great intellectual debate of those days centering in the conflict between authoritarian conservatism and Hegel's new philosophy regarding the inevitability of change in all things, especially in the realm of ideas. Marx soon became a Hegelian materialist and atheist. This brought him into disfavor with the university authorities. Only outside Prussia at the University of Jena, where opposition to Hegel had not yet crystallized, was Marx' thesis for his doctorate acceptable. He mailed it to them and graduated in 1841. Too radical for a conventional academic career he went into journalism to make a living.

In 1842 Marx joined the staff of the Rheinische Zeitung at Cologne (a middle-class liberal newspaper) and soon became its editor. This paper promulgated socialistic doctrine in a philosophical strain. It was suppressed in 1843 because of his militant atheism and its scathing criticism of the new divorce law. The same year he married Jenny von Westphalen.

When an effort to revive the newspaper failed, Marx went to Paris to study. He found the socialist movement in great intellectual ferment, and contacted Proudhon and Bakunin, the leaders of socialist and anarchist thought. He also met Friedrich Engels, the son of a wealthy German textile manufacturer, and they commenced a lifelong friendship that resulted in "the most important literature partnership of the nineteenth century, and perhaps of all time.[4]

Engels became Marx's "alter ego," the great developer and popularizer of his ideas. He brought an independent mind to their partnership and had much to contribute. While working for his father in Manchester, England, he made a detailed study of that city. He discovered two Manchesters. One was an attractive city of the upper-class with its comfortable homes, fascinating shops, numerous churches and theaters. The other Manchester was unbelievably sordid. It was jammed with a "stunted population living in a state of filth and despair, turning to gin and evangelism and doping themselves and their children with laudanum against a life that was hopeless and brutal."

Engels explored Manchester until he knew "every last hovel and each ratlike abode." He published his findings "in the most terrible

[4]R. N. Carew Hunt, *The Theory and Practice of Communism*, p. 253.

verdict ever passed on the world of industrial slums": *The Condition of the Working Class in England in 1844.* On one occasion Engels tried to describe the misery of the slums to a prosperous Manchester acquaintance. After listening quietly he was given the following brush off, "And yet there is a great deal of money made here; good day, sir."[5]

In 1845 Marx was expelled from France. He took refuge with Engels in Brussels. They joined the Communist League in 1847 and issued their famous *Manifesto* late that year. The timing of this brilliant publication was striking, for on February 18, 1848, revolution broke out in France, the monarchy fell and the movement spread to Germany, Austria, and Italy. Marx went to Cologne to direct things, but was arrested, tried, and banished. He went to England as an exile in 1849.

From 1850 his life was uneventful. For the next twenty years Marx fully expected the revolution to break out "the next day." His life in London was filled with much suffering. Poverty dogged his steps and only Engels' faithful gifts sustained him. He passed his time studying, writing, organizing an international working-class movement, and feuding with all who had the courage to differ with him. An "isolated and bitterly hostile figure" his impatience and irritability increased with old age, and he took care to avoid the society of men who bored him or disagreed with his views.[6]

And yet, Marx was a man of conviction. He was intellectually honest and "absolutely incorruptible." He felt a strong sense of moral indignation over the social injustice he saw on every hand. England in the early decades of the Industrial Revolution, as interpreted by Engels, made Marx see red. "Why are the laborers the poorest class?" he would ask himself. "Their labor produces wealth, yet they do not share in it. Most of it goes to the capitalists. Here is the monstrous crime: the capitalists are enriching themselves by robbing the laboring classes and the laboring classes are becoming increasingly bitter." "I can see," he would add, "that these two classes are deeply opposed to one another. Inevitably their conflict will erupt into the violence of revolution. This is the law of life: this is the law of economics."

[5] R. L. Heilbroner, *The Worldly Philosophers*, p. 133.
[6] Isaiah Berlin, *Karl Marx: His Life and Environment*, p. 253.

With the crushing of the Commune of Paris in 1871 and the growing prosperity of the latter half of the Victorian Era, Marx lost hope in an immediate revolution, and devoted his closing days to his major work, *Das Kapital*. He died in 1883. Eight attended his burial and heard Engels declare, "The greatest living thinker will think no more. His name will live for centuries to come."

B. Marxism

1. Its Philosophical Basis

At the University of Berlin, Marx came under the influence of Hegel's philosophical system in which the world was regarded as irresistibly propelled upward by an all-powerful "It" or world-spirit. Although drawn by the rational principle and optimistic thrust of this dynamic concept, Marx was repelled by the implication that the "It" was a nonmaterial force. It sounded dangerously theistic to him even though Hegel himself deliberately resisted the temptation to equate the "It" with the God of traditional religion. In reaction Marx was attracted to the atheistic position of those who regarded themselves as "left-wing" Hegelians.

In *The Holy Family* (1845) he attributes his conversion to atheism to the influence of three of these men. Two were liberal theologians. David Strauss was the founder of the mystical theory of the origin of Christianity and author of *Leben Jesu* (1835), the most powerful rationalistic repudiation of the deity of Christ ever written. Bruno Bauer, Marx' favorite professor, wrote *Religion of the Old Testament* (1838) dealing with the origins of Judaism in the same fashion. He explained everything in terms of myths and dogmas he alleged were clever inventions of early Jewish leaders to give ancient authority and sanction to the ethical standards they felt should characterize their emerging national culture. The third was Ludwig Feuerbach, a popular philosopher whose major work, *The Essense of Christianity* (1841), reduced all religious convictions to mere outward projections of man's inward nature. "God is made in the image of man," he thundered as he championed a purely psychological and pragmatic approach to religion. Besides confirming Marx in his atheism Feuerbach influenced him to claim that all the products of the human mind could be regarded as but reflections of the material conditions under which man lived and worked.

Recalling the satanic aspect of Communism's origin and development, it is rather significant that these three men who gave Marx an intellectual basis for his atheistic and materialistic views were likewise extremely influential in initiating the anti-Bible, antisupernatural revolt within the Protestant Church which later had a deadening influence on spiritual life and missionary passion.

In one aspect Marx and his left-wing Hegelians were loyal. They accepted without hesitation Hegel's dialectic. He had stated that the path of the ascent of mankind is a sort of predestined, fatalistic zigzag. This dialectic or "theory of the union of opposites" declares that every state of things is inevitably followed by an opposing state, its "negation" which will in turn yield to another opposite, "the negation of the negation." The process is one of thesis, antithesis, and synthesis. All things are in a state of change. All ideas are in the state of becoming other ideas. All past history can be broken down into periods in which there existed but two forces: the protagonist and the antagonist with the conflict eventually resolving itself in the sudden emergency of the synthesis of the two, "the unity of opposites." There must always be this eventual reconciliation, but even this synthesis is just as automatically followed by the emergence of the new antagonist. All is relative; the absolute with its complete absence of inner conflict is only possible in the distant future. Dialectics appeared to Marx to be the science of all laws of motion both of human history and of human thinking.

But what was the "It" behind this dialectical process? While in Paris, Marx was continually pressed by Engels to discover scientific reasons for believing in the certain overthrow of capitalism and the inevitable evolution of society into the ideal that the socialists had been describing so gloriously, wherein all willingly worked for the common good and were rewarded in accordance with the principle "from each according to his ability, to each according to his needs."

One day the thought gripped Marx that economics might be the great "It" of Hegel's system. Days of feverish study followed. Then, one day, Marx told Jenny that he had made the most staggering discovery in centuries, the discovery that economics is the only force that rules the world. Marx regarded himself now as the author of the final philosophic system and eagerly began to develop its details. Everything seemed to fit together: all recorded progress in the past had been the result of economic forces developing according to the dialectical pattern. Past history now had to be restudied and rewritten on this basis. But more, the future course of the world could now be plotted with the mathematical accuracy such a dialectic allegedly made possible. Throughout his life Marx regarded this discovery as one of the outstanding achievements of the human mind. It was 1844 and he was 26.[7]

2. Its Political Economy

Once Marx settled on economics as the key to all history he began to regard everything in this light.

> Since mankind must first of all eat and drink, have shelter and clothing, before it can pursue politics, religion, science, and art, Marx saw that the production of the immediate material means of subsistence, and consequently the degree of economic development attained by a given people or during a given epoch, form the foundation upon which State institutions, the legal conceptions, the art and even the religious ideas of the people concerned have been evolved, and in the light of which these things must be explained, instead of vice versa as had hitherto been the case.[8]

The first item of significance that gripped Marx in his studies and theorizing was *the class struggle*. Giving way to his common failing of oversimplifying complex matters, he projected the pattern of the zigzag dialectical ascent into the history of the past. In the *Manifesto* he wrote:

> The history of all human society, past and present, has been the history of class struggles. Freeman and slave, patrician and plebeian, baron and serf, guild-burgess and journeyman—in a word, oppressor and oppressed—stood in sharp opposition each to the other. They carried on perpetual warfare, sometimes masked, sometimes open and acknowledged; a warfare that invariably ended either in a revolutionary change in the whole structure of society or else in the common ruin of the contending classes. . . . Modern bourgeois society, rising out of the ruin of the feudal society, did not make an end of class antagonisms. It merely set up new classes in place of the old; new conditions

---

[7]The over-all thrust of this paragraph was taken from an unpublished paper *Communism: The 20th Century's Major Problem,* by David Bentley-Taylor.
[8]Marx, *Selected Works* I, p. 16. From the eulogy at Marx's grave by F. Engels.

of oppression; new embodiments of struggle. Our own age, the bourgeois age, is distinguished by this—that it has simplified class antagonisms. More and more, society is splitting up into two great hostile camps, into two great and directly contraposed classes: bourgeoisie and proletariat.

Marx took this concept and forged it into a revolutionary slogan, a call to arms for the proletariat against the *bourgeoisie*. He felt that the laboring masses should be taught that their misfortunes were all due to the "blood-sucking" capitalists whose machines they served. The class struggle was pressed upon them as evidence of "the unity of opposites," the unstable situation in the dialectical advance of history. He called the workers of the world to unite, to sense their essential unity, and agree to rise up and destroy their capitalist bosses. Their destiny was only to be achieved through actively heightening the class struggle and thus hastening the advance toward the nodal point at which the dialectical leap thrust mankind upward into the socialist stage of mankind's political and social evolution.

Marx might rightly be regarded a philosopher, a prophet of doom, announcing the violent end of capitalist society, and the inevitability of a proletarian revolution. But he was a revolutionist as well. For this reason he has challenged the activist as well as the intellectual.

3. Its Theory and Practice of Revolution

To Marx the basic premises were clear. Capitalist society was doomed. Its internal contradictions manifested in the class struggle were evidence of the relentless operation of the dialectic. In time the tension would mount to the breaking point. Then would come the proletarian revolution. As Lenin later said in *Left-Wing Communism* (1920), "Revolution becomes possible only when the lower classes do not want the old way, and the upper classes cannot continue in the old way." It was all so scientific: the triumph of socialism was inevitable—just a matter of time.

But Marx was not content merely to theorize. He was essentially a revolutionist. As a result he was constantly taken up with the tactical problems confronting the proletariat in their class struggle. He sought to discover a revolutionary method that would accelerate the movement of the dialectic and hasten the revolution. The dialectic itself gave him his chief weapon. If one could heighten the conflict of interest between the proletariat and the *bourgeoisie*, he reasoned, by exploiting each and every issue of conflict, an explosive situation would be generated that in time would produce the "dialectical leap." This became his revolutionary method. From Marx onward each and every intelligent, disciplined communist makes himself the agent of discord in the dying capitalist society. He studies how to provoke strife and ill will between the *bourgeoisie* and the proletariat, while somehow strengthening the togetherness and brotherliness of the proletariat, the very people most likely to suffer from the acceleration of interclass strife. This development of proletarian solidarity is essential to success.

In his call for action Marx emphasized that the only valid political goal for which mankind should strive and sacrifice is the public ownership and control of the means of production, distribution, and credit. Inasmuch, however, as the *bourgeoisie* will not peacefully and willingly relinquish control of these basic elements of its economic structure, Marx was always careful to point out that the proletariat would have to seize them by force. "The immediate aim of the communists," he preached, "must ever and only be the conquest of political power by the proletariat." This would be amplified to mean that they would have to master first the "state apparatus" of the capitalists. Only then could they introduce their longed-for qualitative change of society—the dialectical concept of transforming the means of production into public property.

But what will follow this conquest of political power? The first task of the victorious proletariat will be to decree that the means of production have become the property of the people, represented by a vanguard of "enlightened" leaders having enormous power. In his *Critique of the Gotha Programme* Marx wrote that "between capitalist and communist society lies the period of the revolutionary transformation of the former into the latter. To this corresponds a political transition period, in which the state can be no other than the revolutionary dictatorship of the proletariat." Under its leadership socialism is introduced and all production related no longer to personal profit. (Incidentally, socialism to the Marxist is this historical period immediately following the revolution; it is not solely a particular philosophy of the organization of society, etc.)

During this transitional, socialist period, payment by results will dominate industry. "From every man according to his ability; to every man according to his work." After a considerable period mankind will begin to shed its old bourgeois trappings. Then commences an era of perfection with the fading away of those characteristics of human behavior which formerly necessitated such coercive state functions as military conscription, direction of labor, internal police, penal institutions. domination of the legislative by the executive, limitation of human rights, etc. In time the proletarian dictatorship itself begins to become redundant. The barriers between it and the people commence breaking down. The state starts to "wither away." As Engels described in *Anti-Dühring* (1877), "The interference of the state authority in social relationships will become superfluous, and will be discontinued in one domain after another. The government over persons will be transformed into the administration of things and the management of the process of production. The state will not be abolished; it will die out." People begin to work for the love of working, to serve for the privilege of serving. With this comes, at long last, the dawning of the era of *Communism*.

At this point Marx waxes Utopian. He sees mankind at last the master of his social organization. No longer is he the slave to necessity. He is now free. Marx, the prophet, described this flowering of human history as follows:

> In the higher phase of Communist society after the enslaving subordination of individuals under division of labour and therewith the antithesis between mental and physical labour has vanished; after labour has become not merely a means to live, but has become itself the primary necessity of life; after the production forces have also increased with the all-round development of the individual, and all the springs of co-operative wealth flow more abundantly—only then can the narrow horizon of bourgeois right be fully left behind, and society inscribe on its banners: "From each according to his ability, to each according to his needs."[9]

And yet, Marx repelled many by his revolutionary methods. To him the end justified the use of any means. Both he and Engels presented a closely reasoned defense of this amoral position. Engels wrote:

[9]M. Eastman, *Capital and Other Writings of Karl Marx*, p. 7.

We reject every attempt to impose on us any moral dogma whatsoever as an eternal, ultimate and forever immutable moral law. . . . We maintain that all former moral theories are the product of the economic stage which society has reached at that particular epoch. And as society has hitherto moved in class antagonisms, morality was always a class morality. A really human morality which transcends class antagonisms and their legacies in thought becomes possible only at a stage of society which has not only overcome class contradictions but has even forgotten them in practical life.[10]

Years later Lenin was asked whether or not there was such a thing as Communist ethics and Communist morality. His reply was forthright, and in complete harmony with Engels' position.

It is frequently asserted that we have no ethics, and very frequently the *bourgeoisie* say that we Communists deny all morality. In what sense do we deny ethics, morals? In the sense in which they are preached by the *bourgeoisie,* a sense which deduces these morals from God's commandments. Of course, we say that we do not believe in God. We know perfectly well that the clergy, the landlords, and the *bourgeoisie* all claimed to speak in the name of God, in order to protect their own interests as exploiters. We deny all morality taken from superhuman or non-class conceptions. . . . A morality taken from outside of human society does not exist for us; it is a fraud. For us morality is wholly subordinated to the interests of the proletarian class struggle.[11]

Ever since its inception as a revolutionary movement Communism has consistently adhered to this pattern of ethics. All actions are evaluated as to their rightness or wrongness depending on whether they advanced or retarded the revolution. Prof. Harold Laski, one of their protagonists, has had to admit that communists

act without moral scruples, intrigue without any sense of shame, are utterly careless of truth, sacrifice without any hesitation the means they use to the ends they serve. . . . The only rule to which the Communist gives unswerving loyalty is the rule that a success gained is a method justified. The result is a corruption of

---

[10] F. Engels, *Anti-Dühring* (ed. Burns), pp. 109-110.
[11] Lenin, *Religion*, pp. 55-56.

both the mind and heart, which is alike contemptuous to reason and careless of truth.[12]

This revolutionary ethic, at once so relativistic and materialistic, is the direct issue of the philosophical basis of Marxism. Individualism is deliberately suppressed. Individual Communists find no significance to their lives apart from their identification with the group and its program. Obedience to Party leadership is the only morality. It is in the field of philosophy and ethics that the vast gulf between Communism and Christianity is fully revealed. One condones while the other eschews the use of force to effect the extension of its message and influence throughout the earth.

This then is Communism—a complex of philosophy, economic theory, and revolutionary procedure. But the Marxism one encounters today differs considerably from the original, as delineated by Karl Marx. It has been influenced and altered by the march of time and by Marx's followers. Regarding this development, the orthodox Lenin conceded:

> In no sense do we regard the Marxist theory as something complete and unassailable. On the contrary, we are convinced that this theory is only the cornerstone of that science which socialists must advance in all directions if they do not wish to fall behind life.[13]

Since Lenin and his era gave great impetus to this evolutionary development of Marxism, our investigation must now consider him and his work.

C. Nicolai Lenin (1870-1924)

Lenin was the man who "streamlined the ponderous Marxist doctrine into a fast-moving revolutionary chariot."[14] By the time Marx died in 1883, the Victorian Era had started to blossom into a rapidly expanding prosperity. Gone were the lean, hard times that had provoked the creation of Marx's dogma of inevitable revolution. The lot of the worker was steadily improving instead of worsening as he had predicted. Even the most zealous socialists were succumbing to the pressure of a reality that demanded the revision of their revo-

---

[12]Quoted by John C. Bennett in *Christianity and Communism*, 1949, p. 36.
[13]Quoted by M. Eastman on p. xix of *Capital and Other Writings of Karl Marx*.
[14]E. Rogers, *A Christian Commentary on Communism*, p. 183.

lutionary program. Today communists call this form of apostasy the
mortal sin of "revisionism."

However, as the years passed, this prosperity began to wane. The
working classes became restive. Once again their future began to
look dark. They no longer were drawn to those who had liberalized
Marx. And yet their leadership was unable to cope with the petty
bickerings and jealousies that plagued their ranks. But where was
the leader who really understood the course they should follow?
Where was the man strong enough to command and secure their
allegiance? In 1895 he suddenly appeared in remote St. Petersburg,
Russia, distributing mimeographed sheets denouncing the betrayers
of Marx. He was Vladimir Ilyich Ylyanov, better known by his
political name, Nicolai Lenin.

Lenin was born in Simbirsk on the Volga, being the third child
of a primary school inspector. His mother was the daughter of a
land-owning physician. Despite his father's government position
the political thinking of the home was strongly socialistic. Shortly
after Lenin graduated (with honors) from Simbirsk gymnasium at
the age of seventeen, a shadow fell upon the home. His eldest
brother, Alexander, who had joined a terrorist society (the Narodo-
voltze), took part in an unsuccessful attempt on the life of Tsar
Alexander III, was captured and executed. This caused the whole
family to be brought into public disrepute. A police ban was placed
on them. From that time forward Lenin was determined on the life
of a revolutionary to bring down the regime responsible for his
brother's death.

Even though embittered, he did not give way to irrational, passionate action. Although still quite young, he appraised rather objectively the whole matter of political assassinations. He was impressed with the relative futility of terrorist acts by individuals
against highly placed persons as a policy for achieving fundamental
social changes. He soon decided that instead of attacking individual
tyrants, a better course would be to make the workers aware of themselves as a social class and then instill in them the definite objective
of rising up en masse and seizing political power. From that time
onward Lenin became increasingly impressed with the importance of
organization, if a revolution was to be successfully carried out.

In 1887 Lenin entered Kazan University to study law but was

sent home by the authorities for affiliating with the local Marxist group. By dint of hard study at home he finally prepared himself to take the law examinations and was successful, being awarded his degree in 1891.

After graduation Lenin began to study systematically all that Marx had written, and eventually drifted to St. Petersburg (renamed Petrograd during World War I, and Leningrad shortly after his death in 1924). There he began conducting a vigorous campaign against all who had deviated from Marxist orthodoxy. His zeal made him a marked man. At twenty-six he was arrested, imprisoned, and subsequently banished to Siberia. While there in relative freedom he married Nadzehda Krupskaya, a fellow collaborator of St. Petersburg days. Later they were exiled to Switzerland. Wherever he went Lenin injected a new spirit into the revolutionary movement. He was a dynamic leader, calling continually for the immediate formation of a centralized "underground" revolutionary party, which would train and lead the proletariat in an organized struggle against the Tsar's government.

Then came the great 1903 split in the international labor movement. The minority (Mensheviks) wanted a liberalized eclectic Marxian dogma, a loose party organization that would receive all sympathizers and would seek to gain political power through uniting proletariat and liberal *bourgeoisie* policies. Opposing these political opportunists were the majority (Bolsheviks) demanding orthodox Marxian dogma, a tight, disciplined party organization that would work toward only one goal, the sudden, violent acquisition of power through armed revolution. Lenin at thirty-three was the undisputed leader of the Bolshevik section. (In 1918 the name Bolshevik was dropped in favor of communist.)

In October, 1905, there occurred an abortive revolution. Due to the humiliating defeat of Russia by Japan in the 1904-1905 war, agrarian disturbances at home, general government incompetence, and the tragic shooting by apprehensive soldiers of many innocent workers peacefully demonstrating before the Tsar's palace ("Bloody Sunday"—January 22), the Russian people became increasingly more restive and sudden "spontaneous, not directed" strikes broke out all over Russia. It seemed as though the time for the armed uprising of the proletariat had come. Frantic efforts were made to channel this revolutionary spirit. A general strike was ordered, power was seized, and local Soviets (councils of workers, soldiers, and peasants' deputies) were hastily formed to exercise the functions of government. The people began to taste the joy of using force against their oppressors. However, due to inadequate central leadership (Lenin arrived too late to take charge), the opportunity faded and the Tsarist government, backed by the army, regained control. The revolutionary spirit dwindled. For the next decade the State's counterrevolutionary activity—arrests, executions, and banishments—enabled it to maintain control of the lower classes. During this period Lenin lived abroad for safety's sake.

Lenin never felt that the 1905 uprising had been in vain. In his work *Left-Wing Communism* (1920), he wrote: "Without the dress rehearsal of 1905, the victory of the October Revolution of 1917 would have been impossible." To him this failure pointed up the complete vindication of the Bolshevik contention that a disciplined unified revolutionary party was absolutely mandatory.

From 1906 till 1914, Lenin, the exile, devoted all his strength and time to perfecting the revolutionary movement in Russia. He did this by correspondence, by clandestine contacts with key men, and through seeking to seize control of all workers' organizations. Soon his disciplined Bolsheviks had penetrated all key positions. This internal victory was achieved by 1912. By a legal press (Pravda) and an illegal, underground press, he provided his men with a "party line" that was always up to date and always directed toward the one great objective: the seizure of political power by the proletariat. And he never forgot to stress continually the thesis that Marxist, now termed Bolshevik, dialectical materialism was the most enlightened, most scientific thought in the Western world.

When World War I began, Lenin was certain that the revolution could not be too distant. He denounced the warring capitalist nations for fighting solely that they might destroy their economic competitors and grab new markets overseas. Patriotic appeals were exposed as so much groundless sentiment to deceive the working classes. He sought to stir up the workers everywhere to transform what he termed the "international, imperialist war" into many separate civil wars. He was especially successful in Russia. After years of heavy military reverses the impoverished, suffering Russians became desperately war-weary. In the early part of 1917, the revolutionary spirit once again manifested itself. On March 15, the Tsar abdicated and a provisional government was established under Alexander Kerensky's leadership. Although this new government captured the imagination and loyalty of the people, Lenin's Bolsheviks had done their undercover work too well. In time, the semistable situation began to deteriorate. Lenin struggled to reach Russia to lead the revolutionary movement. Through the connivance of Swiss socialists and German officials he obtained permission to travel across Germany in a sealed car. He arrived in Petrograd on April 4 and in the railway station announced that the revolution against feudalism must move directly to the establishment of the dictatorship of the proletariat. Many of his followers felt this was not "dialectical," since the capitalist stage of Marxist theory was thereby completely bypassed. By sheer will-power Lenin persisted. His slogans, "No Support for the Provisional Government" and "All Power to the Soviets," stirred the people, while his small disciplined Bolshevik team kept undercutting all opposition. Nevertheless, Lenin was fighting against desperate odds. At one point he had to flee to Finland and remain in hiding several months.

On October 25, at the opening of the Congress of Soviets, Lenin felt the fatal hour had struck. It was "now or never." He suddenly appeared, denounced the provisional government and made a bid for the immediate seizure of power. By promising immediate peace and the redistribution of the land he won the soldiers and peasantry. The delegates were overwhelmed by his arguments. The Bolsheviks, now clearly in control, declared that supreme political power throughout Russia was only to be vested in the Soviets through their elected delegates. Kerensky's government was ignored. The delegates were won over. They made Lenin president and victory was complete. It was an almost bloodless conquest. But blood soon began to flow.

Lenin now faced enormous problems. He could only continue to hold the soldiers by commencing negotiations with the German General Staff to end the war. To hold the peasantry he began almost immediately to carve up the lands of the estate owners. To appease the theorists who desired a truly dialectical revolution (from feudalism to capitalism to socialism) he called for the election of a bourgeois-type constituent assembly. This was done but it proved to be too independent of Lenin. It lasted two days and he then dissolved it, affirming doubtless with tongue in his cheek that the dialectical movement had gathered such terrific momentum that it now demanded the immeate introduction of the Socialist era. In the meanwhile, civil war had broken out, and central Russia was soon surrounded by counterrevolutionary "white" Russian armies. Then followed months of incredible chaos. When things were at their darkest for the communists Lenin was shot twice by an anarchist, Fanya Kaplan. To the surprise of all, he made an amazing recovery, and his followers were more determined than ever to stamp out all counterrevolutionary elements.

In all there were three frightful years of "War Communism." Vast numbers of the former bourgeois society were liquidated without even the semblance of a trial. Eventually the government went so far in suppressing the people that another revolution was imminent. The Kronstadt mutiny (January, 1921) by Bolshevik sailors against the Soviet government came to Lenin as a solemn warning. The only way he could save the nation was to return to a limited form of private enterprise. For tactical reasons alone he ordered this retreat. (The missing dialectical "zag" of capitalism was inserted!) This New Economic Policy continued from 1921 to 1925. The nation now began to breathe and develop.

Due to the strain of overwork and a sclerosis attacking his cerebral arteries, Lenin began to decline physically in 1922. Over a period he suffered three strokes and lingered on until January 21, 1924.

Lenin was no social dreamer. He was a revolutionist in the fullest sense. He used Russia to test Marxist theory; the immediate welfare of the Russian people was never allowed to have a primary place in his thinking and planning. Shub says in this connection:

> The enormous sacrifices which his great experiment required were inescapable and irrelevant. Mercy was a bourgeois virtue. The man who loved children, animals and nature seldom lifted a finger to save human beings from Cheka firing squads.[15]

[15]David Shub, *Lenin* (1948 Mentor Abridged Ed.), p. 178.

D. Leninism: Its Contribution to Marxism

Lenin applied Marxist theory successfully to a revolutionary situation. For this reason Leninism is officially defined as "Marxism of the era of imperialism and of the proletarian revolution" (Stalin). And yet, the October Revolution was undertaken in such defiance of Marxist principles that Lenin's exegesis of basic Marxist texts was considerably influenced by his desire to appear orthodox while acting in a completely unorthodox manner. In communist circles today Lenin's writings on revolutionary techniques are studied and revered far more than the writings of Marx and Engels. Lenin would not have approved of this. He regarded himself an orthodox Marxist who drew his chief inspiration from Marx's thesis that "a working-class movement must be revolutionary or it is nothing at all." He seemingly built his whole life on that one text and regarded even his most incidental tactic in the revolutionary struggle to be an expression of correctly applied Marxist dogma.

Much has been written in recent years of the strong influence of Russian history and national temperament on the character of the world communist movement. It was Lenin who Russified Marxism and changed an essentially Western creation into an Asiatic-Byzantine, autocratic, messianic world crusade. Stalin merely followed Lenin's lead. He was a loyal, consistent Leninist.

Lenin was chiefly a politician. His constant emphasis was on revolutionary organization, the development of the Communist Party as both a revolutionary weapon (against bourgeois society) and a suppressive weapon (over the *bourgeoisie*). Economic theory was never allowed to interfere with his practical, pragmatic approach to political problems. For instance, Lenin doubted the inevitability of the breakdown of capitalism. Political power had to be seized or it might never come to the proletariat, dialectics notwithstanding. In this, he went far beyond orthodox Marxism.

Lenin coined the phrase "democratic centralism." He meant that even in the revolutionary proletarian party a central, bureaucratic self-perpetuation core of leadership was mandatory. This leadership not only had the task of maintaining discipline within the ranks of the party but of purging it from time to time so that among its members there would always be complete conformity in thought.

Such doctrinal fanaticism Lenin felt to be essential if a revolution-making party was to succeed.

Lenin developed the concept of "dictatorship of the proletariat" into something strikingly different from Marx's original, democratic conception. To him the term proletariat did not represent the total working-class, but rather those elements within it that supported the program of the Communist Party. According to Lenin, the dictatorship of the proletariat represented the dictatorship of a Communist Party over all the elements of the socialist state: the proletariat, remnants of the former bourgeois class, and what he called the "non-proletarian masses." This is his tragic legacy to his followers: a totalitarian control by a disciplined minority over the whole of society.

> If the dictatorship of the proletariat means anything at all, then it means that the vanguard of the class is armed with resources of the state in order to repel dangers, including those emanating from the backward layers of the proletariat itself.
>
> —STALIN

The application of this principle has resulted in making the welfare of the Communist Party the supreme function of the Communist State.

Lenin is likewise credited with a distinctive contribution to Marxist economic theory. It was he who fitted the post-Victorian era into the dialectic. This he termed the era of imperialism or "monopoly capitalism." He deliberately excluded from his reasoning all reference to the colonial expansion of the seventeenth and eighteenth centuries and argued that imperialism in its twentieth-century form was nothing more than the dialectical reaction against a burgeoning capitalist economy that could not solve the problem of the "boom-trust" cycle other than by creating foreign markets through duplicity or force. He wrote:

> Imperialism is capitalism in that stage of development in which the domination of monopoly and finance capital has taken shape; in which the export of capital has acquired pronounced importance; in which the division of the world by international trust has begun; and in which the partition of all

the territory of the earth by the greatest capitalist countries has been completed.[16]

From this Lenin went on to reason that modern imperialism was the last, final stage of capitalist development. All efforts to develop capitalism further were doomed to failure. The only result will be the eventual dialectical shift to socialism. This theory became very useful as the chief propaganda weapon of all overseas Communist Parties.

Lenin challenged them to become openly anti-imperialistic in those underdeveloped areas of the world where they stood to gain by either fermenting or supporting nationalistic movements. The more restive a colony the more tension could be provoked between it and the mother-country. The more its peoples heard of their exploitation the more they would seek the support of a movement publically affirming its desire to help liberate all subjugated peoples. This anti-imperialist crusade of the Communist Party has given it enormous influence in the colonial areas of the world.

E. Stalin

Following Lenin's death a sharp struggle for power was waged within the communist hierarchy. Eventually Joseph Stalin, the son of a shoemaker, emerged as the supreme dictator. During the almost three decades of his autocratic rule, the strength and prestige of the Soviet Union were greatly increased. But Stalin added virtually nothing of significance to communist theory. Inasmuch as Lenin's Marxism is currently the orthodox line accepted by communists the world over, there is little point in reviewing the minor deviations Stalin made from Lenin's interpretation of Marxist texts.

However, in the realm of communist practice, Stalin made a distinct contribution. He insisted on giving top priority to what he called "socialism in one country." During the first years following October, 1917, Lenin held that unless revolutions were speedily generated in other countries of the world, the weak Soviet Union would collapse. He stressed the work of the Communist Parties abroad. But Stalin felt that effort and strength should be chiefly concentrated in establishing Russia as the powerful heart of a new socialist order. He regarded the task of fermenting revolutions abroad of secondary

[16]Lenin, *Selected Works: Imperialism, The Highest State of Capitalism*, II, p. 709.

importance. He did not believe the world would witness further revolutions until the Soviet Union was sufficiently powerful enough to direct and support them. To achieve his purpose he collectivized agriculture at frightful cost (1929-1933), greatly expanded Russia's heavy industry, strengthened State power and, in the end, fully vindicated his thesis by leading his nation to victory over the previously invincible Nazi armies in World War II. The remarkable and symbolic resistance of Leningrad and Stalingrad, by which the Soviet, Union was saved, gave her immense military prestige. She is feared by many. But it was Stalin's achievement of rapid industrialization of backward Russia that has made Communism attractive to the underdeveloped countries of the world. Indeed, the colossus of today that is the USSR is a tremendous vindication of Stalin's leadership even though he is despised and repudiated in the current party line.

In conclusion, it must be said that through the labors of Lenin and Stalin the dogma of international Communism has been successfully wedded to Russian imperialism. The result is a fearful combination whose very presence does not augur well for the future of this globe in its drift, chiefly through technological development, toward the inevitability of world government.

COMMUNISM AND CHRISTIANITY

We have seen that Marxism is essentially optimistic, a well-articulated body of doctrine—philosophic, economic, political, and social—that is allegedly based on scientific principles. Although its followers firmly believe they are living in a doomed, divided world that is irresistibly rushing toward a final period of violence and tribulation, they manifest a bracing hopefulness as to their eventual triumph. Marxists rarely appear to be troubled with inferiority complexes. They have all the ardor of crusaders. No personal sacrifice is too great to make if thereby the cause is furthered. But in their zeal and enthusiasm they are also capable of fierce hatreds. And this hatred is directed relentlessly toward all those forces which they regard as hindering the movement toward proletarian revolution. It is in this context that the Marxist encounters the Christian. Toward no other movement does he manifest more open scorn, settled opposition, and implacable hatred than he does toward Christianity.

The well-trained communist is neither neutral nor indifferent toward religious systems and their followers. "Communism abolishes eternal truths, it abolishes all religion and all morality."—*Manifesto*. In his pamphlet, *Religion*, Lenin discusses the reasons for this hostility.

> The roots of modern religion are deeply imbedded in the social oppression of the working masses, and in their complete helplessness before the blind forces of capitalism, which every day and every hour cause a thousand times more horrible suffering and torture for ordinary working folk than are caused by exceptional events such as war, earthquakes, etc. "Fear created the gods." Fear of the blind forces of capital—blind because its action cannot be foreseen by the masses—a force which at every step in life threatens the worker and the small business man with "sudden," "unexpected," "accidental" destruction and ruin, bringing in their train beggary, pauperism, prostitution, and deaths from starvation— This is the taproot of modern religion which, first of all and above all, the materialist must keep in mind, if he does not wish to remain stuck forever in the kindergarten of materialism.
>
> . . . Religion is the opiate of the people.[17] Religion is a kind of spiritual intoxicant, in which the slave of capital drowns his humanity and his desires for some sort of decent human existence. . . . To him who toils and suffers want all his life, religion teaches humility and patience on earth, consoling him with the hope of reward in heaven. And to those who live on the labor of others, religion teaches charity on earth, offering them a very cheap justification for their whole existence as exploiters, and selling them at a suitable price tickets for admission to heavenly bliss. . . . Our program is based entirely on a scientific and materialistic world conception. Our program necessarily includes the propaganda of atheism. We shall now probably have to follow the advice which Engels gave to the German Socialists —to translate and spread among the masses the enlightening atheistic literature of the 18th century.

Originally, Lenin advocated using only the ideological weapon to oppose religion, feeling that with scientific enlightenment and the impact of the new social order all religion would soon wither and die. He desired to avoid producing martyrs through making

[17]This phrase was first used by Charles Kingsley, an Anglican clergyman.

religious principles the issue in his conflict with the church. But in time he came to realize that religious convictions could be very deeply rooted, and recommended a cautious and clever "combination of open attack with deceit and subterfuge." Stalin followed this pattern. Realizing its propaganda value, he decided that the organized Church should be allowed to exist, so long as it served completely the interests of the Party and the State. This continues to be the official policy.

And yet, the basic conflict continues. E. Manuilov, a Party spokesman in an official lecture in 1951, emphatically stated: "The destruction of religious survivals is a necessary condition of the training of conscious builders of a Communist Society." The Statutes of The Young Communists' League (1949) affirms that its members should "fight against drunkenness, hooliganism, the survivals of religious prejudices, and an uncomradely attitude against women." This lowering of religion to the level of social vices is an indication of the present point of view of the Soviet Union.[18]

Religious liberty as it is known in the West does not exist in the USSR. While freedom of religious worship is granted, Christians are not free to propagate their faith. All the propagandizing is on the other side. The vast propaganda machine of the State is ceaselessly at work seeking to draw the youth away from the Church so that in time the Church will be in almost complete isolation, out of touch with the people and dying from want of new life and intellectual stimulation. Besides the usual chatter about scientific materialism, this officially sponsored propaganda warfare keeps reminding the people of the close association between religion and capitalism: "Churches are the agents of Western Powers"; "Citizens who frequent churches expose themselves to the ideologies of the disloyal, the reactionary, the enemies of the States," etc. Such propaganda generates fear ,and the timid readily succumb.

Communism cannot simply say there is no God. Since the basic antagonism between Marx and Christ is doctrinal and philosophical, Communism inevitably finds itself saying, "Mankind everywhere must be made to cease believing in God." Feuerbach is quoted with approval: "Human beings have no future before them until they stop regarding themselves as the valets of His Heavenly Majesty." And

---

[18]Quoted from *The Church Under Communism*, p. 10.

yet, the antagonism is not solely theoretical. All too often, in the past, organized Christianity has been a reactionary force in the development of social justice. Jacques Maritain, the Roman Catholic philosopher, in pondering the enmity of the communists toward Christianity, has had to confess that communist hostility and atheism "originated chiefly through the fault of a Christian world unfaithful to its own principles, in a profound sense of resentment, not only against the Christian world, but—and here lies the tragedy— against Christianity itself. . . ."[19]

It has been observed that this conflict between Communism and Christianity is so characteristic of the attitude of one exclusive religion toward another that Communism itself might well be regarded as a religion. Certainly in matters pertaining to the human spirit it is most uncompromising. In this connection, after noting that in political matters Communism has a remarkable capacity for adaptability, Berdyaev observed:

> But there is a domain in which Communism is changeless, pitiless, fanatical, and in which it will grant no concessions whatever. That is the domain of the "world outlook," of philosophy and consequently of religion also. . . . It sometimes looks as though the Soviet government would rather go on to the restoration of capitalism in economic life than to granting freedom of conscience, freedom of philosophic thought, freedom to create a spiritual culture.[20]

But is Communism a religion? John C. Bennett has made an almost classic reply to this query. He writes:

> . . . If religion is defined as man's relationship to whatever he regards as ultimate or to whatever he trusts most for deliverance from the evils and hazards of life, then Communism is undoubtedly religious. . . . It is certainly true to say that Communism occupies the place in life for the convinced Communist that religions occupy in the lives of their adherents. Communism offers a goal for life. It offers a faith in redemption from all recognized evils. It offers an interpretation of life's meaning which may be short-sighted and one-sighted but which at least does provide the kind of guidance that the religious believer secures from doctrine. It even offers the kind of authority

[19]Quoted by J. C. Bennett, *Communism and Christianity*, p. 48.
[20]J. C. Bennett, *op. cit.*, p. 42.

that the more authoritarian churches provide for their members. Many other features of religion, such as sacred scriptures and saints, have their analogies in Communism. The Communist, like the Christian . . . is a man of faith. He is committed to a cause and he has an ultimate confidence that the highest powers, the existence of which he will admit, are on the side of that cause.[21]

To many, Communism presents itself as "the most coherent philosophy and the greatest single emotional drive" with which our generation has to deal. It is a cult which, in its opposition to traditional religious beliefs and patterns, has created its own counterbeliefs and counterpatterns. G. B. Shaw, the playwright, called it "the lay form of Catholicism."

People do not become communists gradually, but abruptly, suddenly through a total commitment of themselves to the will of the Party. They pass through a conversion-type experience in which self-interest is dethroned and there is the total acceptance of Party authority. But why should there be the desire to make so complete a surrender of oneself to his fellow men? A study of the case histories of ex-communists is most revealing. Some of the reasons given might be classified as follows:

A. The Desire for a Meaningful Life.

Human idealism seeks a direct outlet. Communism offers release from a way of living which, because it makes no demands, seems intolerably tame, purposeless, and enervating. Here is an efficient outlet for all the frustration one accumulates through living a selfish, meaningless existence. The lure of the Great Purpose: here is the answer to every question, the removal of all doubt, and a leadership which removes the burden for all individual decisions.

B. The Desire for Security.

In the underdeveloped areas of the world today there is a growing hunger of the masses for revolutionary change. These innumerable peoples, who have suffered so pathetically and pointlessly for centuries, are beginning to realize that their misery, poverty, sickness, and harsh grinding circumstances are altogether unnecessary.

[21]*Op cit.*, pp. 33, 34.

They have had some contact with the capitalistic West; many have seen films, some have read books, all have listened to the speeches in the market places. "Why, they ask, "should America or England be so wealthy when we are so poor? How comfortably they live! Yet while they ruled over us they made little serious effort to help us. We want a change, and we want it now. Look at the Soviet Union! Thirty or forty years ago Russia was a poor, diseased, backward nation. Today, after one brief generation, despite a most devastating war, it is emerging as the strongest nation, the most technically advanced nation in the world. If no one else will help us, the Soviet Union will. Unless we turn to them for safety, the impersonal juggernaut of the political upheavals of our day will crush us."

C. The Desire for Companionship.

People lost in the mass anonymity of Western society are lonely, hungry for fellowship, desirous of belonging to a group as recognized and appreciated members. The fear of being alone, without roots, drives them to the communist red flag with its vision of a united classless brotherhood. Richard Wright, an American Negro novelist, described his conversion to Communism as follows:

> It was not the economics of Communism, nor the great power of trade unions, nor the excitement of underground politics that claimed me; my attention was caught by the similarity of the experience of workers in other lands, by the possibility of uniting scattered but kindred peoples into a whole. It seemed to me that here at last, in the realm of revolutionary expression, Negro experience could find a home, a functioning value and role. Out of the magazines I read came a passionate call for the experiences of the disinherited, and there were none of the lame lispings of the missionary in it. It did not say: "Be like us and we will like you, maybe." It said: "If you possess enough courage to speak out what you are, you will find that you are not alone!" It urged life to believe life.[22]

D. The Desire for Light on Life's Problems.

Communists have great insight into the realities of contemporary political and social problems. They are master diagnosticians. And

[22]Richard Crossman, *The God That Failed* 123, 124.

their words can be very persuasive. One has but to listen to the comments of common people after they have been "exposed" to communist speeches. "These Communists use the correct labels. They call injustice, exploitation, oppression by their true names. They have a basic honesty about things. They look facts in the face.' Arthur Koestler, an Hungarian journalist, described his conversion to Communism as follows:

> By the time I had finished with *Feuerbach* and *State and Revolution,* something had clicked in my brain which shook me like a mental explosion. To say that one had "seen the light" is a poor description of the mental rapture which only the convert knows. The new light seems to pour from all directions across the skull; the whole universe falls into pattern like the stray pieces of a jigsaw puzzle assembled by magic at one stroke. There is now an answer to every question.[23]

In addition there are several lesser reasons why people become communists, but a discussion of them is beyond the scope of this chapter. Suffice it to say it is in analyzing them, one by one, that the evangelical Christian becomes aware of the true nature of the communist problem. When he discerns the religious overtones of Communism's optimistic world-outlook, and comes to understand the appeals it makes to the unregenerate heart, he begins to see that the only vital way of "combatting Communism" (for want of a better phrase!) is through adhering to the commission he has already received from his Lord to "preach the gospel to every creature." The Gospel of a crucified and risen Saviour is more than adequate to meet the basic needs and heart-hungerings of people in this twentieth-century world. But most important of all, the Gospel is able to meet man's greatest though most unconscious need: his need for forgiveness of sin and reconciliation to God.

Realizing all this, the evangelical Christian should seek in a new way to get under the burden of his fellow man. The disinherited of the earth are heart-hungry, hungry for love. But who loves man as does Jesus Christ. There is no power that can resist God's love when it is triumphant in the heart. In contrast, impersonal Communism is loveless. Then too people are hungry for fellowship. What fellowship transcends that of Christian brother with Christian brother,

[23]*Ibid.,* p. 32.

and together with Christ? Christians yearn for fellowship with other Christians, and their very yearning is for the presence of Christ they discern in one another. All the communist talk of "comrade" cannot compare with the spiritual fellowship of the vital, local church. People are hungry for purpose in their lives. What service is so utterly satisfying as doing the will of God? It is a service without regrets, no following of lost causes, no liquidating or repudiating of the ultimate leader. Communism breeds cynicism. While calling for total commitment and sacrifice, its whole fabric rests upon the uncertain framework of purge and counterpurge. In contrast, as the Christian goes through life, experiencing the abiding faithfulness of his Lord and proving the utter trustworthiness of the written Word, the Bible, his faith and heart-satisfaction are steadily enlarged.

Once a person has been recruited by the Communist Party he is given careful individual training. This is twofold, embracing cultural indoctrination and intensive practical discipline. A very severe period of preliminary training must be successfully undergone before there is any substantial recognition by the group. Assigned to the most difficult and unpleasant tasks to test loyalty and devotion, he must "accept and obey to the least detail, without grumbling."[24] Family responsibilities and pleasurse must be subordinated to the Party's interests. And there is tithing too. Unless one is willing to give at least 10 to 15 percent of his income, his devotion to the Party is suspected. The first law of discipline is that rebellion against the authority of the Party is not merely a mistake but a mortal sin—a mortal sin against the Soviet Fatherland and the revolutionary faith of Marx-Leninism. Self-criticism and confession are encouraged. The disobedient or "fractionary" must make public confession before being restored to the fellowship of the group. A kind of quack psychiatry is used: "If you don't reveal your wrong thoughts and bad deeds, they will become an intolerable burden on your shoulders . . . heavier and heavier, until the time comes when you no longer will be able to bear their great weight."[25] To fail to participate in the self-criticism meeting is to expose oneself to the charge of being a "lagging behind particle," a backward element without a genuine

[24]Shades of Philippians 2:14-16!
[25]Edward Hunter, *Brain-Washing in Red China*, p. 34.

sense of responsibility for the revolution. Actual apostasy is rare. Excommunication from the Party generally involves "liquidation" in those areas of the world where communists have political power. All in all, the communist is a man of faith, living in subjection to a fierce hierarchy and bound to them by a dogmatic creed. His is the religion of the scientific, secular man of the twentieth century.

THE CHRISTIAN APPROACH TO COMMUNISM

The basic problem of this age, confronting the Bible-believing Christian, is neither Communism nor world-wide social revolution. It is the unregenerate human heart in its rebellion against God. This is an age in which this spirit of disobedience appears to be manifesting itself in an ever-increasing manner due to the gathering momentum of technological advance with its perfected techniques for expressing the essentially sensate heart of the culture of our day. Since the Christian of this generation is committed to the sole task of evangelizing the peoples of this generation, he must be aware of what men are thinking. And since they are becoming increasingly aware of Communism in its onward march he dare not be ignorant of Communism and its appeals.

An awareness of the twentieth century's world-wide social revolution, the decline of the West, and the shifting of political power to the non-Caucasian races is mandatory to the Christian. Communism must be viewed—on the human level—in the light of this present era of transition. It considers itself the Messianic dynamic of this age and the vanguard of all social revolution and all scientific enlightenment. It cannot be dismissed merely as a power-grabbing conspiracy that is capitalizing on the widespread hungerings of the masses for social change. Although Communism has its demonic elements, a Christian critique should not be confined to an indignant evaluation of the by-products of its atheism. True, it frequently corrupts and betrays its most devoted followers. True, its negation of God eventually results in its repudiation of the dignity of human personality, and permits if not encourages the calculated use of brutal, immoral methods to dehumanize and break the spirit of its enemies. But this is only part of the total picture. In the interests of fairness and honesty, all its aspects must be studied and evaluated objectively.

Within recent decades there have developed a variety of "religious" approaches to Communism. In a real sense they reflect the overtones of religious life in Christendom today with resurgent Romanism, the decline of Protestant liberalism with its false optimism, and the emergence of neo-orthodoxy with its essentially pessimistic outlook on mankind's future. Classification of these approaches is both difficult and dangerous, and space does not permit a discussion of them here, only that of the evangelical Christian is attempted.

His Biblically-oriented approach to Communism might be summarized as follows. He begins with God and His revealed, infallible Word. He thinks vertically and not horizontally. There is only one Cause, and that is God. He is the God of history. And He will consummate history as He has already foretold. Righteousness shall reign on this earth. In the past He has raised up bitter and hasty nations to chasten His people to bring them back to Himself that in turn they might further His purpose among men. The Assyrian and Babylonian nations are cases in point. After using them to accomplish His purpose He punished them for their sins (Isa. 10:5-14, etc.). An omnipotent God has allowed the Communist movement to come into existence to refine His Church and bring it back to active obedience to His will. At this late hour in history when God's people have not yet completed their task of preaching the Gospel to every creature and making disciples of all nations, it is not too difficult to assume that a sovereign God is ordering circumstances so that—perhaps in the midst of a fiery furnace of brutal communist power—His people will at long last give Him the obedience He has been seeking, and witness wholeheartedly to the nations of the earth. In His time, the oppression of the communists will be broken and they too shall be arraigned before His judgment bar.

After reaffirming his settled conviction regarding the ultimate triumph of God in history—for He will win and He must reign—and after realizing the fact that in this day God is not losing sight of His Church's primary missionary obligation, but is working among the nations to hasten the completion of that task, the Christian now is ready to proceed with a sober, thorough study of the theory and practice of Communism. Its philosophy, economics, and political theory should be both understood and appraised as objectively as possible. He should know its weaknesses and inadequacies, and be willing to acknowledge its sources of strength. He should be able to challenge and refute its basic assumptions: its crass materialism which makes no allowance either for objective, eternal truth, or for mind or spirit; its atheism which denies God, His creatorship, and His control of history, and reduces man to naught but the highest of evolved beasts; its underestimation of the reality of evil in man and its naïve belief in human perfectibility; its overemphasis of the economic factor in human life and its predication of the class struggle as the point of departure for all so-called dialectical advance in society.[26]

Furthermore, in the light of the Word of God, the Christian should honestly face and accept the totality of his personal obligation to his brothers and sisters in Christ, to his non-Christian fellow citizens, and to the State authority. He will discover that the Bible has not a little to say about all three of these areas of relationship.

As to his fellow Christians, the dominant element of his relationship will be found to be one of love. He should seek financial independence of them by manual labor. He should especially remember the poor and destitute. He must avoid living in luxurious self-indulgence, recognizing that he is no better than the least member of the Church. In fact, his personal life must be a reflection of the fact that all social and economic distinctions are obliterated in the "household of faith." For love's sake, others are esteemed better than himself and under its compulsion all things are done "for their edification." Since his Lord while on earth unashamedly magnified the spiritual and heavenly above the earthly and material, the Christian seeks by his own example to keep this standard and thereby encourages his fellow Christians likewise to "set their affection on things above, not on things on the earth."

As to his non-Christian fellow citizens, the dominant element of his relationship will likewise be found to be one of love. Under the constraint of Christ's love, he will recognize that his primary obligation is to witness by life and word with a view to leading his neighbor to Christ.

In addition he has the responsibility of being an influence for good in society. He is as "salt" that checks rottenness and as "light" that dispels darkness. But this does not mean that he seeks to in-

[26]Use should be made of such excellent texts as: R. N. Carew Hunt's, *The Theory and Practice of Communism*, and *Marxism Past and Present*, and Sidney Hook's *Marx and the Marxists*.

fluence society to adopt the same standard of conduct that should characterize relationships within the local church. Unregenerate men have no capacity for New Testament (agape) love, although they do have a capacity for justice. Hence, the motivation to engender among them to ameliorate their own social conditions should be on this basis. Society is influenced by example and precept. If an employer, the Christian has certain just obligations to his employees. If an employee, the Christian has certain just obligations to his employer. If unjustly treated he is not permitted recourse to either violence or retaliation. But this proscription does not prevent the Christian from making an appeal on the basis of policy or justice. If, however, it is not granted, the Christian should encourage submission and patience. In all his dealings with the unsaved he should follow his Lord who refused to make either materialism or economic need the basis for His approach to a sinning mankind.

As to State authority, the dominant element of the Christian citizen's relationship will be found to be one of support and submission, so long as Caesar does not seek to usurp the place that belongs to God alone. Civil authority is only to be resisted when it clashes with the revealed will of God. The Christian must faithfully discharge his obligations of citizenship. He is not absorbed in politics, but exercises his right as a citizen to express his convictions on all social matters in the public assembly and by the ballot-box.

He will find that although his dominant responsibility as a witness is clearly defined in the Bible, he will have to weigh carefully its principles and wait much upon God if he is to know what position he should take on matters pertaining to social justice, such as racism, war, trade unionism, etc. And he will have to be charitable toward fellow Christians who conscientiously differ with him. Much humility of mind will be needed to accept graciously their varied opinions. At this point, however, he will begin to realize the impracticability and presumption of the Christian socialist in his assumption that the church be a "prophetic voice" in an unregenerate society. The very silence of the New Testament on this point will now strike him as significant. Were it written in the climate of the ecumenical movement of today it would be filled with calls to collective church action against slavery, against Nero's totalitarianism, and against participation in Rome's imperialistic wars.

All in all, the evangelical Christian must avoid adopting the attitude that the Bible is filled with easy solutions to the grave social problems of our day. Far better to admit one's ignorance. When the great majority of people involved in these social problems are in open rebellion against God, it is never wise to prate superficial judgments allegedly based on the Word of God. It brings dishonor to His name.

In seeking to increase his understanding of what God's Word says his attitude and conduct should be while living in a secular society beset by all the tensions that exist between individuals and the accepted mores of the society, the Evangelical Christian should not lose sight of his commission. In the final analysis his God-given responsibility is primarily not to society, but to individuals. He must never, never lose sight of the Gospel that has been committed to his care. This Gospel must be given to men: he must persuade men to be reconciled to God through Christ. Despite the angry evidence on every side of Communism's dynamic crusade, he must not tolerate for a moment any idea that the Gospel is not more than adequate to meet the basic needs of people today. It is at this point that the Christian socialist shows an unfortunate tendency to minimize the Gospel and think chiefly in terms of the collective needs of society. The Christian socialist is too eager to solve man's immediate needs while overlooking the fact that man's eternal needs are far greater. Christ and His redemptive work—delivering man from the awful consequences of his sins and making eternal life possible for him—this must be kept central.

To stress evangelism is to contribute solidly to the development of a healthy society. Religious revivals have had a greater, more wholesome influence on society than any other force—including Communism. To promote them, by prayer and by preaching, is always the greatest possible contribution the Christian can make to a diseased society, the majority of whose members are unregenerate, not under the rule of Christ.

But effort should continually be made to strengthen one's sense of historical perspective. Christians need to be prepared for catastrophe. This certainly was central in the apostle Paul's training of converts (Acts 14:22). In this day, Christians need to keep before them the record of the past, when for long centuries the Church suffered to maintain its Evangelical witness. They need to regard themselves and their churches as a part of the continuum of the God-given privilege of being burning and shining lights in a hostile world. What if the Communists gain complete control of the world? The Lord can still triumph, as His people, in their suffering, "'out-think, out-live, and out-die" their enemies. Even should organized Christianity be obliterated from the earth, God's people can still further His great missionary purpose. The Flame need not cease spreading from heart to heart.

No one knows what lies ahead. What if the communist movement climaxes in the emergence of that final Antichrist? Will God lose? No, on some dark day, His trumpet will sound and His Son shall return in glory to establish true social justice and righteousness in the earth.

BIBLIOGRAPHY

Basic Sources

Engels, Friedrich, *Anti-Dühring,* Ed. by E. Burns, International Publishers, New York.

Lenin, V. I. *Selected Works.* International Publishers, New York, 1943.

Mao, Tse-tung. *Selected Works.* (four volumes, based on Chinese edition, Peking, 1951). International Publishers, New York, 1934.

Marx, Karl. *Selected Works in Two Volumes.* (Prepared by The Marx-Lenin Institute, Moscow. Editor: V. Adoratsky), International Publishers, New York.

Stalin, J. V. *Foundations of Leninism.* International Publishers, New York, 1932.

———. *Problems of Leninism.* International Publishers, New York, 1934.

Biographical Studies of Leading Men
(These are written from the Communist viewpoint)

Berlin, Isaiah. *Karl Marx.* Oxford University Press, London ,1939.

Deutscher, Isaac. *Stalin: A Political Biography.* Oxford University Press, London, 1949.

Liebknecht, W. *Karl Marx Biographical Memories.* (tr. by E. Untermann), Charles H. Kerr & Co., Chicago, 1901.

Mayer, Gnotav. *Friedrich Engels.* (abr. English ed.), R. H. S. Crossman, London, 1935.

Nehring, F. *Karl Marx—The Story of His Life.* (tr. by E. Fitzgerald), London, 1951.

SHUB, DAVID. *Lenin—A Biography.* Doubleday & Co., New York, 1948.
TROTSKY, LEON. *Stalin.* Hollis & Carter, London, 1947.
WOLFE, BERTRAM D. *Three Who Made a Revolution.* (non-Communist viewpoint). Dial, New York, 1948.

DOGMA AND PRACTICE

ADORATSKY, V. *Dialectical Materialism.* International Publishers, New York, 1934.
BURNS, EMILE. *A Handbook of Marxism.* Random House, New York, 1935.
EASTMAN, MAX. *Marxism: Is It a Science?* McLeod, Toronto, 1941.
EBENSKIN, WILLIAM. *Today's Isms: Communism, Fascism, Socialism, Capitalism.* Prentice-Hall, New York, 1954.
HOOK, SIDNEY. *Heresy, Yes—Conspiracy, No.* John Day, New York, 1953.
———. *Marx and the Marxists.* Von Nostrand (Anvil Book No. 7), New York, 1955.
HUNT, ROBERT NIGEL CAREW. *The Theory and Practice of Communism.* Macmillan, New York, 1954.
———. *Marxism: Past and Present.* Geoffrey Bles, London, 1955.
———. *A Guide to Communist Jargon.* Geoffrey Bles, London, 1959.
OVERSTREET, HARRY AND BONARO. *What We Must Know About Communism.* Norton, New York, 1958.

ECONOMIC THEORY

JOSEPH, HORACE, W. C. *The Labour Theory of Value in Karl Marx.* Oxford University Press, New York, 1923.

NATIONALIST PHILOSOPHY

ACTON, HARRY B. *The Illusion of the Epoch: Marxism-Leninism as a Philosophical Creed.* British Book Center, New York, 1955.
BOBAR, MANDELL MORTON. *Karl Marx's Interpretation of History.* Harvard University Press, Cambridge, 1927.
EASTMAN, MAX. *The Last Stand of Dialectical Materialism.* Polemic Publishers, New York, 1934.
GUEST, DAVID. *A Textbook of Dialectical Materialism.* International Publishers, New York, 1939.

HISTORICAL DEVELOPMENT

BERDYNEV, NICOLAS. *The Origin of Russian Communism.* Scribner's, New York, 1937.
CARR, EDWARD H. *The Bolshevik Revolution 1917-1923.* Macmillan, New York, 1950, 1951, 1952.
MOOREHEAD, ALAN. *The Russian Revolution.* Harpers, New York, 1938. (Also available as Bantam Book.)

REED, JOHN. *Ten Days That Shook the World.* Boni and Liveright, New York, 1919.

SETON-WATSON, HUGH. *From Lenin to Malenkov: The History of World Communism.* Praeger, New York, 1953.

TIMASHEFF, N. S. *The Great Retreat.* Dutton, New York, 1946.

ORGANIZATIONAL AND REVOLUTIONARY METHODOLOGY

BERMAN, H. J. AND KERNER, MIRSLAV, Editors. *Documents on Soviet Law and Adminstration.* Harvard University Press, Cambridge, 1955.

BRZEZINSKI, Z. *The Permanent Purge.* Harvard University Press, Cambridge, 1956.

BUDENZ, LOUIS. *The Techniques of Communism.* Henry Regnery, New York, 1952.

BURNHAM, JAMES. *The Web of Subversion.* John Day, New York, 1954.

COMPTON, BOYD (translator). *Mao's China Party Reform Documents.* University of Washington Press, Seattle, 1952.

DALLIN, DAVID J. *Soviet Espionage.* Yale University Press, New Haven, 1955.

DJILAS, MILOVAN. *The New Class.* Praeger, New York, 1957.

MALAPARTE, CURZIO. *Coup d'Etat: The Technique of Revolution.* Dutton, New York, 1932.

MEYER, ALFRED G. *Marxism: The Unity of Theory and Practice.* Harvard University Press, 1954.

POSSONY, STEFAN T. *A Century of Conflict: Communist Techniques of World Revolution.* Henry Regnery, Chicago, 1953.

ROSSI, A. *A Communist Party in Action.* Yale University Press, New Haven, 1949.

SELZNICK, PHILIP. *The Organizational Weapon.* McGraw-Hill, New York, 1952.

STOWE, LELAND. *Conquest by Terror.* Random House, New York, 1951.

REVOLUTIONARY ACTIVITY

ALEXANDER, ROBERT J. *Communism in Latin America.* Rutgers University Press, New Brunswick, 1938.

CARR, EDWARD H. *The Soviet Impact on the Western World.* Macmillan, New York, 1949.

EINAÜDI, MARIS. *Communism in Western Europe.* Cornell University Press, Ithaca, 1953.

HAINES, C. GROVE. *The Threat of Soviet Imperialism.* Johns Hopkins Press, Baltimore, 1954.

HOOVER, J. EDGAR. *Masters of Deceit.* Holt, New York, 1958 (reprinted by Pocket Books, Inc., 1959).

SCHMID, PETER. *The New Face of China.* Harrap, London, 1958.

SETON-WATON, HUGH. *The East European Revolution.* Praeger, New York, 1951.

SPOLANSKY, JACOB. *The Communist Trial in America.* Macmillan, New York, 1951.

WALKER, RICHARD L. *China Under Communism: The First Five Years.* Yale University Press, New Haven, 1955.

APPEALS

ALMOND, GABRIEL ABRAHAM. *The Appeals of Communism.* Princeton University Press, Princeton, 1954.

CROSSMAN, RICHARD H. S. (ed.) *The God That Failed.* Harpers, New York, 1950.

COMMUNISM AND EDUCATION

COUNTO, GEORGE S. *The Challenge of Soviet Education.* McGraw-Hill, New York, 1957, and LODGE, NUCIA. *The Country of the Blind: The Soviet System of Mind Control.* Houghton Mifflin, Boston, 1949.

EELS, WALTER CROSBY. *Communism in Education in Asia, Africa and the Far Pacific.* American Council on Education, Washington, D.C., 1954.

HUNTER, EDWARD. *Brain-Washing in Red China.* Vanguard Press, New York, 1951.

YEN, MARIA, AND MCCARTHY, RICHARD. *The Umbrella Garden.* Macmillan, New York, 1954.

COMMUNISM AND ORGANIZED RELIGION

BOLSHAKOFF, SEEGEI. *Russian Nonconformity.* Westminster Press, Philadelphia, 1949.

BOYLE, SAMUEL E. *The Church in Red China "Leans to One Side".* Samuel E. Boyle, Hongkong, 1950.

BRADEN, CHARLES SAMUEL. *War, Communism and World Religions.* Harper, New York, 1953.

Church of Scotland, General Assembly on Communism. *The Church Under Communism.* Philosophical Library, New York, 1953.

GSOVSKI, VLADIMIR (ed). *Church and State in Satellite Europe.* Praeger Press, New York, 1955.

MACESIN, GARY. *The Communist War on Religion.* Devin-Adair, New York, 1951.

MARKHAM, REUBEN H. *Communists Crush Churches in Eastern Europe.* Meador, Boston, 1950.

SHUSTER, GEORGE N. *Religion Behind the Iron Curtain.* Mc-Graw-Hill, New York, 1952.

COMMUNISM AND CHRISTIANITY

(a) By "Christian Capitalists"— (theologically conservative) —

BLAIR, MORRIS M. *Christ, Christianity and Communism.* Standard Publishing Company, Ohio, 1950.

KAUB, VERNE P. *Collectivism Challenges Christianity.* Light and Life Press, Indiana, 1946.

(b) By "Neo-Liberal, Neo-Orthodox" writers from various Protestant denominations—

BENNETT, JOHN C. *Christianity and Communism Today.* Association Press, New York, 1948, 1960.

BRUNNER, EMIL. *Communism, Capitalism and Christianity.* Lutterworth Press, London, 1949.

CUNINGGIM, MERRIMON. *Christianity and Communism.* Southern Methodist University Press, Texas, 1959.

HORDERN, WILLIAM. *Christianity, Communism and History.* Abingdon Press, New York, 1954.

MACKINNON, DONALD M. (edited by). *Christian Faith and Communist Faith.* St. Martin's Press, 1953.

MILLER, ALEXANDER. *The Christian Significance of Karl Marx.* Macmillan, Student Christian Movement, New York, 1947.

ROGERS, EDWARD. *A Christian Commentary on Communism.* F. A. Praeger Press, New York, 1952.

(c) By Roman Catholics—

BOYER, CHARLES S. J. and others. *The Philosophy of Communism.* Fordham University Press, New York, 1952.

SHEEN, FULTON J. *Communism and the Conscience of the West.* The Bobbs-Merrill Co. New York, 1948.

(d) By "Christian Communists"—

WEN-HAN, KIANG. *Christianity and Marx-Leninism.* Missionary Research Library, New York, 1952. (translated by Frank L. Cooley).

COMMUNISM AND JUDAISM

MAYER, PETER, et al. *The Jews in the Soviet Satellites.* Syracuse University Press, Syracuse, 1954.

SCHWARZ, SOLOMON J. *The Jews in the Soviet Union.* Syracuse University Press, Syracuse, 1954.

COMMUNISM AND NEGROES

NOLAN, WILLIAM. *Communism Versus the Negro.* Henry Regnery, Chicago, 1951.

COMMUNISM AND MISSIONS

BARNABAS (pseud.). *Christian Witness in Communist China.* Morehouse-Gorham, New York, 1951.

AUTOBIOGRAPHIES OF EX-COMMUNISTS

CHAMBERS, WHITTAKER. *The Witness.* Random House, New York, 1952.

HYDE, DOUGLAS. *I Believed.* Putnam, New York, 1950.

(*Bibliography continued on page 440*)

Fig. 13.—Interior view of the dome of St. Sophia, Istanbul, constructed by Justinian I, sixth century A.D. (Courtesy of the Turkish Embassy.)

Thou, O Immortal, thou didst descend into the tomb, yet didst
thou overthrow the might of Hades, O Christ our God; and thou
didst arise as Victor, saying to the Ointment-bearers—Hail! Thou
didst give peace to thine Apostles, who dost cause them that are
fallen to arise.

Orthodox Easter Hymn

XIII.

Eastern Orthodoxy

by GEORGE YPHANTIS

INTRODUCTION

EASTERN ORTHODOXY refers to the religion or faith of the Eastern Orthodox Church and is employed in the present article synonymously with the latter. After Roman Catholicism and Protestantism it constitutes the third largest branch of Christendom. Geographically, it is the faith and the church of the Christian populations of Eastern Europe, of Western Asia, and of Northern Asia known as Siberia, and of Northeastern Africa. Because of migrations large numbers of its adherents also are to be found in Western Europe, America, and other parts of the world.

Races and nations. Historically, in its earlier period it has been the church of the peoples of the Eastern Roman Empire. For over a thousand years, that is from the fourth century A.D. to the middle

Born in Turkey, MR. GEORGE YPHANTIS received his early education at the Anatolia College. During World War I he left his home, crossed Siberia, and finally made his way to the United States. Upon arrival, he enrolled at Nyack Missionary College. Next he took the B.A. degree at the University of Toronto and later the Bachelor of Fine Arts at the Yale School of Fine Arts. For eight years he served as Professor of Art and Chairman of the Department of Fine Arts at the University of Montana. In more recent years, he has been working as an artist with various engineering firms. Mr. Yphantis has travelled extensively in Asia and Europe. His interest in Eastern Orthodoxy stems from his youth in Turkey and his close association with the Greek Evangelical Mission, of which his brother, K. Paul Yphantis, is Executive Secretary.

339

of the fifteenth century, its fortunes and history were inextricably interwoven with those of the Eastern Empire and its peoples. This is and has been pre-eminently the church of the Greeks. It is also the church of the peoples of the Balkan Peninsula, such as the Southern Slavs, i.e., Serbians, and Bulgarians, and also of the Rumanians. But the peoples of Russia for many years have contributed the largest numbers to its communion. It is also the church of the Armenians, of the Christians of Syria and of Palestine, of the Ethiopians, and the Copts of Egypt, although all of these are known as the Separated Eastern Churches.

The various names by which this church is known throw a great deal of light on its general character.

The Eastern Church. First of all, this title has served to distinguish it from all the churches of Western Europe; at first, from the Western or Roman Church, and later on from the Protestant churches which have emerged from the latter. It is primarily the church of Eastern Europe, and also of the area now known as the Middle East. The genius of the East as distinguished from that of the West, in religious, and theological, and philosophical realms, has been esoteric, mystical, and speculative, rather than logical, dialectical, or practical. The mystical-speculative element is one of the most outstanding factors in the formation of the Eastern Church and its particular aspirations, doctrine, and practice. But the Eastern element is not solely responsible for shaping the character of this church, but shares this function with another important element, namely, the Greek.

The Greek Church. The dominant elements of the Eastern and Western worlds of the Middle Ages were the Greek and the Roman respectively. Each of these implies not only the conspicuous linguistic distinction, but also the vast cultural heritage as well as the temperaments represented by them. This is the church of the Greeks, in which Greek was the dominant language rather than Latin, and has continued to be the official language in some of its important nerve centers to this day. But the Greek heritage is not confined solely to the language, but comprises many another important element inherited from the Greek culture of ancient times. The philosophical outlook and achievement of the ancient Greeks, particularly that of Plato, have been a most powerful stimulus, especially in the early centuries, in the development of the theology and of the creeds not only of the Eastern Church but of the Church Universal. The effect of the Greek heritage is clearly evident in the evolution of ecclesiastical art, which eventually displaced Eastern and Roman elements, though never entirely. The religious influence of the heritage is also unmistakable, and is doubtless also responsible for pagan tendencies in the lower popular strata.

The Orthodox Church. The most emphatic and preferred title of the church among its adherents, as distinguished from heretical or heterodox.[1] Literally, it denotes *right views or beliefs on dogmatic questions.* Originally employed with questions dealing with the Persons of the Trinity and of Christ, it culminated in the final determination of the extent and the forms of the visual means, especially pictorial, to be employed in worship. The final and outstanding crystallization of this title dates from the year 843, the date of the Seventh Ecumenical Council. On the first Sunday in Lent of that year the more than a century-long bitter struggle over sacred images came to an end with their restoration, and that day was assigned a place in the calendar of the church as "The Sunday of Orthodoxy," which it occupies to this day.[2]

HISTORY

There is no single or finally valid division of the history of the Eastern Orthodox Church into periods. The following division into five periods is based on the fact of the interdependence of the Eastern Church and the Eastern Roman Empire, from the year A.D. 330, the year of the foundation of its capital, Constantinople, to the year

[1]That this is the title preferred by the official members of this church, may be seen from the article on Orthodoxy in, *A Dictionary of the Eastern Orthodox Church* by R. Ll. Langford-James, D.D., (London: Faith Press). For lack of space, we can only give short, abbreviated fragments here; but the entire article should be of considerable interest to the student of this subject.

The Orthodox Eastern Church, the "Church of the Seven Councils," has chosen for itself an even more honourable name than the word "Catholic" which the Western Church is proud to bear. The guardianship of the truth is the most honourable of all trusts. The Orthodox Church has the distinction of marking its sense of this honour in the name it has adopted. And its supreme care for the truth, for right belief, is its characteristic mark. Remembering its descent from the Greeks, who more than any have furthered the pursuit of the truth through their philosophy, the fact need occasion no surprise. It is the embodiment of the peculiar genius of the Greek race in an eternal form. The first question that the Orthodox asks, characteristically, of other Christians is, "Are you Orthodox in belief?"

[2]More will be said about this event and the events and causes which led up to it in the historical section of this article.

1453, which marks its capture by the Ottoman Turks and the destruction of that Empire. This period with its three subdiviisons into Early, Middle, and Late periods, constitutes the main body of a history which is preceded by a sort of introductory period of three centuries during which the Church stood alone and in presecution by its future protector. There is also a concluding period which covers the years from the fall of Constantinople to the present. We have, then, five periods, as follows:

A. Early Christian Era—A.D. 30 to A.D. 330.
B. Early Eastern Roman Empire—A.D. 330 to A.D. 717.
C. Middle Eastern Roman Empire—A.D. 717 to A.D. 1204.
D. Late Eastern Roman (or Greek) Empire—A.D. 1204 to A.D. 1453.
E. Modern Era—A.D. 1453 to the present.

A. Early Christian Era—A.D. 30 to A.D. 330.

The roots and origins not only of the Eastern Church, but of *all* Christian churches, are to be found in this era. It begins with the birth of the Church of Jesus on the Day of Pentecost, which is nurtured through her infancy by the labors of the apostles and their successors in labor and persecution at the hands of the pagan Roman Empire for nearly three centuries. Not without some justification, the Eastern Church refers to herself as "The Mother of All Churches," in view of the fact that she remains the heir of many of the original centers and territories of apostolic and post-apostolic activity. Furthermore, this rhetorical title is also a reminder of the fact that all the Universal or Ecumenical Councils were held in territories which continue under her jurisdiction, during the period immediately following this one. Among the many cities which witnessed the work of the apostles, three continue to this day as Patriarchal Sees of the Eastern Church: Jerusalem, Antioch, and Alexandria where the Gospel was preached by Mark, according to tradition. Other similar areas include Macedonia, Corinth, the Islands of the Eastern Mediterranean Sea, and Asia Minor, the familiar mission fields of Paul, the greatest of the apostles.

This period takes us through the era of the Apostolic and Pre-Nicene Fathers, who began to lay the foundations of Christian theology, marked by periodic persecutions and martyrdoms, down to the conversion of the Roman Emperor, Constantine the Great. Due to the danger of Arianism, the first great heresy which threatens to engulf the Christian Church, Constantine calls together the First Ecumenical Council, the Council of Nicaea, in the year A.D. 325, while he is casting about for a site for a new capital of the Roman Empire. This is provided in the Greek colonial town of Byzantium on the shores of the Bosporus, located between the Sea of Marmora and the Black Sea. There, in the year A.D. 330, Constantine lays the foundations of the city which he names New Rome, but which before long assumes a name reminiscent of its founder. (In our day, Constantinople has been officially renamed by the Turks into the abbreviated name of Istanbul.) From that year on, to the present day, the fortunes of the Eastern Church have not ceased to be interwoven with the history of "The City of Constantine."

A person who deserves mention in this connection is Saint Helena, the mother of Constantine, whose Christian piety included a pilgrimage to the city of Jerusalem for the discovery of the True Cross, in which tradition says she was successful. This event, probably more than any other, was responsible for the establishment of the cult of holy relics and their veneration in the traditional churches. From the advent of Constantine on, the history and fate of the Eastern Church are bound with those of the empire, and to a great extent are determined by the dominant political figures and events of the latter.

B. Early Eastern Roman Empire—A.D. 330 to A.D. 717.

Since this period, like the preceding one, belongs almost as much to the Western branch of Christendom, we must pass lightly over it with a bare mention of a few of the great persons and events which stand out prominently. There is the Emperor Justinian, who reigned from 527 to 565: a great ruler, soldier, and lawgiver, besides being a great theologian and hymnographer and the builder of Eastern Christendom's greatest shrine, the Church of Hagia Sophia. There was John Chrysostom, the "golden-mouthed" prince of preachers and a reformer of the Church in the fourth century of our era, whose homilies held the crowds of Constantinople spellbound, but was banished by the Empress Eudoxia, frightened by his great popularity. This is the period of the six Ecumenical Councils, the first of which was at Nicaea. But this period also witnesses, in the seventh century, the rise of one of the most formidable and dangerous foes of Christendom, the religion of the Prophet Mohammed, known as Mohammedanism or Islam. Within a century, so high did the tide of this flood rise that for a while it seemed as if the gates of Hell had burst open to wipe the Church of Jesus Christ off the face of the earth. But divine Providence raised not only Charles Martel to hammer back on the French plains the Moorish conqueror in the direction of Gibraltar, but also raised the formidable Isaurian Emperors who met the Eastern wing of the same foe beyond the Cappadocian plains and mountains.

Contact with the advancing Mohammedan armies resulted directly or indirectly in a number of historical conflicts of overwhelming consequences. One of these was the long controversy over the employment and the veneration of sacred images or icons, and over other practices such as were connected with relics, saints, etc., all of which were repugnant not only to Mohammedans but also to a large number of Christians who had come into vital contact with them. Among the latter were the very men of the armies which defended the empire against Islam, under the able leadership of generals of Eastern origin, who were elected to the Imperial purple. Leo III, founder of the Isaurian Dynasty, and his son Constantine V, became the outstanding champions of reformation directed against many a practice that had gathered momentum over a number of centuries, all of which they considered frankly as idolatrous.

Another indirect consequence of the rise of Mohammedanism, but as a direct result of the controversy over images, known as the Iconoclastic Movement, was the aggravation of the rift between East and West, and the establishment of the Western or Holy Roman Empire.

C. Middle Eastern Roman Empire—A.D. 717 to A.D. 1204.

> The Iconoclastic upheaval, and the Orthodox reaction; use of images in the church; worship and veneration of images, relics, saints.

The Mohammedans, in their application of the Mosaic commandment against images, extended their repugnance of the worship of images to the very art of representation, particularly of the human figure.

Not only among Mohammedans, but also among Christian sects of Asia Minor and of the eastern provinces of the empire, such as the sect of the Paulicians who were neighbors of the Mohammedans, the practice of smashing any and all images, known in history as Iconoclasm, became quite common. It was championed by the emperors, the army, and the people of Asia Minor. The cult of the images, on the other hand, was supported by the two regent queens—Irene the Athenian, and Theodora—the Greeks, and the ranks of the monks.[3]

Briefly, these are some of the persons and their acts connected with this movement. The Emperor, Leo III, who as a general of the imperial armies had stemmed the tide of the Saracen armies and was raised by his own armies to the throne, took the first steps against veneration of sacred pictures by an edict issued in 725. His action provoked a rebellion in Greece and riots in the capital.

An equally great champion of Iconoclastic reforms initiated by Leo, and in some respects greater, was his son Constantine V, under whom a general council, convening in 753, condemned image worship. On the other hand, Irene the Athenian, widow of Leo IV, acting as regent of her son Constantine VI, restored the worship of the images in the first year of her regency. The Iconoclastic Council was reversed by the so-called Seventh Ecumenical Council at Nicaea in 787.

Under the Armenian, Leo V, the Iconoclastic party came into power again. The Phrygian emperors, Michael II and Theophilus, continued to champion the cause of Iconoclasm. Theodora, the widow of Theophilus, finally in the year 843 restored both the images and their worship, nearly 120 years after the initial action taken against them by Leo III.

The two ablest champions of the icons, also known for their theological writings as well as for their hymns, were John of Damascus (*c.* 676-*c.* 756) and Theodore of Studium (799-826).

The Popes of Rome had no sympathy with the image-breaking of the emperors of the East. In this controversy they found an excellent excuse for withdrawing their allegiance to the emperors in Constantinople and transferring it to the Western Frankish kings. On

[3]Among the latter, the economic motive should not be overlooked, as the production of icons was already a thriving industry of the monasteries—which, not without reason, recalls the experience of the apostle Paul with Demetrius of Ephesus!

Christmas Day of the year 800, Pope Leo III placed a crown on the head of Charlemagne, in the Basilica of Saint Peter's in Rome, declaring him Emperor of the Romans. Thus the political unity of East and West was officially terminated, and this was also reflected in the break of relations between the Eastern and the Western Churches, which was completed in the year 1204.[4]

In the matter of images and their worship, Charlemagne's position coincides neither with that of the Iconoclasts nor with that of their opponents, nor yet with that of the popes, but shows a remarkable degree of vigor as well as of originality and independence.

"The general attitude was that the fear of God is shown, not as alleged at Nicaea, in the veneration and worship of images, but in the will and pursuit of the commands of God."[5]

1. Worship and Veneration of Relics.

Side by side with the evolution of the cult of images and their worship, the cult of *Relics* or sacred souvenirs was evolved from humble and scattered instances into a vast and imposing cult. The Council of Nicaea in 787 made obligatory the consecration of a church by the placement of relics under the altar. Even a brief consideration of the implications embodied in the cult of relics cannot fail to convince one that here is the saddest instance of "seeking the living among the dead" that the imagination can encompass.

The short article in the *Dictionary of the Eastern Orthodox Church* is well worth quoting in full, as revealing not only the traditional attitude of the Eastern Church, but also the current faith in the importance and efficacy of relics:

> As one would expect in a fully organized part of the Catholic Church, the cult of holy relics prevails in the Orthodox Church. In ancient times Constantinople possessed more important relics than any other place in the world. There was the True Cross, the crosses of the Two Thieves, Our Lord's sandals, the head of St. John Baptist, the body of St. Stephen, the cruse of St. Mary Magdalene, the body of Samuel, Moses' rod, Our Lady's girdle, the bodies of the Holy Innocents, the body of St. James, the body of Zacharias . . . the Hairs of St. John Baptist, the bodies of the Myrrh-Bearers (the women who went to the Sepulchre on Easter

---

[4] Historians commonly assign the date 1054 A.D. to the split between Constantinople and Rome.
[5] E. J. Martin, *A History of the Iconoclastic Controversy*, p. 233.

morning), and others. In 1204 the city was literally pillaged of relics, which were borne off in triumph to the West. In Cyprus were the rope with which Christ was bound, three drops of the Precious Blood, and the body of St. Anne. The body of St. Andrew was at Patras. Three of St. Luke's seventy pictures are still preserved in various places. The Nails of the True Cross formed part of the halo of Constantine on the famous burnt statue of him at Constantinople. St. Peter's Chains were also to be found in that favoured city. The Constantinopolitan *Menologion* has the following about them: "Taken from his all-holy body a sanctifying and healing power, they fell into the hands of Christians, and were taken to Constantinople and the Emperor, and a feast was yearly kept for the sanctifying of the faithful. From this the holy Church has learnt worship and reverence not only for the dead bodies of the Saints, but also for their clothes, etc." This is quoted as Orthodox official testimony to the ordinary Catholic belief in the healing and sanctifying power of relics.[6]

While on the subject of relics, we should also make brief mention of that which was considered the greatest of all relics, the very cross on which our Lord had been crucified. Saint Helena, the mother of Constantine the Great, early in the fourth century made a pilgrimage to Jerusalem for the purpose of presiding over the construction of the churches erected over sacred places such as the Holy Sepulchre, Bethlehem, and the Mount of Olives. At that time she is said to have discovered miraculously the Actual or True Cross on which Christ had been crucified. Before long a feast was instituted at Jerusalem, known as *The Elevation of the Venerable Cross,* and has been observed ever since on September 14 of each year. This cross, after being carried off by the Persians, was recovered by the Emperor Heraclius in the seventh century, and shortly thereafter was removed to Constantinople to prevent its capture by the oncoming Moslem conquerors.

2. Conversion of the Slavs.

A most important development during the middle period of the Eastern Roman Empire, often referred to also as the Greek Empire, and also as the Byzantine Empire, was the conversion of the Slavic peoples to Christianity. This was brought about primarily by the

[6]R. Ll. Langford-James, *A Dictionary of the Eastern Orthodox Church,* pp. 106, 7.

efforts of the Eastern Church. The great apostles to the Slavs were the two brothers from Constantinople, Cyril and Methodius, who were sent forth as the missionaries requested by Ratislav, the Slav king, in the latter part of the ninth century. They arrived at his court in 863, adequately prepared for the task, because one of the brothers, Cyril, had invented an alphabet of the vernacular Slavic language into which they translated the Gospels and the service books. They labored in Moravia from 863 to 868 against the opposition of the German missionaries who were not entirely free of political aspirations, even in those primitive times. After Cyril's death, Methodius was appointed Archbishop of Moravia and Pannonia. After his imprisonment for three years by King Louis at the request of his German bishops, he undertook missionary journeys among the Bohemians and the Poles. Upon his return to Constantinople he completed the translation of the Scriptures into the Slavic language. The alphabet known as the Cyrillic is in use by Russians, Bulgars, and Serbians to this day.

King Boris I of the Bulgarians, after being defeated in battle by the Greek Emperor Michael III in 863, was baptized with the latter as his godfather, and then compelled his subjects also to be baptized. The Patriarch Photius, famous for his vast learning, was responsible for the conversion of King Boris. As a result, he came into conflict with the Roman See, which had rival claims on the control of Bulgaria. The mutual excommunications of patriarch and pope led to the final schism between the churches each represented.

At the end of the ninth century Photius and his rival, Ignatius, sent missionaries to Russia. But it was not until the year 957 that Princess Olga embraced Christianity. The story is told about her grandson Vladimir, who, after being approached by Mohammedan, Jewish, and Christian representatives of their religions, decided to send a delegation to the city of Constantinople in order to investigate more thoroughly the most desirable religion for Russia. The delegation, upon witnessing the liturgy celebrated in the magnificent cathedral of Saint Sophia, were so overcome by the majesty, the beauty, and the mystery of the worship, that it was decided that here was the religion which their king would be happy to adopt. Accordingly, Vladimir was baptized, together with his nobles, in 988, his people following his example; and thus was the vast subcontinent of Russia attached to the banner of Eastern Orthodoxy at the conclusion of the first millennium of Christian history. In the same year Vladimir and the Greek Princess Anna were married, and thus a powerful link was established between the old Roman Empire and the new Russian state that was eventually to adopt the imperial arms and titles of the Roman Caesars.

We should also note in this connection that with the restoration of orthodoxy and the defeat of Iconoclasm, the religious arts achieved a veritable golden age of profusion as well as of perfection, and of a magnificence seldom equaled. As seen in the case of the Russian delegates to Constantinople, this proved to be an important asset in the appeal of the Church to the primitive but beauty-loving nations of the Slavic race.

D. Late Eastern Roman (or Greek) Empire—A.D. 1204 to A.D. 1453.

1. Separation of East and West

The causes of the conflict between the Eastern Church and the Western Church were geographical, racial, cultural, political, and theological.

There was first of all the vastness of the Roman Empire, which compelled Constantine to create a second Rome on the shores of the Bosporus, which he eventually preferred to the old city on the banks of the Tiber. At the end of the fourth century the empire was divided between the brothers Arcadius and Honorius, the former to be the governor of the Eastern part with Constantinople as his capital, and the latter to govern the Western part with Rome as his capital. The Pope of Rome, being the sole Patriarch of the Western World, considered himself superior to any one of the remaining four of the Eastern World. In 587 the Patriarch of Constantinople assumed the title of Ecumenical, meaning Universal, and thus a fierce competition between the Patriarch of Constantinople and the Pope of Rome was initiated, gathering force and momentum with each passing century.

The theological grounds were not slow to make their appearance. In the year 589, the Western bishops meeting at Toledo inserted a single word into the Nicene Creed, the famous clause known as the *Filioque,* meaning: "And from the Son." It has to do with the Holy Spirit, who, according to the creed was said to proceed from the

Father. The clause of course was added without the consent of the Eastern Church, which has continued to reject it as a theological heresy to this day.

But there were also grievous economic causes, such as the annexation of certain provinces by the Eastern emperor, which were claimed by the Roman Pontiff. We have already mentioned the conflict caused by the mutual claims of Patriarch and Pope over the newly converted Bulgarians. The coronation of Charlemagne by Pope Leo III as a rival emperor to the Eastern monarchs of course intensified the conflict. But the final blow came with the Fourth Crusade, which was sidetracked from its declared goal, i.e., Jerusalem, and was directed to the capture and the pillage of Constantinople in the year 1204. This was followed by the desecration of the very churches of the Eastern Christians by the knights of the cross, who had come from the West. The empire was partitioned among them, and all hope of reunification of the two divisions of the Church was thus completely destroyed. Constantinople became the capital of a Latin Empire, but was recovered by the Greeks in 1261. But a fatal blow had been dealt, which paved the way for the final capture of the capital city and the destruction of the empire by the Ottoman Turks in 1453.

2. Capture of Constantinople by the Turks

The capital for over a millennium had been the chief bastion and stronghold of the empire as well as of the Eastern Church, not to mention the whole world of Christendom. It had successfully resisted repeated waves of onslaught from the Saracen Moslems, as well as from Persians, Slavs, and Normans. But now, following the serious body blow it had received from the knights of the Fourth Crusade, it was doomed to face with vastly diminished strength and resources the most formidable foe ever to launch an invasion of the continent of Europe. This was the Ottoman Turk, who had been but recently converted to the religion of Mohammed, and for which he was inspired with such fierce zeal that not until he had reached the walls of Vienna was his westward march arrested and the menace to all Christendom at long last contained.

The capture of Constantinople, followed by the final destruction of the last remnants of the Eastern Roman Empire, constitutes one of the darkest, most tragic pages in the entire history of the civilized world. The destruction of the temporal power of the empire was succeeded by centuries of religious and political oppression to be endured by all the peoples who had passed under the heel of their Moslem captor and oppressor. This includes all the peoples of Asia Minor and of the Balkan Peninsula. In the meantime the power which was lost by the Greek emperors was steadily concentrated in the growing empire of Russia, which became the chief barrier to the ambitions of Moslem conquerors to our own day. In the realm of religion Russia eventually became the most outstanding exponent and champion of Eastern Orthodoxy.

E. Modern Era—A.D. 1453 to the present.

With the exception of Russia, almost all the nations of the Eastern church came under the tyrannous yoke of the Ottoman Turkish Empire until the beginning of the nineteenth century, when one nation after another through numberless sagas of blood and heroism at last were able to shake off either entirely or in part the cruel yoke which had been imposed on them. While Christendom in Southeastern Europe and in Asia Minor groaned under the heel of its Moslem oppressors, important developments were taking place in the religious sphere of Western Europe, the most outstanding being the Protestant Reformation, spearheaded by a German, Martin Luther, and a Frenchman, John Calvin. Another development, emerging as a reaction to the Protestant Reformation, was the Catholic Counter Reformation. Eventually both of these movements were to find echoes n the religious life of the peoples of the Eastern Church.

Of particular interest to the student of church history is the singular incident of a most remarkable though unsuccessful attempt at reformation, somewhat on the lines of the Protestant Reformation. This was undertaken by a person of unusual talents, learning, and devotion, a man who had served as Patriarch of the Sees of both Alexandria and of Constantinople, Cyril Lucar. He appears on the religious scene at the time the Eastern Church was harassed not only by the pagan Turk but also by the machinations of the Jesuits. These champions of the Counter Reformation enjoyed for a long time special privileges inside the Turkish Empire, and his attempts at reformation are of such significance that they will be given special attention again in the last section of this article, dealing with proposed principles of reformation.

This brings us to the War of Greek Independence (1821-1833), followed by similar uprisings of other Balkan nations, and to the rise of the various national churches associated with each nation.

An event of overwhelming importance for the Eastern Church as well as for the world was the Russian Revolution of 1917, which resulted in the final loss of the protection and the mundane support of the czars enjoyed by the church for centuries in Russia as well as in other countries from that source. With the advent of Communism, another foe of Christianity, perhaps as formidable as Islam, has been added to those already in existence.

GENERAL ORGANIZATION AND GOVERNMENT

The lower clergy are taken from the laity, and include *priests* and *deacons*. They are assisted by *readers* and *cantors*. Priests may marry only once, and that before ordination.

The hierarchy or upper clergy are taken from the monastic ranks, and hence may not marry. Included in ascending order are: Bishops, Archbishops, Metropolitans, Patriarchs.

A. *The Patriarchates.* At the time of Justinian the Great, the hierarchy of the Universal Church was placed under five bishops officially styled Patriarchs:

> Patriarch of Rome, also titled Pope.
> Patriarch of Constantinople, also titled Ecumenical.
> Patriarch of Alexandria, also titled Por
> Patriarch of Antioch.
> Patriarch of Jerusalem.

After the rift between the East and the West the position of the Roman patriarch was ceded to the Patriarch of Moscow, lasting from 1589 to 1700, when it was discontinued by Peter the Great. He substituted for it government by the Holy Synod, which continued until 1917, the year of the Revolution. The Patriarchate of Moscow was again restored by the government.

Although in theory one may consider Orthodoxy a fraternity of churches enjoying the fellowship of each other under the leadership of the above Patriarchates, owing to political necessities a number of national churches more or less independent or autocephalous also have been evolved.

B. *The three groups of churches in Eastern Christendom:*

1. The Orthodox group of about twelve churches constituting one body and in fellowship with each other through a *common faith, government,* and *worship.* Racially classified, these are the following:

    a. The Greek
        (1) Constantinople (Patriarchate)
        (2) Alexandria (Patriarchate)
        (3) Greece
        (4) Sinai
        (5) Cyprus
    b. The Slavic
        (1) Russia
        (2) Bulgaria
        (3) Yugoslavia
    c. The Rumanic
    d. The Arabic
        (1) Antioch (Patriarchate)
        (2) Jerusalem (Patriarchate)
    e. The Church of Georgia—now a part of the Russian

2. The Heretical or Separated group
    a. The Armenian Church
    b. The Syrian Orthodox Church
    c. The Assyrian or Nestorian Church
    d. The Coptic Church
    e. The Church of Ethiopia

3. The Uniate group

The Uniates, though in union with the Pope of Rome, are allowed to observe the Eastern rite. The largest single body of Uniates are the Ruthenians, most of whom are now in Poland, numbering about 3,500,000. Next in number come the Rumanian Uniates, about 750,000. The extreme latitude of worship and practice permitted to the Uniates, conditioned however by the all-important demand of government under the Pope of Rome, gives an important clue to

the chief cause of the continuance of the division between the Eastern
Orthodox and the Western Roman Catholic Churches. The separation from the Protestant Church, on the other hand, revolves about
certain theological differences reflected in corresponding ritual and
practice.

THEOLOGY AND PRACTICE

Includes Creeds and Confessions, Character of Doctrinal
System, Rituals, Sacraments, Fasts and Feasts, Liturgy;
Essential Differences

A. Basis of Faith

The Eastern Orthodox Church, according to her own declaration,
bases her faith on the following sources:

1. The Holy Scriptures
2. The Seven Ecumenical Councils
3. The writings of the Fathers, up to the last one, St. John of
   Damascus, author of *The Orthodox Faith.*

The doctrinal confessions most often referred to are:

4. *The Orthodox Confession,* written in 1638 by Peter Mogila,
   Metropolitan of Kiev.
5. *The Confession,* written in 1672 by Dositheus, Patriarch of
   Jerusalem; and others.[7]

As to the Scriptures, the Apocryphal books of the Septuagint Greek
translation are also included, though referred to as Deutero-canoni-
cal, i.e., below the other canonical books which alone are to be found
in the Hebrew canon.

As to the Seven Ecumenical Councils, most Protestants reject the
so-called Seventh Council which supports the veneration of Images,
Relics, etc., and thus provides the chief reasons for separation between the Eastern Orthodox and the Protestant Churches. On the
other hand, it is important to bear in mind that both the Eastern
Orthodox and the Protestants are at one in the fundamental doctrines set forth in the *Nicene Creed,* which is the preferred creed of
the Eastern Church. This was adopted at Nicaea in 325, was enlarged
at Constantinople in 381, and finally endorsed at Chalcedon in 451.

---

[7]See Schaff, *Creeds,* ii, 273-542.

It constitutes the basis of all Orthodox catechisms and systems of theology, besides being a regular part of worship.[8]

"The Greek theology is most full on the doctrine of God and of Christ, but very defective on the doctrine of man and the order of salvation.[9] The East went in strongly for *Theological* and *Christological* subtleties, but it ignored the soteriological concerns of the West from Augustine to Martin Luther. It was, for instance, intensely interested in:

Ousia and Hypostasis
Homoousion and Homoiousion
The relations of the Persons of the Trinity
The Agennesia, or Nongeneration, of the Father
The eternal Gennesia, or Generation, of the Son
The eternal Procession of the Spirit
The relation of the two natures of Christ
The heresies: such as the Nestorian, the Eutychian, the Monophysite, the Monothelite;

but never seriously troubled about such *Soteriological* doctrines as:

Predestination
Vicarious Atonement
Justification
Conversion and regeneration, etc., which have also vitally absorbed the attention of the West.

A simple comparison of the Nicene with the Apostles' Creed, which is of Western origin, reveals that in the East the *metaphysical,* *rhetorical,* and *objective* predominate, whereas in the West the *practical,* the *logical,* and the *subjective* predominate. The former tendencies have been inherited partly from Asia and partly from Greece. The latter tendencies, on the other hand, have been derived in part from Roman sources, and in part from Teutonic nationalities.[10]

B. Comparison with the Roman Church.

[8]See *New Schaff-Herzog Encyclopedia of Religious Knowledge,* vol. IV, "Eastern Church."
[9]*Ibid.*
[10]*Ibid.*

This will reveal certain outstanding points of difference on which the Eastern church stands with particular emphasis:[11]

1. Single Procession of the Holy Spirit, as against the Double Procession implied in the clause, *Filioque.*

2. Rejection of the Papacy. In the beginning this implied affirmation of the equality of the five Patriarchs.

3. The right of the lower clergy to marry.

4. Communion in both kinds: i.e., in both the bread and the wine.

5. Threefold immersion, the only valid form of baptism, as against baptism by sprinkling.

6. The use of the vernacular languages in worship.

7. Rejection of the doctrine of the Immaculate Conception.

8. Rejection of Papal infallibility.

9. Rejection of the doctrine of purgatory.

C. Comparison with the Protestant Approach.

This may reveal on the part of the Eastern Church, *Indirection, Mediation,* and the employment of *Symbolical Instrumentation,* in contrast to the more *Direct, Immediate,* and *Concrete* Protestant attitude. For instance, the Eastern Church in the access to God seeks, in addition to the mediation of Christ, the aid of a host of mediators of various ranks, in ascending importance, from saints and martyrs to angels and archangels, and finally to the mother of Christ, whom he prefers to address as the Theotokos, or the Mother of God. Undoubtedly these two attitudes account for the vast differences in aesthetic production, both in the quality and in the quantity of the religious arts as practiced by the respective branches of Christendom.

In theological and ritualistic approach, Protestants will be interested to note these striking features of the Eastern Orthodox Church:

1. The Veneration and Invocation of the Saints.

In the practical application of the article on the Communion of the Saints, the Orthodox believer invokes the aid and the prayers of the departed saints, with the same assurance in their ability and willingness to help him, as that which he would have in their very physical presence. Hence, he prays to them, venerates their images,

[11]*Ibid.*

and their relics, makes pilgrimages to their shrines, and keeps numerous feasts dedicated to them, though unable to offer adequate scriptural justification in this profound confidence, or for his zeal in the service of the saints.

2. The Theotokos or Mother of God: highest of all helpers, and ever ready to intercede to her Son on behalf of all by whom she is invoked. Dogmatically the position occupied by her is below that ascribed to the Persons of the Trinity; but in the popular imagination very often she occupies the dignity of "The Queen of Heaven," one of her many titles. Numberless hymns of devotion and prayers address her in hundreds of superlative names and titles concerning which the least one can say would be that they are extravagant and prodigious in profusion, in intensity and magnitude. In effect she shares the throne of her divine and almighty Son, in her compassionate and overflowing love. Although the Scriptures have preferred discreet silence concerning her later earthly life and her death, tradition has it that after her death, or Dormition, she was translated to the highest Heaven where she exercises the office of intercessor for those who call on her.[12]

3. The Seven Mysteries or Sacraments:

a. Baptism. As mentioned on page . . ., this is administered by threefold immersion, and in general, to children, as noted in the paragraph immediately below.

b. Chrism, or the Unction of Confirmation. This is administered directly after baptism, as a symbol of the gift of the Holy Spirit.

c. The Eucharist or Communion, far from being a mere memorial, is considered the very means by which the believer receives the benefits of the sacrifice of Christ in an indispensable manner.

d. Penance includes sorrow for sins committed, as well as confession in the presence of a priest. The absolution is not direct, but is expressed in the words: "May God absolve thee."

[12]Perhaps caution should be exercised here to determine to what extent the superlative attributes ascribed to the Virgin are to be taken literally, and whether these be but another instance of the tendency of the East to sacrifice logic and semantics to rhetoric and to poetry. Of course, one would not apply the same rules of criticism to poetic license and hyperbole as he would in the case of prosaic language, where certain restraints are imperative. There is, on the other hand, the danger of transferring the hyperbolic language of ecstatic address to the affirmations of dogma, in which case such language might come under Biblical judgment. On those who choose to address the Virgin as the Queen of Heaven, for instance, would devolve the responsibility of squaring the implications of such terminology with such Scriptures as Jer. 44:18, 19, 25.

e. Holy Orders or Ordination. This sacrament is administered to the clerical members only.

f. Matrimony. Though elaborate, this does not differ in essence from that of other Christian bodies.

g. Unction or Anointing of the Sick. This also is briefly defined in the paragraph immediately following. It is administered by an ordained priest.

The Sacraments are considered both the symbols and the means whereby divine grace is communicated to the believer. With the exception of Holy Orders and Matrimony, all Sacraments are obligatory to every believer. Baptism is generally administered to children, and by immersion, being the symbol and the sacrament of regeneration. The last one of the Sacraments is administered for healing of physical or spiritual maladies, whereas in the Roman Church it is administered chiefly before death.

4. Fasts and Feasts

a. Fasts of the week. From Justinian's time Wednesday and Friday have been set apart for fasting and good works. This is not total but partial fasting, i.e., abstinence from certain kinds of foods, chiefly of animal origin, such as meats, fish, and dairy products.

b. Lent. This too is a partial fast, and it is the longest, ending with the greatest of feasts, i.e.

c. Easter. More than Christmas, this is the Great Feast of the Eastern Church.

d. Saints' Days, including the *Feast of All Saints*.

e. Cardinal Feasts from the life of Christ and of Mary. Twelve of these are frequently depicted together, and usually include the following:

(1) Annunciation	(7) Entry into Jerusalem
(2) Visitation[13]	(8) Crucifixion
(3) Nativity	(9) Resurrection
(4) Presentation	(10) Ascension
(5) Baptism of Christ	(11) Pentecost
(6) Transfiguration	(12) Dormition of the Virgin[13]

[13]These two feasts would be depicted in a church dedicated to the Virgin. If dedicated to Christ, the following three would supply the subject matter necessary for the completion of the cycle: The Raising of Lazarus, The Descent from the Cross, The Incredulity of Thomas. (See D. Talbot Rice, *Byzantine Art*, pp. 125, 126.)

5. The Liturgy is the outstanding expression of Orthodox piety and worship. On Sundays and on feast days the normal service is the Divine Liturgy of St. John Chrysostom, that of St. Basil being employed on ten days in the year. The celebration of this Mass is distinguished by its aesthetic organization, and the mystical nature of the service, supported by a vast amount of symbolical ritual, teeming with visual and audible detail, such as the flood of gentle light from numberless tapers, candles, oil lamps; a profusion of murals representing Christ, Mary, the Saints, Angels, and Archangels. The Iconostasis or picture-screen separates the altar from the main body of the church. There are choirs of men and boys singing antiphonally, chanting, or intoning psalms, portions of Scripture, hymns, prayers, etc. The visitor may also observe priests, deacons, etc., with gorgeous vestments, praying, intoning, or chanting the liturgy, and reading the Gospel or the Epistle for the day. He will see genuflections, kissing of sacred pictures, bowing, standing, and upon occasion, processions. Frequently a priest will emerge bearing a censer which fills the church with the odor of incense. The Eucharist or Mass is celebrated by the priest over an altar which may contain the relics of a saint or a martyr. More recently the service has been supplemented with the sermon. But the sermon does not occupy the central position it enjoys in the Protestant service.

The climax of the entire Liturgy is the consecration of the bread and wine of the Communion as the symbols of the body and blood of Christ, as a "Bloodless Sacrifice." However, in distinction from the Roman Church, the Orthodox Church does not attempt to define the exact nature of the agency employed in the alteration of the elements into Christ's actual body and blood. The consecrated bread is administered to children and adults alike, who file past the priest and kiss his hand as they receive the symbols.[14]

---

[14]"The Eucharist or Communion Service is really a sacred play, portraying the entire life of Jesus Christ, with the priests, the subpriests or deacons, and the people as actors. Of the three distinct acts, the first is the Childhood and the eighteen Silent Years, as Western Christians call them; but to the Orthodox East it is the *Prothesis*, or Preparation of the Gifts. The second act is the *Synaxis*, or Assembly of the Gifts, representing the teaching and healing ministry of Christ; and the final act is the *Anaphora*, or Offering of the Gifts, depicting the Last Supper, the Crucifixion, Resurrection, Ascension and the Gift of the Holy Spirit."—*The Faiths Men Live By*, Charles Francis Potter, 1954.

THE POLITICAL BACKGROUND AND ITS EFFECT

A. The Eastern Roman Empire.

From Constantine the Great to the fall of Constantinople, Orthodoxy enjoyed what might be considered its most normal pattern of political background. Under the latter, the Church enlists and receives the assistance and protection of an Orthodox monarch, as was also the case of the Russian Church under its own Caesars or Czars from its earliest days until the Russian Revolution. Under this arrangement there is a complete union of church and state. The head of the state openly or in effect becomes the determining voice even in purely theological matters. Outstanding examples: Constantine the Great, who presided at important Church Councils; Justinian, emperor, lawgiver, and theologian, he often uttered the last word in the settlement of a theological disputation, and had the power to enforce his decisions.

Under the Christian Caesar, promoting and defending the kingdom of God, the Church enjoys certain advantages which, however, are dearly bought at the price of Christian freedom and of spiritual values. In exchange, the Church promotes loyalty to the temporal ruler of her choice. There can be no complete freedom of conscience in matters of faith or dogma, since heresy becomes not only a sin but also a political crime. Eventually stagnation follows, as it is impossible to pursue spiritual ends by worldly means without paying the inevitable high price involved in such transactions.

B. Orthodoxy under Islam.

Shortly after the death of Mohammed in the year 632, Jerusalem, Alexandria, and Antioch passed under the standards of the Arabian or Saracen Caliphs, but the repeated attacks of the Moslems on the capital city were foiled in part by the use of an efficient weapon known as "the Greek Fire." But the capital, together with the remnants of the empire, finally succumbed to another formidable Moslem foe, the Ottoman Turks. Constantinople was captured in 1453, and the entire Balkan Peninsula and all of Asia Minor passed under the oppressive rule of the Turkish Sultans. For centuries the Church and its adherents experienced the bitter persecution, domination, and the attempt at extinction by one of its greatest antagonists. The political condition has been chiefly that of oppressive captivity, and accounts for the numerous movements of nationalist uprisings in which the Church played a very prominent part.

C. Orthodoxy under Communism.

This political system, far from being a protective power of the Church, acts the role of a persecuting agent in varying degrees, from attempts at extermination by such measures as massacre or confiscation, to extreme contempt and watchful indifference. From the very first, the slogan of Russian Communism has been: "Religion, the opiate of the people," called by Lenin, "the Keystone of Marxist policy." Among the weapons employed by Communism, the following should be mentioned:

1. Removal of financial support—particularly effective against state Churches.
2. The education of the young in Atheism.
3. Intimidation of individuals. Communist attacks on religion are indirect, and may be made on grounds of hostility to state, espionage, currency of offenses, etc.[15]

According to H. H. Stroup, "Communism is like Christianity in at least one respect. It asks for the whole life of the devoted follower. It is not content to have any aspect of the life of the individual or group exist outside its sway. Communism is a totalitarianism of the material order; Christianity is a 'totalitarianism' of the spiritual order."[16]

"In 1917 there were [in Russia] over 40,000 churches and nearly 51,000 priests; in 1941, only 4,255 churches and 5,665 priests. But in 1942-43 a milder policy was adopted by the government, apparently because of the war with Germany. An agreement of some sort resulted in the present compromise arrangement of toleration of the Church at the price of subordination to and control by the government. The same status exists in general in the satellite countries."[17]

D. Orthodoxy in America.

In America, as in Western Europe, Orthodoxy has been estab-

---

[15]Editorial, *The Christian Century*, February 24, 1954.
[16]"Communism Threatens the Churches of Europe," *Christianity and Crisis*, July 10, 1953.
[17]C. F. Potter, *The Faiths Men Live By*, p. 144.

lished by migration, and constitutes very definitely a minority. Hence it has been completely untroubled by political hopes or aspirations. The influence of Protestantism here has often resulted in both external and internal reforms. For instance, the church organ, which together with almost all musical instruments had been banned for centuries, is now being introduced in many of the Orthodox Churches. Greater importance is also given to the sermon and the Sunday school. The sermon in the vernacular Greek is often supplemented by the sermon in English for the benefit of the younger generation. There is also a greater and more direct contact with the Scriptures.

Politically, observation of the total separation of the Church from the State in the United States of America should also have a beneficial effect. On the other hand, the Orthodox Church even in this millieu, continues under the dominance of the momentum created by more than one thousand years. Continuity, rather than deeper, spiritual reform and growth, seems by and large to be its chief concern.

The Orthodox Church in America dates from 1794, when nine missionaries arrived at St. Paul on Kodiak Island, Alaska, and erected a church and a school there. In 1796 the first bishop for Kodiak, Kamshatka and America was consecrated in the Siberian city of Irkutsk.

The first church for Greek nationals was founded in New Orleans among the Greek cotton traders.[18] According to the 1957 edition, *Yearbook of American Churches,* issued in September, 1956, "Greek-speaking Orthodox Christians have parishes in the United States, Canada, and South America. These are under the Patriarchate of Constantinople." There are 353 churches, with Inclusive Membership of 1,000,000. The total enrollment in the Sunday schools, numbering 355, is 25,000. Government is administered through a body of bishops under the Archbishop of North and South Americas, whose headquarters are in New York.

Present State of Russian Orthodoxy in the United States of America.

According to an article in *The Christian Century,*[19] "there are (at present) three branches of the Russian Orthodox Church, all operating independently of one another.

[18]Schaff-Herzog, *Encyclopedia of Religious Knowledge,* Vol. IV.
[19]Anonymous correspondent, *The Christian Century,* December 21, 1955.

"The largest branch of the Russian Orthodox Church in the United States is called the 'Russian Orthodox Greek Catholic Church of North America,' and is under the jurisdiction of Metropolitan Leonty, with headquarters in New York City. It is an autonomous Church, and is independent of the Patriarch of Moscow. It claims to have one million participating members. This branch was represented at the World Council of Churches assembly in Evanston, Illinois.

"The second branch of the Russian Orthodox Church in the United States is the 'Russian Church Abroad.' Ths is the branch which broke with the communists in Russia in 1921 and fled to Yugoslavia. Its present headquarters are in New York. In almost every country outside of Russia there are Russian Orthodox Churches affiliated with this branch. This church has 65,000 members in the United States, and is under the jurisdiction of the Patriarch of Istanbul.

"The third and smallest branch is headed by Archbishop Adams from the Cathedral of St. Nicholas in New York, and under the jurisdiction of the *Patriarch of Moscow,* although without much influence from the latter."

PRINCIPLES OF REFORMATION AND CONCLUDING OBSERVATIONS

Since the days of the Iconoclastic movement, Orthodoxy has not experienced an internal spiritual or religious upheavel comparable with the Protestant Reformation, or even to the Counter Reformation of the Roman Catholic Church. One reason for the absence of a parallel movement was the fact that the Church located in the historical centers of the East was engaged in a life-and-death struggle of survival under the Turkish or Ottoman Empire, while the Churches of the West were able to put their house in order in comparative freedom. On the other hand, the Eastern Church has not been a total stranger to the influences of the Protestant Reformation.

The most outstanding instance of this influence was the attempt of the Patriarch Cyril Lucar to promote a similar reformation within the Eastern Church during the early part of the seventeenth century. Unfortunately his efforts proved unsuccessful and only resulted in his assassination by the Ottoman authorities at the instigation of his opponents.

The reform movement of Cyril Lucar is so unique and incredible as to deserve a brief consideration even in this short survey. He was born in Candia of Crete in 1572, and was first appointed Patriarch of Alexandria in 1602. It is claimed that he adopted Protestant doctrines after three years of study, and in 1613 he was obliged to defend himself against the charge of Lutheranism. Among his adversaries were Roman Catholics whom he opposed with arguments drawn exclusively from the Scriptures. In 1620, he became Patriarch of Constantinople, drawing the friendship of the Dutch Protestants, and the enmity of the Jesuits. In 1616, he had begun to correspond with the Archbishop of Canterbury, and shortly afterward sent him the famous Codex Alexandrinus. Cyril also assisted in the translation of the Bible into the Vernacular Greek, which appeared in Geneva in 1638. In 1629 he published the *Confession of the Christian Faith*. It was branded as heretical, because of its Calvinistic leanings. Under a conspiracy of the Jesuits, he was accused to the Sultan of plotting with the Cossacks and was ordered strangled to death and his body thrown into the sea. Thus a greater reformer and his great work came to an untimely end. In 1672, his doctrines were condemned by means of the so-called "Confession of Dositheuos, or Eighteen Decrees of the Synod of Jerusalem."

History does not record a subsequent attempt at reform within the Eastern Church comparable with that of Cyril Lucar.

In more recent years, a milder reform movement has arisen within the Church of Greece, known as "Zoe" or Life, thanks to the tireless and self-sacrificing efforts of the Archimandrite Eusebius Matthopoulos, who died in 1929, and his ecclesiastical colleagues. It is a brotherhood of theologians which aims to bring new life to the Orthodox Church of Greece by improving the means of communicating the Gospel to the people. To this end they have adopted new methods taken largely from Protestant practice. It made its first public appearance in 1911 through the publication of its periodical, *Zoe*. Its membership includes both clergy and laymen, all of whom are graduates of theology, and work in co-operation with the Greek Church. It also includes lay members who are not professional theologians.

According to an article by Herbert Stroup in *The Christian Century*, (March 16, 1955), the Zoe Brotherhood has employed a variety of means to achieve its purposes; i.e., the spread of the Gospel and the strengthening of Christan leadership n Greece.

Preaching has been organized on a country-wide basis, to supplement the liturgical service. The Zoe men also deliver lectures to students, workers, soldiers, parents, etc. The Liturgy also is interpreted to the laity. The weekly paper, *Zoe* has a circulation of 150,000 copies. The Brotherhood also publishes books, and has printed both the Old and New Testaments, for which it issues commentaries.

It has created *Sunday schools* throughout Greece. The total number of schools in 1952-53 was 1,700 with an attendance of 150,000 boys and girls.

Young men are being *trained* for the ministries of the Orthodox Church.

This author also points out that "they have co-operated with other Christian groups which also seek to serve the religious needs of the Greek people."

It should be pointed out that the Brotherhood was for many years suspected of heresy, and brought to trial twice before the Holy Synod, once in 1914 and again in 1923. The second trial resulted in its recognition by the Synod as a very valuable asset for the religious life of the nation.

* * *

In the endeavor to analyze properly and to grasp the important problems of Orthodoxy, one must never lose sight of the vastness of this institution and of the range of its spiritual condition, extending from the rarest mysticism, saintliness, and spirituality, down to the most abject materiality, superstition, and insolent paganism parading as Christianity. In other words, since there are many levels of spirituality, ranging from highest Christian sainthood to lowest heathen practice, great discernment and differentiation will be called for. Not infrequently one may meet honest and earnest members of the Church who not only disapprove these strata of decay, but also yearn for a thorough purging of elements which either filtered in stealthily or moved in boldly from the vast storehouse of paganism, both of the pre-Christian and the post-Christian world.

The bitter warfare waged between Christianity and paganism ended with the destruction of the most outstanding temples and monuments of the latter under the early Christian emperors. Paganism's cunning forces, realizing the futility of open-front resistance, decided to go underground. The futility of open resistance was made abundantly clear by the attempt of the philosopher-emperor Julian the Apostate to reinstate paganism in the fourth century. But a very large section of pagan society managed to disguise its true nature, and by subtle alterations of names and incidental aspects, to parade as the very owner and heir of the very field wherein the seeds of Christianity had been planted.

The safest and most stubborn refuge of paganism was the countryside, otherwise also known as *pagus* or *heath,* from which we have the terms *pagan* and *heathen.* The rural countryside provided greater concealment, making detection many times harder than in the cities. There paganism in its worst and most stubborn aspects lived on, often claiming to be the very essence of the Christian faith. In metropolitan centers, on the other hand, important pagan shrines were often saved from destruction by Christian authorities, through rededication to a saint or to a personage who in the eyes of its devotees was only a successor to a pagan antecedent. This interpenetration of the seeds of Christianity with the tares of paganism, from which all too often the field had not even been sufficiently weeded, was universal and extremely intricate. Even after an initial weeding process, the seeds of the tares were readily reintroduced from sources ever at hand.

The primary lesson which one must learn and ever keep in mind in this connection is that one must avoid all blanket judgments and statements. Whatever may be truthfully said about a certain level of the Orthodox field would not hold water at another level. For instance, one should be careful not to attribute the mentality and the attitudes, not to say the practices of the crude unchristianized masses to the saintly and often unbelievably refined and Christlike individuals whose sudden discovery comes to one as a most beneficent surprise, "lest while ye gather up the tares, ye root up also the wheat with them" (Matt. 13:29).

On the other hand, it would be an unjustifiable extension of Christian charity or understanding to ignore the fact that real pagan elements, especially in provincial practice, not only exist but are all too often tolerated either as harmless or as inevitable. At times they are even looked upon as picturesque relics or charming indications of racial vitality and continuity.

Such abuses, prevalent among backward or retarded rural or illiterate parishes, might be corrected by reference to the accepted doctrine of the Church. But where the doctrine itself is responsible for such practices, the matter is more serious, and the responsibility falls on the higher or theological levels of the Church.

It would seem that here are several points for careful consideration and analysis, namely:

1. Wherein is *current or popular practice* inconsistent with the fundamental teaching of the theological authorities of Orthodoxy, as well as with Scripture?

2. Wherein does *the generally accepted theology* of the Orthodox Church deviate from the scriptural viewpoint?

3. Wherein is *current practice* affected by contemporary national and political pressures? Have any doctrinal or theological modifications been effected by such pressures?

Needless to say, unless such points of inquiry are clearly distinguished from each other, it is impossible to discover the offending causes for any existing condition.

In conclusion, it should be pointed out that it would be hazardous to indicate any a priori or stereotyped procedures in the effort to bring about a reformation. The field is vast and diversified. The Church itself, on the other hand, is aware of the need of reform; yet is very sensitive on the subject of "proselytism." The honest student of religions, therefore, will avoid shallow, or ready-made answers to serious questions, and any easy solutions to difficult problems. A bibliography has been prepared in the hope not only of filling the many gaps imposed by the brevity of an article dealing with such a vast subject, but also of supplying hints and suggestions toward valid and significant conclusions.

Beyond the region of religious problematics, and transcending the latter in importance, will ever lie the positive tasks of the winner of souls, deeply concerned as he is with the regeneration and salvation of souls. For such tasks, the study and understanding of any religious system is but a preparatory exercise and training. It is only through the unction and the leadership of the Holy Spirit that he shall acquire the capacity to proceed from the religious grounds to those which are unmistakably spiritual, with the appeal of the divine revelation of God's grace in and through His Son Jesus Christ.

BIBLIOGRAPHY

GENERAL

ANDREWS, DEAN TIMOTHY. *The Eastern Orthodox Church: A Bibliography*. Pamphlet No. 6. New York 21: Greek Archdiocese, 10 E. 79th St., 1953.

ADENEY, W. F. *The Greek and Eastern Churches*. T. & T. Clark, 1908. Written from a Protestant point of view, very readable, and full of information.

BACON, F. D. *Eastern Pilgrimage*. Lutterworth Press, 1944. "Written by a Protestant."

BRANDRETH, HENRY R. T. *An Outline Guide to the Study of Eastern Christendom*. London: S. P. C. K., 1951. "This booklet aims at giving English readers a sufficient knowledge of the literature dealing with the life, worship, history, and organization of the Eastern churches."

FORTESCUE, ADRIAN. *The Orthodox Eastern Church*. Montreal: Catholic Truth Society, 1929. Written by a brilliant Roman Catholic author.

FRENCH, R. M. *The Eastern Orthodox Church*. London, New York: Hutchinson's University Library, 1951. An excellent work of an advanced nature.

KIDD, B. J. *The Churches of Eastern Christendom*. London: The Faith Press, Ltd., 1927. Mainly historical, deals with the Eastern Church from the middle of the Fifth century to the present. Contains chapters on the Separated Eastern Churches. Also a final chapter on Faith, Government, Worship, and Re-union.

LANGFORD-JAMES, R. Ll. *A Dictionary of the Eastern Orthodox Church*. London: The Faith Press, Ltd., 1923. Langford-James is a member of the Committee of the Anglican and Eastern Association. With a preface by Joannes Gennadius.

MARTIN, E. J. *A History of the Iconoclastic Controversy*. London: S.P.C.K., 1930.

NEALE, JOHN MASON. *A History of the Holy Eastern Orthodox Church*. London: 1847, 1873.

POTTER, C. F. *The Faiths Men Live By*. Englewood Cliffs: Prentice-Hall. Chapter on the Orthodox Church.

ZANKOV, S. *The Eastern Orthodox Church*. London: S. C. M. Press, 1929. "An English translation of lectures originally delivered in German, dealing mainly with doctrine."

Byzantine History

Byron, Robert. *The Byzantine Achievement*. London: G. Routledge & Sons, 1929. A historical perspective, A.D. 330-1453.

Diehl, Charles. *History of the Byzantine Empire*. (Trans. from the French by George B. Eves.) Princeton University Press, 1925.

The Church of Russia

Berdiaev, Nikolai Aleksandrovich. *The Russian Idea*. New York: Macmillan Co., 1948.

Catechisms and Creeds

Schaff, Philip. *Creeds of Christendom*. New York: Harper & Bros., 1931.

Overbeck, J. J. and Robertson, J. N. W. B. (ed.). *The Orthodox Confession of the Catholic and Apostolic Eastern Church From the Version of Peter Mogila*. Thomas Baker, 1898.

Robertson, J. N. W. B. (ed.). *The Acts and Decrees of the Synod of Jerusalem; Sometimes Called the Council of Bethlehem, Holden Under Dositheus, Patriarch of Jerusalem, 1672*. Thomas Baker, 1899.

Music and the Arts

Brownlee, John (trans). *Hymns of the Russian Church*. Oxford: Oxford University Press, 1920.

Dalton, O. M. *Byzantine Art and Archaeology*. With 457 illustrations. Oxford: Clarendon Press, 1911.

Morey, Charles Rufus. *Christian Art*. London: Longmans, Green & Co., 1935.

Neale, John Mason. *Echoes From Easter: Selections from the Hymns of the Eastern Church*. New York: A. D. F. Randolph & Co., 1885.

———. *Hymns of the Eastern Church*. London: J. T. Hayes, 1882.

Rice, David Talbot. *Byzantine Art*. Oxford: The Clarendon Press, 1935.

Woodward, George Tarcliffe. *Hymns of the Greek Church*. Greek and English in opposite columns. London: S. P. C. K. and also Macmillan, 1922.

Liturgy

Hapgood, Isabel Florence, (comp. and tr.). *Service Book of the Holy Orthodox-Catholic Church*. Compiled, translated and arranged from the old Church-Slavonic Service books of the Russian Church. Boston: Houghton, Mifflin & Co., 1906.

Pullan, Leighton. *A Guide to the Holy Liturgy of St. John Chrysostom*. London: S. P. C. K., 1921.

RELIGIOUS THOUGHT

BERDIAEV, NICOLAI A. (also spelled Berdyaev, Nicolas). *Freedom and the Spirit*. New York: Scribner's, 1935.

———. *The Destiny of Man*. New York: Scribner's 1937. These are but two of a host of significant works by one of the outstanding religious thinkers of our era.

FEDOTOV, G. P. *A Treasury of Russian Spirituality*. New York: Sheed & Ward, 1950.

FRENCH, R. M. (trans.). *The Way of a Pilgrim*. Foreword by the Bishop of Truro. London: S. P. C. K.; Philip Allan, 1931.

MONASTICISM

BYRON, ROBERT. *The Station Athos: Treasures and Men*. London: Duckworth, 1928. Deals with the monasticism of Mount Athos.

Fig. 14.—Upper left: statue of St. Bernadette at the Lourdes Museum. Upper right: the Virgin in the Grotto at Lourdes. Above: the Basilica at Lourdes. (Courtesy of French Government Tourist Office. Photos by Yan.)

*It was our Saviour's privilege to prescribe the conditions on which
our reconciliation with God was to be effected. Now He tells us in
His Gospel that Baptism is the essential means established for
washing away the stain of original sin and the door by which we
find admittance into His Church, which may be called the second
Eden.*

—James Cardinal Gibbons

XIV.

The Roman Catholic Church

by Luis Padrosa

Introduction

THE HISTORY OF THE ROMAN CATHOLIC CHURCH cannot be summarized briefly. This is true for four reasons. (1) It neither has a founder nor a beginning. (2) Its continuing development has always been intermingled with the life of the Christian Church. (3) Until the time of the Council of Trent the dogmatic limits and characteristics of the Roman Catholic Church were not well defined. (4) Even after the Council of Trent they continued to add some new essential dogmas for being a Roman Catholic, dogmas which would exclude from the Church the greatest authors, saints, and theologians of the Christian Church.

For instance, authors such as Origen and Augustine, who did not recognize the supreme authority of the bishop of Rome, as is shown

LUIS PADROSA was one of the leaders of Catholicism in Spain, having founded the Loyola Institute in Barcelona and having enjoyed a great reputation as a psychiatrist, lecturer, and sacred orator. In 1951, while studying Protestantism in order to refute it, he was converted. Thereafter he moved to South America and now teaches at the Evangelical Faculty of Theology in Buenos Aires. Dr. Padrosa received his higher education at universities in Barcelona and Naples. For twenty-three years he was a member of the Society of Jesus.

373

later, have since been considered in Roman history as Catholic authors. Popes such as Honorius, condemned for heresy, as is indicated later, and those who mutually were excommunicated during thirty-nine years of the Western Schism, are considered today as true successors of Peter. And when in some cases, as frequently happens, no one knows who the legitimate pope was, it is said that although the "person" was not manifested, the "function" continued unaltered.[1]

In the section on "Characteristics of the Church" we shall indicate the names of the most authoritative scholastics who were opposed to the doctrine of the immaculate conception of Mary, and in spite of this they are considered doctors and saints of the Roman Church.

The Roman Church has always used a very simple procedure: to take from each author that which favors its doctrines, and to omit from their writings that which is not in accord with the given norms of the Vatican. In this way its history is written. In the histories which the Roman Catholics write about the origins of Roman Catholicism, as in their apologetic treatises, they make sophistic generalizations which lead them to conclusions that are extremely harmful to the knowledge of religious truth.

The word *Catholicism* is used as a synonym for *Christianity,* and on this ambiguous basis Jesus Christ and His apostles are spoken of as the "foundations of the Catholic Church." It is certain that Jesus Christ founded a *catholic Church* with His apostles, but we understand the word *catholic* to be a synonym for *universal* and not a synonym for *Roman.* In the sense of universal, it is fair that we look for the basis of its origin in the New Testament, but absolutely not if by "catholicism" one understands (as all their readers understand and all the Roman writers wish them to understand) "Roman Catholic religion." It is evident, therefore, that its origin ought to be sought, not in the New Testament, but in the history of the subsequent centuries.

That is the first sophism which is used as a basis in all Roman Catholic arguments to prove the divine origin and the universal privileges of the Roman Church. After introducing in this way the concept that Jesus Christ founded the Catholic Church, they continue to show that the fundamental rock upon which Jesus Christ

[1] Cf. Father Buips, *La Iglesia de Jesús.* Barcelona: Editorial Liturgica Española, p. 449 ff.

founded His Church is Peter, the first bishop of Rome and the universal head of the entire Christian Church, and likewise the only representative of Jesus Christ on earth. All the bishops that have succeeded Peter in the government of the Roman Church inherit the same privileges of universal jurisdiction and of dogmatic infallibility. This being the case, in order to recognize the legitimacy of the Roman Catholic dogmas, we must first ascertain (1) if Jesus Christ founded His Church on Peter; (2) if Peter left his privileges of the universal papacy to a successor; and (3) where that successor may presently be found.

It is evident that if the bishop of Rome is the true successor of Saint Peter, and if he received from Jesus Christ the supreme hierarchical authority and doctrinal infallibility, we ought to obey him if we want to be authentic Christians. But is this true? This is the first matter to be considered.

The Founding of the Supreme and Universal Papacy

A. The Promise of the Papacy.

The Bible text upon which the Roman Catholic Church rests to prove the existence of a universal pontiff is Matthew 16:18: Thou art Peter, and upon this rock I will build my church. Roman theologians recognize that this text does not establish the papacy upon Peter but only promises it: "I will build," says the Lord. But they argue that if He promised it, He had to do it. Now there has to be some passage in the New Testament in which Jesus Christ is seen conferring upon Peter the maximum universal pontifical authority. That is to say, He has to fulfill the promise expressed in Matthew 16: 18, 19. They find this promise fulfilled in John 21:15 ff. In every treatise of Roman dogmatic theology and apologetics it is affirmed that the interpretation and sense of Matthew 16:18, 19 is evident. Jesus Christ meant to say that He would build His Church upon the person of Peter and upon his successors. And they constantly affirm that only Protestants find other interpretations.

To the one who is well acquainted with the Holy Fathers and Doctors, and with the history of the primitive church, such affirmations are surprising. Among the most authoritative Fathers one finds the same interpretations that the Protestants have held.

Consider, for instance, what Father Maldonado, the so-called prince of the Catholic exegetes and a member of the Society of Jesus, has to say in his commentary on the Gospel of Matthew:

> "And upon this rock I shall build my church." There are some veterans who affirm that this rock is the faith, that is, the confession of this faith by which "thou hast recognized Me as the Son of the living God" (Hilary, Gregory, Chrysostom, Cyril of Alexandria, and the author of the commentaries on the Pauline Epistles which are attributed to St. Ambrose).
>
> Augustine departs even farther from the usual opinion when he says, "On this rock, that is, on myself," because he says the rock was Christ as the Scriptures indicate: "That rock was Christ" (I Cor. 10:4), "for other foundation can no man lay than that is laid which is Jesus Christ."
>
> Origen says: "Upon this rock, that is, upon all men who have this faith."[2]

After having given this quotation, Father Maldonado tries to give an explanation of these patristic texts, in order to make them mean what Rome wants them to say. But in spite of such endeavors, these testimonies prove that the most authoritative Holy Fathers did not accept the Roman interpretation of Matthew 16. They also prove that the Protestants are not the only ones who give an interpretation distinct from that of Rome. Finally, they show that the text cited by Matthew does not contain any evident promise of a supreme pontiff in the Roman sense, since the noted Fathers did not understand it in this way. The papal interpretation was developed subsequently in the course of the centuries.

Lannoy, a doctor of the Sorbonne in Paris, has calculated that among the seventy-seven most authorized Fathers and Doctors of the Church which have written on the disputed verse of Matthew, there are no more than seventeen who interpret it in the sense of Peter's being the fundamental rock, and sixty interpret it in another sense: forty-four affirm that the "rock" is the confession of faith itself that Peter made; that is, the words, "Thou art the Christ, the Son of the living God" (Among them are Justin, Cyril, Hilary, Chrysostom, Ambrose, etc.). The remaining sixteen affirm that the "rock" is Christ Himself (Athanasius, Jerome, Augustine, and others).

[2]Father Maldonado, *Comentario al Evangelio de San Mateo*, p. 541.

B. The Realization of the Papacy.

In spite of the fact that the text of Matthew is the battlefield where the Roman Church has contended most vigorously, and is the text which is used officially to speak of the Pope, and is the text which is written with huge letters above the throne of the Roman pontiff—*"Tu es Petrus et super hanc petram edificabo ecclesiam mean"*—they recognize that the primacy is not here granted to Peter, but that it is merely announced and promised to him for the future: "I shall build my church."

For that reason they have tried hard to find a text in the Gospels which contains the fiulfillment of the promise, the concession of the papacy to Peter. And it is in John 21:15 where the Roman Church sees an explicit concession of the primacy to Peter.

Let's hear what Devivier, a well-known author in the field of Roman Catholic apologetics has to say:

> We see then that Peter and only Peter is appointed the shepherd of the flock of Jesus Christ, and that on no account is the authority which he receives limited.
>
> Moreover, at the same time that Jesus describes the whole church with the figure of a flock, He distinguishes explicitly between the lambs of the flock and the sheep, indicating by the first term the simple faithful, and by the second term those who engender the spiritual life, and those who therefore have the responsibility to guide and feed them, that is, the priests and bishops.
>
> Jesus Christ then, upon placing Peter at the head of his mystical flock, confers upon him a power, the greatest of all powers, which is the primacy of jurisdiction.[3]

And Father Bujanda, a Jesuit, professor of dogmatic theology at the Theological Seminary of Granada (Spain):

> By these words Peter is constituted by Jesus himself as shepherd of His flock; that is, the one who orders and commands, and not merely *a* shepherd, but the *supreme shepherd*, as is indicated by the question, "Lovest thou me more than these?"
>
> Consequently, from the words in which Jesus promises St. Peter that he would grant him the supreme authority, and

[3]Gualtero Devivier, *Curso de Apologética Cristiana.* Barcelona: Editorial Gustavo Gili, 1925, pp. 378-379.

from those in which He actually confers it upon him, rather than two proofs, one is taken, which is more absolute and perfect than if they were considered separately.[4]

That is all the grounds which the Roman papacy has to stand on. If the text of Matthew does not prove, according to the unanimous opinion of the great Fathers cited above, that the promise of a universal papacy was given to Peter, even less does John 21:15 prove it.

The interpretation of this text is obvious and ought not to be forced to mean what Jesus Christ did not intend it to mean. It was not the concession of a special primacy, but of pardon and a public rehabilitation for Peter. Upon denying his Master three times (Matt. 26:69-75), Peter's friendship was broken with Him. He became unworthy of belonging to the Apostolic college and also of governing the flock of Jesus Christ. He therefore lost all the privileges of an apostle.

With three public manifestations of love he manifests his repentance for the three public denials, and he returns to the place which he previously occupied in the apostolic group. He is able once again, as the others, to preach the Gospel and to guide the sheep and the lambs of Christ's fold. Hence, this text does not prove the primacy of Peter and his successors.

The Catholic dogma of the authority and infallibility of the Roman pontiff is also deduced by the Catholic Church from the fact that the concession of the keys of the kingdom of Heaven was granted by Jesus Christ to Peter: "I will give unto thee the keys of the kingdom of heaven: and whatsoever thou shalt bind on earth shall be bound in heaven" (Matt. 16:19).

This is what Jesus Christ says in the Gospels; but what does the Roman Church say? "I will give the keys to thee and to thy successors . . ." "Upon this rock which thou art and thy successors . . ." "All that thou and thy successors bind shall be bound, and all that thou and thy successors loose shall be loosed."[5]

The Roman Catholic Church knows that Jesus Christ did not say "thy successors," but asserts, as a doctrine of revealed faith, that he meant to say it. It is clear that if the successors of Peter, or the

---

[4]Jesús Bujanda, *Manual de Teología Dogmática*. Madrid: Editorial Razón y Fe, 1941, p. 52.

[5]Denzinger-Bunnwart, *Enchiridion Symbolorum*. Freiburg: Herder & Co., 1928, para. 1824-25.

bishops of Rome, have the keys of the kingdom of Heaven, then the only means of entering Heaven is by doing that which the Roman Church ordains. For this reason it is affirmed decidedly: "Apart from the Church there is no salvation."[6]

Rome constantly repeats "Peter and his successors." But it must be noted that Jesus Christ and His apostles never said it. This is enough to make every person who judges cautiously and who searches sincerely for the truth to think of the possibility of a sophism.

Jesus Christ says explicitly: "I give to *thee* the keys in order that everything which thou dost open may remain open, and that which thou dost close will be closed."

He did not say, "To thee and to thy successors." He did not say, "That which thou and thy successors open will remain open." *Not even once!* Neither did He give the "keys" to the Church. He did say, "Upon this rock I shall build my Church and to her I shall give the keys of the kingdom of heaven." Neither did He give them to the apostolic college. He gave them only to Peter, "to thee." In what, then, do these keys consist which only one man is able to have and to use?

They do not refer to the power of binding and loosing, because this very power was given to all the apostles in the same Gospel of Matthew, (18:18): "Verily I say unto you, Whatsoever ye [you, plural] shall bind on earth shall be bound in heaven: and whatsoever ye shall loose on earth shall be loosed in heaven."

Furthermore: "I say unto you, That if two of you shall agree on earth as touching anything that they shall ask, it shall be done for them of my Father which is in heaven. For where two or three are gathered together in my name, there am I in the midst of them" (vv. 19, 20). There is no reason, therefore, to confuse the privilege of the keys, which is given to one man, with that of binding and loosing, which is given to many. There is only one thing which Peter did in an exclusive way, and no one else was able to do it; namely, to inaugurate the Era of the Christian Church, opening the doors of the kingdom of Heaven, first to the Jews and proselytes of Judaism on the Day of Pentecost (Acts 2:28), and then to the Gentiles in the home of Cornelius (Acts 10:44-48).

Evidently Jesus Christ wanted to give the keys to Saint Peter as

[6]A. Hillaire, *La religión demostrada*. Barcelona: Editorial Luis Gili. 1944, p. 336.

keys are given to a minister or governor for a building that is going to be inaugurated. Peter himself refers, with satisfaction and legitimate pride, to this unique privilege which was granted by his Lord, in the Jerusalem Council:

> And when there had been much disputing, Peter rose up, and said unto them, Men and brethren, ye know that how a good while ago God made choice among us, that the Gentiles by my mouth should hear the word of the Gospel, and believe (Acts 15:7).

Let us observe that Peter does not say: "Men and brethren, ye know that how a good while ago God chose me to be the infallible head of the Church, and therefore I declare and determine *ex cathedra* the matter which is being debated in this council." But he simply says: "God determined that the Gentiles by my mouth should hear the word of the Gospel, and believe." This is the way in which Peter himself interpreted the privilege of the keys. Can we understand it in any other way?

"To thee, Peter," says Jesus, "I shall give the keys." Because it is a singular event, it will be your privilege. Not "to thee and the other apostles," because only one is necessary to inaugurate the event.

But Peter, according to Matthew 16:19, and the apostles, according to Matthew 18:18-20, are able to bind and unbind the powers of heaven as you are here on earth by means of prayer. Not "to thee and to thy successors," since the idea of apostolic succession is totally foreign to the New Testament.

The apostles were an exclusive group of witnesses of Christ until Paul's apostleship was disputed because he had not walked with Christ while He was on earth. He defends himself by declaring that he saw the Lord in His glory and contends that this gives him the right to call himself an apostle (I Cor. 12:1-6; II Cor. 9:1-3). Which one of the Popes has had either of these two privileges? With what reasoning, then, can the bishops of Rome claim apostolic rights? Where is the declaration of Christ or of Peter that such rights could be conferred upon another person outside the group of the twelve?

Jesus Christ speaks with exactness and knows how to express what He wishes. Jesus Christ makes a clear distinction between Peter (thou) apostles (ye) and the Church (she). "Thou, Peter, will be the foundation rock, that is, omitting the metaphor, the founding architect of My Church, the one who lays the first rock of the building with the declaration of My deity and the one who inaugurates it. To thee I shall give the keys, conferring upon thee this special honor.

"You who are apostles, supported by Peter and together with him, will build My Church. What you undertake to do in this building, as you are inspired by the Holy Spirit who will guide you in all truth (John 16:13), I shall perfect. You, the Twelve, together and aided by Peter, whose declaration of faith in My deity is the basis, make up the foundation stone of My Church. She, the Church, will have an aid, a supernatural force, against which the powers of Hell will be shattered. To thee, Peter, I give the keys to open and to inaugurate the Age of Grace. To Her, the Church, I give the power to withstand until the consummation of the ages."

It is clearly seen, therefore, that Jesus Christ knows how to distinguish with propriety, and He aportions to each one what He wills without any confusion.

C. The Transmission or Succession of the Roman Papacy.

In all the treatises of dogmatic theology that are studied in Catholic seminaries, the same arguments are presented to prove the succession of the Roman papacy, and the same ones are propagated among the people by means of popular apologetic tracts and by preaching.

Listen to the arguments of Devivier, one of the best representatives:

> The form which Jesus Christ has given to His Church cannot be modified except by Him. Now, then, Jesus Christ, on founding His Church, has established a primacy in it; therefore, no one is permitted to lay his hand upon it for the purpose of altering it, and much less to suppress it.
>
> This primacy, then, ought to exist continually, not necessarily in St. Peter, since every man must die, but in his legitimate successors.
>
> Jesus Christ made Peter the foundation of His Church and the shepherd of His flock; He did not impose any restriction. His will was, undoubtedly, that the Church should always find sta-

bility in its foundation, and that the flock should not cease from obeying its shepherd.

The foundations of a building, and especially the foundations of this one, ought of necessity to last as long as the building itself, that is, until the end of the world.

Now then, Jesus knew that Peter was not going to live continually; therefore, He wished that his ministry and his primacy might be perpetuated until the end of the ages by means of his legitimate successors.[7]

So, according to Rome, Jesus Christ left His Church resting upon a man of flesh and bone. Otherwise the Church cannot exist. It is the same as if it were a matter of a club or a human society which has no other support than that which mortal men can give it.

This is the reasoning which is found in all the theological treatises. Hence, the act of transmitting the supreme authority of Peter is not based on any part of the New Testament. Roman Catholics only deduce it from the Bible verses indicated above; and as we have already shown that the texts for the founding of the papacy do not prove the existence of any Roman papacy, the arguments for the transmission or the succession of the papacy remain without any support.

D. The Location of the Papacy.

No matter what book on the papacy that we pick up, we invariably find the categorical affirmation that Jesus not only founded a papacy on Peter, but that the latter transmitted his authority and privileges to a successor, and this successor is necessarily the bishop of Rome. For instance, Devivier's *Curso de Apologética,* cited above, says:

The bishop of Rome is the successor of Peter and it does not seem that on this point there can be any doubt. It is evident that the Catholic Church is the only church that obeys the successors of Peter, the first and supreme shepherd given to the Church by Jesus Christ Himself.

Now then, tradition and history offer us, with respect to the coming of Peter to Rome and of his death in that city, a series of testimonies so numerous and clear that for thirteen centuries no one appeared to advance any doubts concerning them.

After the Waldenses, the Protestants were naturally the ones

[7]Devivier, *op. cit.,* p. 473 ff.

who pretended to deny this fact, which is without a doubt of extreme importance in their controversies with the Catholics. Thus it is that these heretics have not spared anything, as the modern unbelievers, in order to tear down this truth, otherwise so well attested to by many and very notable documents, and established even today by the works to which the adversaries have given occasion by their own attacks.

Therefore, I believe it will be very helpful to review briefly some of the proofs summarized by the most authentic documents.

First, the prince of the apostles himself can serve as a witness. In his first epistle, written to the Christians of Asia Minor, he definitely says: "The church that is at Babylon, elected together with you, saluteth you; and so doth Marcus my son." This name Babylon, as in other passages of the Apocalypse, evidently designates the city of Rome, looked upon at that time as the empire of impiety, as oriental Babylon was looked upon by the Jews of the captivity. In this way the Holy Fathers always understood the passage in question, and Renan also agrees completely with this interpretation, as do the Protestants Grotius, Cave, Lardner, etc.

Second, at the end of the first century, St. Clement, bishop of Rome and disciple of St. Peter, speaking of the faithful who were martyred by Nero, named among them Peter and Paul.

Third, forty years after the death of St. Peter, St. Ignatius of Antioch, after being carried to Rome to be fed to wild beasts, addresses the Romans with this stirring request: "I entreat you now to show me no inexpedient mercy; let me be as feed to the wild beasts . . . I do not command you as Peter and Paul; they were apostles, I am no more than one condemned to death."

Then Devivier adds: "These words are of no significance if it is not admitted that the two apostles were governing the Roman Church."[8]

In spite of the fact that all the treatises on the Roman papacy affirm with Devivier[9] that "tradition and history offer us a series of testimonies so numerous and clear . . . ," the same author says on the following page,[10] "Nor should it surprise us that we do not find

[8]*Ibid.*, p. 381 ff.
[9]*Ibid.*, p. 383.
[10]*Ibid.*, p. 384.

in the early times of Christianity more than a few explicit testimonies of St. Peter's stay in Rome."

Devivier then gives his reason for this: "The writings that have come down to us are scanty because at the time no one thought of bringing up for discussion the reality of Peter's stay, and consequently, no one thought of proving it either, since in a time as that, full of persecution, the writers were not engaging themselves in trivial matters of this kind."[11]

The most curious aspect of all this reasoning is that they repeat even to the extent of satiety that the founding of the Roman papacy is that which lends stability and solidarity to the whole Church; and immediately, when faced with the scarcity of proof texts, they say that it is "a triviality" to say exactly where this foundation is, whether in Rome, Alexandria, Corinth, or New York.

History openly contradicts this Roman claim. The Catholic historian cited above, Father Llorca, S. J., in his *Manual of Church History* which is used as a textbook in some theological seminaries of the Jesuits, says in chapter II: "The stay of St. Peter in Rome and his death in the same city are historically well proven, so the majority of modern historians look upon these as indisputable historical facts. . . . It is true that the question is being discussed anew today, and notable authors, such as Lavisse and Bambaud, and particularly Heussi, doubt it."[12] If this is true, how can one say that it is well proved historically?

Again, Devivier confesses that history is not so clear on the point of Peter's arrival in Rome. "With regard to the date of his [Peter's] arrival in Rome, tradition is not so explicit."[13]

The publisher Desclée is publishing a history of the Church that is written by modern historians of considerable renown. These writers set forth or try to set forth the last word of historical criticism concerning the origin and development of the Church. In the first volume, devoted to the early Church and written by the famed Lebreton, we read:

> How long did St. Peter live in the eternal city? We have no
> idea. There is no historical document which supports the tra-

[11]*Ibid.*, p. 384.
[12]Bernardino Llorca, Manual de Historia ecclesiástica. Barcelona. Editorial Labor, 1951, p. 38.
[13]Devivier, *op. cit.*, pp. 384-385.

dition that the Roman episcopacy lasted for twenty-five years. Let us at least agree that his stay in the imperial capital was not constant for those twenty-five years, since in 49 A.D. he attended the Council of Jerusalem, shortly afterwards he was in Antioch reconciling his differences with Paul, and finally, there is neither an allusion to him in the epistle which Paul wrote to the Romans in 58 A.D., nor in the account of Paul's confinement in Rome (61-62 A.D.), according to the book of Acts.

Furthermore, only later authors, whose veracity ought to be questioned, refer the claimed meeting in Rome of Peter and Simon Magus to the beginning of the reign of Claudius (41-54 A.D.).

On the other hand, how can one explain, apart from any direct act of the apostles, that at the time St. Paul wrote to the Romans their church was vigorously flourishing and its importance was so great in Paul's eyes that he dedicated his great doctrinal treatise on predestination to them?

As this apostle could not have been Paul himself, who confesses in his epistle (*c.* 58 A.D.) that until then he had not been able to visit the imperial capital, it seems admissible to believe that St. Peter had previously visited them, even though at that time he may not have had a permanent residence there.

Proofs for substantiating this hypothesis are lacking, and even more so if we claim to set the time as being twenty-five years before his death.[14]

So when the sincere authors speak scientifically to the scholars they confess that the foundations upon which the Roman papacy is constructed could not be any weaker or less certain.

An author of great esteem in the Catholic world, Father Sertillanges, O. P., of the Paris Institute, says in his celebrated work:

And why precisely Rome? Upon arriving here it is only necessary that we respect providence, since our explanations make no claim to scrutinize or judge it. But we can note that Rome, when the Church was born, was for the world what Peter was for the Church, a center of life. And thus as the city par excellence, a metropolis, it spread its light rays in all directions, and diffused the rights of its legislators through towns and villages, as the head of the Church likewise did in the spiritual realm. The pagan city was a figure of the Christian city and was to

[14]Llorca, *op. cit.*, p. 39.

serve as its servant. By placing the church in the heart of the world in which it was born, it was only necessary to follow the pulsations of that heart, and to launch out with it through all the geographical and administrative channels which were secularly prepared and to serve as its blood and soul.[15]

This is the true reason for placing the papacy in Rome. It has no Biblical foundation but is the result of mere circumstances.

And in another part of the same chapter Sertillanges says:

Was this bond of union between the bishop of Rome and other pastors of the Church well established in early times? It is true that it was rather weak. But the embryo is not the man, and besides, the apostolic rule was given to all those who had enjoyed a personal contact with Christ and had heard from His very lips the divine teachings, a kind of universal mission similar to that of Christ Himself: the Church which had as its leader one of the Twelve was considered to be sheltered from all deviation. Now then, this rule was still in effect at the time of the immediate successors of the apostles, whose customs they had acquired and which were profiting them. The recourse to Rome, which was difficult at that time, was not considered indispensible. Nevertheless, many indications are available, *although* relatively weak, of the early authority of the bishop of Rome, and we ought to rely upon these.

Only "indications" and "relatively weak," for the most important and fundamental dogma of the Roman Church!

Father Sertillanges continues:

Well, how did the transition develop? The power of the other bishops became more and more limited to their own particular churches; on the other hand, that of the bishop of Rome became proportionately more universal, meeting with satisfaction the new needs of that unity which continued to grow, and from that functional complication which required a most vigorous concentration.

In spite of such historical evidences, the Roman Church is determined to defend the belief that its existence is found in the very beginnings of Christianity, and that its origin is completely divine. In the ecclesiastical histories of Rome, Clement of Rome, bishop of

[15]Father Sertillanges, *Catechism of the Unbelievers,* Book III, chap. 2.

the same city, is presented as the third successor of Peter, because Irenaeus attests to it, even though they confess that it is only evident that he may have written a letter and that we have no information concerning his life. All the writings which antiquity attributes to Clement of Rome have been considered spurious even by the Catholics themselves, except the letter to the Corinthians. And it seems to them that what this letter exposes—the need for submission to the hierarchy—proves the existence of a Roman pope in A.D. 90.

We know with certainty that in the fifth century churches such as those of Carthage did not recognize the universal papal authority of the bishop of Rome. It is sufficient to remember that the Roman bishop Zózimus (A.D. 417-418) once approved the doctrine of Pelagius and Coelestus, when these men appealed to his authority. But he was later forced to retract his approval when he discovered that the bishops of Africa had condemned it. This same bishop of Rome defended an African presbyter, Apiarius, who had been excommunicated by his bishop, and maintained that he was authorized to do it according to a canon of the Nicene Council. Then a synod convened in Africa and replied that such a canon did not exist. And it was true. The bishop of Rome, Zózimus, had confused the Nicene canons with those of Sardis which figured under the same caption as those of Nicaea in the records of Rome. Zózimus died toward the end of A.D. 418, without having solved the problem of Apiarius. But the issue was raised again in A.D. 426 by the Roman bishop Celestine. Then the bishops of Africa confirmed the condemnation of Apiarius, repeated that the pretended Nicene canon produced by Zózimus was spurious. The canons of Sardis were evidently ignored.

Then they wrote frankly to the Roman bishop Celestine that he should abstain from receiving persons who had been excommunicated by their synod and from meddling in the affairs of their churches. And it must be remembered that at that time brilliant men of Augustine's stature were members of the African episcopacy.

So it can be proved that the Roman papacy has neither Biblical nor historical support for maintaining its *promise,* its *foundation,* its *succession,* nor its *location.*

THE CHARACTERISTICS OF THE CHURCH

Both the Catholics and the Protestants agree that Jesus Christ

founded a church and a human religious society which would be conspicuous among men. This being true, we all believe that the Church
of Jesus Christ must have some characteristics which distinguish it
from all others. The Roman Church emphasizes this argument considerably and tries as skillfully as possible to show that it alone possesses the characteristics of the Church of Jesus Christ.

After many years of discussion, the characteristics sufficient to distinguish the true Church from those which are false have been reduced to four: unity, sanctity, catholicity, and apostolic succession.
And this is their reasoning: the Church is the mystical body of Jesus
Christ, His permanent incarnation among men; consequently, the
mark of the perfections of the God-man ought to be found in the
Church.

Hillaire sums it up in this way:

> First, there is only one Christ; in Him the divine and human
> natures are united by a hypostatic or personal union. In the
> same manner, there is only one church wherein both the divine
> and human, the visible and invisible, are united.
>
> Second, Jesus Christ is the personification of sanctity. He evi-
> denced this sanctity while living in mortal flesh, by means of His
> virtues and miracles.
>
> Third, Jesus Christ is the Saviour of the world; He died for
> all, and wants everyone to be saved. It is essential that His
> Church, as He Himself, be catholic and universal.
>
> Fourth, having been sent by His Father, Jesus Christ sends His
> apostles, who, in turn, send their successors. Thus the Church,
> throughout the centuries, is always apostolic.
>
> The true Church of Jesus Christ, made in His image and like-
> ness, is a society, both human and divine at the same time, which
> He animates by His Spirit and which reflects His divine unity,
> sanctity, immensity and mission.[16]

A. Unity

The Roman Church, as is expected, says that the only church
which evidences the four characteristics is the Roman Catholic
Church. They try to prove it in this way: First, it is *one*. All the
members profess the same faith, participate in the same sacraments,
and obey the same supreme hierarch, the Pope. And as Hillaire says:

[16]A. Hillaire, *op. cit.*, p. 310.

All Catholics admit the same truths, the same precepts, the same evangelical counsel. Travel wherever you may on the earth, and at every point of the globe, you will hear the servant of the Roman Church sing the same creed. Go back through the ages to apostolic times and you will see the same symbol professed for nineteen centuries.[17]

It would be impossible to find a proposition which is easier to refute. If there is a religion or a church that has changed, it is precisely the Roman Church. When has there been unanimity of thought and doctrine among the Roman theologians before establishing a dogma? Never! Those of us who have lived within it and have attended the theological discussions, and have studied the evolution of dogmas, of liturgy, of the precepts of the Church, of the hierarchy, are astonished when we hear it said that the Church claims to have the characteristic of *unity*.

Roman *unity* exists merely on the surface. And in order to appear united, they have recourse to a severe censorship of books and magazines and to the threat of excommunication for the one who defends that which is contrary to Rome.

Where do we find the dogma of the immaculate conception? As late as the eleventh century we find Anselm of Canterbury teaching that Mary was conceived and born in original sin, but that she was freed of it prior to the birth of Jesus.[18]

The clear apparition of this doctrine was in the twelfth century, when, in 1139, the Canons of Lyons celebrated the Conception of Mary (December 8) as the festival of the Immaculate Conception. The festival was in existence already; the only thing that was added was the adjective *immaculate*. Many men of great authority reacted against this initiative, among whom was Bernard of Clairvaux esteemed Marian doctor par excellence.

Bernard of Clairvaux insisted that the Immaculate Conception contradicted the dignity of Jesus Christ, the only one who is totally immune from sin. And he says:

How have these authors discovered such a hidden fact? By means of the same motive and authority they would be able to

[17]*Ibid.*, p. 313.
[18]*Cur Deus homo*, II, 16-17.

speak of the solemnity of the mother and father of Mary and of all their ancestors back through infinity. . . .[19]

Likewise, the greatest scholastics resisted such an innovation until the fourteenth century: St. Anselm, Peter Lombard, Alexander of Hales, Bonaventura, Albert Magnus, Thomas Aquinas.

These struggles were intensified when Duns Scotus, in the fourteenth century, kindled the great agitation with the argument which was to become famous: *"Potuit, decuit, ergo fecit."* "He was able, it was convenient, so he did it."

It was Pope Pius IX, a great devotee of Mary, who defined, as a doctrine revealed from God, the dogma of the Immaculate Conception, in 1854. We do not intend to discuss the expediency or the veracity of such a dogma here. We cite it merely to show that the doctrine has not always existed in its same form; that it has been profoundly changed. Before 1854 one could deny the immaculate conception of Mary without being a heretic. One could even be a saint and a doctor of the Church, as were those whom we have cited above. Now, however, if one denies it he is a heretic and is excommunicated from the Church. Can it honestly be said that nothing has been changed?

Where do we find the obligation of hearing mass on Sundays and the penalty of mortal sin or of eternal condemnation if it is not heard? Where is the obligation of prayer by the Roman Breviary in Latin, for the priests, under the penalty of mortal sin, and therefore, of eternal condemnation? Where is the obligation for believing in the Assumption of Mary to Heaven in body and soul, in order to be able to obtain eternal salvation?

It would suffice to recall the case of Pope Honorius, of the seventh century (625-638), who during several centuries was considered a heretic: first by the Council of Constantinople (the Sixth Ecumenical Council), then by Pope Leo II (682-683) again by the Seventh Ecumenical Council of Nicaea (787), and still again by the Eighth at Constantinople (869). This condemnation was included in the body of the oath which was pronounced by every pope upon being elected, from the eighth to the eleventh centuries, and was included in the editions of the Roman Breviary until the eighteenth century.

[19]Epístola 174, *ad Canonigos Lugduenses De Conceptione S. Mariae.* Editorial Migne I, pp. 332-336.

Following the dogmatic affirmation of the infallibility of the Pope, in 1870, various interpretations were sought in order to make allowance for this extremely important doctrine; but the fact is that for several centuries the Church of Rome officially opposed something which no one can now oppose without being considered a heretic; namely, the papal infallibility in questions of faith and morals.

It is not necessary here to remember that which one finds in any manual of church history: the Western Schism, when for forty years the Roman Church was divided into two series of popes (1378-1417). Each pope affirmed that those who obeyed the other pope were placing their souls in danger of eternal condemnation. The Councils of Pisa, of Constance, and of Basel, explicitly affirmed that the Council is superior to the pope in matters of faith, schism, and heresy. This superiority includes the question of infallibility. Here one may use Bossuet's famous argument, frequently used against the Protestants: "Changes? then, thou canst not be true!"

When I belonged to the Roman Church, for some time I had to take some medicine each evening in order to help me with a certain heart ailment. The following day I was not able to conduct the mass nor to administer communion because of having broken the eucharistic fast which the Catholic Church then considered essential for the participation. So it was considered more important to go without communion and without having mass than to do it a few hours after having taken some medicine. Today fasting is not considered necessary, and one can hold a mass and administer communion after having eaten. The doctrinal change has been realized within five years. Five years ago I was committing a mortal sin if I held a mass after having eaten or drunk anything, no matter how insignificant it might be. Now it is not even considered a venial sin, but a perfectly just act.

It is said that the Roman ecclesiastical hierarchy has authority to proclaim and annul laws, practices, and customs. The astonishing thing is that at the same time they dare to affirm that the same doctrine has always been upheld and that they have "unity of faith," "unity of worship," and "unity of government." How can one say, as Hillaire does, in his *Religión demostrada:*

> All Catholics admit the same truths, the same precepts, the
> same evangelical counsel. Travel wherever you may on the

earth, and at every point of the globe you will hear the servant
of the Roman Church sing the same creed. Go back through the
ages to apostolic times and you will see the same symbol professed for nineteen centuries.

These affirmations can only be made to people who are ignorant
of ecclesiastical and dogmatic history. The rest of us know only too
well the divergencies in essential points for eternal salvation. We
have been thoroughly acquainted with the impassioned struggles between the Dominicans and the Jesuits in the famous *"de auxiliis,"*
in which some endorsed Thomism and others endorsed the doctrines
of Suarez, the Scotistic and Molinistic schools, etc. And let it not
be said that they were purely ceremonial and disciplinary matters,
because it is well known that the question centered around the doctrine of grace and of eternal salvation.

We are well acquainted with the effort exerted by the Society of
Jesus to defend that which it calls "our doctrines," and with the
sternness by which it obliges its members to defend them! No matter
how well versed one may be in Biblical theology, he will lose his
assignment without any hope of regaining it or of publishing books
or theological writings, until he renounces every doctrine which is
not 100 per cent in accordance with the theological doctrines of the
Order. We could present long lists of theologians, Jesuits of considerable talent, who live almost in exile, without being able to hold
positions of any importance in the Order or to exert any doctrinal
influence, only because of not being adherents exclusively to the doctrinal norms which are practiced by the Order. And they speak of
unity of the faith! Such unity is apparent, but is it real?

Let us move on to the sacraments. The theologian, Leo von Rudloff, in his *Dogmatic Theology,* says: "The Church from the beginning has always taught that Christ instituted seven sacraments."[20]
On the other hand, Father Bujanda, also a Jesuit, in his *Dogmatic
Theology,* says:

> For many centuries a sacrament meant not only that which
> the Roman Catholic Church designates today by that term, but
> several other religious actions; however, little by little the use of
> that word came to acquire the exclusive meaning which it has

[20]Leon von Rudloff, *Teología dogmática para laicos.* Buenos Aires: Editorial Descleé,
n.d., p. 131.

today, and ever since the twelfth century this seems to be the accepted meaning.[21]

Do contrary statements about the same subject represent "unity of opinion" and "doctrinal unity?"

According to the Catholic Church, in order for a rite to be a sacrament, it is necessary for Jesus Christ to have instituted it. But what about the sacrament of confirmation? The Roman catechism, part II, chapter 3, says:

> Christ has not only been the author of this sacrament, but as the sovereign pope S. Fabiano affirms, He himself prescribed the rite of the chrism and the words which the Catholic Church employs upon administering it.[22]

On the other hand, the commentator of the *Suma Teológica* of Thomas Aquinas, Father Manuel Mendía of the Order of Preachers, says:

> One cannot determine exactly at what time and in what circumstances Christ formally instituted this sacrament. Some think that He instituted it at the same time as the Eucharist; others, when He blessed the little children placing His hands upon them; others, in the interval which intervened between His resurrection and ascension, during which He gave the apostles the last instructions about the mysteries of His kingdom.[23]

Compelled by this evidence, the Roman catechism, in the above-mentioned chapter, question XII, says:

> Even when it cannot be proven that this is the true form of the sacrament, the authority of the Catholic Church, which with its magistarium has always instructed us in this form, by no means allows us to doubt concerning this.

So it is affirmed that Christ "not only has been the author of this sacrament but that He himself prescribed the rite of the chrism and the words which the Catholic Church employs upon administering it." Then it is said: "Even when it cannot be proven . . ." How can it be lacking proof if Christ Himself established its form and the words which are to be uttered? And we ask furthermore: How

[21]Bujanda, *op. cit.*, p. 375.
[22]From the Council of Florence. See Denzinger-Bannwart, *op. cit.*, para. 697.
[23]Thomas Aquinas, *Suma Teológica*. Rev. and annoted by Manuel Mendía. Madrid: Editorial Moya, 1883, Vol. IV, p. 746.

can one affirm that Christ determined the words and the rite, if one does not even know it was instituted and the apostles never speak of it?

Alexander of Hales, in his *Suma Teológica,* part IV, question IX, edited in Venice, 1575, says:

> This sacrament was instituted by the inspiration of the Holy Spirit at the Council of Meaux with regard to the form of the words and the essential elements to which the Holy Spirit conferred the virtue of sanctifying.

Thomas Aquinas, in his *Suma Teológica,* says in this regard:

> Others say that it was instituted by the apostles. But this cannot be true, because the institution of a new sacrament belongs to a superior power which is only held by Christ. And therefore it ought to be said that Christ instituted this sacrament, that it was not given by the Holy Spirit but that Christ promised the Spirit, according to John 16:7: "For if I go not away the Comforter will not come unto you; but if I depart, I will send Him unto you."[24]

As is clearly seen, that which ought to have been proved is left without proof: who was it that instituted the sacrament of confirmation? Every sacrament which the Roman Church defends as a divine institution has been and still is even now discussed vigorously in its most essential aspects. And they dare to say that they have always defended the same thing and that they have absolute doctrinal unity!

One may confirm what we have just said by consulting any treatise on moral theology; for example, "The Clergy's Adviser," by Berthier; "Moral Theology," by a Jesuit, Father Ferreres, or the *Suma Teológica,* by Thomas Aquinas, which is the principle textbook in every Catholic seminary.

One is able, therefore, to prove with evidence and complete satisfaction that the Roman Catholic Church does not even possess the first characteristic which she sets forth as the characteristics of the Church of Jesus Christ: doctrinal unity in matters of worship and government.

[24]*Ibid.*, p. 746.

B. Sanctity

We shall not discuss here the sanctity of the Roman Church, for unquestionably there are aspects of it and persons in it which are very saintly, but could we not say the same about other religions? They deny this and affirm that in no other church has sanctity flourished as in theirs. It was founded by Jesus Christ, the Saint of saints. Other religions have had men as founders who are more or less sinners, and some, as the Protestants, they say, have been founded by men who are totally degenerate.

Having shown that the Catholic Church does not have its origin in Jesus Christ, and knowing what history affirms concerning the election of popes and of their lives, it is meaningless to say that the Protestants are not saints. Many Catholic leaders were corrupt men, and God could not entrust to them the reform of His Church, which the Catholics recognize was necessary. Could God entrust the government of His Church to Bonifice VI who, as Mourret says in his *General History of the Church*, "occupied for two weeks nothing less than the office of St. Peter, the former being deposed two times, because of being despicable, from the subdeaconship and from the priesthood."[25] Or could it be entrusted to John XII who was placed at the age of sixteen, because of his ambitions and conspiracies, to rule the Church of God in spite of the fact that he was "licentious, dissolute, and a dealer in spiritual benefits. . ."?[26] Or could it be entrusted to Stephen VI who scaled the papal throne in 896, after attempting and achieving the death of Pope Formoso in order that he himself might later die, being strangled the following year in prison.

"To remember this," says Father Labruru, S. J., "crystallizes one's horror and causes one to lower his head in shame."[27] And the most distinguished and authentic historian of the popes, Pastor,[28] says:

> For the sake of publicity and owing to an unprecedented lack of scruples, Alexander VI gave himself over, during the eleven years of his reign, to his own inclinations and appetites which were entirely mundane and frequently reprehensible. His pa-

[25]J. A. de Labruru, *Qué es la Iglesia?* Montevideo: Editorial Masca, n.d., p. 124.
[26]*Ibid.*, p. 125.
[27]*Ibid.*, p. 125.
[28]Pastor, *History of the Popes*, Vol. VI, p. 75.

pacy was a calamity for the Church upon whose prestige it had inflicted the most serious wounds.

Labruru adds: "When dying, the disgraced Alexander VI was called a poisonous plant hated by God and man."[29]

These facts are so well known that even the Catholic historians themselves recognize their veracity. But what is hard to understand is that in spite of knowing this they dare to pronounce accusations and anathemas constantly against the Evangelical Church; for example: "Protestantism has no sanctity, not even in its founders who were all men of infamous and scandalous conduct. This characteristic suffices to judge a religion. *God does not employ a corrupt people to perform such an important mission as the reform of His Church.*"[30]

We would reject, as an argument without value, the statement that the Roman Catholic Church cannot belong to Jesus Christ because of its hierarchs and priests. Neither the treason of Judas nor the denial of Peter argue against the sanctity of the doctrine of Jesus Christ or against the sanctity of the apostolic college. It is the doctrine itself that must be analyzed and shown to be that of Jesus Christ and His apostles. The life of those who propagate, defend, and profess the doctrine of Christ in no way militates against its sanctity and veracity. This unfortunately is forgotten frequently by the Romanists. I know this from experience.

Since I left Roman Catholicism, the personal defamations against me have not ceased, and there is no dishonorable title in the dictionary which has not be applied to me hundreds of times. They do not attack the message which I expound at conferences or that of my book, *Why I Left Roman Catholicism,* because, according to them, its falsehood is too evident. All their energies, their press, their radio, etc., have been employed in a personal attack, in order to bring the individual into disrepute, believing thereby that the cause will remain in bad repute. What a lack of logic! What a lack of Christian love!

C. Catholicity.

It cannot be denied that the Roman Church is catholic in the sense of being universal. But we ask, when the Gospel of Jesus Christ

[29]Labruru, *op. cit.*
[30]Hillaire, *op. cit.*, p. 324.

was not yet preached in all the world, but only in limited regions, did it cease to be the doctrine of the true Church of Jesus Christ? Did the Christian Church fail to be the true Church as long as the Gospel was not preached throughout all the world? Is it not possible for a doctrine to be scattered throughout the world without it being in essence the best and most convenient of all doctrines? Is not Communism becoming catholic in the sense of being universal? Are not the Evangelical Churches scattered throughout the world?

In no period of history has one been able to judge the veracity and divinity of a doctrine by its territorial extension. And furthermore, as we have already shown that the Roman Church does not evidence the characteristic of *unity,* nor of absolute *sanctity,* and above all, nothing of *apostolic succession,* the characteristic of *catholicity* does not prove anything.

It has not come from the apostles, but has been formed gradually during the course of the centuries, and has had to subdue the vigorous resistance of its own members who did not readily accept the innovations which were being added to the apostolic doctrines. This is so evident and certain that a curious theory called "the germ" was elaborated, and then propagated by Cardinal Newman. This he did in order to be able to explain the divine origin of a doctrine, in spite of the fact that nothing is found in the apostolic writings, or in any writings of the early centuries. In this way the dogmatic Roman affirmations which are prevalent today are given validity.

It is admitted that no matter how much one searched for such affirmations, they could not be found in any explicit form, but were hidden as in a germ, and that down through the centuries they came into appearance. But this clearly proves, as George Salmon notes in *The Infallibility of the Church:* "The defeat which the leaders of the Roman Church have suffered in the battle which they pretended to fight on the grounds of history."[31]

THE PRESENT SITUATION

Faced with the exposition of the above arguments and many more which could be submitted, the reader may ask how it is possible for a church whose doctrines are supported on the basis of fallacies to have so many followers and to acquire so many new adherents as has

[31]George Salmon, *The Infallibility of the Church,* p. 32.

happened in reality throughout the past years? It is certain, as statistics affirm, that several thousand converts are won by the Roman Church every year, and among them many Protestants. However, this undeniable fact has an explanation which is independent of its doctrinal contents.

The Roman Church undeniably employs some effective techniques. First, there is *liturgy in its greatest grandeur* and in its most spectacular form. It would suffice to witness the liturgical functions of a Benedictine monastery, or of St. Peter's in Rome, in order to immediately understand the fascinating influence which is exercised in the soul of those who are assembled there. Second, *beautiful art in its most delightful expression* is employed. Who has not been profoundly impressed when facing a Gothic cathedral such as that of Cologne? Or facing the paintings of Raphael, of Michelangelo, of Fra Angelico? or listening to the music of Palestrina or Vittoria? Third, *oratory in its most suggestive and stirring form* is a potent tool. It is sufficient to recall Lacordaire, Bossuet, Bourdaloue, and so many other preachers who have flourished throughout the Roman Church and were prepared especially to move multitudes with the force of oratorical persuasion and with the aesthetics of their overtures. These three devices are employed by the Roman Church as much as possible, for they are convinced that these are decisive measures for attracting new members to their flock.

Once having succeeded in winning persons by these means, they have two others for attracting and conserving them, which are not insignificant in their effectiveness. I refer to schools and hospitals. It is true that in Catholic countries the schools with most prestige are those directed by monks. And in many countries which have been distinguished because of their Protestant tradition, the schools of the religious orders are on a level with the best.

As one can see, the means of obtaining converts are decidedly effective. But once within the Catholic Church, the method is fundamentally that of an absolutist, for they have no security for holding on to the converts which they have obtained. Therefore, there is strict censorship of every book and magazine, with the threat of excommunication if one reads or publishes or sells books which do not have the approval of Rome. And when a book is considered very effective in proving the errors of Romanism, they place upon it an excommunication that is reserved for the Roman pontiff, as they did with my book, *Why I Became a Protestant*. This excommunication means that no ordinary confessor, and not even bishops, can forgive the sin of one who has read, edited, or sold such a book.

The Church is no less absolutist in regard to the use of reason. The spiritual leaders and confessors do not tolerate any discussion against the established dogmas. They must be accepted without being analyzed. The rules of St. Ignatius, the founder of the Society of Jesus (Jesuits), have been applied by the Romanists. From these I should like to cite only two.

Rule One: "Setting aside all judgment, we ought to have a spirit which is prepared and ready to obey completely the true bride of Christ our Lord which is our holy mother, the hierarchical church." So, in order to be a good Christian, that is, "in order to have the true experience which we should experience within the militant church, the following rules must be heeded." This means, dispense with judgment, do not reason, cease thinking, and accept without inquiry the legitimacy of that which is proposed to you.

Rule Thirteen: "We should always be disposed to believe that the white which I see is black if the hierarchical church so declares it."[32]

Even with regard to the reading of the Bible itself, Catholics are not permitted to read it without commentaries or marginal notes that are written by an authorized priest of the ecclesiastical hierarchy. This mandate is given in spite of the fact that the Council of Trent recognized and declared "that the Bible has infallible authority and that it contains a supernatural revelation, written under the inspiration of the Holy Spirit, and that it is sacred and inspired in all its parts."[33] So if a priest writes some notes on John, Matthew, Paul, and Peter, I can read his writings. But unless a priest tells me how I am to interpret what the sacred writers have handed down to us, I cannot read them (the books of the Bible) and must submit such writings to the Index of prohibited books until a Roman priest gives them an approved meaning often an interpretation contrary to the literal statement of Scripture.

[32]Ignatius of Loyola, *Edición de las Obras completas*. Madrid: Biblioteca de autores cristianas, 1952, pp. 235-237.
[33]From the Vulgate Edition, ratified by the Council of Trent, Session IV; Denzinger-Bannwart, *op. cit.*, paras. 784-785.

Therefore the Catholic has no means of escaping from his error. He is not allowed to reason for himself; he is not allowed to read anything that is not Roman in character, or to compare anything for himself; to attend Protestant services or those of other religions. He is not even allowed to study the Bible by itself without being guided by a specialized Romanist. Only in this way is one able to understand why, in spite of so many fallacies, the Roman Church maintains itself. Freedom of thought is not permitted, nor freedom of reading, because their error would become too evident and the masses would abandon the Church in a short time.

Fortunately, time has changed many things since the Middle Ages. People read, investigate, and reason much more than formerly. Dogmatic affirmations are losing more and more force each day. The Roman Catholic Church itself recognizes that the popular and working masses are no longer Catholics. The percentage of those who attend mass on holidays and special occasions is reduced considerably, and the prestige of the clergy has diminished extremely even in countries where Roman Catholicism is strongest. In South America, the Catholics themselves confess that the priests have no prestige in the eyes of the public. In Catholic Spain during the civil war which brought Franco to power, the people killed the priests and friars and burned churches and convents. Therefore the Roman clergy is interested in conquering governments in order to have the support of military and civil forces. Only in this way can they maintain themselves.

In these last days, the greatest crisis of all history is being witnessed. When the governments cease to lend their support to Romanism in preference to other religions, and the people ignore the excommunications of Rome and make use of reason and read religious and historical books, regardless of whether or not they are ecclesiastically censured, in that day the last hour will strike for that church which has pretended to be the only true one.

BIBLIOGRAPHY

As indicated in footnotes, Dr. Padrosa's sources were all written in Spanish and Latin. A few of the more helpful works in English are listed here; both Catholic and non-Catholic viewpoints are represented.

BERKOUWER, GERRIT. *Recent Developments in Roman Catholic Thought.* Grand Rapids: Wm. B. Eerdmans Publishing Co., 1958.

BLANSHARD, PAUL. *American Freedom and Catholic Power.* Boston: Beacon Press, Rev. Ed., 1958.

———. *Communism, Democracy and Catholic Power.* Boston: Beacon Press, 1951.

The Catholic Encyclopedia. New York: The Encyclopedia Press, 1913.

CHINIQUY, CHARLES. *Fifty Years in the Church of Rome.* Grand Rapids: Baker Book House, n.d.

DENZINGER, HENRICI. *Sources of Catholic Dogma.* Trans. by Roy Deferrari. St. Louis: Herder, 1957.

GIBBONS, JAMES CARDINAL. *Faith of Our Fathers.* New York: P. J. Kenedy & Sons.

HAMMOND, T. C. *The One Hundred Texts.* London: Society for Irish Church Missions, 3rd ed., 1950.

HOWARD, GEORGE P. *Religious Liberty in Latin America?* Philadelphia: Wesminster Press, 1944.

HUGHES, PHILIP. *A popular History of the Catholic Church.* New York: Macmillan, 1949.

POHLE, JOSEPH and PREUSS, ARTHUR. *Dogmatic Textbooks,* 12 vols. St. Louis: B. Herder, Vol. 12, 1950; other vols., previous dates.

REYNOLDS, ARTHUR G. *What's the Difference?* New York: Abingdon Press, 1954.

VAN DOORNIK, N. G. M., JELSMA, S., and VAN DE LISDONK, A. *A Handbook of the Catholic Faith.* Garden City, New York: Doubleday & Co., Inc., 1954.

FIG. 15.—John Witherspoon, a leader in American Presbyterianism. Dr. Witherspoon was president of Princeton (1768-1794), was first moderator of the General Assembly of the Presbyterian Church in this country, was active in the Committees of Correspondence, was a member of the Continental Congress and was the only clergyman to sign the Declaration of Independence. (Courtesy of Presbyterian Historical Society.)

*The greatest wonder ever on earth is, that the Son of God died
the shameful death of the cross.... Therein recognize that the
merciful Lord God and Father so loved the poor condemned world,
that he spared not his only begotten Son, but gave him us for
us all, that whosoever believeth in him should not perish, but have
everlasting life.*

Luther's Table-Talk, CCXXVIII.

XV.

Protestantism

by KENNETH S. KANTZER

AT HIGH NOON ON October 31, 1517, a brilliant young professor walked up to the door of the town church in Wittenberg, Saxony, and, as was the custom in that day, tacked to the door frame a paper containing ninety-five debate topics—a challenge to all comers. Little did Martin Luther realize that thereby he had started the Protestant Reformation. His debate topics were in themselves innocent enough. They dealt mainly with abuses relating to the sale of indulgences, which he attacked as permits in advance to sin without fear of God's judgment or punishment.

Beneath these surface questions regarding indulgences, however, lay two great principles—the principles which were to serve as the basis of the Protestant Reformation. The first of these Reformation principles was that of justification by faith or the idea that man may be received into the loving favor of God on condition of personal

KENNETH S. KANTZER, A.B. (Ashland College), M.A. (Ohio State University), B.D., S.T.M. (Faith Theological Seminary), Ph.D. (Harvard University), is chairman of the division of Biblical Education and Apologetics at Wheaton College (Ill.). He is also a consulting editor of *His* magazine and a member of the Young Life Institute staff. Recently Dr. Kantzer spent a year in Europe, studying at the University of Goettingen, Germany, and the University of Basel, Switzerland.

commitment of himself to God through Jesus Christ unhindered by the baggage of ecclesiastical or legalistic "good works."

Undergirding this first principle was a second—a new principle of authority. According to the new Protestant principle of authority, the Bible is the only infallible rule of faith and practice and provides for the simplest believer an immediate guidance of the Holy Spirit for his moral and spiritual life.

Martin Luther had been brought to these new convictions through deep agony of soul. As an Augustinian monk he had for years sought to find his way to peace with God through the intricate maze of medieval and monastic religious devotions. But he sought in vain. In spite of emptiness of soul, his earnest zeal and brilliant mind brought continual advancements wthin his order. Early in the year 1514, as professor of theology at the University of Wittenberg, he became exceedingly interested in Biblical exegesis, especially of the books of Psalms and Romans. Through his influence, new grammars, dictionaries, and Bible commentaries were added to the University library in the castle. As his studies progressed, he became increasingly repulsed by the decadence of the sixteenth century church, which had substituted sterile ecclesiastical works for the gospel of God's free forgiveness.

The Tetzel indulgence, harked through Germany to raise funds for the building of Saint Peter's Cathedral in Rome, merely served as the occasion for Luther's growing convictions to manifest themselves. As a result of his stand against indulgences, Luther came immediately into conflict with the organized church. The surface issue of the validity of the papers of indulgences soon dropped into the background before the fundamental questions of how man is rightly related to God. For Luther, and for all his true followers, man is a sinner who through repentance and personal commitment to Christ receives immediately full and free forgiveness and acceptance into the favor of God. For the Romanist, on the contrary, salvation was dispensed horizontally through the agents and means of a divinely established church.

Much of medieval theology, of course, Martin Luther had no desire to overthrow; for he considered it thoroughly Biblical and essential to the basic structure of his own newly found Christian faith. Jesus, the man of Galilee, is also God, uniting in His one person a completely human nature and a completely divine nature. The pre-existence, virgin birth, sinlessness, miracles, substitutionary death, bodily resurrection, and second coming of Christ, Luther defended with a zeal surpassing that of his Roman protagonists. New was the complete sufficiency of Jesus Christ as a living Saviour. For him and his followers, Jesus Christ was not only the divine Lord in heaven, He was also the divine Saviour who out of infinite love for guilty and wretched sinners came down from Heaven to become incarnate among men, here to live and suffer and die, in order that He might redeem lost sinners for Himself. As the resurrected, living Saviour, Jesus Christ now through His Spirit offers to all men forgiveness from sin, full restoration to divine favor, and hope for the life to come. This promise of grace is not bestowed upon those who have first made themselves worthy of it through self-righteous "good works," for no man can earn his way into the favor of God. It is rather, good news for sinners. Jesus Christ faces men in their rebellion and calls them to decision—not a decision to be good, for that they cannot do while they remain alienated from Him. But He calls them to repentance, to surrender of themselves to Him in that whole-soul commitment the Bible calls faith.

This is the gospel which Luther discovered—the evangelical principle of justification by faith. For Luther and all true protestants it is *the* great fundamental of the Christian religion.

It took the debates between the papal Legate, Eck, and Luther for the further issue of authority to be brought into clear perspective. The medieval Church's way of salvation rested upon the grounds of ecclesiastical authority—the exclusive right of the Roman Church to interpret revelation and to administer its grace. Before long, however, it became apparent that Luther could defend his gospel "the just shall live by faith" only if he were willing to deny the whole structure of Roman authority—its creeds, its conciliar decisions, and its pope. From Medieval traditions Luther appealed to the ancient fathers of the church, from Roman councils he appealed to a universal council, from Pope he appealed to the original deposit of revelation—Christ and the Holy Scriptures.

The final authority of Holy Scripture thus came to be the formal principle of Protestantism as the gospel of Christ was its material principle. Its authority rests upon the fact that it is God's own Word spoken to man by inspiration through prophets and apostles of old.

For Luther, the Bible was not a second fundamental alongside of Christ, but rather an adjunct to the Christian gospel. Holy Scripture is the source of man's knowledge of Christ and together with the sacraments is the instrument through which He provides blessing and guidance for the believer. It is from beginning to end a book about Jesus Christ and His gospel. To interpret it in any other way is for Luther to destroy the Bible.

Romanists have derided both Luther and his followers for advocating a book religion. No true protestant has ever worshiped the Bible; but the fact remains where the Church of Christ has drawn its nourishment from an open Bible, there evangelical Christianity has flourished.

Modern students of religion have frequently charged that Luther merely replaced one pope with another—and a dead paper pope at that instead of the living personal Pope at Rome. Nothing was farther from Luther's intentions. He accepted the Bible as the infallible rule of faith and practice, but for him the Bible was no dead Book. Rather it was the living Word of God as the Holy Spirit took that which He had inspired in time past, recreated it by His living voice to become His contemporary Word in the hearts and minds of men of every age.

The gospel of Christ and the authority of the Bible thus came to the fore as the great twin themes of the Protestant Reformation. The newness of these principles however, was not absolute, but only a relative newness. Whatever may be said of its political and sociological ramifications, Protestantism was a true reformation, not a revolt. Luther never for a moment looked upon himself as having made any new religious discovery. He rather was re-discovering the truths of the ancient Church and especially of the Scriptures—truths that had become lost or obscured during the Middle Ages.

By 1520, nonetheless, when Luther publicly burned at Wittenberg Square a notice of excommunication from the Pope, it became evident that his reform within the church had become an irreparable break. After the Diet of Worms in 1521, Luther became a fugitive in the Empire of Charles of Spain. No doubt the tiny movement would have been crushed in its infancy had not numerous powerful princes come to the support of it. Some of these princes were motivated less by exalted religious convictions in siding with Luther than by a desire for independence from cumbersome financial ties with Rome. Of those who lent their support to the new Lutheran movement, few did so from purer motives or with more loyalty than did Luther's own elector of Saxony, Frederick.

The term "Protestantism" was derived rather accidentally as a result of the so-called second Reichstag of Speyer, called by the Emperor of the Holy Roman Empire in April 19, 1529, in order to quash this Lutheran revolt against the authority of the church. The catholic majority voted to prohibit all innovations in the field of religion and to make the support of the Lutheran heresy grounds for forfeiture of the right to hold office throughout the entire empire.

The Lutheran representatives naturally objected to this attempt to destroy them and prepared a "protest." The charge sometimes made that Protestantism was from the start a negative movement is thus partially true. Luther's initial thesis had been directed against abuses which he felt were conducive to sin and which obscured the free grace of God. The protest of the Lutheran princes was directed against a denial of their right to confess the gospel of Christ. Their protest and Luther's original thesis as well, were also a "protest" in the sense of a "witness before." As these princes made clear, the basis of their protest was their personal right, yea, God-given duty— to believe and to preach the pure gospel of Jesus Christ. Positively, at its very beginning Protestantism was a solemn witness to the gospel of Christ as a central affirmation of Christianity.

Meanwhile the new movement begun by Luther was spreading rapidly. Furthering the teaching of Luther at first were his students, converted monks, businessmen, and the Wittenberg faculty. Soon the influence of the Lutheran movement in Saxony penetrated into every nook and cranny of the Empire. Other leaders, encouraged by the reception accorded to Luther, seemed to spring up spontaneously almost everywhere.

A prodigous flood of Protestant literature appeared on the book markets of the Western Empire. For the half century before the reformation scarcely forty publications a year were produced in all Germany. But in the single year 1518 the number of publications suddenly doubled. In five years the volume of German literature had increased one thousand per cent over the preceding century. It is not too much to say that Martin Luther and the Protestant Reformation made the German language. And many of these publications were translated into the vernacular of all the language groups in Western Christendom.

As a direct result of this prodigous flood of literature the new ideas spread like fire into Scandinavia, England, Scotland, Switzerland, France, Holland, Poland, Bohemia, and even into Italy and Spain. Eventually Lutheranism came to be the accepted doctrine and practice throughout much of northern Europe, including most of northern Germany and the Scandinavian countries. Even where Luther's teachings did not finally triumph, they prepared the way for later victories of the younger Calvinistic churches in Switzerland, Holland, Scotland, and Germany and of the Anglican Church in England.

Today Lutheranism is the largest Protestant denomination in the world with seventy million children and adults. Old World Lutheran diversity was brought to America by great waves of immigration from central and northern Europe in the eighteenth and nineteenth century. Language barriers and variations in theology promoted separate developments within the Lutheran heritage. Since 1910, however, there has been an increasing solidarity among Lutherans on national, continental, and global levels.

In the United States, Lutherans are approaching the seven million mark. They now consist of seventeen denominations of which the largest is the United Lutheran Church, formed in 1918 by the joining of several strands of Lutheran communities extending back into the colonial rootage. Nearly equal to this body in size are the Missouri Synod with well over two million adherents and the newly formed denominations (1960), The American Lutheran Church, uniting three older bodies: The Evangelical Lutheran Church (Norwegian), the American Lutheran Church (German), and the United Evangelical Lutheran Church (Danish), to which may soon be added the Lutheran Free Church. Since 1918 most Lutheran groups except for the Missouri Synod have co-operated through a common agency known as the National Lutheran Council, in missionary work, relief and educational work.

the major American denominations. Neo-orthodoxy however, has gained considerable foothold, especially in the United States. This is the greatest deterrent at the moment to a union of all major Lutheran synods.

CALVINISM

While the Lutheran Reformation was starting in central Germany, a similar movement was getting underway among the tiny states of the Swiss Confederation. Its original leader was Huldrich Zwingli, a brilliant humanist and dissolute priest, who found the gospel message through his humanist researches into the original documents of Scripture. Soon the mantle of the Swiss Reformation fell upon the man who gave his name to the second of the great divisions of Protestantism, namely—John Calvin.

As a man, Calvin was entirely different from Luther. Luther was full of energy, spirit, and emotion. John Calvin was a wispy French intellectual with an introspective syllogistic mind. Born in France he was forced to flee to Geneva, Switzerland because of his heretical "Lutheran" views. There for twenty-three years he held sway as civil ruler, burdened pastor of the city cathedral, professor and head of the most famous theological school of all times, and acknowledged light of all Protestantism.

The great contribution of the Geneva reformer was to reduce the Protestant movement to theological coherence. In 1536 he published the first edition of his *Institutes of the Christian Religion*. Calvin shared with Luther the basic tenets of Protestantism, and this work has stood through subsequent centuries as the outstanding systematic formulation of Protestant theology. The first edition consisted of only six chapters, but Calvin kept adding and expanding as long as he lived. At his death in May, 1564, the *Institutes* contained 104 chapters organized in four great books.

The doctrine which Calvin propounded from his citadel in Geneva penetrated throughout western Europe and bore fruit in the Reformed churches of Germany, Holland, Bohemia, in the Presbyterian Church of Scotland, in the Puritans of England and in the Huguenots of France.

In America the Reformed group is divided into three main subgroups: (1) Congregational Churches descended from Calvinistic Separatists and Puritans in the Church of England who came to New England in the early days of the colonies; (2) Presbyterian churches descended from English and Scotch Presbyterians who settled in southern New England and spread across the continent with the growing nation; (3) the Reformed churches, followers of Calvin from continental churches in Holland, Germany, and Hungary, who migrated and brought their own national churches with them.

There are at present twelve different Presbyterian bodies in the United States with a total membership of about four million. The largest of these is the United Presbyterian Church, U.S.A., numbering just under three million. The next largest is the Presbyterian Church in the U.S. which split off from the parent body over slavery and has never returned. To this total the three closely related Reformed churches add less than a half million.

Although stemming in the beginning from a strongly Calvinistic and Puritanical background, Congregationalists have passed through many variations. Torn in the early nineteenth century by Unitarianism, the denomination had scarcely recovered from this until it was again swept by "Liberalism" in the latter part of the nineteenth century and early twentieth century.

In 1931, the denomination merged with the Christian Church, a colonial church of rather anti-creedal background. In 1957, again, the Congregational Christian Church united with the Evangelical Reformed Church to form the United Church of Christ with well over two million members. To what extent this new body ought to be listed among the Reformed churches is difficult to determine.

Reformed theology has often been identified with the so-called five points of Calvinism, brought to the memory of every seminary student by the letters *t u l i p.* In this mnemonic device *T* stands for *total depravity:* man is unable in his own spiritual strength to do anything to bring himself into a right relationship with God. *U,* for *unconditional election:* man's salvation is ultimately a gift of God's choice not dependent upon anything that He sees worthy of reward in man. *L* represents *limited atonement:* the provision of salvation in the work of Christ is limited to those whom God had thus chosen to salvation, *I,* for *irresistable grace:* God brings the grace of his salvation irresistably and certainly to all whom He has chosen, and *P,* for *perseverance of the saints:* those who thus are brought into salvation, will never ultimately fall from the grace of God.

In authentic Calvinism, however, these are not central affirmations.

The central message of Calvinism like Lutheranism is the gospel of salvation through personal faith in Christ. The authority of Scripture is the second fundamental of Calvinism as it is for Lutheranism. The doctrines suggested by the word *tulip* do not represent the essence of Calvinism, but are rather the differences between authentic Calvinism and the teachings of Arminius, a Dutch thinker who in the early years of the seventeenth century departed from the strict Calvinism of his forefathers. His views were condemned by the famous Synod of Dort in Holland in 1619, but they lived on to have a profound influence not only on the Continent, but especially in the Church of England.

The distinctive genius of Calvinism is found in its doctrine of the sovereignty of God and the necessity for absolute submission of the believing Christian to the will of God. As a result of this emphasis upon the sovereignty of God, Calvinists have always laid a tremendous stress upon ethics and upon the Lordship of Christ in practical affairs of the Christian life. This aspect of Calvinism is symbolized in John Calvin's personal crest, a flaming heart in an open hand. Man offers himself to his God in a life of sacrificial and obedient service. In the words of the Westminster Shorter Catechism, "Man's chief end is to glorify God and to enjoy Him forever."

ANGLICANISM

The reform movements spreading rapidly over Europe in the sixteenth century were slow in reaching England. According to popular legend the Protestant Reformation in England originated in the lustful desires of an autocratic monarch, Henry VIII. Frustrated by his Spanish wife's inability to provide a male heir to his throne, Henry fell in love with one of his wife's attendants, Ann Boleyn. Under pressure from the Spanish Emperor, the pope refused to dissolve the marriage. Henry then took matters into his own hands and declared himself to be the head of the Anglican Church, thus establishing Protestantism in England.

Actually the English Church had long exercised considerable autonomy in its relations to the papacy, and Henry himself had no intentions of rejecting the spiritual authority of Rome. He wrote a vindictive pamphlet against the Reformation on the continent and persecuted the reform movement in his own territory. During the reign of Henry no doctrinal changes occurred.

The true reformation in England did not occur until the boy King, Edward VI came to the throne. At this time the Archbishop of Canterbury, Thomas Cranmer, began to institute reforms to mark the beginning of true Anglicanism. In 1552, Cranmer brought about the adoption of the thirty-nine articles of Faith, a clear statement of Protestant principles. English was substituted for Latin in worship services, Celibacy of the clergy and confession were discontinued, and the Zwinglian symbolic interpretation of the Eucharist was adopted. An attempt at a Roman Catholic restoration by the next ruler, "Bloody" Queen Mary, ended with her death. Under Queen Elizabeth, Protestantism, now wholly identified with political interests and the rise of nationalism, became rooted. At this time such men as Richard Hooker and Jeremy Taylor formulated the Anglicanism that we know today.

Since the time of the Elizabethan settlement the Church of England has mothered many divergent movements. No one of these has been able to determine the character of the church as a whole, but each has left a permanent mark upon the Anglican Church. First to come was the Puritan Revival of the early and middle seventeenth century, culminating in the overthrow of the middle-of-the-road church set up under Elizabeth and in the establishment of a Puritan Church under the Roundheads of Cromwell.

When in turn Puritanism was overthrown, the Restoration of 1660 gave the Anglican Church a vigorous thrust in the direction of Catholicism. Many indeed thought that the second Charles intended to unite with the Roman papacy.

In the eighteenth century came the Evangelical revivals under the Wesleys. This Wesleyan movement brought quickening of spiritual life into every part of the church. In the mid-nineteenth century came the Anglo-Catholic revival and Oxford movement, which again pushed the church in the direction of Catholic doctrine and practice. Finally at the end of the nineteenth century came liberalism.

As a result of this religious interplay across the centuries, three rather loosely defined theological groups have developed within the Anglican communion. First are the descendants of the Puritans and of the Evangelical revivals of the eighteenth century. Generally speaking those influenced by this movement within the Church of England fall within what is called the Low Church or evangelical church movement. In the middle comes the Broad Church, which seeks to bring all factions into a working harmony by playing down doctrinal distinctions. Representing a third group are the High Church Anglicans with their emphasis upon Catholic doctrine, church tradition, and sacramentalism. This group culminates at the far right in the Anglo-Catholic segment of the church which is Roman Catholic in practically everything except recognition of an infallible Pope.

The genius of Anglicanism is to be found in this ecumenical spirit. While it has produced almost no great theologians or systematizers of doctrine, from its ranks have risen many exegetical scholars and linguists, as well as numerous great apologists and philosophers of religion. It has excelled at the production of outstanding churchmen. In the contemporary ecumenical movement in the World Council of Churches Anglican Churchmen have consistently taken the lead.

It has often been said that Anglicanism seeks to preserve a theological *via media* between Catholicism and Evangelical Protestantism. This is really an oversimplification. It would be better to say that Anglicanism seeks to allow freedom of doctrine in all these areas within the framework of the original creed of the church.

Today the Anglican communion comprises some twelve national churches of forty million children and adults all over the world. These churches are in communion with each other and with the See of Canterbury, but they preserve their separate autonomy. The Protestant Episcopal Church in America has nearly three million children and adults. As the sixth largest communion in America this church alone of the major Protestant denominations has had no important schisms. Of all the colonial denominations, it alone preserved its unity during the divisive American Civil War.

Closely related to the Anglican Church and growing out of it as a parent body is the Methodist Church. Methodism began with the Holy Club, dubbed so by taunting fellow students at Oxford University in the early days of the eighteenth century. The first leaders of the Holy Club were John and Charles Wesley and George Whitfield, who as students at Oxford preparing for the ministry gathered together for daily Bible reading and study. Somewhat later in his life, John Wesley came into contact with Moravians from Germany and with the doctrine of justification by faith as set forth by Luther in his commentary on Galatians. This discovery transformed Wesley's life and ministry. Immediately he began preaching the necessity for conversion, for the new birth, and for holiness of life. With tremendous zeal he carried the gospel up and down the length of Britain, especially to the poor and needy of the land. His brother, sweet-singer for the movement, produced over six thousand hymns by which they sang their way into the hearts of the people of England and America.

In England the Wesleyan revival soon became identified with the Low Church party. John Wesley himself never left the Anglican Church, but many of his followers soon were forming new churches among the poor people of the cities of Britain. The real fruitage of Methodism is to be found in the United States where Wesley, Whitfield, Francis Asbury and others, preached up and down the colonies and spread themselves westward with the growth of the nation. These itinerant Wesleyans stressed sanctification of life and the need for practical and methodical culture of the devotional life. From this latter emphasis they received their name Methodists.

The Methodist denomination, numbering ten million, is the largest single Protestant body in the United States. There are approximately two dozen smaller Methodist groups, the largest of which is the African Methodist church containing around a million members. Among smaller groups perhaps the best known are the Free Methodist and the Wesleyan Methodist, two very evangelical groups, the former of which split off from the parent body in order to preserve strict standards of doctrine and practice in the face of a growing liberalism within the larger body. The Wesleyan group split originally over the issue of slavery, but at the present time Wesleyan and Free Methodists are in process of union. The total number of Methodists in the United States is approximately twelve million with a membership of sixteen million around the world.

ANABAPTIST

After the original impetus of Protestantism had expended itself, the religious situation in the Western Empire tended to solidify in four basic types of Christianity, Roman Catholic, Lutheran, Reformed, and Anglican. In each political division, the ruler determined which of these churches was to be the legally approved church in his particular territory. Once this was determined on this principle of *Cuius regno cuius religio,* no other form of worship was permitted. All who dissented from this state church were liable to persecution.

Large elements within these national churches, however, came to feel that Protestantism had stopped short of the thorough reformation which they themselves would like to see. They desired a more radical break with Roman Catholicism than was made by Lutherans, Reformed or Anglicans. Out of this tension there soon developed a fourth distinct group among the Protestants, which came to be known as the Anabaptists.

The Anabaptists, of course, maintained that their way of thinking went back to the original Church. They had no founder but Christ. It is true that the term Anabaptist was quite well known even in the ancient church, but no direct historical connection is traceable between these earlier groups bearing the name and the Anabaptists of Reformation time.

Throughout the course of Church History, nevertheless, there had been in continuous existence an underground movement of those dissatisfied with the shallow spiritual life of the Catholic Church. The Brethren of the Common Life, for example, had flourished for several centuries in northern and central Europe. Clear affinities with such groups, many of whom remained within the outward framework of the Catholic Church, are traceable—in the later Anabaptist movement.

The Protestant Anabaptist movement, as we know it today, began in Zurich, Switzerland, in 1524 and 25 among the followers of Zwingli. These early Anabaptists became dissatisfied with the elements of popery, formalism, and intellectualism still remaining within the state church as set up by Zwingli. They demanded complete freedom of conscience to interpret the Word of God for themselves. Adult baptism soon became the issue over which these Anabaptists and the early Reformed leaders came to blows. The Swiss Anabaptists insisted that adults must be re-baptized because true baptism is only possible upon confession of faith and commitment to discipleship. They were persecuted with great cruelty; but in spite of all opposition, the movement grew and spread with tremendous rapidity from Switzerland throughout western Europe.

Meno Simons, an Anabaptist leader, fled under persecution to Holland, which had become an oasis of religious freedom during this intolerant era. Here the cause of the Anabaptists flourished; and under the tutelage of Meno Simons, disciples went out from Holland as missionaries spreading Anabaptist doctrine over the whole of northern and central Europe. In 1608 English Puritan refugees in Holland affiliated with Dutch Mennonites in Amsterdam and organized the ancestor of the English Baptist Church. The Anabaptist movement driven by the double force of persecution and missionary zeal spread to Alsace, the Palatinate, all of southern Germany, and eastern France. Many groups from Germany migrated farther into the Ukraine and southern Russia and there became the mother of large Mennonite groups in these areas, which in a later generation moved again to the prairies of the United States and western Canada.

In most places the whole Anabaptist movement during the sixteenth and seventeenth centuries remained more or less underground. This circumstance, coupled with its rapid spread throughout the whole of the Protestant world, left it without literary guidance or central organization which could tie the various groups together and hold them in solidified communion. The Anabaptist movement therefore, was characterized by tremendous diversity. All sorts of doctrinal abberations and peculiar practices made their appearance. Some developed anti-trinitarian tendencies. Others turned to eschatological fanaticism. In their opposition to persecuting governments many became anarchists in their attitude toward the state.

The large mass of orthodox Anabaptists suffered greatly by identification with the radical fringes of their own movement. Anyone who did not acknowledge one of the officially approved state churches was inevitably lumped together with the despised Anabaptists. In contrast with "classical Protestantism" of the Lutheran, Calvinistic, and Anglican variety, the Anabaptists were labeled sectarianism and "radical Protestantism." In Europe, this method of classification has maintained itself with some force even until today. Because of the continued existence of state churches in Europe, no doubt such a procedure makes sense; but in America it becomes preposterous. It is quite senseless, for example, to place side by side as representative of "classical Protestantism" such divergent groups as the very liberal minded Congregational Church, the extremely strict Missouri Lutherans, and the separatist Bible Presbyterian Church and then by contrast in a sort of theological Noah's ark, to lump together as "radical Protestantism" the Southern Baptists, the Amish (whose distinctions are largely cultural and sociological rather than doctrinal) and the Jehovah's Witnesses.

The really amazing thing about the Anabaptist group was the fact that the large bulk remained essentially true to all the basic tenets of Protestantism. The Bible was taken as the final authority by which doctrine and practice were to be determined. The essential principle of Protestantism, the gospel of Christ, His deity, the Trinity, and related doctrines were likewise preserved by the vast majority of the Anabaptists.

By and large however, the Anabaptists were not a creedal church. In revolt against a mere lip service to doctrine, which neglected the spiritual and ethical side of Christianity, they developed a repugnance to creedal statements of any kind. They stood, so they affirmed, for the whole Bible. And by this they meant the Bible interpreted literally and with special regard to its ethical injunctions. Anabaptists, nevertheless, did put forth several confessions of faith. The most famous of these was the New Hampshire Confession adopted by Baptist bodies of the United States. This Baptist confession was largely patterned after the Puritan Westminster Confession of Faith with appropriate changes for Baptist doctrine.

The Anabaptists also insisted upon personal holiness as mandatory for every member of the Church. In contrast with the Lutheran stress upon the enjoyment of salvation as a present experience, they set forth a demand for radical discipleship on the part of every believer. This was often accompanied by an insistence upon literal obedience to the commands of Christ and the New Testament. In many cases external characteristics such as dress became the thumbnail test for righteousness.

The distinctive of the Anabaptist group, of course, is to be found in its central idea of the gathered church as opposed to a folk church. The Church is limited to those who make a personal commitment to Christ. This stress on individual responsibility engenders within the Anabaptist Church a holy enthusiasm for the cause of Christ and leads to a pure type of church which can serve as a conscience for many of the state churches. Other distinctive emphases of the Anabaptist Churches can best be understood as corollaries of this central principle of the gathered church. The insistence upon adult baptism flowed directly from it, for baptism conceived as identification with the church must necessarily be given only to those who have made personal religious decisions. The state church, taking everyone into membership, inevitably was looked upon as worldly and filled with the unconverted. The Anabaptists as a body, therefore, stood for separation of the church from the state. Because of their persecution by the state church the Anabaptists emphasized the necessity for complete freedom of worship. They demanded this for themselves and, quite consistently, they were willing to grant it to others. Many of the Anabaptists, especially followers of Meno Simons, became pacifists; and in their opposition to the state and its domination over the church renounced all use of force in any way. They also frequently became "quietists." In their withdrawal from the world, they insisted that man should have no part whatsoever in the state government. This extreme is not typical of the Anabaptists, however. Many of them, as an outgrowth of their insistence upon holy living, have been active in the social work of the church and have not been adverse to extending their activity into the political realm. The Anabaptist influence upon the social minded followers of John Wesley must not be forgotten. In more recent times the labor party in England has been motivated in considerable measure by the English Baptist movement.

In America the Baptist movement is generally traced to Roger Williams. Roger Williams himself was not really a Baptist. He was rather a separatist minister violently opposed to the union of church and state in the colony of Massachusetts. Forced to flee because of his strong anti-state church views, he journeyed with a few devout followers to Rhode Island and there built a new community. His followers soon developed Baptistic doctrines.

Large settlements of Anabaptists also came from central Europe to Pennsylvania, lured there by the promises of William Penn that they could secure complete religious freedom. During colonial days the Baptist church made some strides, but it did not catch fire. With the setting up of the new nation, however, the Baptist movement began its swift advance across the continent. Baptists and Methodists became the two churches of the frontier. In the South they won the Negroes, who were frequently neglected by other denominations. Well over half of all Negro church members in the United States today are Baptist and most of the rest are Methodists. At the present time there are approximately thirty million Baptists throughout the world, twenty million of which are in the United States. The Southern Baptist, the largest of all the groups, is also the fastest growing major denomination in the United States. Except for Missouri Lutherans, it is also the most conservative of the large denominational groups in America. In recent years the Southern Baptist church has become widely known for its Sunday School work and for its tremendous publication program. In a single year the Southern Baptist denomination distributed over sixty million different publications through its educational agencies. The over-all figures for the Baptist Church are somewhat misleading for this church includes only adults on its roll books, and its principle of the gathered church (not always adhered to) tends to make the membership figure smaller than for many other denominational groups. This is reflected in the per capita giving of the Anabaptists and Baptists in the United States, which for the most part, though they do not come from the most wealthy groups in the country is much larger than that of the other major denominations.

Down through the centuries Anabaptists have been characterized by continual splintering and by organizational variations. Although approximately twenty million Baptists are united more or less directly with the Baptist World Alliance founded in 1905, there are in the United States nearly fifty separate Baptistic organizations, to say nothing of the dozens of Mennonites and Brethren groups, all of which can be traced back originally to the Anabaptist movement. The remarkable thing about this, however, is that there is still an amazing unity in spiritual life and in fundamental doctrine. In recent times these small denominations lying within the Anabaptist tradition have been less hit by Modernism than any of the major denominations.

The Anabaptist branch of Protestantism has often been called the cradle of modern democracy as well as the source of modern religious liberty. There is much truth in these claims. Certainly, Anabaptist churches did much to foster democratic ideals and to provide work-

ing laboratories for the practice of democracy. All too often they
likewise displayed the evil features which may accompany democracy
in action. The Anabaptists have been the almost forgotten forerun-
ners of much that is commonly accepted by Protestants especially in
England and in the United States.

PROTESTANT SECTARIAN GROUPS

From time to time since the initial impulse of Protestantism, small
groups have split themselves off from the older and parent bodies to
form new denominations. From the very nature of Protestantism,
such activity is quite understandable. Contrary to Roman Catholicism, which finds the essence of the church in a visible and outward
organization, the true Protestant considers the Church to be a spiritual entity, determined by God; and it includes all who are loyal to
Jesus Christ and recognize Him as Lord and Saviour.

Many of these small, militant denominations, thus formed, though
popularly linked among the sects, are in reality firmly insistent upon
both the formal and the material principles of Protestantism. They
are opposed to the formalism of the older established churches. They
wish to free themselves from the deadness of these churches. They
rebel against Modernism and Liberalism in these churches; but in
their main doctrines they are solidly in the stream of historic and
orthodox Protestantism.

The I.F.C.A. (Independent Fundamental Churches of America),
for example, are mildly Calvinistic churches whose membership
would have been right at home among the extreme separatists who
landed at Plymouth Rock three hundred years ago. The Nazarenes
are simply twentieth century followers of John and Charles Wesley.
Neither of these groups is a sect in the ordinary sense of the term.
They are part and parcel of historic Protestantism in its Calvinistic
or Wesleyan branch. The only difference between them and their
seventeenth century progenitors is two hundred years of history.
The so-called holiness sects fall within the same category.

Removed a step farther to the left are the rapidly multiplying
Pentecostal denominations now claiming nearly five million adherents in the United States and many more in other parts of the world.
By and large, Pentecostalists are in complete agreement with the
basic tenets of historic Protestantism. On all points held in common

by the original national churches, the Pentecostalists also would agree. They insist, however, that "speaking in tongues" is a spiritual gift to be exercised today, contrary to the older churches which insist that this was a phenomenon limited to the apostolic Church.

The affinity of these Pentecostalists with the older groups, especially with the Anabaptists, is seen in the fact that the largest Baptist church in Sweden is Pentecostal in doctrine. Although no precise figures are available from behind the Iron Curtain, the Baptist Church of Russia is alleged to be one of the fastest growing in the world.[1] Despite its name, however, it is strictly Pentecostal in its insistence upon the exercise of the "gift of tongues."

The "Christian Denomination" likewise frequently reckoned among the sects is made up of followers of Alexander Campbell in the eighteenth century. Their chief difference from the Baptists, with whom they have often been confused, lies in their doctrine of baptismal regeneration in which they accept a view held by many High Anglicans and Lutherans.

In the same general classification fall most of the "Healing Cults." These groups retain all basic evangelical and Protestant doctrines but also insist that healing of body is offered on exactly the same basis in the gospel message as is forgiveness of sins.

However lamentable some of these deviations may be, these groups have every right to the name Protestant. They accept without reservation the basic principle of authority, the Scripture, and also the basic message of the Christian gospel, justification by faith in Jesus Christ.

Clearly on the other side of the theological fence are those groups which, though giving lip service to the Protestant principle of Scripture, set forth a radically different gospel from that of traditional Protestantism. In such cases they deny the material principle of salvation by grace, or if they do not deny it outrightly, they obscure it by encrustations basically at odds with the essential gospel of Jesus Christ.

In the early days of the Protestant Reformation, a number of Unitarians under their founder, the Socini brothers, settled in Poland and from there slowly infiltrated both Roman and Protestant Europe. Early in the nineteenth century, a relatively independent Unitarian movement sprang up within the Congregational Church of New

[1]Marcus Bach, *God and the Soviets* (New York: Thomas Y. Crowell Company, c. 1958), p. 204.

England. In recent years of course, the Unitarian Church has moved far to the left, theologically speaking, and in its formal statements does not adhere either to the formal or to the material principle of Protestantism. Far more militant and also more prolific than either of these is a contempory Unitarian sect, the Jehovah's Witnesses.

A borderline case difficult to classify as historic Protestantism or as sectarian is the Seventh-Day Adventists. Although this group does not deny the Christian gospel, it demands the worship of God upon Saturday instead of upon Sunday as the necessary complement and evidence of salvation. It thus seems to be in danger of confusing the material principle of the gospel. Quite recently however, there has been an increasing tendency to place the Seventh-Day Adventists within the Evangelical Protestant framework.

Many present day sects do not even claim to be Protestant in any sense of the term. Some represent attempts to unite the best elements drawn from Christian faith with insights into truth gleaned from various Oriental religions, and thus to promote a new religious synthesis superior to any of the others. Others, like many spiritualist churches, are simply new religions founded without reference to the doctrinal content of historic Protestantism.

Quite a number of present-day cults owe their origin to some great prophet or leader who claimed to have received a new supernatural revelation from God such as Mary Baker Eddy put forth in her *Science and Health with Key to the Scriptures*. Or as Joseph Smith provided in his translation of the Golden Plates let down from Heaven. In all such cases there is an explicit denial of the formal principle of Protestantism. Authority for the religious life is derived outside Holy Scriptures. Along with this denial of the formal principle of Protestantism comes also a denial of the material principle of Jesus Christ as Lord and Saviour. Unitarians, Jehovah's Witnesses, and Christian Scientists are, therefore, not true Protestants at all. They deny the basic principles of historic Protestantism and ought not to be numbered among specifically Protestant sects.

On the whole, there is little co-operation between these various groups and Protestantism. They tend to look upon the historic Protestant denominations as a vast mission field from which to glean new adherents for their own cult. In spite of a high mortality rate, especially among educated youth, the actual growth of the cults is phenomenal. No doubt this is in large part due to the stagnation of the older Protestant denominations, which often seem unable to cope with the spiritual needs of twentieth century man. Whatever may be the explanation, their enthusiasm and zeal have made these cults the fastest growing element in the nominal Christian Church today both in the United States and around the world.

THE MODERNIST—FUNDAMENTALIST CONTROVERSY

The most significant development in the Protestant church since the days of the Reformation is without doubt the Modernist—Fundamentalist controversy, which has now for almost a century raged within every major branch of historic Protestantism.

The roots of Modernism lay in the critical philosophies of Hume and Kant with their radical disavowal of any supernatural elements in religion and their unbounded faith in an autonomous man who can decide for himself with unaided reason what he will believe without dependence upon divine revelation.

The modern revolution in scientific thinking also contributed its bit to undermine the religious faith of Protestantism. It did this first by creating in men the conviction that its methodology in contrast with the authoritarian methodology used by the church was the only proper channel through which useful knowledge might be gleaned. Another effect of the scientific revolution was to produce vast bodies of scientific fact (or sometimes of philosophical ideas which passed as scientific facts). Frequently these facts (or alleged facts) were not readily assimilable into evangelical Christian tradition. At first the Church would resist them as Luther in his day fought against the views of Copernicus. But in the end the Church inevitably succumbed. As one Modernistic spokesman puts it: "The Bible is full of things that to intelligent educated persons of today are either quite incredible or at best highly questionable. From the account of creation in the first chapter of Genesis to the description of the heavenly city in the closing chapter of Revelation, statements abound that even the most tortuous interpretation cannot reconcile with modern scientific conceptions of the universe."[1] Many came to believe that one must choose between taking his science straight and

---

[1] Millar Burrows, *An Outline of Biblical Theology* (Philadelphia: The Westminster Press, 1946), pp. 9, 44.

holding blindly to Christian faith. Said they, a committed Christian cannot possibly be an honest student of twentieth century science.

A third significant factor in the rise of Modernism was the reconstruction of Biblical material so as to harmonize the origins of the Hebrew-Christian revelation with the newly popular theory of evolution. The Hebrew-Christian revelation was forced into place within the history of naturalistic evolution of religion. The effect of this naturalistic straight-jacket was devastating to the traditional Protestant view of the authenticity of the Biblical text and the truth of the Christian message.

Modern study in comparative religions seemed finally to destroy the uniqueness of Christianity. World wide exploration and increasing rapid means of communication brought East and West together. Sympathetic understanding of the ethnic religions, freed from the bias of Western provincialism, demonstrated that all religions were on exactly the same level. Christianity, so it was concluded, is simply first among equals of the religions of the world.

Such a drastic transformation did not take place overnight. Only gradually and reluctantly was evangelical Protestantism led down the road to a thoroughly non-miraculous Christianity. But the end result was a complete denial of the fundamental principles of historical Protestantism.

Modernists, of course, did not consider themselves in any sense disloyal to Christianity. In most cases they were convinced, quite sincerely, that they stood squarely within the tradition of their fathers. They looked upon themselves simply as defenders of the faith. From their own point of view, they were not denying Christian faith. Rather, they were sloughing off unessential baggage handed down from the past in order to discover the true essence of Christianity. This basic Christianity they could then defend more effectively than ever against onslaughts from the modern secular world. A contemporary writer describes Modernism as a "Yes, but" religion. *"Yes,* we accept Christianity, *but* we do not believe all those silly and indefensible doctrines for which Christianity has stood in the past."[2]

This concessive nature is one of the fundamental characteristics of Modernists. It explains why they wish to retain the title Christian.

[2]Willard Sperry, *Yes, But: The Bankruptcy of Apologetics* (New York: Harper, 1932).

It also explains why, to the exasperation of Fundamentalists, they continue to express their faith in conservative orthodox vocabulary. It explains likewise the extreme diversity in Modernism with its continual changing from one form to another. There is no uniform Modernistic theology or philosophy of religion, but only a recurring series of attempts by different Modernists to find a new way of presenting the Christian faith in defensible form.

The Orthodox reaction to Modernism has been violent and continuous. Step by step through the nineteenth century, conservatives had fought doggedly against each Modernistic concession to Western secular culture. In 1909 two laymen subsidized the publication and distribution of a large number of apologetic papers by leading evangelical scholars. The work appeared in twelve short readable volumes under the title *The Fundamentals*. Although the word Fundamental had been used earlier with this same meaning, it now gained general acceptance as the name for the defenders of strictly orthodox Protestantism.

Among these Fundamentalists were to be found many thinkers of high order. The greatest of them all were Herman Bavinck in Holland, James Orr in Britain, and Benjamin B. Warfield in the United States. Ably supporting these leaders were Kuyper, Lang, Le Cerf, Patton, Hodge, and Machen among the Reformed, Keyser and Pieper among the Lutherans and Mullins and Robertson among the Baptists.

Most of these men never considered themselves Fundamentalists. In fact some expressly rejected the term. They were simply defending orthodoxy against a non-Christian movement which had entered like a fifth column into the Protestant church and was threatening to take over the whole of that segment of Christianity.

Controversy centered around six points of doctrine: the virgin birth, deity, substitutionary atonement, bodily resurrection, and second coming of Christ (all related to the material principle of the reformation) and the inerrant authority of Scripture (related to the formal principle of the reformation). All of these points, of course, had been held in common by the original Protestant bodies and had been set forth in the major creeds of the Protestant church. They became, therefore, a rallying cry for conservatives in opposition to a rapidly growing Modernism.

In spite of the vigor of the orthodox attack (sometimes it must be admitted it was more vigorous than wise), Modernism continued to grow and eventually captured for its viewpoint academic institutions, missionary societies, and denominational leadership in large areas of historical Protestantism. In Europe, Modernism reached its peak about the time of World War I. In the United States its development was delayed somewhat, and it did not attain its zenith until after 1930.

Deep within Modernism, however, were the seeds of its own destruction. Although its leaders sincerely attempted to remain within the structure of the older tradition, it became increasingly obvious as time went on that Modernism had made a radical break with all that was essential to the earlier Protestant faith. Emil Brunner but echoed the substance of Fundamentalist apologetic when he declared: "[Anyone] possessed of a reasonable correct knowledge of Christianity will have little difficulty in proving that Modernism teaches, under the label of Christianity, a religion that has nothing in common with Christianity except a few words and that those words cover concepts which are irreconcilable with the content of the Christian faith."[3]

It became increasingly apparent, moreover, that the basic structure of Modernism, which short decades before had appeared so convincing and durable by contrast with tottering orthodoxy, was in fact utterly inadequate to withstand the pressures built up against it in the turbulent mid-twentieth century. Two world wars and world depression of devastating consequences made clear to all that the plight of man is truly desperate. Universal brotherhood could hardly be argued with a straight face while those "brothers" were tearing each other to bits on the battlefield of western Europe. The atomic bombs dropped on Hiroshima and Nagasaki destroyed more than several thousand Japanese. They destroyed man's hope in man. As man's needs appeared greater, so the solution to his need became more radical. The Jesus of Modernism, a kindly man who walked up and down the land of Palestine proffering bits of good advice to all who would hear, presented a figure which (being free from all supernatural elements) was quite "defensible" to contemporary man. But such a Jesus was no help to desperate men sick of soul, and Modernism collapsed primarily because it was unable to provide

[3]*The Theology of Crisis* (New York: Charles Scribner's Sons, 1929), p. 9.

any adequate substitute for the material principle of historic Protestantism—salvation for sinners through faith in a divine Christ.

The most obvious predicament of Modernism was its lack of authority. The Bible had become a mere scrapbook of Jewish devotional literature, suitable, in the time honored custom of preaching, as a source book for sermon texts, but utterly unfitted for proclamation in ancient prophetic style, "Thus saith the Lord."

Karl Barth, a former Modernist turned Neo-orthodox, tells how in the early days of his ministry he gradually became disillusioned with the milk-toast "good advice," which was all he had to offer to his parishioners. Faced with the crushing realities of war time life, he discovered to his consternation he possessed only a frothy palaver of superficial human guesses. As he mounted the sacred pulpit on a Sunday morning to deliver his sermon, the table of the law would slip between his fingers. He stood there before his people a mere man, pleading to them a man's wisdom which even he only half-believed.

Neo-Orthodoxy: Mid-Twentieth Century Compromise

As the religious bankruptcy of Modernism became more and more obvious, disillusioned leaders began to look back with nostalgia upon historic Protestantism with its strong note of authority and its comforting gospel for sinners. "Our grandfathers, after all, were right," Barth declares, "when they struggled so desperately in behalf of the truth that there is revelation in the Bible. . . . And our fathers were right when they guarded warily against being drawn out upon the shaky scaffolding of religious self-expression. . . . We live in a sick old world, which cries out from its soul, out of deepest need: 'Heal me, O Lord, and I will be healed.' In all men, whoever and where-ever and whatever and however they may be, there is a longing for exactly this which is here within the Bible."[4]

This new movement soon separated itself off clearly both from Modernism and from Fundamentalism. Commonly dubbed Neo-orthodoxy, it represented a hybrid of Modernistic thought and of the old redemptive religion of authority. Most of those who go loosely by the title, Neo-orthodox, agree with orthodox Protestantism that man is a sinner; they are convinced with the Modernist, however,

[4]*The Word of God and the Word of Man* (Grand Rapids: Zondervan, 1935), pp. 44, 50.

that historic Christianity is not defensible at the bar of reason; neither is the Bible an infallible rule of faith and practice. True knowledge of God, so they affirm, can only be secured through a personal encounter. This necessary encounter with God, however, is made possible through the instrumentality of the Bible, specifically through its story of Jesus Christ, who is the supreme revelation of God to man. The Christ who thus reveals God does not become known through the study of history; but rather as a living contemporary, He makes himself known to men in immediate and personal encounter.

With respect to the formal principle of traditional Protestantism, therefore, Neo-orthodoxy accepts the authority of Scripture, but only to the degree that the Holy Spirit here and now constitutes the Bible as God's Word to the individual believer. In the more liberal minded among the newer group, like Niebuhr and Tillich, the Bible is simply a convenient instrument which the Holy Spirit may use, along with other instruments, to bring men into the encounter with God. To more conservative Neo-orthodox thinkers like Barth, the Bible alone is the place where God by His own free choice, lets Himself be found by men. Barth does not recognize the Bible as infallible in all its teaching, but for him it is the standard by which all teaching and preaching in the church of Jesus Christ must be judged, for it is Biblically grounded preaching alone which brings men to the encounter with Jesus Christ.

With respect to the material principle of Protestantism, Neo-orthodoxy speaks with many voices. Differences are so great and so confusing that the very term, Neo-orthodoxy, has become almost meaningless. For the more liberal type of Neo-orthodoxy the deity of Christ is only symbolic, and other elements of the doctrine of Christ are relegated to the sphere of the mythological. Reinhold Niebuhr, for example, insists that salvation is by grace through faith, but the object of saving faith is emphatically not the God-man of an historical incarnation. By contrast, Karl Barth accepts the deity of Christ without reservations (although he holds to a unipersonal trinity). The virgin birth and bodily resurrection of Christ he defends. Strangely, on the basis of Biblical teaching regarding universal atonement, he hopes for a universal redemption of all men.

The Neo-orthodox movement, liberal and conservative, has effected a tremendous revival of theological interest. Biblical and theological studies of every kind are flooding the market in amounts not known since the heyday of Protestantism. The relevance of the Bible to the great issues which perennially engage the minds of serious men is once more being acknowledged on every hand.

In Europe the rising tide of Neo-orthodoxy has swept away the lingering traces both of nineteenth century Modernism and of the older orthodoxy. In Britain and America its progress is slower. Here too it has made deep inroads into the Modernistic leadership of the past generation and has exerted considerable influence upon some Fundamentalists.

Especially in America, however, Neo-orthodoxy has not escaped deep and searching criticism. By Modernists it was attacked as a step back toward the obscurantism and authoritarianism of medieval Christianity. "A return to the dark ages," one disillusioned liberal decried it. Its extreme emphasis upon the transcendence of God, its apparent irrationalism exhibited in its excessive use of snappy theological paradoxes, and its radical subjectivism, resulting in not one Neo-orthodoxy, but in fundamentally divergent types of Neo-orthodoxy, were exposed in scathing polemics stemming both from Modernist and Fundamentalist sources.[5]

The latter, especially, were quick to point out inconsistencies in Neo-orthodox departures from historic Protestantism. The Bible is the authority for faith and practice, so the Neo-orthodox vociferously affirm. But at the same time they disregard Biblical authority when it comes to the Bible's testimony as to the nature of its own inspiration and authority. Cutting still more deeply, the Fundamentalists charged the Neo-orthodox with basic inconsistency in their attitude concerning Jesus Christ. In opposition to Liberalism, the Neo-orthodox argue with convincing cogency for the divine Lordship of Jesus Christ. But, so asked the Fundamentalist, if Jesus Christ is really Lord must we not also accept His view of the authority of the Scripture? Does not the Neo-orthodox failure to enunciate with clarity the Protestant principle of authority, jeopardize his retention of the material principle of the Reformation, the doctrine of salvation

[5]See Henry Nelson Wieman (ed.), *Religious Liberals Reply* (Boston: Beacon Press, 1947); and Cornelius Van Til, *The New Modernism: An Appraisal of the Theology of Barth and Brunner* (Philadelphia: The Presbyterian and Reformed Publishing Company, 1946).

through Christ? Such would seem to be the case, particularly among leading American representatives like Reinhold Niebuhr and Paul Tillich.

In spite of these attacks against it, Neo-orthodoxy either in its liberal or more conservative form, is the dominant trend in the theological schools of America seems destined inevitably to take over leadership in the major denominations in America just as it has done previously in Europe.

The Ecumenical Movement

William Temple, former Archbishop of Canterbury, once called the ecumenical movement "the great fact of our time." Certainly no survey of Protestantism would be complete without reference to this significant movement. Occasional attempts at church union are to be observed within the Protestant church from its earliest beginning. A despotic King in Prussia compelled Lutherans and Calvinists to unite in a single state church. All during the nineteenth century, evangelical bodies in America had co-operated in various educational, charitable, and missionary work. Likewise the British and Foreign Bible Society was broader than the mere Church of England in the support of its work and in the groups to which its services were made available. Until the twentieth century, however, Protestantism had tended to perpetuate the great historic divisions of the Reformation and indeed within these broad groupings to divide and sub-divide into ever smaller factions each seeking to preserve its own denominational loyalties and traditions. Within the last half century has come for the first time a significant trend in the opposite direction towards the re-union of Protestant denominations.

Many factors led to the rise of ecumenicalism within the modern Protestant world. The liberal emphasis upon the practical work of the Church to the neglect of doctrinal commitments made sheer folly any retention of petty denominational differences. World-wide communications brought Christians from every national group more closely together and rendered possible the inter-play of ideas necessary for inter-church co-operation. Again the resurgence of powerful forces molded together against Protestant Christianity tended to force Protestants to unite in self-defense against a common foe. The anti-Protestant dictatorships on the continent of Europe, the spread of Communism into central Europe, and the astounding growth of the Roman Catholic Church throughout the world in recent decades, have driven many Protestants to an apparent choice between union or extinction. Finally, the modern missionary movement in its contact with heathen religions throughout the world brought increased necessity for co-ordination of efforts in the various mission fields. A single message, a common policy, mutual co-operation, and sharing of responsibilities were demanded not only on the mission field itself but also in the national churches at home.

Whatever may have been its causes, the ecumenical movement caught fire in the early part of the twentieth century. The first formal attempt to unite the Protestant churches of America was made in 1908, in which year the Federal Council of Churches of Christ in America was brought into existence in order to combine all Protestant strength in religious matters. In 1950 the Federal Council was dissolved in favor of the newly formed National Council of Christian Churches in America. The latter organization is composed of thirty-three different denominations with a total membership of slightly under forty million. It brought together under one single roof the work previously done by twelve inter-denominational agencies.

On the world front the ecumenical movement was likewise moving ahead with great strides. Various international missionary conferences had been held such as those at Edinburgh in 1910, at Lausanne in 1927, and at Oxford in 1938. These preliminary international meetings were consumated in 1948 by the formation at Amsterdam of the World Council of Churches. This Council is a federation of Lutheran, Reformed, Anglican, Anabaptist and Greek Orthodox Churches. The Council links together one hundred and sixty denominational groups spread throughout forty-seven countries of the world.

Thus far the meetings of the World Council have proved to be more theological discussion groups than anything else. They have, however, brought together the Neo-orthodox movement of Europe and liberal churchmen from America. The result of this ecclesiastical marriage has been to bring about an increased influence from conservative Neo-orthodoxy upon the liberal theology of the American denominations.

For theological platform, the National Council of Churches in America, followed also by the World Council, acknowledges Jesus Christ as Lord and Saviour. This formula is understood in various ways by the co-operating groups. Among the more liberal members of the group, especially in America, it is taken so loosely as scarcely to be anything more than a pious approval of Jesus Christ as a good example for moral and spiritual life.

In recent years conservative Protestants have formed two smaller groups in opposition to the older Federal and later National Council of Churches. The American Council of Christian Churches was first formed in 1941 in order to bring together orthodox Protestants within the various denominations. The American Council has become a strictly separatist body, however. It has extended its influence beyond the United States by means of the International Council, which has representatives among separatists in various parts of the world.

Conservatives also formed the National Association of Evangelicals which attempted to bring together non-separatists among conservative Protestants. It appealed generally to conservatives within denominations whose leadership tended to be liberal and to the smaller denominations who were repulsed by the militantly separatist American Council.

THE UNSOLVED PROBLEMS OF PROTESTANTISM

Ever since the day of its inception Protestantism has been in constant battle against the prevailing culture in which it has found itself. Never has this been true more than today. Chief among the problems facing contemporary Protestantism are (1) the problem of its relationship to the modern scientific world view. J. S. Haldane put the matter bluntly when he declared, "To most modern scientists like myself religion will never make any appeal until it comes to terms with science." Many of the finest trained minds in Europe and America find themselves uncomfortably alien in the atmosphere of traditional Protestant theology. How to meet the up-and-outer has come to replace the former problem of how to reach the down-and-outer.[6]

The second problem facing contemporary Protestantism relates to

[6] J. S. Haldane, *The Philosophy of a Biologist* (Oxford: The Clarendon Press, 1935), pp. 111 ff.

social action. Communism appeals not only to the downtrodden racially but to the laborer as well. By a mere exchange of economic systems, so the Marxist promises, revolution will transform society immediately and will usher in the good life for all. Protestantism with its insistence upon individual conversion and its impractical regard for love, seems hopelessly pedestrian in this modern world.

A third difficulty confronting the Protestant is that of preserving his own religious traditions. In many parts of the world, public school systems are dominated by an alien religious or secular tradition. Even in those parts of the world where nominal Protestantism is in control an evangelical Protestant can rarely propagate his faith actively through public institutions especially where, as in this country, separation of church and state have come to mean that public schools may not participate in religious instruction of the young. With the increasing financial pressure on denominational colleges and lower level private schools, the problem becomes even greater.

Fourthly, the Protestant is forced to acknowledge radical divergences from traditional viewpoints often existing side by side within the framework of his own denomination. Fundamentalism, Modernism, Neo-orthodoxy, to say nothing of the two hundred and fifty odd sectarian groups within the contemporary church, make the problem of religious co-operation particularly difficult. The right choice between an over-rigid separatism and an extremely lax co-operation would take the wisdom of Solomon and the patience of Job—and descendants of these two gentlemen are indeed rare in the contemporary churches. Between a National and World Council, blind to the importance of any theological affirmation, and a fundamentalism, some of whose adherents (though not all) see every issue as of supreme importance, this particular problem seems almost impossible of solution. Historic Protestantism seems doomed not to present a united voice to the world. Rarely enough can it even gain a hearing of men.

Finally, the Protestant is faced with the necessity for freeing his own religious faith from the onus of Western culture. On the mission fields of the world Protestantism by and large is reckoned merely an adjunct of British and American imperialism. The repudiation of Western imperialism and of Western culture therefore frequently carries with it also a repudiation of Western religion and specifically of Protestantism.

THE GREAT TASK

Before problems of such staggering gravity, the Protestant of the mid-twentieth century is tempted again and again to shirk his divine calling. But God has "called out" his *Ekklesia* and has commanded it to protest to (witness before) all the world of the good news of salvation through Jesus Christ. In this generation as in the past, many who call themselves Protestants seek to withdraw from contact with an evil world which threatens to destroy them. Such craven hearts do not follow in the steps of him who stood alone before the mightiest ruler of his day and cried, "Here I stand; I cannot do otherwise! God help me."

Others equally disloyal to their Protestant forebears, seek to water down their message to what will give no offence to the world. This no true Protestant dares to do. His message is not his own; he is under written orders from His Lord to declare the message of the Book—the Christ of the Bible. Such a commission no doubt lays special duties upon the Protestant true to his task. If he is to be a witness to the Christ of the Bible, he must know the Christ of the Bible. This demands serious study of the Bible, not merely by the scholar who aspires to become a theologian but also by the man in the pew who longs to become a useful servant of God. For the Protestant, Bible study is not an extra-curricular activity: it is his major textbook. In the pages of this sacred Book, the Holy Spirit meets the simplest believer, to instruct him in Christ and in all His benefits.

Faithfulness to his divine call to witness demands also that a Protestant must experience for himself that to which he would point others. His Christian faith must not be something external to himself, but it must be something that he holds in conviction because he has made it a part of himself. He must be able to say with the blind man of old, "One thing I know, that whereas I was blind, now I see."

Last of all a Protestant must possess a heart filled to overflowing with love for God and for his fellow men. This alone can drive him into an alien world to witness even though it cost him his life. The true Protestant must go and find his fellow man wherever he is, witness to him of the Christ of Holy Scripture, and passionately love

him into the Saviour's kingdom. This is the great task of Protestantism, to bear witness to Jesus Christ and to persuade all men
everywhere to turn from their twentieth-century idols to the living
God.

BIBLIOGRAPHY

BARTH, KARL. *Church Dogmatics.* Vol. 1:1, 2; 2:1; 4:1, 2. Edinburgh:
T. & T. Clark, 1936-1958. The definitive statement of conservative
Neo-orthodoxy.
———. *The Knowledge of God and the Service of God.* Tr. by J. L. M.
Haire and Ian Henderson. New York: Charles Scribner's Sons, 1939.
A clear, readable statement of conservative Neo-orthodoxy.
BERKOUWER, G. C. *The Triumph of Grace in the Theology of Karl Barth.*
Grand Rapids: Wm. B. Eerdmans Pub. Co., 1956. v, 414 pp. The
ablest analysis of Barth's thought from an evangelical viewpoint.
BRUNNER, HEINRICH EMIL. *The Christian Doctrine of Creation and Re-
demption.* London: Lutterworth Press, 1952. x, 386 pp.
———. *The Christian Doctrine of God.* London: Lutterworth Press, 1949.
361 pp. These two volumes by Brunner represent a clear, readable
defense of conservative Neo-orthodoxy by one of its two ablest repre-
sentatives.
CAIRNS, EARLE EDWIN. *Christianity Through the Centuries.* Grand Rapids:
Zondervan, 1954. xxxiii, 511 pp. A panorama of Christianity with good
summary of all major movements in the Church, ancient as well as
modern, by a thorough-going conservative.
CARNELL, EDWARD JOHN. *The Case for Orthodox Theology.* Philadel-
phia: Westminster Press, 1959. 162 pp. A controversial defense of
Protestant orthodoxy concentrating largely on the formal principle of
Scripture.
———. *An Introduction to Christian Apologetics.* Grand Rapids: Wm.
B. Eerdmans, 1952. 379 pp. An able defense of Fundamentalism.
———. *The Theology of Reinhold Niebuhr.* Grand Rapids: Wm. B. Eerd-
mans, 1950. 250 pp. The best analysis of Niebuhr by an evangelical.
The Christian Hope and the Lack of the Church: Six Ecumenical Essays.
New York: Harper, c. 1954. Besides these six essays, this volume also
contains numerous lesser reports—all representative of the Second
Assembly of the World Council of Churches.
CLARK, GORDON HADDON. *A Christian View of Men and Things.* Grand
Rapids: Wm. B. Eerdmans, 1952. 325 pp. A defense of Calvinistic or-
thodoxy.
DE WOLF, LOTAN HAROLD. *The Case for Theology in Liberal Perspective.*

Philadelphia: Westminster Press, 1959. 206 pp. A warm-hearted, keen-minded defense of Liberalism—unreconstructed but influenced by and alert to contemporary trends.

———. *A Theology of the Living Church.* New York: Harper, 1953. 383 pp. A splendid contemporary presentation of unreconstructed Modernism.

FERM, VERGILIUS. *The American Church of Protestant Heritage.* New York: Philosophical Library, 1953. 481 pp. An interesting sketch of the main groups within American Protestantism, fairly presented by a liberal.

HEBERT, ARTHUR GABRIEL. *Fundamentalism and the Church.* Philadelphia: Westminster Press, 1957. 156 pp. The ablest attack against Fundamentalism in print.

HARNACK, ADOLPH. *What Is Christianity.* Introduction by Rudolph Bultman. New York: Harper, 1957. 319 pp. The finest presentation of liberal Christianity ever written, by the renowed Church historian and liberal (Ritschlian) theologian, who at the turn of the twentieth century spoke as mouthpiece for his whole movement.

HENRY, CARL F. H. *The Protestant Dilemma.* Grand Rapids: Wm. B. Eerdmans, 1949. An analysis of the current theological confusion within Protestantism, especially 'on the basic issues of revelation, sin, and Christ.

HORDERN, WM. *The Case for a New Reformation Theology.* Philadelphia: Westminster Press, 1959. 178 pp. The New Reformation Theology is conservative Neo-orthodoxy and is capably presented.

———. HORDERN, WM. *A Layman's Guide to Protestant Theology.* New York: Macmillan, 1955. 222 pp. The clearest survey of contemporary Protestant theology on the market, by a liberal evangelical.

JEWETT, PAUL KING. *Emil Brunner's Concept of Revelation.* London: J. Clarke, 1954. x, 190 pp. The best evangelical analysis and critique of the theology of Emil Brunner.

KIK, JACOB MARCELLUS. *Ecumenism and the Evangelical.* Philadelphia: Presbyterian and Reformed Publishers, 1958. 152 pp. The problem of ecumenicalism from a thoroughly orthodox viewpoint.

LATOURETTE, KENNETH SCOTT. *History of the Expansion of Christianity.* 7 vols. New York and London: Harper, 1937-1945. A brilliant survey of Christianity and its mission from a semi-liberal viewpoint.

LINDSAY, THOMAS MARTIN. *A History of the Reformation.* 2 vols. Edinburgh: T. & T. Clark, 1906-08. An old but well-written and authoritative survey of reformation history.

MACHEN, J. GRESHAM. *Christianity and Liberalism.* Grand Rapids: Eerdmans, 1946. 189 pp. The definitive answer to Modernism.

MEAD, FRANK S. *Handbook of Denominations in the United States.* Rev. and enl. ed. Nashville: Abingdon Press, c. 1956. 255 pp. A mine of information and "vital statistics" of all the American churches.

NIEBUHR, REINHOLD. *The Nature and Destiny of Man.* 2 vols. New York: Charles Scribner's Sons, 1941-43. The classic document of liberal Neo-orthodoxy in America.

ORR, JAMES. *The Christian View of God and the World.* Grand Rapids: Wm. B. Eerdmans, 1954. 480 pp. A classic statement of the orthodox viewpoint.

PACKER, JAMES INNELL. *Fundamentalism and the Word of God.* Grand Rapids: Eerdman's, 1958. 191 pp. A reply to Hebert's volume, *Fundamentalism and the Church of God,* by a clear-thinking orthodox Calvinist.

ROBINSON, CHARLES HENRY. *History of Christian Missions.* New York: Charles Scribner's Sons, 1915. xiv, 533 pp. A useful survey especially of the modern missions movements.

SCHLEIERMACHER, DAVID FRIEDRICH, *On Religion: Speeches to Its Cultured Despisers.* Tr. John Oman with an introduction by Rudolph Otto. New York: Harper, 1958. 287 pp. A classic statement of Liberal Theology by the acknowledged "Father of Modern Theology."

VAN BAALEN, JAN KAREL. *The Chaos of Cults.* Grand Rapids: Wm. B. Eerdmans, 1956. 409 pp. A popular survey of the leading cults.

WIEMAN, HENRY NELSON (ed.) . *Religious Liberals Reply.* Boston: Beacon Press, 1947. A vigorous attack against Neo-orthodoxy from the modernistic viewpoint.

General Bibliography

Following is a list of some of the more useful general works on world religions. Only those books are included which deal with several religions.

ANDERSON, J. N. D. (ed.) *The World's Religions*. Chicago: Inter-Varsity Christian Fellowship, 1950.

BRADEN, CHARLES SAMUEL. *The Scriptures of Mankind*. New York: The Macmillan Co., 1952.

———. *The World's Religions*. New York: Abingdon-Codesbury Press, 1939.

BUNCE, WILLIAM K. *Religions in Japan*. Rutland, Vermont: Charles E. Tuttle Co., 1955.

CHAMPION, SELWYN GURNEY. *Eleven Religions and Their Proverbial Lore*. New York: E. P. Dutton and Co., Inc., 1945.

CHAN, WING-TSIT. *Religious Trends in Modern China*. New York: Columbia University Press, 1953.

FERM, VERGILIUS. *Religion in the Twentieth Century*. New York: Philosophical Library, 1948.

FINEGAN, JACK. *The Archeology of World Religions*. Princeton: Princeton University Press, 1952.

HOCKING, WILLIAM E. *Living Religions and a World Faith*. London: A. Allen and Unwin, Ltd., 1940.

HUME, ROBERT ERNEST. *The World's Living Religions*. New York: Charles Scribner's Sons, 1925.

JAMES, E. O. *History of Religions*. New York: Harper & Bros., 1957.

JURJI, E. J. *The Great Religions of the Modern World.* Princeton: Princeton University Press, 1947.

KRETZMANN, P. E. *The God of the Bible and Other "Gods."* St. Louis: Concordia Publishing House, 1943.

LYON, QUINTER M. *Great Religions.* New York: Odyssey Press, 1957.

NOSS, JOHN B. *Man's Religions* (rev. ed.). New York: The Macmillan Co., 1956.

REICHELT, KARL LUDVIG. *Religion in Chinese Garment.* London: Lutterworth Press, 1951.

RING, G. C. *Religions of the Far East.* Milwaukee: Bruce Publishing Co., 1950.

SOPER, E. D. *The Religions of Mankind.* New York: Abingdon Press, 1938.

SPIEGELBERG, FREDERIC. *Living Religions of the World.* Englewood Cliffs, N. J.: Prentice-Hall, Inc., 1956.

TROOD, S. M. E. *The Religions of Mankind.* London: Christophers, 1939.

COMMUNISM—BIBLIOGRAPHY

(*Continued from page 337*)

KOESTLER, ARTHUR. *The Invisible Writing.* Macmillan, New York, 1954.

KRAVCHENKO, VICTOR A. *I Chose Freedom.* Scribner's, New York, 1946.

ANTI-COMMUNIST NOVELS

DOSTOEVSKY, FYODOR. *The Grand Inquisitor.* Haddam House, Association Press, New York, 1948.

KOESTLER, ARTHUR. *Darkness at Noon.* Macmillan, New York, 1939.

ORWELL, GEORGE. *Animal Farm.* Harcourt Brace (or Penquin 838), New York, 1945.

Index

441